This is a study of the history of linguistics in North America. It begins before the First World War and surveys the whole field up to the 1990s. It then explores in detail the development of grammatical theory from Bloomfield's first book (1914), through his *Language* (1933) and the work of Harris and other 'Post-Bloomfieldians', to the latest ideas of Chomsky. The last chapter in particular is an account of Chomsky's intellectual development since the 1950s. One of the main objects is to trace the origins of a set of ideas that are often taken for granted. The first is the Bloomfieldian concept of constituency structure, which includes that of the morpheme as the ultimate constituent. The second is the attempt by the Post-Bloomfieldians and their successors to separate the study of syntax from the study of meaning. The third is the more recent Chomskyan theory that the object of linguistics is to study a genetically inherited universal grammar. These three ideas have come to dominate linguistics, and for anyone who wants to understand how they have arisen this book will be essential reading.

CAMBRIDGE STUDIES IN LINGUISTICS

General Editors: J. BRESNAN, B. COMRIE, W. DRESSLER, R. HUDDLESTON, R. LASS, D. LIGHTFOOT, J. LYONS, P. H. MATTHEWS, R. POSNER, S. ROMAINE, N. V. SMITH, N. VINCENT

Grammatical theory in the United States from Bloomfield to Chomsky

In this series

35 MARTIN ATKINSON: *Explanations in the study of child language development*
36 SUZANNE FLEISCHMAN: *The future in thought and language*
37 JENNY CHESHIRE: *Variation in an English dialect*
38 WILLIAM A. FOLEY and ROBERT VAN VALIN JR: *Functional syntax and Universal Grammar*
39 MICHAEL A. COVINGTON: *Syntactic theory in the High Middle Ages*
40 KENNETH J. SAFIR: *Syntactic chains*
41 J. MILLER: *Semantics and syntax*
42 H. C. BUNT: *Mass terms and model-theoretic semantics*
43 HEINZ J. GIEGERICH: *Metrical phonology and phonological structure*
44 JOHN HAIMAN: *Natural syntax*
45 BARBARA M. HORVATH: *Variation in Australian English: the sociolects of Sydney*
46 GRANT GOODALL: *Parallel structures in syntax: coordination, causatives, and restructuring*
47 JOHN M. ANDERSON and COLIN J. EWEN: *Principles of dependency phonology*
48 BARBARA A. FOX: *Discourse structure and anaphora*
49 LAUREL J. BRINTON: *The development of English aspectual systems*
50 DONNA JO NAPOLI: *Predication theory*
51 NOEL BURTON-ROBERTS: *The limits to debate: a revised theory of semantic proposition*
52 MICHAEL S. ROCHEMONT and PETER W. CULICOVER: *English focus constructions and the theory of grammar*
53 PHILIP CARR: *Linguistic realities: an autonomist metatheory for the generative enterprise*
54 EVE SWEETSER: *From etymology to pragmatics: metaphorical and cultural aspects of semantic structure*
55 REGINA BLASS: *Relevance relations in discourse: a study with special reference to Sissala*
56 ANDREW CHESTERMAN: *On definiteness: a study with special reference to English and Finnish*
57 ALESSANDRA GIORGI and GIUSEPPE LONGOBARDI: *The syntax of noun phrases: configuration, parameters and empty categories*
58 MONIK CHARETTE: *Conditions on phonological government*
59 M. H. KLAIMAN: *Grammatical voice*
60 SARAH M. B. FAGAN: *The syntax and semantics of middle constructions: a study with special reference to German*
61 ANJUM P. SALEEMI: *Universal Grammar and language learnability*
62 STEPHEN R. ANDERSON: *A-Morphous Morphology*
63 LESLEY STIRLING: *Switch reference and discourse representation*
64 HENK J. VERKUYL: *A theory of aspectuality: the interaction between temporal and atemporal structure*
65 EVE V. CLARK: *The lexicon in acquisition*
66 ANTHONY R. WARNER: *English auxiliaries: structure and history*
67 P. H. MATTHEWS: *Grammatical theory in the United States from Bloomfield to Chomsky*

Supplementary volumes

MICHAEL O'SIADHAIL: *Modern Irish: grammatical structure and dialectal variation*
ANNICK DE HOUWER: *The acquisition of two languages from birth: a case study*
LILIANE HAEGEMAN: *Theory and description in generative syntax: a case study in West Flemish*

Earlier issues not listed are also available

GRAMMATICAL THEORY IN THE UNITED STATES FROM BLOOMFIELD TO CHOMSKY

P. H. MATTHEWS

Professor of Linguistics, University of Cambridge

Published by the Press Syndicate of the University of Cambridge
The Pitt Building, Trumpington Street, Cambridge CB2 1RP
40 West 20th Street, New York, NY 10011–4211, USA
10 Stamford Road, Oakleigh, Melbourne 3166, Australia

© Cambridge University Press 1993

First published 1993

Printed in Great Britain at the University Press, Cambridge

A catalogue record for this book is available from the British Library

Library of Congress cataloguing in publication data

Matthews, P. H. (Peter Hugoe)
Grammatical theory: from Bloomfield to Chomsky / P. H. Matthews.
p. cm. – (Cambridge studies in lingustics: 67)
Includes bibliographical references and index.
ISBN 0 521 43351 7 (hardback) – 0 521 45847 1 (paperback)
1. Linguistics – United States – History – 20th century.
2. Grammar, Comparative and general – History – 20th century.
I. Title. II. Series.
P81.U5M38 1993
410′.973–dc20 92–41067 CIP

ISBN 0 521 433517 hardback
ISBN 0 521 458471 paperback

CE

For Lucienne
with love and gratitude

Contents

Preface

Parts of this book are based on earlier publications. Chapter 2 substantially reproduces a paper with the same title that is about to appear in the *Transactions of the Philological Society* (Matthews, 1992); I am grateful to the Secretary for Publications for allowing that earlier version to go ahead. In the first two sections of Chapter 3 I have incorporated some material from my contribution to a Festschrift for R. H. Robins, edited by F. R. Palmer and Th. Bynon and published by Cambridge University Press (Matthews, 1986). A preliminary and much shorter version of Chapter 4 appeared with a different title in *An Encyclopaedia of Language*, edited by N. E. Collinge and published by Routledge (Matthews, 1990a). It has been rewritten almost entirely, but I am grateful for their permission to incorporate material from it.

John Lyons has very kindly read and commented on the final typescript. I dedicate the book to my wife, Lucienne Schleich; she has not only commented on most of it but, more importantly, she has taught me the self-discipline needed to write it.

October 1992 P.H.M.

Note on the text

In citing works I have sometimes used later editions or reprintings; in such cases, I have added the original date of publication in square brackets. There are also times when the publication of a work has been substantially delayed; if the original date of composition is important, I have again added it in square brackets.

In the citations themselves all indications of emphasis, whether by italics or small capitals or by spaced or bold letters, have been reduced to italic. Where I have expanded or altered a passage for explanatory reasons, this is indicated by square brackets, including empty brackets where letters, for example, have been removed.

Abbreviations

FL	*Foundations of Language*
Harris, *Papers*	Harris, 1981
IJAL	*International Journal of American Linguistics*
JAOS	*Journal of the American Oriental Society*
JL	*Journal of Linguistics*
LBA	*A Leonard Bloomfield Anthology* (Hockett (ed.), 1970)
Lg	*Language*
LIn	*Linguistic Inquiry*
MSLL	*Monograph Series on Languages and Linguistics*
RiL	*Readings in Linguistics* (Joos (ed.), 1958)
SIL	*Studies in Linguistics*
TPhS	*Transactions of the Philological Society*

1 *Introduction*

Many readers will be familiar with the classic historiographic study by Walter Carruthers Sellar (Aegrot. Oxon.) and Robert Julian Yeatman (Failed M.A. etc. Oxon.), in which they set out 'all the parts you can remember' of the History of England (Sellar & Yeatman, 1930). What 'Every student can remember' of the history of linguistics is not perhaps so bad, and sadly less hilarious. But it would not be difficult to put together an account of '1957 and All That', in which developments in the twentieth century are quite seriously garbled.

It would contain at most two 'memorable dates'. One is that of the publication, in 1957, of Chomsky's *Syntactic Structures*, in which Structuralism, or (according to some authorities) American Descriptivism, was overthrown. The other date, which careful research might well reveal not to be memorable, is that of Saussure's *Cours de linguistique générale*. Before this, at the beginning of the century, linguists were only interested in the history of languages. But according to Saussure, who is known as the Father of Modern Linguistics, the subject had to be synchronic, and we had to study 'la langue', which is just an arbitrary inventory of signs. This was at first a Good Thing, since it led to a lot of important work especially on American Indian languages. But in the long run structuralism was a Bad Thing. One reason is that the structuralists did so much work with American Indians that they came to believe that languages could differ from each other in any way whatever. Therefore they were interested only in techniques for classifying data. Another reason is that the American descriptivists ignored meaning. This is mainly the fault of Bloomfield, who was the First to Make a Science of Linguistics. But he decided that meaning could not be studied scientifically. It also has to do with their work on American Indian languages, which were so strange that one could not get at them reliably unless one paid no attention to what the words meant.

All this was swept aside by the Chomskyan Revolution. This was the

Best Thing that has happened to linguistics in the past 2500 years, since, as soon as Chomsky became top linguist, anyone who was anybody worked in an entirely New Paradigm. From the beginning Chomsky has seen language as a Window on the Mind. Therefore he insisted that a grammar had to be generative, and should include meaning. He is the first linguist since the eighteenth century to be interested in Universal Grammar, which he has shown to be innate. He is therefore a Rationalist and not an Empiricist, and this is a Good Thing because it explains why any child learns any language equally fast. He was also famous at one time for his theory of Deep Structure and Transformations. But this turned out to be not such a Good Thing, and according to some authorities may even have been a Bad Thing, because transformations were too powerful.

Of some of the statements that make up this pastiche it might perhaps be said with charity that they are no worse than gross over-simplifications. Others are nonsense, or can easily be proved wrong. But assertions like them do appear in students' essays; and, what is worse, although they are in part perversions of the account in sources that are broadly reputable, much of this story could be cited in inverted commas from other books that are, unfortunately, quite widely read. Nor am I confident that there are no teachers and examiners who will not give an 'A' to more specious versions of it.

One of my aims in writing this book is to try to bring home to colleagues who teach the subject what the currents of ideas in twentieth-century American linguistics have in reality been. I am not sure that I can reach their students directly, since, despite the admirable work of Hymes and Fought (1981 [1975]), which has exploded many of the myths that are told about the period up to 1960, we will still need to discuss in detail texts that are sometimes difficult and not always on students' reading lists. I shall also offer some interpretations that may be genuinely contentious. But I hope that, even in so doing, I will persuade my readers that the recent history of linguistics is a serious topic; that it can be treated as more than just a chronicle of individuals and schools; and that, in going beyond this, we can do better than to trust the official histories of dominant theories, or the polemics of one faction against another, or the haphazard comments of compilers of books of readings, or the attempts by middle-aged scholars to disguise what they believed when they were young, or any of the other sources that are often uncritically followed.

My main purpose, however, is to trace the development and continuity of three dominant ideas. One is that the study of formal relations can and should be separated from that of meaning. It has appeared in many variants: in the insistence that a description of a language must be justified by distributional criteria; in the belief that there are syntactic facts or syntactic arguments for syntactic rules that are distinct from semantic facts or semantic arguments; in a theory of levels in which one component of a grammar accounts for the grammaticality of sentences and another supplies their semantic interpretation; in other weaker concepts of the autonomy of syntax. Not every scholar I will refer to has subscribed to such ideas. But it is a motif that runs through American linguistics from the 1940s onwards, and where similar views are current elsewhere it is largely under American influence.

The second idea is that sentences are composed of linear configurations of morphemes. Strictly, this involves three propositions: firstly, that relations are basically of sequence; secondly, that they hold within and between the units in a hierarchy of constituents; thirdly, that morphemes are the elementary units in this hierarchy. But these propositions usually go together, especially in the potted expositions of grammatical theory that are read by students. They have in consequence become so widespread, at least or above all in English-speaking countries, that many scholars have to be reminded forcibly that there might, in principle, be arguments against them. But their origins, as we will see, lie in the specific preoccupations of American theorists earlier in this century.

The third idea is that many aspects of grammar are determined genetically. This is more recent, and has arisen independently of the others. But, like them, it is widely held, and all three are commonly held by the same people. It is not, of course, my business as a historian to say whether these ideas are right or wrong, or to discuss any criticisms of them that are not themselves part of their history. But I would be disingenuous if I did not confess that my account will be in part what might be called an 'anti-Whig' interpretation. I have selected these ideas because they have come to dominate grammatical thought in the late twentieth century, because their history fascinates me and because existing accounts are partly misleading. But the dominance of the first two, in particular, is not (to return to the language of Sellar and Yeatman) a Good Thing, and I would not be disappointed if my study of their origins were to lead more scholars to question them.

The time span of this study runs approximately from the appearance in 1911 of the first part of the *Handbook of American Indian Languages* to the late 1980s, but will deal in greatest detail with the middle of this period. Its geographical scope will be limited to the United States. This has in practice been an easy decision, since the main stream of American linguistics has for much of this century had few tributaries. It will also concentrate on Bloomfield and Chomsky, who, if nothing else, are the most influential figures in our story. But they are, of course, much more; and the reading and rereading undertaken for this book has only increased my admiration for their subtlety, originality and ingenuity of mind. They are therefore the only scholars whose contributions to grammatical theory will be studied systematically over their whole lifetime. Others have played a dominant role at various times: in the term used in the ancient analysis of the *Iliad*, there is an ἀριστεία or moment of glory of one group in the 1940s, of another in the late 1960s, and so on. The contribution of Harris, in particular, is central to the history of American linguistics for nearly twenty years, and, over that period, will be discussed in the same detail. But neither for him nor for others will I attempt a rounded intellectual biography.

For, finally and most importantly, this is a history in which ideas will generally loom larger than people. In that respect the echo of Ranke, which may have been detectable some paragraphs back, was serious. Particular ideas will often be seen to persist as the personnel who hold them change, and as other ideas change also. This is especially the case, and especially understandable, when an idea is not itself the immediate focus of debate. There is no doubt, for example, that Bloomfield's views on meaning and the psychology of language changed radically between his first book (1914) and the one for which he is best known (1935 [1933]). But as I will try to show in Chapter 2 (§§2.1–2), much of his detailed concept of grammar survived, in a new form and with a new justification. There is also no doubt that the goals of American linguistics were transformed in the early 1960s, when Chomsky's partial critique of Post-Bloomfieldian work sank in. But that did not affect ideas which he did not criticise, such as the concept of constituency structure (see §2.3); or that of the morpheme, which, as we will see in §§2.4–5, most American scholars have continued to take for granted; or a commitment to distributional criteria (§3.2). There is nothing odd about this, nor, in the illustrations I have given, anything that will not be accepted at once by anyone who has read the primary sources. But the secondary sources tend to deal in schools and individuals, and emphasise the discontinuities between them. They also tend to treat the thought within each school as a unit. It is therefore worth stressing that ideas often persist, evolve and may be abandoned on a time scale that does not correspond to the transitory intellectual hegemony of one group of scholars or another.

There is also a logic of ideas that is not always obvious from the explicit reasoning of those who hold them. When a new theory of the morpheme was developed in the 1940s, it was said to remedy defects of the existing theory developed by Bloomfield. But when we look at this episode more closely, we find that the defects were not strictly as they were said to be, and that the real motives, as I will suggest in §2.3, lie deeper. A quarter of a century later, the main issue among Chomsky's followers was whether semantics was 'interpretive' or 'generative'; and, since the latter view did not prevail, it is often seen as an aberration. But I will suggest in §3.4 that it was a natural consequence not just of the way that transformational grammar developed in the early to mid-1960s, which is undoubtedly how its proponents saw it, but of a view of form and meaning whose roots lie earlier and which Chomsky, in developing the theory of transformations, had accepted and supported. This kind of history becomes increasingly difficult from the early 1970s onwards, as the arguments are too recent and for the most part continue. But for the earlier period it is feasible and, controversial as it may be, is more interesting than any other.

1.1 American linguistics 1900–1990

Let us begin with a general historical survey. This will include some statements that either need or deserve more detailed discussion and documentation, which, where the leading scholars are concerned, will be reserved for later chapters. But the main stream of American linguistics is naturally not the only stream. I will therefore have to allude briefly to the work of other schools, good or in its day important, to which I will not be able to return.

Our history may conveniently begin around 1910. This is just before the publication of the first part of the *Handbook of American Indian Languages* (1911), which included Boas's 'Introduction', and four years before Bloomfield's first book; it is also the date when Sapir took up his first post, in Ottawa. Insofar as it is possible to divide the century into periods, the first might then be said to run from 1910 to the foundation, at the end of 1924, of the Linguistic Society of America. No division can serve as more than a skeleton for the exposition of ideas. But the latter date is also chosen by Andresen (1990) to end a survey of American linguistics that begins in the mid-eighteenth century. It is also worth remarking that, although he was active until much later, Boas had by then reached a normal age of retirement; and that in 1925 Sapir moved from relative isolation in Ottawa to a chair in Chicago. This led to new contacts and a new role, and, as Darnell's recent biography makes clear, an accompanying shift in his interests (Darnell, 1990).

In the light of what was to come, the most important intellectual trend is the emergence of what we now call structuralism. The term itself was not used until later; but, in reviewing Sapir's *Language* in the early 1920s, Bloomfield spoke already of the 'newer trend of linguistic study' with which Sapir's work was associated (Bloomfield, 1922: *L[eonard] B[loomfield] A[nthology]* 92). Its 'theoretic foundation' had, he said, been given by Saussure, and in the following year, in a review of the second edition of the *Cours de linguistique générale*, he stressed the value of Saussure's work as a 'clear and rigorous demonstration of fundamental principles' (Bloomfield, 1923: *LBA* 106). 'Most of what the author says has long been "in the air" and has been here and there fragmentarily expressed'; but, he adds, 'the systematization is [Saussure's] own'. The precise contribution of Saussure is still a topic of debate, into which we need not enter. But some of these ideas had been 'in the air' especially in America, and American structuralism thus had partly native origins. It also had some biasses and characteristics of its own, which were to set American linguistics on a distinct course.

One central structuralist idea is that every language has a structure of its own, in which individual elements have a role distinct from that which superficially similar elements have in other languages. For example, a [ð] in English does not have the same role as a phonetically similar [ð] in Spanish. In phonology, this point was definitively made in Sapir's classic paper on sound patterns (1925); and in his major review of Sapir's posthumous *Selected Writings*, Harris speaks of the 'patterning of data' as the 'greatest contribution' of Sapir's linguistic work. The 'fact of patterning' he sees as 'the overshadowing interest' from 'de Saussure to the Prague Circle and Sapir and Bloomfield' (Harris, 1951b: 292, 297). In semantics, Boas had laid great emphasis, at the beginning of our period, on the very different principles of classification to be found in the vocabularies of different languages, and the striking ways in which grammatical categories may vary (n.d. [1911]: 19f., 28ff.). Earlier in his chapter on 'The characteristics of language', Boas too had shown how distinctions made in one 'phonetic system' may be quite foreign to another (n.d.: 11ff.).

Boas's 'Introduction' was written with such good judgment that much of what it says, on these and other matters, now seems simply obvious. It would therefore be tiresome for a commentary such as this to do more than remind readers of his contribution and influence. The same is true of much of Sapir's work. Many will acknowledge the brilliance of his classification of grammatical concepts, and the typology based on it (1921: 101f.; Ch. 6); many more will highlight passages in which he talks of 'the relativity of the form of thought' or of 'no two languages' representing 'the same social reality' (Mandelbaum, ed., 1949: 159 [1924]; 162 [1929]). But for the history of linguistics generally what matters most is not the part that is controversial, but the basic finding that languages do differ radically in phonology and grammar, in ways that make sense only when they are analysed in their own terms. This was shown most strikingly by Boas and Sapir, and went hand in hand with the greater understanding of native American languages that Boas inspired.

Another central structuralist idea is that the scientific study of language could be, and in the first instance had to be, synchronic. For Bloomfield, this was one of two 'critical points' that the 'newer trend of linguistic study' affected; and for a historian it stands in particular contrast with the view of Paul (1920 [1880]: 20). In Bloomfield's words, 'we are coming to believe that restriction to historical work is unreasonable and, in the long run, methodologically impossible' (1922: *LBA* 92). The other 'critical point' concerned the autonomy of linguistics. As Bloomfield put it, 'we are casting off our dependence on psychology, realizing that linguistics, like every science, must study its subject-matter in and for itself . . .'. 'In other words, we must study people's habits of language – the way people talk – without bothering about the mental processes that we may conceive to underlie or accompany these habits'. This is again from his review of Sapir's *Language*, in which Sapir had made clear, in a passage that Bloomfield cites at length, that it is desirable and profitable to study language 'as an institutional or cultural entity, leaving the organic and psychological mechanisms back of it as something to be taken for granted' (n.d. [1921]: 11).

Bloomfield is talking of a broad trend in linguistics, for which Saussure had given a foundation, and not of the *Cours* directly. Nevertheless the singling out of these points is of interest for what is omitted as well as what is included. To most structuralists in Europe, other aspects of Saussure's thought were to seem at least as important – in particular, his distinction between 'langue' and 'parole', and the concept of a language as a system of signs. In Europe these have been and still are very influential. But structuralism in America was to develop differently, and although there was little published discussion, both ideas were often implicitly rejected.

The notion that words and other units are signs did not, of course, begin with Saussure; and something in part resembling the relation between the two sides of the Saussurean sign is naturally implied by any account in which distinct forms are associated with stable meanings. In that sense, I will talk later of a 'sign relation' in Bloomfield's mature work. But the term 'sign' has not been general in American linguistics (or, for that matter, in linguistics in other English-speaking countries), and the principle of parallel substitution of both forms and meanings, which is familiar in Europe from its formulation by Hjelmslev, was not American either. According to Sapir, the 'question of form in language' might be addressed independently either by looking at 'the formal methods employed' (at the types, for instance, of morphological process) or by 'ascertain[ing] the distribution of concepts with respect to formal expression' (n.d. [1921]: 57). From a European viewpoint, one is reminded more of scholars who were not structuralists, like Jespersen. For Bloomfield, it became a central principle that distinctions of meaning were established by the analysis of form. 'Linguistic study', as he put it in words which were to be the inspiration of his successors, 'must always start from the phonetic form and not from the meaning' (1935 [1933]: 162).

The concept of 'langue' is mentioned by Bloomfield in his review of the *Cours*, but there was to be nothing truly resembling it in his own theory or that of his leading followers. In Bloomfield's writings, linguistic units have a status like that which they had in ancient accounts of language: that is to say, they were recurring units of speech. A 'phonetic form' is a 'combination of phonemes that occurs in a language' (Bloomfield, 1935: 138). It is thus the equivalent of what the ancients called an 'articulate vocal sound' (in Latin 'vox articulata'), made up of the minimal units that they called letters. Where such a form has meaning it is a 'linguistic form': as I have pointed out in an account of ancient models, this is the equivalent of what the Stoics called in Greek a *logos* – a phonetic form or one 'pronounceable in [a] language' (Bloomfield, 1935: 162) that in addition has meaning (Matthews, 1990b: 222, 293). Linguistic forms are thus in turn recurring units of speech, from the sentence, which is the largest, to the smallest, which is Bloomfield's 'morpheme'. It may or may not have been clear to Bloomfield how far this diverged from

Saussure's view. But in a critique of Saussure in the late 1940s, Wells picks almost unerringly on passages in the *Cours* which can be read as saying something similar. In Wells's account of Saussure's theory, 'speech (la parole)' is 'made up ... of two linear sequences', one composed of '*tranches de sonorité* ... which are in turn sequences of one or more phonemes', the other 'a sequence of meanings'. A *signifiant* is a '*tranche de sonorité* ... which is associated with a concept'; this concept, which is an element in the other sequence, is a *signifié*. The implication is that the sign is basically a unit of speech: 'words, word-groups, and sentences are all signs' (Wells, 1947a: 7f.). Wells's paper cannot be recommended for its exegesis of Saussure, but for a student of American views in its own time it is very revealing.

A final, more specific feature of structuralism as it developed in America is that the sentence remained a central unit. The sources of this view are evident in Bloomfield's first book, and will be discussed later (§2.1); it is also clear in Boas's 'Introduction' (1911: n.d. 21f.). In his review of Saussure, Bloomfield says that 'in detail, I should differ from de Saussure chiefly in basing my analysis on the sentence rather than the word; by following the latter custom de Saussure gets a rather complicated result in certain matters of word-composition and syntax' (1923: *LBA* 107f.). For Bloomfield, a crucial stage in the emergence of an autonomous linguistics, which he refers to several times in writings from the early 1920s onwards, was the formulation by Meillet (1912) of a definition of the sentence which was not grounded in psychology. This primacy of the sentence is, of course, linked to the implicit rejection of Saussure's distinction between 'langue' and 'parole'. For the Saussurean tradition, sentences (since the range of combinations was unlimited) could only be units of 'parole'. But in one line of thought in the United States, which runs from Bloomfield in the 1920s through to Chomsky in the 1950s, the notion of a sentence or utterance is the basis for the definition of a language. As Bloomfield put it in a paper that stands at the beginning of our next period, 'the totality of utterances that can be made in a speech-community is the *language* of that speech-community' (1926: *LBA* 130, Def. 4).

The late twenties and thirties

If the period up to the mid-1920s saw the initial growth of structuralist ideas, the next fifteen years are distinguished in particular by the emergence of structural linguistics as a distinct discipline. From a modern viewpoint, these years are dominated intellectually by Sapir, who taught many of those who were to become the leaders in the 1940s, and by Bloomfield, whose new book (1933) was taken as a unique guide to linguistics almost as soon as it appeared. The influence of these scholars has been assessed by Hymes and Fought (1981 [1975]), Anderson (1985) and Darnell (1990: Ch. 14), among others. But it is perhaps important to underline their role in successive Linguistic Institutes in the late 1930s, and that of the Institutes in general, in bringing scholars together and fostering a common view of the subject. In looking back on the first twenty-one years of the Linguistic Society, Bloomfield was to suggest that its existence had saved American linguistics from 'the blight of the odium theologicum and the postulation of "schools"' (1946: *LBA* 493). But when we look at matters in a wider perspective, there was very clearly an American school, of which he was the acknowledged leader, by the beginning of that decade.

The Linguistic Society of America was not founded, of course, to promote structuralism. In his address to the inaugural meeting, its first president divided the domain of linguistics into three subdivisions. One is concerned with the 'permanent conditions' of language and includes, in particular, general phonetics and general or 'philosophical' grammar. The second deals with history and evolution, and includes both comparative study and that of single languages, 'of dialects, of single authors, of special grammatical topics'. As examples of works which survey both subdivisions, he cites 'the well known lectures of Max Müller and of W. D. Whitney', von der Gabelentz's *Die Sprachwissenschaft* (1891), and the more recent books by Bloomfield (1914) and Jespersen (1922). The third subdivision might be called '"practical" or "applied" linguistics'. It includes the practical study of grammar; also topics such as the relation of speech and writing, or the construction of artificial languages (Collitz, 1925: passim). The first number of *Language* begins with an essay by Bloomfield (1925) which is much better known. But, despite a different view of the subject and a very different emphasis, he too is describing a united science of language to which each of these branches belongs.

The true scope of the society is revealed most clearly by its journal. Of the 172 papers published in the first ten volumes of *Language*, about twelve can be said to deal with general topics, and of these twelve, two by Bloomfield (1925, 1926), two by Sapir (1925, 1929) and one by Swadesh (1934a) are well known from reprintings. Of the other seven, a cautiously behaviourist essay by Weiss in the first volume (1925) finds no echo except in Bloomfield's 'set of postulates' in the second; the others are untouched by what he had called the 'newer trend'. The remaining papers deal overwhelmingly with comparative or historical problems in particular families and languages, and with philological topics in a broad sense. Well over half are on the ancient Indo-European languages, including nearly thirty on Hittite (mostly by Sturtevant), nearly twenty on Latin and Italic and about ten on Ancient Greek. Fewer than ten papers are purely descriptive: I am including in this figure two very different phonetic studies, by Heffner of Icelandic and by G. S. Lowman of Albanian, as well as a few brief sketches of unwritten languages. Altogether there are twelve papers, including two by Bloomfield and one by Boas, on native languages in North and Central America.

At the end of the 1920s, in a discussion of the terms 'linguistics' and 'philology', the first editor of *Language* contrasts 'the study of man's speech-habits' with two other fields: 'the study of what his speech-habits have enabled man to accomplish' and 'the establishment and interpretation', where necessary, of texts. To the first of these three 'corresponds the *Linguistic Society of America*'; it is one, he adds, in which 'a tendency to subdivision has hardly as yet set in' (Bolling, 1929: 27f.). But by the mid-1930s descriptive phonology is recognisable as a distinct trend. Volume 10 of *Language* includes Swadesh's paper on 'The phonemic principle'; also Trager's on 'The phonemes of Russian' (1934) and a second by Swadesh, on 'The phonetics of Chitimacha'. Swadesh 'recommend[s] to the attention of the reader that this paper succeeds in remaining entirely within the limits of phonemics. No attention is given to historical considerations, nor is the argument anywhere made to depend on the morphological interrelation of phonemes' (1934b: 345). It was not until well after the war that *Language* ceased to be a major vehicle for philological papers. But from 1935 most volumes include at least one contribution to what became known as 'descriptive' linguistics.

One of the marvellous things about Bloomfield's *Language* is the way in which it reconciled so much that was already the established wisdom in the discipline, and therefore the main interest of most of the early membership of the Linguistic Society, with so much that was strikingly new. Its scope is what one might expect from Collitz's address to the inaugural meeting: fifteen chapters on what he had called the 'permanent conditions' of language (Chs. 2–16), eleven on comparative and historical problems (Chs. 17–27), and one (Ch. 28) on 'Applications and outlook'.

When we compare this table of contents with that of Bloomfield's first book (1914), it is remarkable that *Language* gives proportionately more space to the comparative and historical part (215 pages out of 509, compared with 96 out of 325). That is also more space than it had had in Sapir's *Language* (70 pages out of 232).

In the text itself, what is obviously new is Bloomfield's account of the foundations of the subject. This included, in particular, a new theory of meaning, and an exposition of the basic concepts of grammar which was original and involved a good deal of new terminology. But what was built on these foundations was more familiar and often not in dispute. It is instructive, for instance, to look at Bloomfield's actual use of new or newer terms. The concept of the phoneme was becoming general; and, if one accepted it, there was no other term. It is therefore used throughout the book, including the chapters on comparative method (Ch. 18) and phonetic change (Chs. 20 and 21). But 'morpheme' is used far less. From Ch. 16 onwards it appears three times, twice in saying or implying that all languages have morphemes, and again when Bloomfield says that in Chinese 'each word is a morpheme' (509). It is not used at all in his account of analogical change (Ch. 23). Nor is it frequent in his chapters on synchronic morphology and 'Morphologic types' (Chs. 13 and 14). He makes the same remark about Chinese (207), and describes forms like *man* as 'morpheme-words' (209); also forms like plural *sheep* as 'secondary morpheme-words' (218). Later he distinguishes simple roots from those, like *flash* or *flame*, that include 'root-forming morphemes' (245). But only once (212) is 'morpheme' used of an inflectional ending. Otherwise, everything is explained in terms of 'bound forms', 'affixes', 'suffixes' and so on. The term is really needed only in the chapters dealing with the foundations of grammar and the lexicon, mainly Ch. 10 ('Grammatical forms') and, more briefly, Ch. 16 ('Form-classes and lexicon').

The same is true of the terms that Bloomfield invented, such as 'taxeme' and 'tagmeme'. The latter appears once in the final chapter (the 'morphemes and tagmemes' of a foreign language); but it is not used, for example, in the chapter on syntax (Ch. 12). This talks instead of constructions, which have been defined as one of three great classes of tagmeme. 'Taxeme' is used more widely, in the first two sections of the chapter on 'Sentence types' (§§11.1–2), at several places in the chapter on syntax, and in the chapter on morphology. As we will see later, this is the part of Bloomfield's account that caused most difficulty. But neither 'taxeme' nor 'tagmeme' appears in the comparative and historical chapters, and the sections in which any invented term is important are at most a sixth of the whole.

For the structuralists who followed Bloomfield these were very important sections; so too were the dozen or so pages (25ff., 139ff.) in which a theory of meaning is grounded in a model of reactions to stimuli. But the account of meaning elsewhere is quite neutral, precisely because Bloomfield acknowledges that, in practice, one could only proceed by existing methods. For example, there is no trace of this theory in his discussion of semantic change (Ch. 24). It is not surprising, therefore, that his contemporaries found little to object to. Hockett recalls that when it came out, Bolling told a class that 'for the first time since I began giving this course there is a textbook that completely satisfies me'; and then proceeded to read it with them, chapter by chapter (Hockett, ed. 1970: 258). Bloomfield had, of course, been Bolling's colleague at Ohio State University, before moving to Chicago in 1927. But the reviews that Hockett reprints add only a few qualifications. Sturtevant comments on the many new terms and 'new definitions of old terms', and the difficulty they will give beginners. But 'any person who masters this book will get as sound an outlook upon language as can be had' (1934: *LBA* 265). Kent 'cannot commend [it] too highly' (1934: *LBA* 266), and confines his critique to the topic of phonemic transcription. Edgerton says that it is 'sound and authoritative', and 'presents the best opinion of linguistic scholars on all important aspects of their science' (1933: *LBA* 258). He too was worried about 'such terms as *taxeme*, *tagmeme* and *episememe*'. But 'if this be called a criticism (and I do not suggest that I could have avoided the difficulty), it applies to form alone' (259). His only real disagreement again concerns the phonemic representation of American English. Kroesch talks of Bloomfield's 'independence and objectivity' and the 'outstanding merit' of his work (1933: *LBA* 261, 264). In reviewing the British edition, Bolling says that it 'seems to me the only notable advance beyond the position reached in [Paul's] work', on which he sees it as 'built' (1933: *LBA* 277). Two foreign reviews, by Meillet (1933) and Debrunner (1936), are merely less fulsome.

It will be obvious from this analysis that Bloomfield's *Language* was designedly not a revolutionary manifesto. Nor was it simply an amalgam of ideas that were well established with others that were novel. Instead it showed with great skill, through a chain of definitions largely unobtrusive and often subtly refined from chapter to chapter, how the foundations for what was familiar could be established in a radically new way. 'The man is a poet', as a professor of English at Yale remarked (*LBA* 545). But the consequence was that scholars of his own generation were able to take one thing from it, and those who read it as students quite another. In his obituary notice, Bloch described it as 'a shocking book: so far in advance of current theory and practice that many readers [this is still Bloch's impression] . . . were outraged by what they thought a needless flouting of tradition' (1949: *LBA* 529). But the whole was not shocking; only the parts which, taken in isolation, were those on which Bloch's generation were to build.

What they got from it was, above all, a set of general assumptions and attitudes. Bloomfield's detailed account of grammar and the lexicon was abandoned in the 1940s, and replaced, as we will see, by a new theory of levels (below, §2.3). Of the associated terms, only 'phoneme' and 'morpheme', which had not been peculiar to him, were to survive, and the latter was redefined. But they retained his general assumption that recurrent patterns belonged to grammar. The lexicon (insofar as his followers distinguished a lexicon at all) was, as Bloomfield himself had put it, 'really an appendix of the grammar, a list of basic irregularities' (1935 [1933]: 274). This assumption was to dominate almost all American thinking from the 1930s until late in the 1970s. Bloomfield's followers also took from him and from Sapir the general structuralist assumption that a given state of a language may and should be studied in abstraction from its history. The consequence in practice, though it is hard to believe that it is one which Bloomfield would have welcomed, is that many leading theorists did not concern themselves with problems of history at all, and passed on to the next generation a view of linguistics either wholly or largely synchronic. Above all, they retained Bloomfield's positivist attitude to science, and in particular the view of meaning inspired by it.

It is perhaps no longer necessary to shoot down the 'canard', as Hall describes it in his recent biographical sketch, 'that Bloomfield neglected or opposed the study of meaning in linguistics' (Hall, 1990: 8). But it is important to separate the features peculiar to his particular theory of meaning from those that were common in the discipline generally. He was not the only scholar to insist that the semantic units of a particular language are those that have formal expression in it. This is a general tendency in twentieth-century linguistics, exemplified by writers as different as Hjelmslev and Jespersen. Nor was he alone in practice in basing the analysis of a language on distinctions of form. For Bloomfield this principle was 're-inforce[d]' (1935: 162) by the difficulty in implementing the description of meaning that he saw as his ideal. But it is not clear that it would have been any different if he had assumed that existing methods of describing meanings were quite satisfactory. It was agreed by all that the semantic distinctions in one language might not and in general did not correspond to those in others. Therefore, in practice, one would have to start from the phonetic forms to find out what they were.

It is instructive, both in this connection and for the understanding of later developments, to read Harris's assessment of Sapir's work on the semantics of English and other European languages. This was undertaken around 1930 in collaboration with the International Auxiliary Language Association (Darnell, 1990: 272ff.), and includes his posthumous paper on 'grading' (Sapir, 1944), as well as two Language Monographs (Sapir, 1930; Sapir & Swadesh, 1932). Harris distinguishes three main problems that are tackled in these investigations (1951b: 300f.). Firstly, 'There was some analysis of the purely semantic relations among the meanings themselves'. For example, 'more than' and 'less than' are based on the perception of 'successively inclusive bounds'. Secondly, 'we find analysis of the precise meanings' of words in a given language. Thirdly, 'from his analysis of the total meanings which are expressed in each word', Sapir isolated individual 'factors of meaning'. This 'isolating of "elements of meaning"' is praised as an 'empirical linguistic investigation' (301), which does not flow from 'some deductive system of presumed basic meanings'. Starting from such studies we can obtain a general 'picture of how meanings are expressed in languages, and a suggestion of how other ways can be constructed'.

What was peculiar to Bloomfield was his definition of meaning itself. It is often described as behaviourist; and certainly, through his association with the psychologist Weiss during his years at Ohio State University, Bloomfield had been converted to a form of behaviourism. But that view of psychology is simply one reflection of the positivist concept of science which developed in an extreme form in the decades between the wars. In an address to the Modern Language Association in 1929, Bloomfield made clear his belief that 'in the near future – in the next few generations, let us say – linguistics will be one of the main sectors of scientific advance' (1933: *LBA* 227). It is in this sector that 'science will then win through to the understanding and control of human conduct' (compare *LBA* 230). He does not fully explain in this paper what he takes science to be. But in a later presidential address to the Linguistic Society, he adheres explicitly to what he calls the 'hypothesis of *physicalism*' (Bloomfield, 1936: 325). 'One cannot read modern writings without meeting [this view] again and again, expressed by students who, to all appearance, have reached it independently.' In the first part of his paper he refers particularly to the philosophy of science and language in the Vienna School. They have 'found' (as Bloomfield puts it) that 'all scientifically meaningful statements are translatable into physical terms – that is, into statements about movements which can be observed and described in coordinates of space and time'. Other statements are 'either scientifically meaningless or else make sense only if they are translated into statements about language' (323). It is a task of the linguist to show, 'in detail, that [a] speaker has no "ideas"', but only words, which 'act with a trigger-effect upon the nervous systems of his speech-fellows' (325).

Bloomfield's account of meaning is best read in the context of this paper. He starts, in Ch. 2 of *Language*, with the observation of a single utterance. This might be analysed in various ways; but 'we, who are studying language, will naturally distinguish' the act of speech itself from various 'practical events' which either precede or follow it. In his example, Jill asks Jack to pick her an apple. She was hungry, Jack was by her side and so on: these are the practical events we call the 'speaker's stimulus'. On hearing her speak, Jack vaults a fence and so on: these are the practical events we call the 'hearer's response' (Bloomfield, 1935: 23). The source of this analysis is not given specifically in the notes (512). But in his 'Set of postulates' he made clear that he derived it from Weiss (Bloomfield, 1926: *LBA* 129 and n. 6).

The meaning of a single utterance is then defined in terms of the relevant stimuli and reactions. It thus 'consists of the important things with which the speech-utterance ... is connected, namely the practical events' (27). At the beginning of the chapter which deals specifically with meaning, Bloomfield talks equivalently of the '*meaning* of a linguistic form as the situation in which the speaker utters it and the response which it calls forth in the hearer' (138). But our main concern is not, of course, with individual acts of speech. We also assume that the same form can recur with the same meaning in many different utterances. We therefore have to 'discriminate', in any individual case, 'between *non-distinctive* features of the situation' and 'the *distinctive*, or *linguistic meaning* (the *semantic* features) which are common to all the situations that call forth the utterance of the linguistic form' (141). Thus, in Bloomfield's example, the 'size, shape, color, and so on' of the apple are features that are not part of the linguistic meaning of the form apple. What are distinctive are 'the features which are common to all the objects of which English-speaking people use [it]'.

This definition of linguistic meanings rests on an assumption, which, in his 'Set of postulates', Bloomfield had placed at the very beginning (Assumption 1; Bloomfield, 1926: *LBA* 129). In *Language*, it is said to be the 'fundamental assumption of linguistics': namely, that in every speech-community some utterances are alike in form and meaning' (78, equivalently 144). It implies, as Bloomfield makes clear, that each form 'has a constant and specific meaning' (145), and in that sense I believe it is right, as I suggested earlier, to see a parallel with the sign relation of other structuralist schools. But what is unique to Bloomfield's treatment is his radical attempt to locate 'semantic features' elsewhere than in what was ordinarily called the mind of a speaker. Naturally that does not mean that they must be located outside the speakers themselves: it is made clear that 'a very important part of every situation is the state of the speaker's body' (141). Thus, in Bloomfield's initial example, one 'practical event' was that Jill was hungry. 'That is, some of her muscles were contracting, and some fluids were being secreted, especially in her stomach' (23). But in the same example the apple, which is physically there on the tree, is also part of the 'situation'; and, although Jill might have spoken of an apple even when no apple was present, that would be seen by Bloomfield as an 'abstract' or 'displaced' use of speech (30, 141f.) derived from 'its primary value'. Bloomfield recognises that there is an alternative view, which is that of the adherents of 'mentalist psychology'. But from his viewpoint, this is an attempt to 'avoid the difficulty of defining meanings' (142) by positing non-physical processes such as ideas or feelings or volitions. In the period which follows there is little detailed or original discussion of meaning. But even where his followers seem to imply a theory of meaning which is not precisely the same as his, this negative view of an appeal to mental concepts persists.

The Post-Bloomfieldians

This next period begins at the end of the 1930s. Of the protagonists in the decades between the wars, Sapir died early in 1939, and although Bloomfield was very active until 1947, his contribution to the *International Encyclopaedia of Unified Science*, also in 1939, virtually completed the achievement of his mature years as a theorist. The most important external event was the outbreak of the Second World War. This affected the development of American linguistics in two ways. Firstly, it drove to the United States a number of established European scholars, of whom Jakobson, in particular, was to remain. Jakobson's immediate influence was limited: it is hard, for example, to see specific points of contact between his article on Russian conjugation in 1948, though headed in his *Selected Papers* by an apposite quotation from Bloomfield, and the contemporary and equally important contributions to morphology of Bloomfield's own followers. But his ideas were to have a wider impact by the end of the 1950s.

Secondly, the United States did not enter the war until two years after it had disrupted academic life in most of Europe; and, when she did come in, many younger linguists were not dispersed in the armed forces, but set to work, mostly in close contact with others, on the languages of allies and adversaries. Their intellectual development was not interrupted, no one whose ideas were important in the early 1940s was killed, and the flood of important papers towards the end of the decade follows smoothly from those published in 1942. Moreover, linguistics was seen to be useful, and after the war there were jobs. One of the leading scholars of the post-war school remarks with justice that he was 'the moral equivalent of a war millionaire' (Hockett, 1980: 99).

I will describe this school as 'Post-Bloomfieldian'. Many commentators have preferred to say 'Bloomfieldian', and, provided we remember that Bloomfield could have had no direct influence on its development from 1947 onwards, I have no wish to quarrel over labels. But, as Robins remarks in his *Short History of Linguistics*, 'it cannot be said that every one of its characteristics can be directly traced back to Bloomfield's teaching' (1990 [1967]: 233). Indeed there are points at which its members seem to contradict him, and in later chapters (§2.3 and §3.1) I will try to bring out and explain the most important discontinuities.

Whatever we call it, it was very much a school, and one that had become inward-looking. Bloomfield himself was a catholic scholar, as a mere glance at the notes and bibliography of *Language* will show. For his chapters on grammar he refers, for example, to both books by Ries (1927 [1894], 1931), to Jespersen's *Philosophy of Grammar* (1924) and Wackernagel's *Vorlesungen* (1926), to Saussure, to Sapir and to Hjelmslev's first book (1928), as well as works on particular languages and other general studies that are now less read. But the next generation seems to have taken his own book as a fresh starting-point, and to have referred to others as at best supplementary. This is clear already in Bloch and Trager's *Outline of*

Linguistic Analysis, published by the Linguistic Society nine years later. Their annotated reading list recommends European works on phonetics; also, among the references for grammar, two by Jespersen (one said to be 'illuminating but rather superficial ...'). But for grammar Bloomfield's *Language* is 'far more rewarding than any other treatment'. It is also 'the best introduction' to language in general; for their introductory chapter they further recommend *Linguistic Aspects of Science* (Bloomfield, 1939a) and a late article (1942), with five other readings which are all American. It is again the 'best introduction' to phonemics; surprisingly, when one compares articles in the 1930s, there is no reference to European work on phonology (Bloch & Trager, 1942: 80–2).

For the decade or so that follows it is instructive to count actual references. In Harris's *Methods in Structural Linguistics*, which is basically a book of the late 1940s, the references for phonology are comprehensive; there is also one impressive list for grammar (Harris, 1951a: 197, n. 1). But in the remaining notes to his chapters on morphology and syntax, Bloomfield is referred to far more frequently than any other author: for *Language* seventeen times, for other works nine times. In contrast, Sapir's *Language* is referred to four times and articles by him another four times. A further sixteen references are to theoretical work – I exclude factual notes on individual languages – by other scholars writing in the Bloomfieldian tradition (Bloch and Trager, Hockett, Harris himself, Wells, Voegelin, Swadesh and Voegelin). Only fourteen are to general contributions by Europeans (three of them to Jespersen). For a sampling of articles we may turn to Joos's 1958 collection, *R[eadings] i[n] L[inguistics]*. This includes twelve important papers on morphology and syntax published between 1942 and 1954. Of these all but one refer to Bloomfield at least once; *Language* is mentioned nine times and articles by him eight times. The other references include over a hundred to the authors themselves and their American contemporaries (Bloch, Trager and Bloch, Hockett, Harris, Wells, Swadesh and Voegelin, Nida, Pike). Six are to Sapir, two to Boas, two to Jespersen; there are none to other general works by European scholars, contemporary or earlier. The bias is continued by textbooks. In his second edition Gleason recommends Bloomfield's *Language* as 'long, and deservedly ... the standard handbook in American descriptive linguistics', suggests American readings for morphology and syntax, and mentions European work by Firth, Hjelmslev and Uldall, and Martinet at the end of a section in the bibliography headed 'History of linguistics' (1961 [1955]: 484ff.). Hockett tells us that, although he has 'intended no adherence to any single "school" of linguistics, the influence of American linguistics, and especially that of Leonard Bloomfield, will be apparent on every page' (1958: vii). His references are too erratic for serious analysis; but, in contrast, the reader will learn nothing of Saussure, Hjelmslev, Trubetzkoy, Firth, or Daniel Jones.

This isolationism was criticised within America, notably by Haugen in a presidential address to the Linguistic Society (1951). It must also be borne in mind that many scholars, including leading specialists in native American languages, did not belong to this group. But the post-Bloomfieldians set the agenda for general linguistics in America for some fifteen years, and with scant attention, especially in the field of morphology and syntax, to anything that anyone else had thought or was thinking. We must therefore focus on their ideas.

One general feature of this period is the formal separation of 'descriptive' linguistics from other branches of language study. The term 'descriptive' was usual at the time, and since commentators have connected it with the practical problems of describing unfamiliar languages, it has led to misunderstandings. But what was meant was above all 'not historical'. In a scheme devised in concert with others in the late 1940s, Trager divided linguistics in a strict sense into descriptive linguistics, whose concern is the 'descriptive grammar' of a language, and 'contrastive linguistics', in which two or more descriptive grammars are compared (Trager, 1949: §3; for participants in discussion, 8, n. 1). 'Historical linguistics' is a phase of contrastive linguistics in which two systems are compared which 'differ[ ] in time, but [are] known to be, or suspected of being geographically identical or in historical connection' (6). Another such phase is 'dialect geography', which is 'directed at the investigation of the differences between very similar linguistic systems which are geographically or sociologically contiguous'. By contrast, a linguist making a descriptive grammar of a language proceeds 'as if it were completely uniformly used by all speakers, and as if he were dealing with it at a single point in time'. In an important textbook of the late 1950s, Hockett equates 'descriptive' with 'synchronic'. 'The study of how a language works at a given time . . . is called *descriptive* or *synchronic* linguistics' (1958: 303).

Descriptive linguistics was never, of course, the whole of the discipline, even in what I have called the strict sense. In Hockett's textbook, the parts that deal with synchronic phonology, grammar and morphophonemics are less than half of the whole (15–300, Chs. 2–35), and those on 'Synchronic dialectology', 'Phylogeny' and 'Linguistic prehistory' (Chs.

38–40, 42–59) are still roughly a third. But the descriptive branch was seen as fundamental to all others. As Hockett had put it in one of his first articles, 'historical and comparative study implies first the completion of *descriptive* analysis of each of the temporally or spatially or socially grouped ranges of material' (1942: *RIL* 98). To study sound change, for example, is to compare an earlier set of phonemes with a later set of phonemes. In Bloomfield's words 'the assumption of sound-change can be stated in the sentence: *Phonemes change*' (1935 [1933]: 351). Accordingly, descriptive inquiries must establish both sets of phonemes, before a comparison can be made.

Descriptive linguistics therefore had priority; and, since many of its problems were unsolved, it was natural that the greatest effort should be devoted to it. If we look at the journal *Language* in the years that follow the war, we still find many papers dealing with comparative and historical problems in particular languages. There are also a few on general issues in historical linguistics – two by Hoenigswald (1946, 1950), one by Haugen (1950) and one by Hockett (1950b), in the period to the end of the decade. To these we must add an earlier paper by Hoenigswald (1944), in the new informal journal *Studies in Linguistics*. But they are a small haul in comparison with those of the same years, sometimes much longer, which sought to advance synchronic linguistics. The decade that follows closes with Hoenigswald's book (1960). But this was clearly grounded in contemporary synchronic theory; and, if we can perhaps pass over the brief stir caused by glottochronology, his is the only important study, over this period, of the principles of historical linguistics.

By the mid-1950s descriptive linguistics had its own full-length textbook, in which it is described as 'the basic branch of linguistic science' (Gleason, 1961 [1955]: 11). It is not surprising, therefore, that in the years that follow the term 'linguistics' is used more and more, without qualification, to refer to synchronic linguistics only. I have referred already to Trager's division of the subject in the late 1940s. But it is worth remarking that in his presidential address to the Linguistic Society in 1960, he gave a list of 'things that linguists do' that does not include work on the history of languages (1963: 7ff.). The 'basic thing' they do is 'analyze linguistic structures', and since this is the 'first and principal task', it alone has to be discussed 'in terms of theory and methodology' (7). Ten years earlier, Harris had described the field in which he worked variously as 'descriptive' or 'structural' linguistics (Harris, 1951a). But his pupil Chomsky simply talked of 'linguistic theory' (1957: esp. Ch. 6). By the end of the

1960s, many students in America were reading an introduction to 'theoretical linguistics', admittedly by a scholar who was not himself an American, which scarcely mentions comparative and diachronic work except in a brief history of the discipline (Lyons, 1968: 21ff.). Nor did that usage seem strange, in other countries as in America, at the time.

In insisting on the priority of synchronic inquiry the Post-Bloomfieldians were at one with other structural linguists. But the field of descriptive linguistics was also limited for many scholars by the complete or partial exclusion of meaning. In the scheme that Trager published in 1949, what I called 'linguistics in a strict sense' is, more precisely, 'microlinguistics'. This deals with 'the analysis of language systems', which are systems of 'arbitrary vocal symbols by means of which the members of a society interact' (Trager, 1949: 4). But an account of meanings belongs to what Trager called 'metalinguistics'. This deals with relations between such systems of vocal symbols and other aspects of the culture of the society. As Trager put it, 'the full statement of the point-by-point and pattern-by-pattern relations between the language and any of the other cultural systems will contain all the "meanings" of the linguistic forms, and will constitute the metalinguistics of [the] culture' (7).

This is Trager's formulation and was not general, even among the group with whom he had worked. But Harris's view was similar. 'The meaning of any domain, whether morpheme or larger', is defined as 'the common feature in the social, cultural, and interpersonal situations in which that interval occurs' (Harris, 1951a: 347). To study meaning is therefore to study correlations between linguistic units and social and other features (§12.41, 172f.; appendix to §18.4, see again 347). But the units themselves are part of what he later called a 'distributional structure' (Harris, 1954b), which is established solely by the formal relations between them. The 'main research of descriptive linguistics' is into such relations (1951a: 5). It is also worth citing Gleason's textbook. Descriptive linguistics is defined in the preface as 'the discipline which studies languages in terms of their internal structure' (1961 [1955]: iii). He makes clear later that, as the term is 'ordinarily' used, it is concerned with 'the expression side of language' (11).

Despite Hymes and Fought's correction of the record (1981), it may still be necessary to stress, firstly, that the extreme view was not universal and, secondly, that it had little to do with the study of hitherto undescribed languages. It is also important to distinguish three issues, which though clearly related and perhaps confused to some degree in the minds of some participants, are in part independent.

The first is a matter of what precisely belonged to 'linguistics'. For Trager, it was legitimate to equate this term with 'microlinguistics', and that, as we have seen, excluded the description of meanings. It also seemed to some foreign observers that this view was held more generally. As early as 1950, Firth remarked that 'certain leading linguists, especially in America, find it possible to exclude the study of what they call "meaning" from scientific linguistics'. They arrive at this conclusion 'by deliberately excluding anything in the nature of mind, thought, idea, concept' (Firth, 1951 [1957: 225]). But it would be hard to find many who said precisely that in print. Moreover, the exclusion of meaning from descriptive linguistics ostensibly had nothing to do with the rejection of mentalism. The reason Trager gave was that the study of meanings was necessarily interdisciplinary. It was 'dependent on the formulations of other cultural systems than language' (1949: 7). Similarly, in Harris's account of meaning, one would have to depend on other disciplines for the identification of 'social, cultural and interpersonal' features.

The second issue is whether an account of the formal structure of a language can be given independently of an account of meanings. It seems that the general answer would have been 'yes'. In practice, of course, examples would be translated; one would also supply a gloss for individual morphemes, and perhaps some indication of the semantic roles of constructions. In practice, too, one might arrive at this structure partly on the basis of semantic evidence. But a systematic description of the 'internal structure' or 'expression side' of a language could, in principle, stand on its own. Not only was this widely assumed by Post-Bloomfieldians. It was the most important assumption that Chomsky took from them, and was scarcely questioned until the late 1960s.

The third issue is whether it is possible, in theory, to determine this structure without in part relying on meaning. The words 'in part' are important, since it was not disputed that formal evidence was paramount and that in general, as Bloomfield had said, analysis should start from form rather than meaning. In a paper which follows Bloomfield much more closely than most, Fries insisted that, in carrying out an analysis based on distribution and substitution, 'certain uses of particular kinds of "meaning" seem necessary and legitimate'. In particular, it is 'necessary to control . . . enough of the lexical meaning' and 'enough of the structural meaning' to determine whether forms or arrangements are 'the "same" or "different"' (1954): 67f.). But he also insists that 'any use of meaning is unscientific' if it 'leads us to stop short of finding the precise formal signals' that convey it.

The words 'in theory' are also important. Those whose concept of linguistic analysis Fries was implicitly attacking were, in particular, Harris and Trager; but both acknowledged that appeals to meaning were legitimate in practice, as a source of hints or what were sometimes called 'short cuts'. In his chapter on 'Morphemic segments', Harris remarks that 'linguists often use apparent differences or identities of meaning (or of translation) as hints in their search' for these elements. Nor does his own view imply that they 'cannot be used'. What is important is that 'these hints must always be checked' with the purely formal operations that he proposes, so that 'meaning never functions as a full-fledged criterion for morpheme segmentation, on a par with' formal criteria (Harris, 1951a: 189). That was also the view of Trager and Smith, in an influential monograph on the structure of English. 'In the present state of morphemic analysis it is often convenient to use the meanings of utterance fractions as a general guide and short-cut to the identification of morphemes.' But when the going gets tough, 'the theoretical basis of the analysis ... becomes evident: it consists of the recognition of the recurrences and distributions of similar patterns and sequences.' An analyst must therefore remember always that 'his hunches ... are really short-cut conclusions about distributional facts' (Trager & Smith, 1951: 54).

Why was this view adopted? It is worth stressing once more that it was not overtly connected with a distaste for mentalism. In a brief discussion at the beginning of the decade, Hockett said that it was 'important to see how far we can go' with either 'no resort to meaning, or ... small resort of a specific and well-defined kind'. 'To say this', he goes on, 'is far different from labelling semantic considerations "unscientific", "mentalist", "mystical", or "unbehavioristic", none of which they need be' (Hockett, 1950a: 55). It is also clear that, however much the Boasian tradition may be said to have shaped the course of American linguistics, this view was not inspired by experiences in field work. Of the scholars cited, Trager and Hockett had worked on native American languages. But the most able advocates in the 1950s were Harris, who was originally a Semitist, and Chomsky (1957: 93ff.), whose work focussed on English.

The real issue was how, in principle, a description could be validated. A descriptive linguist dealt, as we have seen, with the formal or 'internal' structure of a language. But how could one ensure that it was described correctly? Part of the answer clearly lay in the reliability of the data. But the rest was thought to require the development of rigorous procedures for analysing it. 'Rigour' was a word particularly used by Harris. In his first article on morphology, Harris suggested a 'technique for determining the morphemes of a language, as rigorous as the method used ... for finding its phonemes' (1942: Harris, *Papers [on Syntax]* 23). In the introduction to *Methods in Structural Linguistics*, he contrasts the 'cumbersome but explicit procedures offered here' with the 'simpler intuitive practice' traditionally followed; by using his methods, one can arrive at the same system 'with greater difficulty – and greater rigor' (Harris, 1951a: 3). Where a procedure 'seems more complicated than the usual intuitive method (often based on the criterion of meaning)', the reason is again 'the demand of rigor' (1951a: 8).

If a description was to be justified procedurally, it was vital that procedures should be followed in a stated order, and that no procedure should have as its input the results that might be expected from another procedure that had yet to be applied. Where the analysis started was in part a matter of convenience. As Harris points out, it was theoretically possible to begin with either phonemes or morphemes (1951a: 195f.). But to begin with phonemes was the 'usual method'; and, if one followed it, the phonology of the language would have to be established by operations on the phonetic data only. One could not refer, for instance, to word boundaries or to contrasts between morphemes, since they could not be established rigorously until a later stage of the analysis. At that stage one could in principle go back and reconsider aspects of the phonology: this was described by Hockett at one stage as a process of 'normalization' (1947: *RiL* 231f.). But the procedures had to be applied without, as it was said, 'mixing levels'. When the analysis of phonology had been completed, one could go on to identify morphemes. That would involve a series of operations on the phonemic transcription of the data, and they in turn could not rely on what was as yet a purely intuitive understanding of larger grammatical units. No one expounded such procedures as fully as Harris. But Trager and Smith describe a similar sequence of operations (1951: 8), and later stress 'the extreme importance of levels' in investigating 'the whole field of human behaviour'. Microlinguistics, as they see it, must deal with the distribution of elements 'rigidly observed on ascending levels of complexity of organisation' (81).

This programme was criticised, especially – where phonology was concerned – by Pike (1947; also 1952). But Pike was the linguistic director of a society of Bible translators; and, in replying to him on this and related matters, Hockett saw him as conditioned by his role in training missionaries for field analysis. 'It is important', Hockett stressed, 'to keep clearly in mind the distinction between *theoretical frame of reference* and *actual sequence of operations in the field*' (Hockett, 1949: 49). The same distinction is crucial when we assess the attempt to develop procedures of analysis independently of meaning. Not everyone was convinced that it could succeed. But it was widely assumed that a descriptive linguist had to have available procedures of analysis that were as rigorous as possible. Only then could findings be shown to be valid. It was also assumed that a description of the formal structure of a language should be separate from and should precede an account of meanings. Therefore, although one might in practice use semantic evidence to discover this formal structure, the demand of rigour required that one should be able to show, in principle, how the same results could be obtained without it. Otherwise the formal analysis would have to anticipate what could only be known intuitively.

Once the logic is set out, it is obvious that the basic assumptions can be challenged. One can argue, on the one hand, that form cannot be separated from meaning. That tended to be the starting-point of European critics, of whom Haas (1954) was one of the most effective. It had also been the published view of Bloomfield in the 1930s (details in §3.1 below). On the other hand, one can argue that a description does not have to be justified by a procedure of analysis. That was the essence of Chomsky's critique (1957: Ch. 6), which by the early 1960s had won the day in America itself.

But the criticism did not come until the Post-Bloomfieldian programme had been carried to what seemed the point of success. It had begun in the early 1940s with Hockett's account of criteria for phonemes (1942), which, in particular, involved 'no grammatical fact of any kind' (*RiL* 107). Above all, he relied on concepts of distribution, which had been introduced by Swadesh in his article on the phoneme eight years earlier (Swadesh, 1934a: *RiL* 35). This was followed after the war by Bloch's 'postulates for phonemic analysis' (1948). In wording these, Bloch 'avoid[ed] all semantic and psychological criteria', and argued that, provided there is some redundancy – as it would later be called – in the distribution of phonemes, 'theoretically it would be possible to arrive at [a] phonemic system . . . without any appeal to meaning' (1948: 5 and n. 8). He also remarked that a chief difference between his approach and

Bloomfield's is that Bloomfield did 'invoke[ ] meaning as a fundamental criterion' (6). The chapters on phonology in Harris's *Methods* set the seal on this approach to the phoneme. Meaning is rarely mentioned (see index) and never crucially. In particular, whereas Bloch had seen reliance on meaning as a 'shortcut' which it would be a waste of time not to follow (1948: 5), Harris says nothing about a need for hints or heuristic procedures. Some years later his pupil Chomsky specifically attacked the notion that 'phonemic distinctness' could in principle be established by differences and identities of meaning (1955a, 1957: 95f.).

When the phonology of a language had been worked out, the next step was to identify its morphemes; then, after that, their classification and the constructions in which they stand. The latter problems were addressed by Harris in an article immediately after the war, which was the first contribution to grammar to eschew all reference to meaning. In Harris's words, 'the method described ... require[d] no elements other than morphemes and sequences of morphemes, and no operation other than substitution, repeated time and again' (1946: *Papers* 45f.). This article supplied the nucleus of his treatment in *Methods* (Harris, 1951a: Chs. 15 and 16), and it must have seemed that, once the morphemes had been identified, the remaining problems of grammar could be solved. This initial problem was more difficult. In the early 1940s, Harris still relied on meaning both in dividing forms into what were later called morphs, and in assigning them to morphemes (1942: *Papers* 24ff., §§2.1 and 2.2). So did Hockett after the war (1947: *RiL* 229f.). In *Methods* Harris tried to work out purely formal procedures; but it is in these chapters that the use of hints and short cuts is particularly acknowledged, and it is on them that doubts about his programme tended to concentrate. But Hockett returned to the problem in the following year, with a detailed formalisation of a procedure for converting sequences of phonemes into sequences of morphs (Hockett, 1952a). In this paper he referred to the 'brilliant discussion' in Harris's book in general (27). Finally, Harris himself proposed what would have been seen as a definitive solution (1955), which indeed he still relied on in his last book (1991).

The 1960s and the first Chomskyan school

The start of our next period is marked by no external event; and, since Chomsky's ideas were to dominate it, it is natural to date it from the publication of *Syntactic Structures*. But this is potentially misleading. In

1957, two important books in the Post-Bloomfieldian tradition had yet to appear (Hockett, 1958; Hill, 1958), and although, with Joos's *Readings in Linguistics*, they may appear to later generations as the tombstones of an era that had ended, that is not how they were meant or received at the time. In addition, Chomsky's ideas were original, and although an enthusiastic review by Lees made sure that they were well known, it took time for them to win through. Only from 1960 is there evidence of widespread conversion to his movement.

Soon afterwards Kuhn published a short book (1962) on the nature of what he called 'scientific revolutions'. I confess that if I were still in a Sellar and Yeatman mood I would unhesitatingly describe this as the Worst Thing that has happened to the historiography of twentieth century linguistics; not, of course, because of what Kuhn said, though one had to be pretty naive if one could not see that his concepts of science and history were highly controversial; nor because I do not believe that the main stream of American linguistics changed course at this time; but because it led so many of Chomsky's supporters to make events fit Kuhn's model. In an ordinary sense of the word there had, of course, been a revolution. But we will not understand it unless we realise that the impact of Kuhn's book became a part of its history, and partly obscured its real origins.

If we look first at American linguistics in general, one obvious feature of the 1960s is the growth of separate schools. Earlier in this survey I referred to Bloomfield's essay on the occasion of the twenty-first anniversary of the Linguistic Society, in which he suggested that it had helped it to prevent such a development. He went on to explain that 'when several American linguists find themselves sharing some interest or opinion, they do not make it into a King Charles's Head, proclaiming themselves a "school" and denouncing all persons who disagree or who merely choose to talk about something else' (Bloomfield, 1946: *LBA* 493). But these words would have brought a wry smile to the face of anyone who read them twenty-one years later. By that time those who followed Chomsky formed one close-knit group, critical if not contemptuous of others. In syntax they already had their own textbook (Bach, 1964), and the first in phonology (Harms, 1968) soon followed. Pike and his missionaries formed another group – numerous, though historically and intellectually less important. The final edition of Pike's massive work was soon to appear (1967), and this school too had its own introduction to grammar (Longacre, 1964). A third group were the 'stratificationalists', led by

Lamb. Lamb's outline of his theory also appeared in the middle of the decade (1966), and for a few years, from 1964 onwards, he was very prolific. Each of these schools had its own theory of linguistic levels, its own terminology, its own way of seeing problems, even its own notations. By the 1970s further groups had emerged that were distinguished only by their treatment of one aspect of language. In particular, the first generation of Chomsky's followers had split over the issue of grammar and meaning. The warring between schools was frank and often bitter in a way that few earlier arguments had been.

Another obvious feature of this period is the growing interest in fields bordering on other disciplines. When Bloomfield had sought to distance linguistics from psychology, his aim was to free it from dependence on changing psychological theories (preface to *Language*, 1935: vii–viii), and throughout the Post-Bloomfieldian period there are remarkably few references to them. Nor does it seem that psychologists were much concerned with linguistics. Miller's *Language and Communication* (1951) shows wide knowledge and wide reading, but its references even to leading linguists are sparse. For phonetics and phonology he refers to Bloch and Trager's *Outline* (22); also to Jakobson, who was by then a colleague and is cited in the preface, for distinctive features (24). The index suggests that he meant to refer to Bloch and Trager for words, sentences and related notions (82f.); note that he does not mention morphemes. Bloomfield's *Language* is listed at the end of the chapter on learning as 'a classic text ... which favors the behavioristic description of verbal behavior' (173); elsewhere it is mentioned only once, for sound change (194). The selected readings for another chapter include a popular work by Bodmer, which Bloomfield (1944) had excoriated.

Twenty years later matters were very different. The field which Miller had promoted was a distinct branch of inquiry, and the name 'psycholinguistics', which he had also promoted, was firmly established. Those who worked in it, whether by origin psychologists or linguists, had to be at home in both disciplines. As Brown saw it, it was 'one of the very few hybrids in all of behavioral science that ha[d] penetrated to the hard truth that a dilettante interest in another field is not enough to support interdisciplinary work' (Brown, 1970: ix). A mere glance at the references in his next book (1973) confirms that it had done so.

The late 1970s also saw the growth of sociolinguistics, as conceived by Labov especially. Labov's thesis was published in 1966, and by 1972 he alone was able to put together two collections of papers. For linguistics in general, one important aspect of early sociolinguistics is the fresh interest that it gave to the question of how languages change. By the end of the decade, a few of Chomsky's followers had tried to apply their synchronic theory to diachrony (especially King, 1969). But it was largely just that – the application to history of a theory developed for other reasons. It was thus at one with a tradition that goes back to the applications of phonemics to diachrony in the 1930s (in America by Hill, 1936). In contrast, Labov was a pupil of Weinreich, whose own thesis (1953) had been supervised by Martinet at the height of his work on diachronic phonology. His first publications had dealt with sound change (Labov, 1963 [1972: Ch. 1]; 1965 [1972: Ch. 7]), and in a major theoretical study begun by Weinreich, the structure of variation within a speech community, which had been seen as lying outside both Post-Bloomfieldian descriptive linguistics and its Chomskyan successor, was proposed as a vital principle of explanation (Weinreich, Labov & Herzog, 1968).

Two final external features are worth underlining. One is the increasing volume of publication. In the first years of the 1960s a young scholar could buy and read everything written in the field of general linguistics. I was a young scholar and did so. The polemics in the middle of this decade at least took for granted that one studied what other people were saying. But by the mid 1970s linguistics had drifted into an era of specialisation, in which it was hard to keep up in detail with everything that appeared. The other feature is the growing prestige of American linguistics in other countries. From the late 1950s it became a common thing for foreign scholars to visit the United States, and for foreign postgraduate students to take degrees there. The effect of this on currents of thought within America does not seem to have been great, since few established scholars, with opinions formed already in another tradition, settled permanently. But it had a profound influence on thought elsewhere, through the spread of Chomskyan ideas specifically.

Of these ideas, the most general centred on the concept of a grammar as a system of rules. The term 'rule' had been avoided by Chomsky's predecessors, and although other terms like 'statement' are found in contexts where 'rule' would have been normal later, the notion that the nature and interaction of rules was the central topic of linguistic theory would have been, and indeed in the late 1950s was, foreign to most scholars. The units of grammar (phonemes, morphemes, and so on) were important; also the kinds of relation obtaining between them. In the final set of statements towards which a descriptive linguist was aiming, these would be set out for a particular language. But the main problem, as we have seen, had been to develop procedures of analysis which would ensure that that account would be valid.

There is more to be said about the continuity and discontinuity of ideas at this juncture, and we will return to it later (§3.2). But the basic change lay precisely in Chomsky's analysis of the problem of validation. In a brilliant discussion in *Syntactic Structures*, he distinguished three requirements that might in principle be placed on a linguistic theory, and argued that it only had to meet the weakest. In particular, it did not have to specify the kinds of procedure that Harris and others had tried to develop. In Chomsky's terms – and it is perhaps important to stress that they are his terms and were new to linguistics – it did not have to provide a 'discovery procedure'. Instead it was sufficient that it should provide an 'evaluation procedure' which, 'given a corpus and given two proposed grammars', will 'tell us which is the better grammar of the language from which the corpus is drawn' (Chomsky, 1957: 51). A description is therefore justified in just the sense that, for a given body of data, no better grammar has been found.

This simple argument stood Post-Bloomfieldian linguistics on its head. It had always been important, naturally, that what Trager had called a 'descriptive grammar' (1949: 4) should describe the language accurately. But in Harris's programme it could be assumed that this would follow if the data on which it was based were gathered scrupulously, and rigorous procedures of analysis, if followed scrupulously, would give it as their result. As Harris put it in a passage to which I will return in more detailed discussion, 'the work of analysis leads right up' to a synthetic 'description of the language structure' (1951a: 372). But in the Chomskyan programme, this became not the end but the beginning. A grammar was 'essentially a theory' of a language (Chomsky, 1957: 49), and the first test was whether, in the term that he had taken from mathematics, it generated the set of sentences that were grammatical in it.

It had also been important, naturally, that a descriptive grammar should give an account that was as simple as possible. But in the earlier programme it could be assumed that simplicity would be achieved if rigorous procedures of analysis were followed. These included procedures which would minimise the inventory of units at all levels, would simplify the description of, for example, morphological alternations, and in general give what Harris called 'a compact statement of what utterances occur in the corpus' (1951a: 361). But in Chomsky's programme simplicity could be tested only by comparing alternative grammars. Therefore, a linguistic theory had, again as one of its first objectives, to define 'simplicity'.

The consequence of both changes is that grammars had to be formalised. When Chomsky became a leading figure, some commentators mistook this concept of a grammar as betraying an interest in computers. Equally, had the computers of the 1960s been a reality in the early 1950s, it might have been supposed that Hockett's attempt to formalise procedures for the identification of morphemes (1952a) was also inspired by the desire to run them on a machine. But although dreams of what computers might do were part of the academic culture of the age, the reason in both cases had to do with the aims of linguistic theory. For Chomsky, the aim was to validate grammars by an evaluation procedure. To determine how far the sentences of the language were distinguished correctly, it had to be clear what each rule or statement in a grammar allowed, and how they related to one another. Therefore the form and interpretation of rules had to be laid down exactly. To define simplicity was to prescribe a measure that would assign a higher or lower value to a grammar. Therefore something – rules, units, categories, steps in derivations, or whatever – would have to be counted, and to make that possible the form of rules, including their notation, had in turn to be prescribed.

Finally, to propose such a formalisation was to propose a hypothesis about languages in general. Any descriptive linguist naturally assumed some general scheme of linguistic levels. For example, all languages were believed to have a level of organisation at which the basic units were morphemes. Such schemes could be made explicit, as by, among others, Joos (1950) or later Trager (1963). If not, they were implicit in procedures of analysis. For example, there was a set of procedures for identifying morphemes and that again assumed that all languages had morphemes. But a theory of the forms of rules went far beyond that. In particular, it was possible to show that one such theory could not yield a grammar for a language which had certain properties, or that another theory would yield one which was simpler or more revealing. Since it was essential to propose a formalisation, the initial problem for any linguistic theory was to find the form of grammar that was appropriate to languages with the properties that all human languages do have.

This chain of argument has been set out without direct quotations, both because the individual points are well known and because we will return to Chomsky's work in later chapters. But it was in these radical reversals of priorities that its impact was first felt. Moreover, although the first fruit of this programme was the addition of transformations to a formalisation of Post-Bloomfieldian syntax, its next fruit was a theory of phonology, originally proposed by Halle (1959), in which the phoneme, which of all the achievements of structural linguistics had been the most solid, had no place. In later chapters I will try to bring out elements in Chomsky's thought which continued that of his predecessors. But there can be little doubt that, in the relatively closed community of American linguistics, whose history must have seemed one of cumulative and collaborative progress since the 1930s, this was revolution. In the words of the Jews in Thessalonica who believed not, those who had turned the world upside down (οἱ τὴν οἰκουμένην ἀναστατώσαντες) were come among them (Acts 17.6).

At the general level there was little effective criticism. One reason, possibly, is that anyone who reflected on the philosophy of science would have realised that the earlier positivist account had been discredited, and that a scientific theory was widely seen as a deductive system which, like a grammar as Chomsky saw it, was confirmed or falsified by the facts. It is perhaps worth noting that the English translation of Popper's *Die Logik der Forschung* (1959 [1935]) appeared as Chomsky's ideas were taking hold. Other reasons may be simply that the ablest theoreticians, Harris especially, were not inclined to polemic or not wedded to the inductive method. But whatever the explanation, published discussion tended to concentrate on matters that either were not central, or, if they were, did not affect his programme only. One topic, in particular, was that of the grammaticality of sentences, and whether a native speaker's intuitive judgment, including in the case of their native language that of linguists themselves, was reliable evidence for it. This was discussed repeatedly at a conference on the analysis of English in 1958, Hill's record of which is invaluable (Hill, ed. 1962; see especially 18ff., 73–8, 158f., 169, 180ff.). A little later, Hill reported on his own failure to devise tests which would elicit reliable judgments from subjects (Hill, 1961). But although the problem was genuine, and later members of Chomsky's school were often to be criticised for basing rules on judgments that were unsafe, it was a problem that no programme of research on syntax could be expected to avoid. It arose because a grammar was bound to make predictions beyond a corpus; and, as we will see below in §3.2, Chomsky neither was nor claimed to be the first to see that.

Another topic debated at this conference was the role of meaning in description and analysis (Hill, ed. 1962: 23–8, 59), on which Chomsky's view was the same as that of Harris. But the picture which emerges most often is that of a noble effort by the other participants, most of whom were specialists in English rather than linguistic theory, to understand what Chomsky was saying. At one point, for example, he was questioned as to where, in the words of Hill's summary, 'one enters the language system for purposes of analysis' (183). But the discussion seems to have been at cross purposes. At first, Chomsky could only take it as a question about 'the history of the states inside myself that occurred when I began to analyze' (173). Later he tried to answer it by making clear that his data were sentences (175). But his concept of linguistic research was so different from any that had been usual that the question intended no longer made sense.

After 1960, the Chomskyan school grew and gathered momentum. I will call it the 'first Chomskyan school', since many of its members have since abandoned his ideas, and few are active in the new Chomskyan school that emerged in the 1980s. But for a dozen years they were the storm troops of a new order. By the middle of the decade, several specific problems of English syntax had been tackled in a new way, especially processes of nominalisation (Lees, 1960a), adjectives with infinitive complements (Lees, 1960b), comparative constructions (Lees, 1961), pronouns (Lees & Klima, 1963), relative clauses (Smith, 1964) and coordination (Gleitman, 1965). Many of these were to remain standard topics of transformational grammar, with important later studies by Lakoff and Peters (1969 [1966]), Langacker (1969), Ross (1969, 1970) and others. Like the earlier Bloomfieldian school, this group became inward-looking. In 1970 many of its leading members were represented in a collection of papers edited by Jacobs and Rosenbaum, in which over half the studies referred to were by contributors to the volume and only one-seventh by anyone whose general views were different. In addition, half the items in the bibliography were unpublished and at best circulating privately.

The middle of the decade is marked by the adoption of the model of grammar by which for many years Chomsky was to be best known. It is in effect the last great structuralist scheme. Like those of Hjelmslev and others that had gone before, it is remarkably symmetrical. It has an expression side and a content side: in Chomsky's terms, a grammar describes a formal relation between meanings and sounds. Meanings are to be analysed into minimal distinctive features, just as sounds are; and, just as phonetic features are drawn from a set of universal categories, so are semantic features. The relation between them is mediated by a level of syntax, which divides into a level of 'deep structure' related to the content side and a level of 'surface structure' related to the expression side. Like earlier models, it is one where, in a phrase whose origin is explored by Koerner (1989: 404ff.), 'everything holds together' ('ou tout se tient'). Every form of rule has its allotted place, and there is no redundancy in the representation of sentences at different levels, or among rules of any one kind, or between rules of different kinds.

There was also no part of it on which substantial progress had not been made. Halle's theory of phonology was a proposal about the kinds of rule that related surface structures to representations of sounds. It was beginning to attract criticism, by Householder (1965) and from adherents of other schools. But it had been applied to divers languages, and a definitive study of English (Chomsky & Halle, 1968) was announced. Work on syntax since the mid-1950s had revealed the nature of deep structures and the rules of transformation relating them to surface structures. Although individual contributions had been criticised (that, for example, of Lees, 1960b by Bolinger (1961)), it seemed that the general case for transformations, and therefore for a distinction of levels between deep structures and surface structures, had been established. Finally, the relation of syntactic structures to meanings had been studied in a preliminary way by Katz and Fodor (1963) and Katz and Postal (1964).

At the same time, Chomsky explicitly linked a theory of the universal properties of languages, to which this work was directed, with an explanation of how a native language developed in children. The topic of 'linguistic universals' had been in the air since the end of the 1950s, and the proceedings of an important conference, with a wide range of participants, had been published by Greenberg (ed. 1963 [1961]). As one observer remarked, there had in the past been 'a tide toward uniqueness and incomparability; now there is a swelling of emphasis on the essential sameness of language' (Hymes, 1961: 21). But Chomsky gave new zest to their study by suggesting – in the terms in which it was first put – that a knowledge of linguistic universals was innate. This idea captured the imagination not only of his followers within linguistics but of many within other disciplines. By the end of the decade he had an influence on general academic culture greater by far than that which any earlier linguist had had.

The study of linguistic universals involved both 'formal universals', which concerned the 'character of . . . rules . . . and the ways in which they can be interconnected', and 'substantive universals', which concerned the categories and features forming 'the vocabulary for the description of language' (Chomsky, 1965: 29). By the early 1970s it was to become clear that formal universals had a vital role in Chomsky's argument, and that 'universal grammar', as he conceived it, was essentially a theory about them. But in the late 1960s the most exciting proposals dealt with substantive functions in syntax. In his own work, Chomsky had sought to give definitions, to be 'thought of as belonging to general linguistic theory', of terms such as 'subject' and direct object' (1965: 71f.). But the semantic roles of elements such as these are varied: in *I jumped off*, the subject refers to someone performing an action, in *I heard it* to someone undergoing an experience, and in *I got it through the post* to someone receiving something. In this light, Fillmore in particular proposed that the description of sentences should be based directly on functions such as 'actor', 'experiencer', or 'recipient'. In his terminology, these were abstract 'cases'. They formed 'a set of universal, presumably innate, concepts' grounded in human judgments about events (Fillmore, 1968: 24).

This was important work, which would have been valuable in whatever theoretical framework it had been cast. But with other contemporary studies it formed part of a current which was to lead many in the first Chomskyan school to abandon the assumptions with which it had started. I will try to explain the details of this movement later (§3.4); but what lay at the heart of it was a new and unconstrained enthusiasm for the semantics of grammar. The subject had been virtually neglected since before the war: for, although Bloomfield had talked of constructions having meaning, and his successors had at least envisaged some form of correlation between the meanings of sentences and their formal structure, little had been said within this tradition about the actual meanings of particular constructions. Bloomfield's 'fundamental assumption', however intended, had in effect set a lid on the problem. But in the mid 1960s the lid was taken off. In Chomsky's general model, a representation of the syntax of a sentence had to be related to a representation of its meaning. For example, a representation of *I heard it*, as consisting of a pronoun followed by a verbal constituent and so on, had to be related to a representation of meaning in which it could hardly be maintained that, in this specific sentence, *I* refers to an actor, *heard* to an action, or *it* to the goal of an action. The meanings which these elements actually did have had to be investigated.

It did not follow that, in sentences like *I jumped off* and *I heard it*, *I* had a different syntax. But in the view that emerged among some of Chomsky's followers, the only identity in construction lay at the level that he had called surface structure. How then was the relation between surface structures and meanings to be described?

The answer in Chomsky's model was that there was an intermediate level of deep structure. Following the treatment of syntax that he had developed ten years earlier, deep structures were a set of representations of sentences generated by what he called the 'base component' of a grammar. Another component specified a set of operations which would relate deep structures to surface structures: that was the role of transformations. Another component again would relate deep structures to meanings. But why were deep structures needed? In a series of articles from 1967 onwards, McCawley and Lakoff argued that there was no case for such a level of representation. There were simply meanings and surface structures. It was then assumed that, as in the existing account of syntax, surface structures were derived by transformations. Therefore they had to be derived directly from meanings, and the base component of a grammar had to generate a set of semantic representations of sentences.

That, briefly, is the origin of what was at first appropriately called 'generative semantics'. But an obvious problem, or one that at least in retrospect should have been obvious, was whether it was any longer possible to defend a concept of grammaticality. In Chomsky's programme, the rules of syntax had to generate a set of sentences that could be shown to have this property. But did that still make sense if they were based on a description of meanings?

The first years of the 1970s are (and were) extremely confusing. One has the feeling that if only the main participants could have been persuaded to write less, and to have taken a little longer doing it, the argument would have been clear. But the crucial finding was that questions about grammaticality could not be answered in abstraction from the knowledge, beliefs and so on of a speaker. Take, for example, the distribution of *who*, which is one of the illustrations discussed in a paper by Lakoff. One cannot simply say that, as a relative pronoun, it can only relate to nouns classed in a lexicon as human. *Cat*, for example, is not 'human', on the evidence of phrases like *the cat which I saw*. But if a cat is seen as an animal with human attributes, phrases like *my cat, who believes that I am a fool*, are perfectly possible. As Lakoff put it, if 'the distribution of *who* and *which* is a question to be dealt with in a field called "grammar", then one's judgments of grammaticality seem to vary with one's assumptions and beliefs' (1971a: 332). In this and many other cases, 'it makes no sense to speak of the well-formedness or "grammaticality" of a sentence in isolation' (329).

Lakoff concluded in this paper that Chomsky's notion of grammaticality had to be replaced by one of grammaticality relative to a set of 'presuppositions' (1971a: 336). In another contribution to the same volume, these were included with other things in the semantic representations of sentences (Lakoff, 1971b: 234f.). But let us take another example of a kind that Lakoff made famous. *His next insult was to call me a Republican* presupposes that being a Republican is a bad thing (for the example compare Lakoff, 1971a: 333). It is therefore grammatical only if the speaker thinks that. But is it? The speaker might be ironic: for example, the person doing the 'insulting' thought it was a bad thing and assumed wrongly that the speaker thought the same. Alternatively, it is only the hearer who takes such things as truly insulting, and so on. If what is known or assumed by someone who might utter this sentence is part of the meaning to be represented in a grammar, how many varying semantic representations has it got?

The last agonies of generative semantics are hard to document. But the natural conclusion was first reached (I think) in a review article by McCawley whose preprint was distributed privately in 1973. At the beginning he says simply that 'strictly speaking, generative semanticists are not engaged in "generative grammar"'. The reason is that 'while there was general agreement about the notion of "grammaticality" around 1967', they had now 'come to dispute the notion that one can speak coherently of a string of words ... as being grammatical or ungrammatical or having a degree of grammaticality'. Instead they 'hold that a surface structure can be "grammatical" only relative to the meaning that it is supposed to convey and the (linguistic and extra-linguistic) context in which it is used' (McCawley, 1975 [1982: 11]). The disintegration of the first Chomskyan school was then complete.

The latest period

By 1975, most of the movements that had seemed exciting ten or even five years earlier had fizzled out. Halle's theory of phonology had been carried to its logical conclusion in the late 1960s, and from then on the reaction to it was increasingly critical. The details are discussed by Anderson (1985: Ch. 13) and need not concern us. But one important factor is that

Chomsky and Halle were unable to justify a purely formal measure of the simplicity of phonological rules (Chomsky & Halle, 1968: Ch. 9). The quest for an evaluation measure had been a mainspring of Halle's argument in the early 1960s (see especially Halle, 1961, 1962); moreover, generative phonology was the only branch of generative grammar in which the requirement that linguistic theories should provide a measure had been developed beyond a programmatic stage. As Halle's theory was abandoned, this goal was effectively set aside. In the mid 1960s it had still been central to Chomsky's thinking (Chomsky, 1965: 30ff. and elsewhere). Ten years later, in the Whidden lectures which form the first part of *Reflections on Language*, the term 'evaluation procedure' appears only in a note (Chomsky, 1976 [1975]: 233, n. 15).

Generative semantics had also reached its logical conclusion, as we have just seen. In later years its best proponents were to find new roles, with assumptions very different from those they had taken from Chomsky when they began. But at the same time, the received account of transformational syntax was being undermined by other developments, above all in Chomsky's own work. The classic concept of a transformational grammar is enshrined in textbooks in the middle 1970s, notably the second by Bach (1974), those of Akmajian and Heny (1975) and Culicover (1976), and, outside America, Huddleston's (1976). But within one or two years they were clearly out of date.

These developments had not seemed so damaging at first, partly because the apparent controversy in the Chomskyan school in the early 1970s, as to whether or not semantics was 'generative', had tended to overshadow them. But from the beginning of the decade the scope of transformations was progressively reduced, firstly at the expense of a new concept of the lexicon and, subsequently, by a shift in the relation of syntax to semantics. In Chomsky's original conception, a theory of a language had been a theory of syntax above all. He had inherited from Bloomfield a view of the sentence as a primary unit; from Bloomfield again a concept of the lexicon as an inventory of minimal units; and from Bloomfield's successors an assumption that semantics was external to what Harris had called distributional structure. All this was still assumed in 1965, with the sole change that the distinction between a distributional syntax and what Chomsky now called an 'interpretive' semantics became internal to a grammar. The argument for transformations partly rested on the assumption that, if there was a distributional regularity, it would have to be stated in syntactic terms.

But in 1970 Chomsky argued that some regularities were lexical and not syntactic. His main example was the relation between verbs (like *destroy*) and derived nouns (like *destruction*); and, since this had generally been said to belong to derivational morphology, and in other traditions had always been a relation between words rather than constructions, the argument seemed striking only in contrast to the views of the generative semanticists, who were at that time pushing syntax to extremes. In reviewing the volume in which Chomsky's article appeared, I described it as 'refreshingly conservative and responsible' in tone (Matthews, 1972b: 135). But once there were rules relating words within the lexicon, they could in principle handle other kinds of process. They could clearly deal with many phonological or morphophonological alternations, like that of *destroy* and *destruc(t)-*: that is the starting-point for what was later developed as a theory of 'lexical' phonology. They could also describe inflections independently of syntax: this was suggested by Halle in 1973 (discussed in §2.5 below). Finally, they could deal with any other case in which a systematic relation between words is associated with a change of syntax. Take, for example, the relation of active and passive. This had been one of Chomsky's earliest transformations: first an active structure was derived by rules of syntax, then a verbal and other lexical morphemes were inserted in it, then a passive was derived from it by a further syntactic rule. But the relation could now be looked at in another way. On the one hand, there are active forms of verbs, like *own* in *The government own it*. On the other, there are passive forms, like the participle *owned* in *It is owned by the government*. Like *destroy* and *destruction*, they appear in different constructions. But such structures do not have to be related syntactically. Like *destroy* and *destruction*, active *own* and passive *owned* can be related as different words within the lexicon.

This possibility was eventually exploited by Bresnan (1978), and became a partial foundation for what surveys in the 1980s (Sells, 1985; Horrocks, 1987) present as one of three main successors to the classic Chomskyan model. But by then the status of semantic rules had also changed. In Chomsky's earlier account, their role had simply been to 'relate[ ] a structure generated by the syntactic component to a certain semantic representation' (Chomsky, 1965: 16). The semantic component of a grammar, when it was first added, was in that sense 'purely interpretive', and the problem of which structures were those of grammatical sentences remained, by implication, one of syntax. But by the mid-1970s it had become clear that, in Chomsky's current conception, a structure which was ungrammatical might be characterised as such by principles or rules at either level. Take, for example, the rules for reflexives. In the early days of generative grammar, a sentence like *He cut himself* was derived by a syntactic transformation from *He cut him* (compare Lees, 1960a: 103, rule T65). But through restrictions whose precise formulation became a subject of intense research, the rules could not derive, for example, *He said that himself did it* from *He said that he did it*. If the role of semantics lay outside the grammar – as had at first been envisaged – or was 'purely interpretive', as envisaged later, that had to be the solution. But suppose it is not 'purely interpretive'. In that case there is no need for a transformation. We can say that a sentence like *He cut himself* makes sense. That is because, among other things, *himself* can be construed as having to refer to the same person as *he*. But through restrictions which remained the subject of intense research, and which indeed in other respects did not change in the slightest, sentences like *He said that himself did it* do not make sense. That is, *himself* cannot in this position be construed with *he*; and, since reflexives must have antecedents, the grammar can exclude such sentences that way instead.

We will return to this development in §4.3. But what with it and with the new role of the lexicon, the technical case for transformations dissolved. A theory of grammar might still distinguish something in part resembling the classic level of deep structure from something in part resembling surface structure, and, in published work up to the time of writing, Chomsky himself has continued to do so. But it could no longer be argued, as it had been argued in the teaching tradition in particular, that, if it was to 'capture' regularities, it had to.

Finally, and again by the mid-1970s, it had become clear to most parties that Chomsky's earlier concept of the meaning or 'semantic representation' of a sentence could not be defended. It had been in origin Katz and Fodor's concept, in a paper (1963) which we will discuss in a later chapter (§3.4). But, as Chomsky was to put it later in the 1960s, individual sentences had 'intrinsic meanings' that were determined by the rules of a generative grammar (Chomsky, 1972b [1968]: 71). These were 'intrinsic' in precisely the sense that they were given by the grammar, and were therefore independent of any non-intrinsic meaning that a sentence might have when it was uttered by a particular speaker on a particular occasion. At the time, this did not seem to him to be controversial. 'It is quite obvious', he remarked in a lecture in the same year, 'that sentences have an intrinsic meaning determined by linguistic rule' (Chomsky, 1972b: 115; date in preface (viii)).

The generative semanticists were among those who had taken this idea seriously, with the result that we have seen. But many others had concluded that the scope of the semantic component of a grammar could not be as comprehensive as that. To meet Katz's requirement, it had to include a dictionary which defined exactly each of an exact set of senses for each word. It also had to indicate exactly in how many ways, for whatever reason, a sentence was ambiguous; when, in whatever respect, its meaning was anomalous, and so on. If generative semantics had shown anything, it was that these things could not be done. In practice, therefore, the programme was dropped. By the later 1970s, many scholars had rejected Katz's account of lexical meanings, and, insofar as the topic was studied in America thereafter, the work which attracted attention was in terms of a theory in which they were characterised by 'prototypical' referents or instances (see, for instance, Coleman & Kay, 1981) and not by exact definition. As in other fields, a textbook account of what had been accepted readily a dozen or so years earlier can now be seen as a tombstone (Fodor, 1977).

At the same time, the scope of semantics was further restricted by a division between it and 'pragmatics'. I have put this term in inverted commas, since it was not at first used and its definition was to remain a matter of debate. But the general drift was that a grammar was concerned only with what may be called the propositional structure of a sentence. In Chomsky's account, the structures generated by a grammar are said, from about the middle of the decade, to be 'associated with "logical forms"' (Chomsky, 1976 [1975]: 43). By definition, these comprised 'those aspects of semantic interpretation that are strictly determined by grammar, abstracted from other cognitive systems' (Chomsky, 1977a: 5), and what belonged to them was at first made clear only by illustrations. But, for example, the logical forms of *Who said Mary kissed him?* and *Who did he say Mary kissed?* are said to be respectively, 'for which person *x*, *x* said Mary kissed him?' and 'for which person *x*, he said Mary kissed *x*?' (Chomsky, 1976: 99). By implication, other aspects of meaning belonged to other 'cognitive systems'.

Other writers began to see semantics as an account of the conditions under which a sentence with a given structure would be true. The source of this idea lay in a philosophical theory, but it was promoted in linguistics by studies like that of Partee (1975), which sought to incorporate attempts by logicians to analyse aspects of ordinary language. In this article, Partee did not claim more than that a definition of truth-conditions 'must be a *part* of any adequate semantic theory' (209). But by the end of the decade the view had developed that semantics, in a strict sense, was concerned with nothing else. Other aspects of meaning belonged to pragmatics, and there was therefore a pragmatics for a particular language, apart from its grammar, whose topics included many that, ten years earlier, had been generally seen as part of the 'intrinsic meanings' of sentences. Semantics in turn became a domain of formal theories, in which the interests of one school in linguistics and a corresponding school in philosophy had virtually merged.

For all these reasons, it is convenient to see the middle 1970s as the start of a new period, distinguished less by the emergence of a single positive idea than by the decay of several old ones that in the past had been perhaps fortuitously linked. This new period is harder to characterise than those that have preceded, the main reason being simply that it is too recent. Another reason, however, is that, as the subject expanded in the 1970s, it also fragmented. In the 1960s new specialisations had already arisen, like sociolinguistics. But early sociolinguistics had been conceived within a structuralist frame, and the theoretical problems which Labov addressed before and after 1970 concerned the nature of rules and grammars, and the nature of change in language conceived as change in a grammar, in a way that entered directly into debate with Chomsky. As late as 1973, in Brown's book on children's speech, that part of psycholinguistics was also clearly integrated with linguistics in general. The unity of the subject was perhaps most clearly seen in Chomsky's domination of it. As Lyons wrote at the end of the 1960s, his school was 'not just one among many'. One might agree or disagree, but 'no linguist who wishe[d] to keep abreast of current developments ... [could] afford to ignore Chomsky's theoretical pronouncements'. Every other school 'tend[ed] to define its position in relation to Chomsky's views on particular issues' (Lyons, 1991 [1970]: 9).

What Lyons says was undoubtedly true, at least of the English-speaking world, when it was written. But it has become increasingly untrue over the past fifteen or so years. Chomsky's ideas are certainly important, probably (though in the light of history I may be proved wrong) as important as the work he did in the 1950s. The second Chomskyan school, as we may call it, is large and very active. But Chomsky no longer bestrides the discipline like a colossus. In syntax, in particular, there are at least two major schools in the United States, one his, the other the typological school on the West Coast, whose ideas developed from work by Greenberg in the same creative period in the early 1960s. Both are concerned with 'linguistic universals' or 'universals of language', terms first used at about the same time both in Chomsky's work (1961b: 219) and in the conference in 1961 whose proceedings Greenberg edited (1963). It is therefore tempting at first to see them as proposing rival treatments of the same problem. As Comrie put it in the early 1980s, 'two major methodological approaches to language universals' had been adopted in recent work (1981: 1). In one approach, data are drawn from 'a wide range of languages', universals tend to be statable in 'relatively concrete' terms, and the kinds of explanation offered tend to be 'open, or at least eclectic'. That is the Greenbergian approach, which Comrie himself follows. In the other, it is argued that 'the best way to learn about language universals is by the detailed study of an individual language', they are best stated 'in terms of abstract structures', and 'innateness' is 'favour[ed]' as an explanation.

But Comrie's own account makes clear that these are in reality approaches to two different problems. In Chomsky's case, the problem is to understand how speakers can develop a knowledge of a language. We will look at the details in a later chapter; but the first step in the argument is that their knowledge involves things that cannot come from experience. Therefore it must develop partly under genetic control, and, since *homo sapiens* is a single species and there is no evidence that different populations are predisposed to acquire different types of language, we may assume that the genetic factors are common to all of them. In this chain of argument, 'universals' are not explained by 'innateness'. Rather innateness – that is, the hypothesis that the development of language in the speaker is in part genetically controlled – implies universality.

In Greenberg's programme, the first step is to establish that 'universals' exist – to be precise, that certain features tend at least to be common to different languages. That is all he at first did, notably in his paper to the conference on universals in the 1960s (Greenberg, ed. 1963: 73–113). Alternatively, we find that languages which have one feature also tend, at least, to have others: to the extent that features cluster languages can then be divided into types. By the late 1970s Lehmann, Greenberg and others also argued that, as languages change, they will tend, all else being equal, to evolve towards one type or another (Lehmann in Lehmann, ed. 1978; Greenberg in Greenberg, ed. 1978: 61–91). If all this is so we then ask why, and the explanation may indeed be of any kind whatever. For example, certain tendencies of word order may be explained by psychological factors bearing on the perception of sentence structure (Hawkins, 1990), other findings by the ease with which one pattern or another may be learned, and so on.

Since the problems are different the methods of research are naturally different too. But, what is more important, programmes such as these are logically independent. In principle, it may be that both schools are partly right. That is, the development of language in the individual is genetically controlled by principles of the kind that Chomsky and his followers have proposed; and, in addition, the features of a language that are determined by experience include some, of the sort that Greenberg or Comrie have studied, which are general or even universal for other reasons. A clash may have to be resolved in the 1990s. But for most of the past fifteen years, despite occasional disparagement from one side or another, each school has in practice had little reason to refer to the other. It is worth noting, for example, that Croft's recent introduction to *Typology and Universals* (1990) cites no work by Chomsky. Seven years before, Newmeyer, in a book on *Grammatical Theory* whose references are wide-ranging and which is in places gratuitously polemic, mentioned Greenberg and his school once (1983: 71).

Part of our problem, therefore, is that if a history of linguistics in this latest period is to do justice to the work that seems important, it will itself fragment, far more than our account of any earlier period, into a chronicle of separate trends. But finally, in the past two decades the main movements have also become international. The history of the first Chomskyan school can be and was told without reference to work outside the United States. Although there were transformationalists elsewhere, notably Bierwisch and his colleagues in what was then East Germany, the current of ideas within America was self-contained. This is less true of the second Chomskyan school: although its leader is American, and its base is firmly on the East Coast where he is, a detailed history would distort matters if it were limited in the same way. It is still less true of the Greenbergian school; or, for instance, of the study of formal semantics. Where we can pick out American ideas that seem important, they are those that have sparked a wider response.

For all these reasons, a true history cannot be written confidently. But as we look back over the past fifty years that precede it, it is tempting to see this as a period in which the dominance of structural linguistics, which had come in in the 1920s and had reached its apogee in the decades after Bloomfield's *Language*, finally weakened. The issue is obscured by different uses of the term 'structuralism', which has often been applied especially to the linguistics of Bloomfield and his immediate followers. Many will therefore be minded to talk less of a decline of structuralism in the 1970s and 1980s, than of its overthrow at the end of the 1950s. But many deep-seated structuralist ideas were not overthrown, nor questioned until later.

One obvious instance is the structuralist preoccupation with theories of levels. General schemes were rife in the middle decades of the century, and a striking feature of most of them, not only in America, was the attempt to model the account of semantic units on that of phonology. 'If it is possible to discover any aim common to all linguistic schools', as Bazell wrote in the early 1950s, it is 'the reduction', by what he called 'terminological devices', of 'the fundamental asymmetry of linguistic systems' (Bazell, 1953: iii). One example, which Bazell gives and which we will examine in §2.3, is the modelling of the Post-Bloomfieldian theory of the morpheme on a previous account of the phoneme. Another is the modelling of 'semantic features' on phonetic features. The notion of distinctive features in phonology was barely established in America when Bazell wrote. But through the influence on Halle of Jakobson's work in the 1950s (Jakobson, Fant & Halle, 1952; Jakobson & Halle, 1956), it came to play a central role in generative phonology, and in the mid-1960s was explicitly taken by Chomsky (1965: 80) as a model for features in syntax. At the same time, an explicit parallel was drawn between the semantic 'interpretation' of sentences in terms of universal features of meaning and their phonetic 'interpretation' in terms of a universal phonetics (see especially Chomsky, 1966a: 12). Among other schemes, the most striking illustration is that of the aptly named 'stratificational' theory (Lamb, 1966). In its developed form this had six levels, each with a fundamental unit in '-eme' (phoneme, morpheme, and so on), a set of minimal components in '-on' ('phonons', for example, are distinctive features of phonemes), appropriate relations of arrangement or 'tactics', and other aspects that were terminologically parallel.

As I remarked earlier, the scheme of Chomsky's *Aspects* is the last great scheme of this kind, at least up to the present. What eventually replaced it in his own works was and is a 'modular' conception of a language in which different modules are characterised above all by different universal principles. This is an idea that emerged in his writings at the beginning of our latest period (Chomsky, 1980: 28, 40ff.), and a crucial feature, as we will see in §4.4, is that the modules are separate and interact. To justify them individually there is no need for a comprehensive scheme, and the spectrum of modules has in practice been left open. Although this is the explicit view of just one scholar and his followers, it has not been criticised from the viewpoint that had inspired earlier schemes, and, perhaps in part through the growth of specialisation, new schemes have not been proposed. There is also far less eagerness to project insights from phonology onto the rest of language. Since the collapse of Halle's classic model of generative phonology, what has replaced it has been interesting. But it is work within a specialist field, and specialists in others have not generally responded to it.

In other, more central respects a decline in structuralist preoccupations is less striking and less widespread, and its importance may be disputed. But a central structuralist idea, whose importance we noted in the 1910s and 1920s, is that the categories of a language have to be established in terms of its own structure. One consequence is that categories in different languages which may seem similar will be defined by different networks of relations: for example, a 'present tense' which stands in opposition to a 'future' and a 'past' is not the same as one which is opposed to a 'past' only. This does not imply that there are no general tendencies or universals. In a review of the 1930s, Bloomfield talked of 'look[ing] forward to a larger synthesis, a General Grammar, which will register similarities between languages' (1934: *LBA* 285); and, despite the occasional loose remark by later scholars, that remained a responsible view. But such a synthesis would not only be delayed until we had more data. Its terms would have to be defined at a more abstract level of discourse, at which systems that were individually different could be compared.

The Greenbergian school may seem at first to have realised a 'larger synthesis'. But from the very beginning much of their research has been based on assumptions that are opposed to those of structuralism. Greenberg's leading study was concerned especially with the order in different languages of 'subject', 'verb' and 'object'; and, if a structuralist view had been accepted, he would have had to put these, as I have just done, in inverted commas. To justify applying the same terms to, say, English and Tagalog would have required a profound theoretical study that no one had undertaken. But it is evident that Greenberg saw no need for it. He simply lists the logically possible orders of these elements, and proceeded directly to look for them. In the most recent account by Croft, 'single-language analyses' are compared with 'cross-linguistic' generalisations, and it is made clear that the 'classic typological approach' is to 'begin[ ] with cross-linguistic comparisons' (Croft, 1990: 4ff., 250). The basic assumption, apparently in either mode of analysis, is that many or most categories can be identified directly 'by semantic means' (12) or 'on an intuitive basis' (13). The most problematic are 'fundamental grammatical categories' such as subject and object. But, despite the lack of any 'obvious functional (semantic and/or pragmatic) definition' and despite the fact that they 'vary considerably in their structural expression across languages', it seems that these too can be identified 'cross-linguistically by semantic-pragmatic heuristics' (13). At the beginning of the century this is precisely what Boas would have been telling his students not to do.

The decline of structuralism in a Boasian sense is perhaps characteristic of this one school. But the idea that every language must be analysed in its own terms is closely linked to the further thesis that the language system exists independently of other mental structures. In a structuralist view, there is an opposition in English between, say, *look* in *They look* and *looked* in *They looked.* When this is established we may say, on notional grounds, that it is an opposition of tense, and that one form is present and the other past. But suppose we see 'tense' as, in effect, a recurring phenomenon: it is 'found' in English in one manifestation, in Latin in another, and so on. Then what is its nature? The answer will be given in terms of a common human perception of time, and in that way one is led to describe the language in terms that go back to the tradition before structuralism, as a direct expression of aspects of experience.

It is perhaps appropriate to refer here to the recent work of Lakoff (1987) or Langacker (1991). Both are former generative semanticists, Langacker's first book having been an introduction in which syntactic rules related surface structures and 'conceptual structures' (1967: 91). But Langacker in particular has since developed the view that 'language is neither self-contained nor describable without essential reference to cognitive processing' (1991: 1), and in an ambitious contribution to the larger field of 'cognitive science' Lakoff argues, among other things, that 'the core of our conceptual systems is directly grounded in perception, body movement, and experience of a physical and social character' (1987: xiv). These may be straws in a wind that will die down or prove to be blowing elsewhere. But there is potentially the ground for a serious critique of ideas that lay at the heart of structuralism.

1.2 Prospectus

This introductory chapter has surveyed American linguistics in general. Although theories of grammar have played a large part in it, that is because they have, in fact, attracted a great deal of attention throughout much of the century. The remaining chapters, however, will concentrate on grammar and especially on the three main ideas that were picked out at the beginning.

Since there are also three more chapters, I ought perhaps to stress that they do not take these ideas strictly one by one. The next deals specifically with morphology, and therefore with the concept of the morpheme. It will begin with Bloomfield's ideas, both in his first book (§2.1) and his mature work (§2.2), and since these are bound up with his concept of grammar generally, this will also be the best place to discuss his general view of syntax. The remaining sections of the chapter will deal with the Post-Bloomfieldian concept of the morpheme (§2.3), with morphology in early generative grammar (§2.4) and with accounts based on the morpheme from the early 1970s onwards (§2.5). It will therefore cover our whole period, though in a more sketchy and more tentative way towards the end.

The third chapter will explore the history of distributionalism, and especially its influence on views of syntax. We will begin with its origins, which, according to the original proponents, lay in Bloomfield's concepts of form and meaning in the 1930s. The first section (§3.1) will therefore ask why the idea arose and why Bloomfield was seen as its source. The next (§3.2) is concerned with the concept of a generative grammar, and will look especially at the continuity between Post-Bloomfieldian thought and Chomsky's programme in the 1950s. The remaining two deal with technical models that, historically at least, are associated with distributionalism. One is that of constituency or phrase structure grammar (§3.3), and we will follow its development through from Bloomfield into the 1970s. The other is the transformational model (§3.4); we will follow this from its origins in work by Harris in the early 1950s to what appeared to be its logical conclusion, in the work of the generative semanticists.

Finally, the last chapter will look at Chomsky's general ideas, and try to trace the ways in which they have unfolded and changed over almost forty years. His career will be divided into four periods, the first (§4.1) centred on *Syntactic Structures* (1957). This will already have been covered partly in §3.2, but we will now need to consider it in relation to the future rather than the past. The second (§4.2) is an extraordinarily creative period in the 1960s, marked for our purposes by, in particular, the first chapter of *Aspects of the Theory of Syntax* (1965) and by *Language and Mind* (1972b [1968]). It was at this time that many of the ideas for which Chomsky is best known, among linguists and even more among scholars in other disciplines, were first presented. The third section (§4.3) will cover the 1970s, seen as a period of transition centred, insofar as one can point to any one publication, on *Reflections of Language* (1976 [1975]). Finally – though with the consciousness again that very recent history is very risky – I will try, in §4.4, to interpret his latest phase, as represented in particular by *Knowledge of Language* (1986).

Throughout this book references will be mainly to the primary sources. It will be obvious that I have learned a great deal from early secondary treatments, notably from Hymes and Fought (1981 [1975]), from Lepschy's general survey of linguistic schools (1982 [1970]), from Anderson's valuable study of phonology (1985), from the brief account in Robins's *Short History of Linguistics* (1990 [1967]), and from numerous articles. I have also acquired insight from some contributions with which it will be obvious that I do not generally agree, notably Newmeyer's history of the generative school (1980). All this will, as I say, be obvious; and I hope I will therefore be forgiven if, in the interest of allowing the primary texts to speak as directly as my own interpretation permits, I do not generally discuss others.

In addition, I will not refer systematically to contemporary European assessments of American work. This decision has been a hard one, since there will be many occasions when comments that I make as a historian reflect those made by critics at the time. Many were made by scholars who I have known personally, notably by Bazell in *Linguistic Form* (1953) and a series of articles from 1949 onwards. There are even a few for which I might refer to work of my own. But pietas and self-esteem are one thing, and the need to keep this book within bounds is another. I have therefore had to ask whether such assessments can themselves be seen as part of our history. The answer is in effect what makes this study possible: that linguistics in the United States has for much of this century been remarkably self-contained. It developed an internal momentum in the 1930s, and new or contrary ideas have in general mattered only when they arose in response to a problem recognised in America at the time, and come from members of the American community.

2 *Bloomfield's morphology and its successors*

The concept of the morpheme is central to much of twentieth-century linguistics, and its history, especially in America, has been told before. But there are reasons for looking at it again. One is that, in interpreting the account in Bloomfield's *Language*, few commentators have made detailed reference to the earlier book, *An Introduction to the Study of Language*, which it replaced. But I will try to show that the comparison is interesting, for morphology and for grammatical theory generally. Another reason is that many have accepted far too readily the critique of Bloomfield's theory by American scholars since the 1940s. I will argue in §2.3 that it was in part mistaken, and that the weaknesses of his treatment, though real and serious, lay elsewhere. A third reason is that, although morphology was largely neglected in the heyday of generative phonology, a new chapter in its history began in the 1970s. I will therefore try to explore the connection between the work of the past twenty years and what had gone before. Finally, I would like to place the theory of the morpheme in what I believe to be its historical context. This can be seen as part of a wider tension or conflict, discernible sporadically throughout the century, between the concepts and techniques of grammar inherited from earlier Western traditions, and the doctrines or (if we prefer) the insights of structuralism.

In morphology, the tension lies particularly between two views of the status, or the primary locus, of grammatical categories. Let us take, for illustration, the English plural *cats*. In one view, the category 'plural' – the meaning 'plural' as one tradition might see it – is primarily, at least, a property of the entire word. We may say, in addition, that *cats* can be divided into *cat* + *s*, that *s* is added specifically to form the plural, and that, by virtue of this, *s* is the exponent or marker or realisation of plural. But we do not have to say so and, if we do, the relation between *s* and plural remains derived or secondary. Plurality, to repeat, is basically a property of the word as a whole.

In the other view, plurality is assigned directly to *s*. The form *cats* has two smaller forms, *cat* and *s*, as its constituents, and the second of these is, or is the form or realisation or the appropriate allomorph of, a plural morpheme. We may also say that *cats*, like any other word, is a syntactic unit and, since it includes the plural morpheme, it is also, as a whole, plural. But it is now that statement that is secondary. The primary statement is that *cats* consists of a noun morpheme followed by a plural morpheme.

In the light of later studies, by myself (1991 [1974]) among others, these have emerged as two alternative models, which have different implications and between which we must choose, either absolutely or according to the nature of particular languages or types of language. But it is tempting, at the outset, to suppose that they have simply got hold of different ends of the stick. Is it not possible to start from a more comprehensive view, in which the whole stick, at both ends, is grasped at once? On my reading of Bloomfield's *Language*, that is precisely what he did, and it is from that that the complexity of his treatment, which has struck most serious readers and commentators, largely springs.

2.1 Bloomfield's *Introduction*

We must begin, however, with Bloomfield's first book (1914). He was twenty-seven in the year that it was published and, as is well known, it was written within the framework of a psychological theory that he later abandoned. It is therefore natural for historians to see it as a juvenile work, which, though interesting in itself, and perhaps of special interest because Bloomfield wrote it, will shed no light on, nor in general help us to understand, the larger and undoubtedly very different book which replaced it. As Mounin remarks (1972: 114), it is in general little read. But there are good reasons to read it, especially for its handling of more technical issues. In the preface to *Language*, Bloomfield himself presents his new work as a 'revised version' of its predecessor (1935 [1933]: vii), and, although this wording may well strike us as unduly and perhaps perversely modest, it reminds us that, in rewriting or replacing any book with such a wide scope, one is bound to recast part of what was expounded earlier. Bloomfield is no exception and, when we look at the first version, we can sometimes see the point of things that scholars who refer only to the second version have found puzzling.

For the relevant sections of the *Introduction* we must refer to four chapters. Ch. 3 ('The mental basis of language'), introduces the concepts of a sentence, of a word and, within the word, of a 'formational element'. It goes on to distinguish syntactic and 'morphologic' categories. In Ch. 4 ('The forms of language'), we will refer particularly to a discussion of what we would now call phonaesthetic patterns, and to a further account of words and parts of words. Ch. 5 is specifically on 'Morphology' and deals with the parts of speech and other kinds of word-class, with inflection and derivation and the formal processes they involve, and compounds. Finally, in Ch. 6 ('Syntax'), we will need to refer, especially in the light of what is to come in *Language*, to sections dealing with the realisation or expression of syntactic relations.

Let us begin with the sentence. In a traditional definition, this is 'a series of words ... forming the grammatically complete expression of a single thought' (*OED*, *s.v.*, §6). But for the younger Bloomfield it is rather the *analysis* of a thought, or, to be exact, of what he calls a 'total experience'. Both humans and animals can 'form' experiences (Bloomfield, 1914: 56), and in man a great many different types of experience are associated with 'distinctive sound-reaction[s]' (57). For example, there is a type of experience 'which we call a "rabbit"'. Once such sound-reactions exist, there is bound to develop a process in which 'expression-relations' are assimilated to 'experience-relations' (59). Thus, in Bloomfield's schematic illustration, the utterance connected with the experience of a white rabbit might change in such a way that it became identical in part with that connected with the experience of a white fox, and, when this happens, each would have two parts, one 'corresponding to the perceptual element "white"' and the other to the element 'rabbit' or 'fox'. The utterance *white rabbit* or *white fox* then 'involves an analysis of the total experience into these two elements', and it is such an 'utterance analyzing an experience into elements' that we call a sentence (60).

There are echoes in these pages of older sources, from Aristotle onwards. But the specific theory of the sentence derives from that of Wundt. Bloomfield himself refers to Wundt's *Die Sprache* (1911–12 [1900]) as a 'great linguistic work' (1914: 316), and makes clear in his preface that for his 'psychology, general and linguistic' he has depended 'entirely' on him (vi). It is therefore worth glancing at part, at least, of Wundt's own argument. In Ch. 7 ('Die Satzfügung'), he rejects as 'psychologically untenable' a view of the sentence either as the combination of a set of ideas ('eine "Verbindung von Vorstellungen"') or as the combination of a set of words ('eine "Verbindung von Wörtern"'). He is thus implicitly opposed to Paul, who defines it (I will summarise loosely) as the linguistic expression by which a speaker transmits a combination of ideas to the hearer (1920 [1880]: 121). Instead a sentence is the analysis into its parts of something that exists as a whole in the consciousness of the speaker ('die Zerlegung eines im Bewußtsein vorhandenen Ganzen in seine Teile') (Wundt, 1911–12, Vol. 2: 243). This independently existing whole is a total thought or idea (a 'Gesamtvorstellung') (244).

Syntax is therefore primarily a study of the units and relationships established by this process of analysis. As Wundt explains, the process is not simply of division ('Teilung') but involves an 'articulation' or division into members ('Gliederung'), in which the parts of a sentence are placed in specific 'logical relations' (244f.). In his full definition (248), a sentence is 'the linguistic expression of the arbitrary articulation of a total thought into its components placed in logical relations to one another' ('[der] sprachliche Ausdruck für die willkürliche Gliederung einer Gesamtvorstellung in ihre in logische Beziehungen zueinander gesetzten Bestandteile'). But the components between which the relations hold are what will later be called immediate constituents. Furthermore, Wundt declares later in this chapter (324) that the articulation of any relation is invariably binary ('die überall durchgeführte binäre Beschaffenheit der Gliederung geschlossener Verbindungen'). That is because 'a logical relationship is of its nature restricted to the two ideas between which it holds' (325). Soon afterwards (333), he introduces a form of diagram which can easily be seen as the precursor of a binary phrase structure tree.

Likewise, as Percival has pointed out (1976), for Bloomfield. The relation between the elements of a sentence is the 'logical' or 'discursive' relation, and 'consists of a transition of attention from the total experience . . . to the successive elements, which are one after another focused by it' (60). Again the process of analysis proceeds 'by single binary divisions' between an element that is 'for the time being focused' and 'a remainder' (61). For example, in *Lean horses run fast*, the experience is first divided into a subject, *lean horses*, which is the part being focussed, and a predicate, *run fast*, which is 'left for later attention'. On further analysis, these parts are in turn divided into a smaller 'subject' or focussed element (*horses*, *run*) and an attribute (*lean*, *fast*). The reason why the analysis is binary is that 'the attention of an individual . . . is a unified process: we can attend to but one thing at a time' (60). That thing is the 'part being focused' and what is left is the 'remainder'.

This theory of the sentence forms the context, as we will see in a moment, for the distinction between syntax and morphology. But before we read the chapter further, we may perhaps reflect briefly on the later history of constituency analysis. The notion of immediate constituents is introduced in *Language* in a passage which we will discuss later (1935 [1933]: 161). But it is no longer founded in Wundt's account of the psychology of the speaker and, in particular, there is no reason to expect that all divisions should be binary. Bloomfield himself allows that, 'rarely', more than two forms may combine in a construction (169). It is therefore remarkable that, although its original justification has collapsed, and new arguments have hardly ever been given, most writers have assumed, with Bloomfield, that divisions between constituents are normally binary, and, in analysing or proposing rules for complex phrases, have continued to take this as a guiding principle. By 'most writers' I mean, of course, most writers within a tradition whose origins can be shown to lie, both on the evidence of who learned directly from whom and by the analysis of successive references in books and articles, in Bloomfield's work. He does not say, in *Language*, why constructions are rarely other than binary. To understand this, I believe we have to look back to his first book and its main source.

With that hint in mind, let us now turn to his theory of the word. The analysis of the 'total experience' proceeds, as we have seen, in successive stages. But in the end there is no absolute distinction between what is analysed 'discursively' and what is merely associated, as a single perceptual element, with a single form. Take, for example, words like *flare* or *flash* or *flicker*. They are not divisible in the way that, say, *lean horses* is divisible. But neither are they strictly unanalysed. In them we find, 'corresponding to [a] common half-emotional, half-perceptual element, the common initial sound-group *fl-*'. The *-icker* of *flicker*, 'which expresses to our feeling the small repeated movements of the flame, performs a similar function in *snicker*'. In *flash*, the sounds *-ash* express a different kind of movement 'also conveyed' in *clash*, *dash* and so on (Bloomfield, 1914: 79). Such forms are neither wholly analysed nor wholly unanalysed. In Bloomfield's terms (62), 'discursive analysis is not an absolute thing: associational identification shades into it'.

These examples are cited from Ch. 4, where the immediate context is different. But forms like *fl-* and *-ash* are similar, in Bloomfield's reasoning, to any element that cannot be spoken independently. *Suddenly*, which is his first illustration, 'divides itself into *sudden* and *-ly*'; but 'since the latter cannot be used alone, the analysis is not discursive but merely associative'

(62). In *ran* and *run*, the vowels [æ] and [ʌ] 'are felt to express the relative time of the action', but neither they nor 'an abstract *r*-vowel-*n*' are conceivable separately. *Father*, *mother* and *brother* share a form *-ther* which 'expresses a common element of all three'. But that too cannot be 'used alone in some such sense as "near relation": there is but the suggestion of an analysis'. In later passages Bloomfield makes clear that there is a gradation. The form *flash* 'relates the experience' to those expressed by *flame* or *crash*, but 'it does this subtly, without analytic consciousness on the speaker's part' (93). Nor can *fl-* be 'added at liberty to any other utterance, but occurs fixedly and exclusively in certain words' (94). In the plural *fires*, the parts 'at once appear to possess a much greater degree of independence'. 'Even the normal speaker', Bloomfield goes on, feels the connections between *fire-* and the singular *fire*, and between *-s* and the similar sounds in *fathers* or in *cats* and *peaches* (94f.). In the possessive *father's*, *-'s* has more independence, since it can combine with phrases (95); *-teen* in thirteen has still more, since we can speak of 'a girl in her *teens*' (96). But still there is not full independence. As Bloomfield puts it earlier (62), all these are 'imperfectly separable elements'.

The fully independent elements are, of course, words. In Bloomfield's definition (103), the word is 'a semantically independent and recurrent element which can be dealt with as a conceptual whole'. It will be obvious that, if we remove the parts of this argument that derive from Wundt's conception of the analysis of a 'Gesamtvorstellung', what is left is the precursor of the definition given in *Language*, as 'a free form which does not consist entirely of ... lesser free forms' (Bloomfield, 1935: 178). The 'imperfectly separable' forms are called 'formational elements'. Thus *fl-* and *-ash* are formational elements; likewise *-s* in *fires*, and so on. It will be clear that Bloomfield's concept of these is not the same as his later concept of the morpheme. But the morpheme in *Language* is in one way closer to the earlier formational element than to the morpheme as it has been generally conceived since the 1940s. For the later Bloomfield, *fl-* and *-ash* remain 'minimal linguistic forms'. With the *gl-* of *glow* and *glare*, or the *-ump* of *bump* and *lump*, they are part of 'a system of initial and final *root-forming morphemes*', though (he adds) they are morphemes 'of vague signification' (1935: 245). But most successors have agreed that words like these are lexically and grammatically simple. In Bolinger's account (1975 [1968]: 219), they show no more than 'a vague resemblance in sound – too hazy to carve out as a definite morpheme'.

The last of the sections which concern us in this general chapter deals with the notion of a category. The process of analysis, as we have seen, establishes types of experience, and, in this process, 'certain types may become habitual and finally universal in a language' (Bloomfield, 1914: 67). For example, in analysing a total experience 'we who speak English always speak of an actor performing an action', even, as Bloomfield makes clear, when no actor and action are 'really involve[d]' (67f). On this basis, actor and action 'are grammatical *categories*' in English. Such categories, 'which universalize certain relations between words, are *syntactic* categories'.

Likewise for 'morphologic' categories. For example, an English verb-form 'always contains an imperfect analysis into a formational element expressive of the action itself and one expressive of its relative time' (68). On that basis, 'the formational expression of present or past time with actions is a morphologic category in English'. In general, then, a category is the generalised expression of a particular type of experience. Alternatively, it is itself the type of experience that is generalised. In the formulation cited actor and action 'are' categories, and on the next page (69) Bloomfield underlines that both they and tense 'must be formally expressed'. The object of the verb 'to express', in his theory, is again a 'type of experience'.

With these foundations in mind, we can turn to the chapter which deals specifically with morphology (Ch. 5). It begins with a comprehensive survey of word-classes, including some – such as parts of speech – which, Bloomfield explains, are 'really ... syntactic phenomen[a]' (120, 128). But if we set these aside the main distinction is between smaller classes whose members share both a common meaning and a common phonetic form, and larger semantic classes whose phonetic basis is only partial. An example of the former is the class of regular plural nouns in English: all these express 'a plurality of objects with the common phonetic element [z] and, by an automatic sound-variation peculiar to this ending, [s] and [əz]' (134). Another class has the members, *dance*, *dances*, *danced*, *dancing* and *dancer* (135), and another, to which Bloomfield again gives prominence, is that of *flash*, *flicker*, *flame* and so on (132f). An example of the second type is the class of all plural nouns; another, since singulars and plurals stand in a 'uniform semantic relation' (137), the class of singular nouns. These are examples of 'categoric classes' (136), or classes established by a categorial distinction.

Morphology in general has already been defined as 'the phase of linguistics that studies [word-]classes – that is, the structure of words'

(110), and divides into inflection, derivation and composition. The reason for separating composition from syntax is that, in compounds, the analysis of the total experience is still marginally imperfect. We have seen, for example, that the *-'s* of *father's* has more independence than the *-s* of *fires*, and that the *-teen* of *thirteen* is yet more nearly independent (93ff.). In the compound *bulldog* (96f.), the elements do appear independently. But still, Bloomfield says, 'there is a reservation' in that, when *bull* is used independently, it has a different meaning: 'bull', not [dog] 'like a bull'. In this expression, it is 'not fully independent, for, though closely associated with the independent use of the same sound-sequence', it has a slightly different value. 'Consequently', the compound 'retains a considerable degree of unity'. Composition therefore receives a semantic definition similar to that which was later given by Jespersen (1942). It 'consists of the use of two or more words in a combination that has a different meaning from that of the simple words in syntactic collocation' (159).

Inflection and derivation are distinguished by reference to categories. If a class of words 'differ only in an element of relational content such as is categoric in the language ... it is customary to speak of ... the relation between them as *inflection*' (140). Inflection, then, 'could be defined as variation between words to express relational differences which involve appurtenance to different categories' (141). But if words differ in an element 'expressing material meaning', and 'the relation between them [is] not merely a difference of categoric function', that relation 'is called *derivation*'. Thus the relation between *flash* and *flare* is derivational; also between *eat*, *eater*, and *eatable* (141). In a briefer and perhaps a clearer formulation, 'when the relation between words of a phonetic-semantic class is not a difference of category, we call it derivation' (150).

For the rest, we must look carefully at two sections. The first, which follows directly on the definition of inflection, is a cross-linguistic survey of the 'commonest categories' as they were known at that time (141–50). Categories are founded, as we have seen, in types of experience and, to the extent that experience as such is universal, it implicitly makes sense to talk of the same types of experience being the basis for what can be called the same category in different languages. Thus many languages 'have ... genders', though their number varies (142f.); case 'appears ... in English especially in the personal and anaphoric pronouns' (143) and is also a category in German. It also makes implicit sense to talk of the same type of experience being expressed differently in different languages. For example, 'the local relations of objects' which English 'analyze[s] fully out of the experience' and expresses by prepositions 'are in many languages inflectionally included in the object-word, which thus varies categorically' for case (144). Sanskrit and Ancient Greek both had three numbers, but in Greek 'the distinction between dual and plural ... was not categoric' (though it is called inflectional), since the use of the dual was restricted and never obligatory (142). The second section, which follows after a very brief discussion of derivation, deals with 'The phonetic character of morphologic processes' (151–9). These include variations of pitch, of stress, of vowels and consonants; affixation; reduplication; 'homomorphy' (i.e. identity) and suppletion. At the beginning of the section, variation which is of morphologic significance is said to be 'sharply distinguished' from the 'automatic sound-variation' found, for example, in *Will you?* ([ju]) and *Won't you?* ([ʃu]) or, we can add, in *dog*[z], *cat*[s] and *hors*[əz].

Is Bloomfield's account of these matters morpheme-based or word-based? The question is not only anachronistic but, even if I were to word it more carefully, would be unfair. On the one hand, words are analysed into formational elements. In that sense, a formational element can be associated directly with an element of experience, and we can talk, as Bloomfield does talk, of forms like *flash* and *flicker* having in common one 'element expressing material meaning' but differing in another (see again the top of 141). But, on the other hand, the discursive analysis of words is always imperfect. In that sense, *flash* and *flicker* are associated as wholes with types of experience that can be seen as unitary. Likewise for relations involving categories. On the one hand, 'even the normal speaker' can say that *-s* in *fires* 'expresses plurality' (95). On the other hand, nouns as a whole 'must express whether one object or a plurality is meant' (142). 'We may say', Bloomfield goes on, 'that each of these "words" has two inflectional "forms", a singular and a plural.' The critique of Bloomfield's *Language* was to lead much later to accounts of morphology based strictly on the morpheme, and the critique of that in turn to a revindication (at first in European work) of accounts based on the word. But within the theory to which Bloomfield subscribed in 1914, either would have been a distortion.

Nevertheless it is worth noting that the concept of a formational element plays little or no role in these sections. The term itself is not used, though affixes are, of course, identified as 'phonetic elements' (153). Instead Bloomfield tends to talk of meanings, or of differences of meaning, being expressed by formal variation. Inflection can be defined, as we have seen, as 'variation between words to express relational differences which involve appurtenance to different categories' (141). In the preceding paragraph, we are told that 'words related by inflection' are so closely associated in 'the habits of speakers' that they are felt as 'necessary variations in the expression of a material concept'. For 'the naive speaker', they are 'really', in the traditional formulation, '"forms" of one "word"'. In the section on phonetic expression, Bloomfield remarks that 'one and the same semantic relation between two words – such as in English the difference of present and past tense – may find expression in the most various formal processes' (157). On the same page, the process of reduplication 'may denote repetition, continuity, or intensity'; it may also '[have] diminutive sense', while in other cases it 'expresses perfective action' or past tense. The more Bloomfield is dealing with details, and can take his underlying theory for granted, the more his way of putting things can fall into a traditional word-based mode.

With this we can leave his earliest treatment of morphology. But it is also necessary, as I remarked at the beginning, to bring into view one aspect of his account of syntax. Syntax in general is said to study 'the interrelations of words in the sentence' (167), whose 'substratum' (168) 'is formed by the binary discursive groupings of predication and attribution' and by relations of coordination or 'serial grouping'. These are variously expressed in different languages. In Latin, for example, an 'actor-subject' and 'action-predicate' may both be 'included in one word'. So, in a sentence such as *Cantat* 'He (she) sings', 'the predication does not receive syntactic expression, but only morphologic' (168f.). In English, however, 'at least two words are needed to express a predication'. One (the subject) must be a noun or pronoun, the other (the predicate) must be a verb (169f.). Bloomfield then turns to the expression of 'emotional relations'. 'The emotional substratum of sentences is', he says, 'to some extent independent of ... discursive relations' (170). Its 'natural expression ... seems to be greater stress'. For instance, in *To'day is my birthday* or *Today 'is my birthday* the sequence of words are spoken with a different 'distribution of emotional value'. However, 'differences of word-order, also, may be used to express' similar emotional relations (171).

Later sections distinguish five 'formal means of expressing syntactic relation' (176). The 'unity and the word-interrelations of the sentence' may also be expressed by 'modulations of pitch and of stress'. For example, *in He 'failed com'pletely to make his meaning clear*, the 'even stress' expresses the role of *completely* as the attribute of *failed* rather than *make* (178). More usually, however, they are 'expressed in various other ways'. The 'most obvious and most cumbersome' (178) is by cross-referring constructions, in which an element is expressed doubly, 'first relationally in connection with another word and then explicitly in a separate word expressing the material content'. Thus in the Latin construction *Puella cantat*, 'literally ..." (The) girl she-sings"', the subject element is expressed by both the noun and the verb (179). Another is by congruence, which has been illustrated earlier (128) in terms of the effect which classes of words, 'possess[ing] no distinguishing characteristics, by themselves, as to form or meaning' have on other words in the utterance. The examples here are of agreement in gender, also in number and case (181). The fourth means of expression is by government or rection, defined as 'the process by which a word has a different form according to its relation to other words in the sentence' (184). For example, *He loves her* 'shows by the form of the pronouns who is the actor, who the object affected' (183). The last means of expression is word-order (186–8).

Distinctions like these reappear in *Language*, where they are introduced as 'ways of arranging linguistic forms' (Bloomfield 1935: 163). We will therefore have to discuss them further in the next section. But one obvious general comment is that these 'means of expressing syntactic relations' are treated quite separately from the formal 'morphologic processes' (affixation and so on) which supply, in effect, the parallel sections of the preceding chapter. That is hardly surprising, given the different origins of these notions. The division of the word is quite old, and concepts such as those of root and affix, which had been borrowed from the Renaissance onwards through the study of Hebrew and subsequently of Sanskrit, had been successfully integrated with the ancient Western tradition of the oppositions of whole words within a paradigm. The topic of 'syntactic means' belongs to the emergence of syntax, late in the nineteenth century, as the independent study of sentence-structure. Ries (1927 [1894]: 140) speaks of 'die *Lehre von den syntaktischen Ausdrucksmitteln*', which addresses the question of what syntactic content is expressed by what forms of construction. Paul's great work, which is naturally in Bloomfield's list of recommended reading (1914: 315), introduces a typology of 'means of sentence construction' (Paul, 1920 [1880]: 123f.). These are means 'for the linguistic expression of the combination of ideas' ('[z]um sprachlichen Ausdruck der Verbindung von Vorstellungen'). Bloomfield is following in that tradition.

At the beginning of Ch. 6, Bloomfield remarks that syntax 'cannot entirely be separated' from morphology. This is partly because 'it is not always possible to determine what is one word, what a combination of words', but also, and more importantly, because 'to the extent in which the words of a language include relational content, to that extent the morphology of a language involves questions of syntax' (Bloomfield, 1914: 167). We have already seen how, in Latin, the discursive relation of predication may receive only morphologic expression (see again 168f.). But in principle, and above all in the techniques of describing formal structure, the fields are as distinct as they are in other works which stand in the nineteenth-century German tradition. It is only in the 1920s that what many scholars might see as the implication of such remarks began to be thought through.

2.2 Bloomfield's mature theory

Between 1914 and 1933 Bloomfield published various papers and reviews that bear on our theme. A pair of articles, on 'Sentence and word' (1915) and 'Subject and predicate' (1917) belong with the *Introduction* and either clarify or modify part of what we have already discussed. The first stresses the primacy of the sentence, explicitly rejecting the traditional account derived from (pseudo-)Dionysius Thrax and Priscian (Bloomfield, 1915: *LBA* 63). The division of a sentence into smaller elements is said to be established by 'the associational connections of the parts of the sound-sequence which constitutes' it (*LBA* 64). For example, when a Roman said *exibant* 'They were going out', the sound-sequence had parts such as [nt] which would have occurred in many previous utterances and would always have 'corresponded to an element of meaning which is present also in [the] new experience'. These past occurrences 'exercise on the [present sound-sequence] the subtle force known to psychologists as simultaneous association or fusion: they give [such parts] a tone of recognition which we . . . may speak of as their meaning'. Likewise if an English speaker says *They were going out*: [ðej], among other parts of the sound-sequence, will have occurred previously in utterances such as *They denied it*, 'where also there was a third person plural actor' (*LBA* 65). The difference, however, is that only sequences like [ðej] can, where appropriate, receive 'full and explicit insistence'. When sequences like this are stressed ([ðéj wr gowiŋ awt], [ðej wŕ gowiŋawt]), we 'show a consciousness of [the] division [of the sentence] into parts and try . . . to arouse the same consciousness in the hearer'. A Roman could not have done the same with *-nt*. In addition,

-nt was tied to its context, 'after an element expressive of action'. *They*, by implication, is not (*LBA* 66).

This is the difference, 'of course', between a word and a 'formative' (= morphologic) element. Both 'recur as the expression of a constant element of meaning', but the latter 'is bound to certain positions with regard to the other elements, while the word may occur in all kinds of connections'. Also, and 'above all', 'the word may be focused by the attention (clearly apperceived), while the formative element never rises to this explicit recognition' (*LBA* 66). In the second of these articles, Bloomfield stresses once more that 'a single word can express only one separately apperceived element' (1917: *LBA* 71). His example is Latin *cantat*, which we have already met in the *Introduction*. When this is spoken as a sentence, 'the speaker's experience is simply that of a known and definite person's singing'. Whatever parts it has are not separated, in the speaker's mind, into a 'logical judgment' of predication (see also *LBA* 74). But it is different in the case of English *She is singing*. Although both sentences are 'expressions of actor and action', which again are elements of experience, only in the English example is there an analysis into the linguistic elements subject and predicate (*LBA* 75).

Within five years of the publication of this second article, Bloomfield's views on grammar and on linguistics generally had changed, in line with what we now call structuralism. As we have seen in §1.1, one feature of this 'newer trend of language study' was that 'we are casting off our dependence on psychology' (Bloomfield, 1922: *LBA* 92). Whereas in his Wundtian phase he had taken notions like 'association' and 'apperception' as an essential foundation, he now argued that, as linguists, we must simply 'study people's habits of language – the way people talk – ', and assign the psychology of language to a 'separate investigation, in which our results will figure as data alongside the results of the other social sciences'. In a review of the second edition of the *Cours de linguistique générale*, Bloomfield speaks of 'a desperate attempt', in earlier linguistics, 'to give a psychologic interpretation to the facts of language'. But Saussure 'proves ... that psychology [also phonetics] do not matter at all and are, in principle, irrelevant to the study of language'. Indeed this is exemplified 'in [Saussure's] own person', since he 'seems to have had no psychology beyond the crudest popular notions' (Bloomfield, 1923: *LBA* 106f.).

These reviews date from Bloomfield's first years at Ohio State University, where, as has often been emphasised, he was converted to the behaviourist psychology of A. P. Weiss. Later in the decade, in what more recent American scholars would have called a survey of the 'state of the art', he again says that 'a psychology is not necessary in linguistics' (1927: *LBA* 176). But, following Weiss, he gives a sketch of what he 'take[s] to be the implications of the actual practice, in purely linguistic problems, of all linguists'. This involves the hypothesis that, 'given an ideal equipment', 'any human act' could be described as follows. First, a physiologist will describe 'the individual's predisposition (channels of nervous discharge) due to earlier stimulations and responses'. Next the psychologist 'traces the formation of this predisposition, act by act, from the individual's birth', and the social psychologist, whose discipline has been distinguished from 'individual psychology' (*LBA* 175), 'identifies the persons who were concerned in these earlier stimulations and through them traces the ancestry of this type of act'. Finally (and on the assumption that we are dealing with an act of speech), 'the linguist defines those features of the act . . . which are habitual in the group, places them in the habit system (language), and traces their history'. Linguistics is again distinct from both individual and social psychology and, as Bloomfield has already stressed, 'remains upon the plane of abstraction' (*LBA* 175). We do not trace linguistic usage act by act, but assume that, once individuals have 'acquired the habit of using a certain linguistic form', they will continue to utter it in similar circumstances. But, for psychology itself, the hypothesis 'implies the postulates of behaviorism'.

It is against this background that Bloomfield reshaped the theory of grammar, first in his 'Set of postulates' of the previous year (1926) and then in *Language*. In the preface to *Language*, he makes clear his general commitment to what he later called the 'hypothesis of *physicalism*' (Bloomfield, 1936: *LBA* 325; see above, §1.1). 'Mechanism', as he calls it at this stage, 'is the necessary form of scientific discourse' (1935: vii). Accordingly, psychology itself must be founded on the study of bodily processes. But Bloomfield also says that, since the publication of his first book, 'we have learned . . . what one of our masters [Delbrück] suspected thirty years [before], namely, that we can pursue the study of language without reference to any one psychological doctrine'. He therefore tries to present the 'facts of language' without a supplementary account 'in terms of mind'. In that way the requirements of mechanism will be met. But this is not just because he himself believes in mechanism. It is 'also because an exposition which stands on its own feet is more solid and more easily surveyed than one which is propped at various points by another and changeable doctrine'. His object, in brief, is to 'avoid dependence' on any specific psychological theory.

Despite such passages, some commentators have claimed that 'for Bloomfield', in the words of one of them, 'linguistics was a branch of psychology, and specifically of the ... brand of psychology known as "behaviourism"' (Sampson, 1980: 64). Even in a more exact account, it might plausibly be disputed whether, in ensuring that his account would be at least compatible with mechanist psychology, and committing himself, in particular, to a model of stimuli and reactions that he ascribes directly to Weiss, he succeeded in presenting the facts of language in a wholly neutral way. But this need not concern us. What matters for our purpose is that his account of grammar could no longer be founded on the psychological theory of Wundt. For, though it may be wrong to read it as a behaviourist work, *Language* is certainly a work within the 'newer trend' of linguistics, as Bloomfield had described it.

This has two immediate consequences. The first is that the sentence can no longer be defined in terms of the discursive analysis of a 'Gesamtvorstellung'. An alternative was offered by Meillet, who had defined it simply as the largest grammatical unit. In Meillet's formulation, the sentence could be seen as 'a set of articulations' which were 'bound to each other by grammatical relations' and were also self-sufficient, in that they did not 'depend grammatically on any other set' ('un ensemble d'articulations liées entre elles par des rapports grammaticaux et qui, ne dépendant grammaticalement d'aucun autre ensemble, se suffisent à elles-mêmes') (Meillet, 1937 [1912]: 355). This was explicitly a definition 'from a linguistic viewpoint, in abstraction from any consideration of logic or of psychology' ('au point de vue linguistique, et abstraction faite de toute considération de logique ou de psychologie'); and as such it had already been praised by Bloomfield in his review of Sapir (1922: *LBA* 93). In his own reformulation, the sentence was 'a maximum construction in any utterance' (1926: *LBA* 132) or, in his definitive version, a 'linguistic form' (= 'phonetic form which has a meaning') which is not part of a larger 'linguistic form' (1935: 170).

The second consequence is that the word cannot be defined in terms of an 'imperfect' discursive analysis. A linguist can no longer see words as conceptually independent; they are simply formally independent. But then it is hard to see how elements which appear only within minimal free forms – Bloomfield's earlier formational or morphologic elements – have a semantic status different from that of any other. *Many fires* (to choose an example at random) is a linguistic form – that is, a 'phonetic form which has a meaning' (Bloomfield, 1935: 138). Within it, [z] is a minimal linguistic form: it has a meaning 'more than one', which, like other meanings, is a 'feature of the practical world' (162) that is assigned to it. Likewise *many* is a minimal linguistic form: its meaning might be represented similarly as 'more than just a few'. In such an account the elements are equally meaningful. We are saying of each that there are certain features of a situation in which speakers will utter it and a constant response which it will call forth in the hearer (74, 139 and elsewhere). The only difference is that [z] is distributionally bound, while *many* is free.

In Bloomfield's terminology, [z] and *many* are equally morphemes; their meanings 'more than one' and 'more than just a few' are equally 'sememes'. Both, moreover, enter into what we can loosely call constructions. The immediate constituents of *many fires* are *many* and *fires*; those of *fires*, in turn, are *fire* and [z]. In the larger unit, *many* is ordered before *fires*; similarly, in *fires*, [z] is ordered after *fire*. In this construction, the selection of a form like *many* carries with it the selection of [z] or its semantic equivalent. For Bloomfield, these are 'habits of arrangement' (166), and, once the notion of 'imperfect' analysis is abandoned, it is hard to see how habits of arranging morphemes within words can differ in principle from habits of arranging words as wholes.

Bloomfield did in fact retain a division between morphology and syntax. This is because, '[i]n languages which use bound forms ... the constructions in which free forms appear in phrases differ very decidedly from the constructions in which free or bound forms appear in words' (183). But both kinds of construction are now described in basically the same way. In the *Introduction*, as we have seen, syntactic relations were said to be expressed by formal means like order, congruence or modulation, while distinctions in morphology were marked by processes like suffixation or reduplication. The formal models, as a later generation might have called them, were different. But in the new account the treatment of morphology has changed. Let us take again the form *fires*. [z] is a suffix; that is, a bound form 'added' to an 'underlying form' in what is described as 'secondary derivation' (218). But these notions are in turn defined in terms of immediate constituents (209). *Fires* is a 'derived secondary word' because it includes, as one constituent, a single free form *fire*, and this form *fire* is 'underlying' because it is so included. Nor should we see this as a primitive operation of 'addition' or suffixation. In terms of an earlier chapter, the bound form [z] would be 'selected'; that is one 'smallest feature of grammatical arrangement', or, in Bloomfield's terminology, one taxeme. It would also be ordered after the underlying form; that is another taxeme. Similarly, in *many fires*, we must distinguish the selection of a 'numerative' (*many*) and its ordering before the noun. These too are taxemes, and together, in both the word and the phrase, features such as those of selection and order form a basic constructional unit, which Bloomfield called a 'tagmeme'.

It is clear already that we are dealing with a rather subtle theory, in which familiar notions, such as suffixation, are characterised not directly but on the basis of more primitive notions that are in part obvious and in part novel. It is also, at root, a difficult theory. In a retrospective discussion published many years later, Hockett confesses that, 'to many of us in the 1940s', Bloomfield's basic 'frame of reference' did not make sense (1968: 21). He remarks that Pike is 'the only post-Bloomfieldian who has tried to develop' it. But Pike's attempt is itself revealing. In an early article, he began by arguing that there was no clear-cut distinction, in Bloomfield's own practice, between taxemes and tagmemes (Pike, 1938: §1); and, although 'tagmemics', as a label for his mature theory of language, is derived from his own use of 'tagmeme' for his basic grammatical unit, he makes clear that his sense and Bloomfield's should not be confused (Pike: 1967: 490). We must therefore look at Bloomfield's theory in some detail. We must also clear our minds of what was to follow, especially in the work of Hockett and others of the later Bloomfieldian school, and try to address the problem as he himself must have conceived it.

Let us first confine our attention to syntax, and let us begin, in particular, by comparing Bloomfield's new account with the one he had given earlier in his *Introduction*. In 1914, what is now a 'habit' or 'feature' of arrangement' – for example, the ordering of *many* before *fires* – had been one of the various means by which, as we have seen, a logical or discursive relation is expressed. Thus, in a sentence such as *Many fires break out*, a total experience is analysed in English into the elements actor and action, and the semantic relationship between them is realised by the formal relationship between the subject and predicate. Within *many fires*, there is another logical relation, which the order of words in part realises, and so on. As we saw in the last section, Bloomfield set out a typology of means of expression. In *Many fires break out*, the relation between *many fires* and *break out* is expressed by word order; also by a 'cross-referring construction' in which both *fires* and *break* are plural; also by the intonation or 'modulation' of the sentence.

But by the 1930s Bloomfield had concluded that a linguistic description could not start from meanings. Their statement, as he remarked in a famous passage, was 'the weak point of language study, and [would] remain so until human knowledge advance[d] very far beyond its present state' (1935: 140). Let us therefore take a form like *many*. We can identify it as a linguistic form, or 'phonetic form which has a meaning' (138). We may not be able to say exactly what that meaning is: at best we may be able to resort to no more than a 'makeshift device' like circumlocution, 'in the manner of our dictionaries' (140). We must simply assume that it exists, and is a stable feature of the situations in which the form *many* is uttered. The basis for this is Bloomfield's 'fundamental assumption of linguistics', that in every speech-community there are different utterances which are 'alike in form and meaning' (78, 144).

As for individual units, so for the relations between them. In *Many fires break out*, we may not be able to describe exactly the meaning of the construction linking *many fires* and *break out*. We assume that a meaning exists; but we cannot take it as the basis for our description. We must again abide by the 'principle', as Bloomfield puts it in his basic chapter on grammar, 'that linguistic study must always start from the phonetic form' and not from meaning directly (162). So, our starting-point must be the formal features which make up the construction: that is, the formal features of word-order, cross-reference and modulation which, in Bloomfield's earlier account, had been the separate means of expression. Together these form a unit, which then has a meaning.

We will return to the details and the terminology in a moment. But it will be clear from this that Bloomfield's new theory of syntax is at heart his old one turned round and presented from a new angle. In the earlier account, the basic concept is that of a logical or discursive relation, and the formal side of language realises it. In the new one the basic concept is that of a formal unit, composed of the erstwhile features of realisation, and the erstwhile logical relation is its meaning. There is also a considerable similarity between Bloomfield's old typology of 'means of expression' and the classification in his new account of types of 'features of grammatical arrangement'. One of these is 'order', which, except that it now includes the order of morphemes within words, corresponds to 'word-order' in the *Introduction*. Another is 'modulation': this too is the same formal type as modulation in the *Introduction*, except again that it now includes accentual patterns within words. Another is 'selection': thus, in *many fires*, the selection of a form of the class of *many*, or, within *fires*, the selection of [z]. In the *Introduction* this was not a distinct type. But agreement is part of it, and Bloomfield now proposed a subdivision of agreement into three types – congruence or concord, government and cross-reference – which is plainly a reworking of what had earlier been three of five separate 'means of expression' (1935: 191ff.; 1914; 178ff.). In *many fires*, the congruence of *fires* with *many* is one means of expressing an attributive relation; alternatively, it is one of the features of grammatical arrangement that make up the meaningful unit called (1935: 202) a 'limitation-substance' construction.

If Bloomfield's own formulation seems more complicated, it is mainly because he tried to draw a detailed parallel between grammatical units – like the 'actor-action' or the 'limitation-substance' construction – and units of the lexicon, like *many* and *fire*. Let us again begin with *many*. It is a morpheme, as we have seen. As such, it is a smallest lexical unit, or, to use the term which Bloomfield uses in his final summing-up (264), 'lexical form'. It is a unit which has a meaning, that meaning (again, say, 'more than just a few'), being a 'sememe'. It is also made up of more primitive units, which are the phonemes [m], [e] and so on. Although the morpheme as a whole is meaningful, the phonemes, on their own, are not meaningful.

Similarly (according to Bloomfield) for grammatical units such as constructions. Like morphemes, they have meanings. For example, that of the 'limitation-substance' construction in *many fires* is different from that of the 'quality-substance' construction (202) in, say, *large fires*. Like morphemes, they are composed of more primitive units: these are the individual 'features of grammatical arrangement', such as that of congruence or the ordering of the numerative before the noun. These again, according to Bloomfield's theory, are not individually meaningful. For example, the congruence in *many fires* does not in itself have meaning, any more than the phoneme [m] in *many*. What again is meaningful is the 'limitation-substance' construction as a whole.

The rest is then a matter of terminology. Firstly, as *many* and *fire* are 'lexical forms', so a construction, like that of *many fires*, is a 'grammatical form'. To be precise, the term 'construction' refers to one of three 'great classes' of grammatical forms (169). As lexical forms like *many* or *fire* are phonetic forms with a meaning, so a grammatical form is a 'tactic form' with a meaning; and, just as phonetic forms are made up of phonemes, so 'tactic forms' are made up of individual features of grammatical arrangement, like the order of numerative and noun, or the feature of congruence. Both Bloomfield's model and his terminology unfold as the book proceeds, but in his final formulation (264) the term 'linguistic form', which had originally referred specifically to a phonetic form with a meaning, like *many* or *fires* or the whole form *many fires*, is used to cover both 'lexical forms', on one level, and 'grammatical forms', on the other.

Secondly, just as *many*, for example, is a minimal 'phonetic form with a meaning', so a 'limitation-substance' or the 'actor-action' construction is a minimal 'tactic form with a meaning'. In neither case can the unit be divided into smaller 'forms', respectively phonetic and tactic, which are also meaningful. By this criterion, *many* is a 'morpheme': this is the 'smallest meaningful unit of linguistic signaling' at the lexical level (264). By the same criterion, each of these constructions is a 'tagmeme'. This is similarly the 'smallest meaningful unit of linguistic signaling' at the level of grammar. The meaning of a morpheme, as we have seen, is a 'sememe'. For example, *many* is associated with a sememe which we have identified, in 'makeshift' fashion, as 'more than just a few'. Correspondingly, the meaning of a tagmeme is an 'episememe'. For example, a 'limitation-substance' construction is a tagmeme whose associated episememe might be identified, again in makeshift fashion, as the limitation of the potential scope of reference of one element ('two fires', 'three fires', 'four fires' and so on) by another. Finally, morphemes are made up of smaller 'unit[s] of linguistic signaling' which are themselves meaningless. These are phonemes, or minimal units of 'phonetic form'. Similarly, tagmemes are made up of smaller elements of 'tactic form', which are likewise meaningless. These are the individual features of selection, order and so on; and, as we have seen, they are the units that Bloomfield called 'taxemes'. The construction of *many fires* thus comprises, among others, a taxeme of order (numerative before noun) and a taxeme of congruence. In Bloomfield's general model, grammar and lexicon are the branches of semantics (138), which is the 'phase' of description that relates forms to their linguistic meanings. In his detailed model, he attempts in these ways to make them completely parallel.

The account which results is complex and difficult, even when, as so far, it is applied to syntax alone. But in 1926 Bloomfield had already talked of 'morphologic' constructions' (*LBA* 132), and in *Language*, as we have seen, the model of taxemes and tagmemes applies in both branches of grammar. When forms are affixed it applies exactly as in syntax. Thus, in *fires*, the suffix is a morpheme, which is selected and placed after a noun morpheme; these are among the features which make up a tagmeme, and the meaning (plural noun, or noun inflected as plural) can be ascribed partly to the sememe ('more than one') and partly to the construction in which *fire* and [z] stand. The problem, of course, is to give a similar account of what had previously been other forms of 'morphologic expression', such as, for example, vowel-variation.

Bloomfield's solution – and it was perhaps the only solution that was possible – was to describe the modification of, say, *man* to *men* as itself a feature of 'arrangement'. Let us think, for a moment, of somebody arranging flowers in a vase. They might pick up a white rose; that is an act of selection. They might put it at the edge of the vase in front of a frond of greenery; that is a matter of order. But before they do so they might take the secateurs and trim the stem, perhaps to shorten it, perhaps to make a better shape. That too is part of the process of arrangement. One has available a stock of roses, greenery, and so on. One chooses items from it, one places each one in relation to the others, and, as one does so, one may also modify some of them.

We can take this as a model for the construction of a word like *duchess* (Bloomfield, 1935: 167f.). This is formed by the arrangement of two lexical forms. One is the morpheme [djuwk]: that, as it stands, is like the white rose as it comes from the garden. The other is the morpheme *-ess* or [is]. In the construction in general, a noun is selected from a 'special class' (*count*, *prince* and so on) whose members can combine with *-ess*, and the forms are arranged in that order: for example, [kawnt] + [is]. But in the case of *duke* there are also phonetic modifications: [juw] → [ʌ] and [k] → [tʃ]. This is like the trimming of the white rose, and is a feature of a specific arrangement which does not recur in, for example, *dukes* or *archduke*. A 'phonetic modification' is accordingly a further 'feature of grammatical arrangement'. It is a fourth kind of taxeme, alongside selection (the selection of *-ess* and a noun from the class of *count*), modulation (the retention of stress on the noun, with the following *-ess* unstressed) and order.

We can then say that, in a construction like that of the plural *men*, there are two features of arrangement. One is the selection of *man* – a member, that is, of another 'special class'. The other is the phonetic modification by which [a] becomes [e]. A noun of this 'special class' combines with this feature of phonetic modification just as, in the case of *fires* or *countess*, a noun of another class combines with a feature of selection.

The rose is thus selected; it is trimmed, and it is set in a vase by itself.

That is the whole 'arrangement'. But although this may be a satisfactory account of the formal pattern – and let us, for the moment at least, assume that it is – there is a problem in stating the relations between forms and meanings. A regular plural, like *fires*, is as a whole 'plural'. In Bloomfield's terms, it is a member of the form-class 'plural substantive'. But it has within it a morpheme [z], and [z] specifically has the meaning 'more than one'. By Bloomfield's definition, 'more than one' is a sememe. Now a plural derived by vowel change, such as *men*, is also a 'plural substantive'. But what carries the meaning elsewhere carried by the morpheme? Its only constituent is the noun, and that has the single meaning 'member of the species *homo sapiens*', 'adult male member of said species', or whatever. There is the change of [a] to [e], but in Bloomfield's model a phonetic modification is a taxeme, and taxemes, like phonemes, do not in themselves have meanings. To what then can the meaning 'more than one' be ascribed? The only solution is to say that it belongs to the entire construction. The taxemes of selection and phonetic modification will together form a tagmeme. Tagmemes do have meanings, and this one must mean 'more than one individual'. That meaning is not a sememe, but an episememe.

If Bloomfield's model is as I have said, and as it is, I believe, quite plainly expounded in his general chapter on 'Grammatical forms', it also follows that we can talk of alternation on two levels. We can talk, on the one hand, of an alternation among phonetic forms that are related by phonetic modifications. For example, [djuwk] as in *dukes* is modified to [dʌtʃ], as in *duchess*; 'strictly speaking', Bloomfield says, the morpheme 'has two ... different phonetic forms, and ... each of these *alternants* appears under certain conditions' (1935: 164). That is how the notion of alternation is first introduced. On the other hand, we can talk of an alternation among grammatical forms that have the same meaning. Take, for example, the German plurals (211). A form like *Hüte* is 'derived from' the singular (*Hut*) by a process of suffixation and a vowel change. In strict terms, the selection of *-e* (a morpheme with the meaning 'more than one'), its ordering after the noun morpheme (*Hut* + *e*) and the phonetic modification of *u* to *ü* (*Hüt* + *e*) are individual features of grammatical arrangement (taxemes) forming part of a tagmeme which again must have a plural meaning. In a plural such as *Jahre* there is no phonetic modification (*Jahr* → *Jahre*); thus the tagmeme is different. In plurals such as that of *Frauen* (← *Frau*) it is different again. But the tagmemes are semantically equivalent: all three have a plural meaning as their episememe, and *Hüte*, *Jahre* and *Frauen* will all be members of a form-class 'plural substantive'.

We can therefore speak of an alternation, which is not between phonetic forms, but between sets of processes, or, in Bloomfield's underlying model, sets of primitive features of grammatical arrangement.

The problem for commentators, and indeed all readers of Bloomfield's chapter on morphology, is that, unfortunately though understandably, he does not spell this out. In the case of *Hüte*, *Jahre* and *Frauen* he says that the 'alternants' are '[-e] with vowel change, [-e], and [-en]' (211). Now by the expression '[-e]', we might conceivably understand 'the addition of [e] in a suffixal position', and that reduces, as we have seen, to taxemes of selection and order. But if we read the passage in context, it has to be confessed that this interpretation seems forced. In the preceding paragraph Bloomfield has dealt with the alternation in English plurals between '[-z]', '[-iz]' and '[-s]'. These are alternants related by phonetic modification – in that respect they are just like [djuwk] and [dʌtʃ] – and are thus, more precisely, 'phonetic alternants'. In the German examples, the 'alternation ... is not phonetic', since '[-en]' is not 'phonetically akin' to the other alternants. That is, [en] and [e] are different morphemes, not a basic and a modified form of the same morpheme. A reader might take this point but naturally assume, since Bloomfield has said nothing to the contrary, that the alternation between '[-e]' and '[-en]' is seen as being directly between linguistic forms, just as the alternation of '[-z]', '[-iz]' and '[-s]' is directly between phonetic variants.

In the case of *man* and *men*, Bloomfield says at one point that a feature of phonetic modification 'appears to express a meaning which is usually expressed by a linguistic form'. The 'modification of the vowel', he goes on, 'takes the place of the plural-suffix' (209). Note, in particular, that it 'appears' to express the meaning: it cannot strictly express it, in the sense that it might be related directly to the sememe 'more than one', since, once more, features of arrangement, like phonemes, are individually meaningless. But when Bloomfield returns to the topic seven pages later, the qualification has disappeared. In such plurals, 'a grammatical feature ... expresses a meaning (namely, the sememe "*more than one* object") which is normally expressed by a linguistic form (namely, the morpheme [-iz], [-z], [-s])' (216). This implies that the alternation is between a morpheme on the one hand ([iz] and so on) and, on the other hand, a process ([a] → [e]). Compare his account of plurals such as *knives*, where 'voicing of final spirant plus suffix [-iz, -z, -s]' is said to be describable as 'an *irregular alternant* of the regular plural suffix [-iz, -z, -s]' (214). In *men*, he also talks, as we have seen, of the modification 'tak[ing] the place of' the suffix. So, just as, in the irregular plural *oxen*, another morpheme might be said to take the place – that is, have the same role as – the regular suffix, so again the place of a morpheme is taken by what apparently should be a taxeme. Compare his corresponding account of plurals such as *sheep*, in which the plural suffix is said (209) to be 'replaced by' zero.

In his standard account of structural linguistics, Lepschy remarks that 'the chapters devoted to morphology in Bloomfield's *Language* were far from explicit' (1982: 113). To many they have seemed to contain clear contradictions. But in reading them we have to bear in mind the kind of book that Bloomfield was writing. He tells us in his preface that he has 'tried everywhere to present the accepted views' (viii), and it seems clear that, in matters of formulation as well as fact, he was striving not to say things that were gratuitously odd or controversial. There is also little doubt that, where morphology was concerned, the accepted way of talking was to say that processes like vowel change could express an elementary feature of meaning, just as suffixes, or suffixal morphemes, expressed meaning. That is indeed what he himself had implied in the earlier book of which *Language* is a 'revised version'. But while he may have wanted to preserve that style of formulation, it had to be grounded in his model of grammatical and lexical forms, whose terms did not directly allow it.

In this light, it would perhaps be charitable to suppose that, when a statement is inexplicit, it can be taken as a form of short-hand for a stricter formulation which, if spelled out, would have seemed exotic or cumbersome. A statement that 'the plural is derived from the singular by suffixation' is effectively short-hand, as we have seen, for 'the grammatical form of the plural involves the selection of a lexical form that on its own would be a singular with, in addition, the selection of a bound form meaning "more than one" and their arrangement in that order'. The statement that, in *men*, the vowel change 'takes the place of' the suffix is short-hand for 'whereas in regular plurals the grammatical form involves the selection of [iz] etc. and its placement after the noun morpheme, in this exceptional instance it involves instead the phonetic modification of [a] in the noun morpheme to [e]'. In the same spirit, the statement that the change of vowel 'expresses the meaning' elsewhere expressed by the suffix can be taken as short-hand for 'the tagmeme one of whose component taxemes is the phonetic modification of [a] to [e] has as its meaning an episememe " more than one individual" which is identical to the sememe (again "more than one individual") which, in the regular plurals, is the meaning of the bound morpheme'. I have no direct evidence to confirm this; but if Bloomfield did not in fact say that, it is perhaps because, for any contemporary, the short-hand formulation was familiar and would lead to less confusion.

If such interpretations are correct there is no underlying inconsistency. But there is, rather obviously, a duplication. In a regular plural the bound morpheme, which for Bloomfield had the basic form [iz], has a meaning ('more than one individual'). The selection of this morpheme is in turn a taxeme, which, like the modification of [a] to [e] in *men* or, in *knives*, the accompanying change of [f] to [v], is itself a meaningless feature of grammatical arrangement. But it is part of a tagmeme, and tagmemes do have meanings. What then is the episememe? In *men*, on the interpretation given above, it is again the meaning 'more than one individual'. So that must also be the meaning of the regular construction. In *horses*, for example, [iz] has the meaning 'more than one individual' and, on the level of grammar, the selection of a noun like *horse*, the selection of [iz], the order *horse* + [iz] and the retention of stress on *horse*, have the same meaning 'more than one individual'. Now sememes and episememes are both primitive. So, by the logic of the model, the same meaning is assigned twice, first to a lexical form and then to a grammatical form.

This duplication, if it is there, is never explicit, and it might well be said that Bloomfield's short-hand formulations, if I am right so to regard them, serve to obscure it. But one is left feeling that the description of meaning could be simpler. If plurality is primarily a sememe, can one not say that the plurality of the construction as a whole – Bloomfield's episememe – is secondary? *Horses*, in short, is plural because it has [iz], which is plural, within it? If it is primarily a feature of the whole construction, can one not say instead that the plurality of the suffix – Bloomfield's sememe – is secondary? [iz], in short, is plural because it is part of the construction of a word which is itself plural?

Each solution now has it proponents, as we will see in part in §2.5. But such a critique of Bloomfield's *Language*, whether fair or not, is clearly only similar in part to the critique which underlies the work of his immediate successors, in what is widely known as the 'Bloomfieldian' school. Their solution was also radically different, and it is this that we must explore next.

2.3 The Post-Bloomfieldians

The main features of the new solution are familiar, and can be summarised very briefly. Where Bloomfield talked of [iz] in *horses* as a morpheme, his successors saw it as an allomorph or alternant of an abstract unit ('plural') which subsumed, in one way or another, all the means by which, in earlier formulations, the meaning 'plural' (Bloomfield's '*more than one* object') was expressed. But this abstract unit, 'plural', is itself a unit of form, not of meaning. Whether it does or does not have a consistent semantic value – whether, in Bloomfield's terms, there is a sememe associated with it – is a separate question that need not be directly addressed.

Why were these changes made? The leading argument, and possibly the only one that was explicit at the time, is to be found in Harris's paper, 'Morpheme alternants in linguistic analysis' (Harris, 1942). 'In essence', we are told, 'the present treatment [of the morpheme] uses the following criterion', for which reference is made (n. 1) to Bloomfield (1935 [1933]: 161). The criterion, as Harris gives it, is that 'every sequence of phonemes which has meaning, and which is not composed of smaller sequences having meaning, is a morpheme' (1942: §1; Harris, *Papers* 23) But 'in some cases' this 'dissociates certain morphemes which we wish, because of the grammatical structure, to unite'. For example, Tübatulabal *puw* 'to irrigate' and *u·-buw* 'he irrigated' 'must be analysed as containing different morphemes, since the phoneme sequence /puw/ does not occur in the second word'. But 'we wish to consider' sequences like /puw/ and -/buw/ 'a single morpheme', since in corresponding forms like *wə·ˀin* 'to pour' and *ə·-wə·ˀin* 'he poured' we find an identical form in both positions.

'Various methods', Harris says, 'are used at present to get around this contradiction.' In cases such as that of *puw* and *-buw* 'different sequences of phonemes are considered as different forms of the same morpheme' (§1.0). More precisely (§1.1), 'we say that there is a regular alternation in the language: a voiced stop is replaced by the homorganic voiceless stop in word-initial'. In other cases, other 'methods' are employed. For example, in Greek *lé-lu-k-a* 'I have loosed' or *me-mén-e:k-a* 'I have remained', 'the meaning of the reduplication is the same'; therefore, by implication, different sequences of phonemes (*le-*, *me-* and so on) should again be united. But in cases such as this we do not talk of an alternation. 'Instead, reduplication is often called a morphological process, a special kind of affix, and the like.' To replace this 'present treatment', Harris proposes a 'technique for determining the morphemes of a language' which, he says, 'will simplify the arrangement' or, as he puts it at the beginning of §2, will 'arrange the morphemes of a language more clearly'.

Five years later, Hockett set out to 'develop further the theory of morphemic analysis' presented by Harris (Hockett, 1947: *RiL* 229), apparently without feeling that its merits had be argued. But in a retrospective article (1961) he effectively repeats, with reference to English *knife* and *knives*, the argument that Harris had illustrated with the forms in Tübatulabal. 'The simplest and earliest assumption', Hockett says, 'was that a morpheme is *composed* of phonemes.' This is 'either explicit, or implicit but very close to the surface, in much of the early Prague discussion and in Bloomfield's postulates [Bloomfield, 1926]'. But /naif/ and /naiv/ are different sequences of phonemes; so, on that assumption, they must be different morphemes. Alternatively, they are the same morpheme; but then the assumption must be wrong, unless (despite appearances) they are composed of the same phonemes (Hockett, 1961: 29f.). Harris's solution, as Hockett saw it, was to establish a kind of pseudo-morpheme which did meet the criterion. This is what he himself (1947: *RiL* 229) had later called the 'morph'. The morpheme itself was 'represented by' a single morph, or by two or more different morphs (like /naif/ and /naiv/, or /z/, /s/ and /iz/ as representations of the morpheme 'plural') under different circumstances (Hockett, 1961: 31).

Such arguments do not seem to have attracted direct criticism, either from Bloomfield himself, who could have commented on Harris's leading paper, or from others. But, as they stand, the objections to what Harris called 'the present treatment' were not fair. Take, first of all, the case of *knife* and *knives*. In Bloomfield's account, [naiv] is derived from [naif] by a process of phonetic modification, and this is part (as Harris correctly points out for the examples in Tübatulabal) of a regular alternation. But it is not clear why that should be seen as a 'method ... to get around [a] contradiction'. Let us return to the analogy of flower arranging. The white rose does not become a different rose when it is shortened or trimmed. Nor does the morpheme [naif], with its accompanying sememe 'instrument with handle and blade etc.', become a different morpheme when the [f] is changed to [v]. It is the same morpheme; but, as part of the construction of the word as a whole, it is phonetically modified.

Why then did Harris see a contradiction? One answer, perhaps, is that he misunderstood the scope of Bloomfield's definition. In Bloomfield's own words, which are not identical to Harris's reformulation, 'a linguistic form which bears no partial phonetic-semantic resemblance to any other form, is a *simple* form or *morpheme*' (1935: 161). *The knives* can thus be divided into three such 'simple forms', [ðə], [naiv] and [z]; *the knife* into two, [ðə] and [naif]. But although this definition does provide a criterion for dividing forms into successive morphemes, it says nothing about the identity or non-identity of simple forms appearing in different contexts. Moreover, it is quite clear, from the remainder of Bloomfield's chapter on 'Grammatical forms', what the criterion for identity is. In English, [naiv] and [naif] are the same morpheme because, firstly, they have the same meaning and, secondly, we can derive one form from the other by a process of phonetic modification. In Tübatulabal, [puw] and [buw] are the same morpheme because both have the meaning 'irrigate' and one can be derived from the other by the devoicing of [b]. The contradiction, in short, does not lie in what Bloomfield said, but simply between what he did say and what he did not say.

The case of *puw* and *u·buw* is the first of six that Harris considers, and in others Bloomfield did distinguish different morphemes. In his account of English plurals, he makes clear that the [n] of *oxen* is not a phonetic alternant of [iz]. It is a 'suppletive alternant' (1935: 215), and is thus a different lexical form. Similarly, as Harris points out, there is a 'special mutual relation of suppletion' (1942: §1.6) between such forms as *is* and *be*. But again it is not obvious why this notion must be seen as a device for getting around a contradiction. As Bloomfield saw it, [n] and [iz], though different morphemes, both had the meaning 'more than one object'. They were therefore not 'dissociated', but related by a common sememe. They were also related further, on the interpretation suggested in the last section, in that the corresponding features of selection make the only difference between two tagmemes sharing the same episememe. The alternation between [n] and [iz] is not then established separately, in order to connect forms which would otherwise be unconnected. It is defined by their identical meanings. If two simple forms have the same semantic value, but we have no grounds to derive one from the other by a process of phonetic modification, then, we say, there is a suppletive alternation between them.

Harris also considers the case of *take* and *took*, where, as in that of *man* and *men*, Bloomfield's own account is more problematic. In the 'present treatment' as Harris saw it, forms like these are 'not the same morpheme, having different meanings' (§1.6). 'Such vowel changes', he goes on, 'are usually described as special kinds of morphological modification, though they may alternate with additive suffixes like *-ed* "past time".' Now, in the model of Bloomfield's *Language*, *took* is derived from *take* by a process of phonetic modification; but, unlike the change of [f] to [v] in *knives*, which does not, in itself, carry meaning, this is one of many cases where 'we find substitution of various syllabics taking the place of [-id, -d, -t]', (Bloomfield, 1935: 216). That is, either a modification expresses the same meaning as a morpheme; or, if we interpret this as short-hand on the lines suggested in the last section, the tagmemes of which the vowel change and the selection of the suffix respectively form part have the same episememe. In either interpretation, the difference in meaning is ascribed to something other than the verbal morpheme, and in either case the relation of *took* to *take* is united – whether in terms of sememes or of episememes – with that of *baked* to *bake* or *waited* to *wait*.

Harris's article was published nine years after Bloomfield's *Language*, and refers in addition to two intervening contributions, that of Swadesh and Voegelin (1939) and Bloomfield's later study of Menomini (1939b). We must therefore take it that, in criticising what he calls the 'present treatment', he is basing his argument not solely on a reading of that book, but also on the way its concepts had been interpreted and applied by others, perhaps, in part, in conversations and oral presentations that are lost to us. Nevertheless, his criticism does seem to involve a new assumption. For Bloomfield too it had been essential that forms should be united if (to paraphrase Harris's wording) the grammatical structure required it. But he did not find it necessary to unite them in the lexicon. The morpheme, which was the basic unit of the lexicon, was only one element in Bloomfield's theory. There were others, and equivalent forms, grammatical or lexical, might be brought together at any level. Some were indeed united (contrary to what Harris said) as the same morpheme: thus [naif] and [naiv], [puw] and [buw], or [iz], [z] and [s]. Others were different morphemes, but united in that they had a common sememe: thus the [n] of *oxen* and the regular plural suffix, plus (on a literal reading) the vowel change in *men*. Others were united in that their constructions, or tagmemes, had a common episememe. It is worth adding that, in the grammar as a whole, forms could also be united by their membership of a form-class. For example, *horses*, *fires*, *knives*, *oxen*, *men* all belonged to the form-class 'plural substantive'. But for Harris and those who followed him, it was evidently not sufficient that forms should be united in the grammar, or even in the treatment of morphology, as a whole. They had to be united specifically as morphemes. In Harris's own words, his critique is directed against 'the present treatment of morphemes' (1942: title of §1). He does not say 'the present treatment of morphology'. For it is only if we assume that all forms which are grammatically equivalent must be a single unit at the level of the morpheme that the 'contradiction' which he finds in Bloomfield's criterion can arise.

Why was this assumed? The reasons lie deep, and it is not easy to reconstruct a chain of thought which was not made explicit. But it seems clear that what Hockett was later to call the 'Item and Arrangement' model of grammar (1954) did not emerge historically in the wake of Harris's new criteria for the morpheme. On the contrary, his arguments make sense only if that model, as a whole, is taken for granted. The subject-matter of grammar must be no more than 'a stock of morphemes, and the arrangements in which they occur' (Hockett, 1958: 137). Meanings, such as 'more than one individual' or 'male human adult', must be seen as belonging not to grammar but to a separate and, as Hockett describes it in the same work, a 'peripheral' system (138). Finally, by 'the arrangements in which [morphemes] occur' we must envisage no more than the position of one morpheme relative to another. Then indeed, if *men* or *oxen* are to be united in a grammar with, on the one hand, *man* and *ox* and, on the other, *knives* and *horses* and all the other plurals, it is only at the level of morphemes that it can be done.

This was a major shift, and there is probably no single explanation for it. One factor, no doubt, is reflected in Hockett's frank confession, cited in the last section, that the theory in Bloomfield's *Language* 'did not make sense'. The obscurity, as he saw it, 'is perhaps best represented by the first part of the chapter "Form-Classes and Lexicon" [Bloomfield, 1935: 264ff.]', which begins with Bloomfield's summing up of the distinctions drawn and illustrated in earlier chapters, between lexical forms and grammatical forms, between phonemes and morphemes and taxemes and tagmemes, and so on. Grammatical forms involve features of arrangement, and 'to render this even more complicated', Hockett goes on, 'it turns out that by "arrangement" Bloomfield does not mean merely the geometrical location of elements relative to one another', but also features of selection, modulation and phonetic modification (1968: 20). In a later paragraph, Hockett argues that there was no genuine parallel between the morpheme as a combination of phonemes, and the tagmeme, seen by Bloomfield as a combination of taxemes (21f.).

This may explain why Bloomfield's theory was thrown over. It does not, of course, explain why it was replaced by the 'Item and Arrangement' model: there are other solutions, as the earlier and later history of the subject show. But when younger scholars cannot understand entirely what their mentor is saying, they will tend to latch more firmly onto the parts that they do understand. One thing that Bloomfield does say is that morphemes are the 'ultimate constituents' of every 'complex form' (1935: 161). Any 'linguistic form' – that is, any 'phonetic form which has a meaning' (138) – can accordingly be divided, via successive stages of immediate constituents, into morphemes. If this is read in isolation, the clear implication is that, in describing a 'complex form', a linguist's task is simply to identify the morphemes of which it is ultimately composed, and show how each morpheme is related, through the hierarchy of immediate constituents, to the others.

But this is only one factor, and it is hard to disentangle it from others. The most obvious is the decision to model the morpheme on the phoneme. In the first sentence of his paper, Harris says that its purpose is 'to suggest a technique for determining the morphemes of a language, as rigorous as the method used now for finding its phonemes' (1942: *Papers* 23; *RiL* 109). In developing his theory, Hockett (1947) invented the terms 'morph' and 'allomorph' by explicit analogy with the 'phone' – a term that he had himself introduced a few years earlier (1942) – and the 'allophone'. This last term had been introduced by Whorf in an unpublished paper at the end of the 1930s (Carroll, 1956: 126). In yet another retrospective passage, Hockett has remarked that, 'in attacking the grammatical-lexical aspect of languages', he and others in the 1940s and 1950s adopted 'a series of working assumptions' (essentially those of the 'Item and Arrangement' model), derived by 'following a pattern that had proved eminently successful in dealing with their sound aspect' and so proposing 'that *morphemes* are, on the grammatical level, what phonemes are on the phonological level' (Hockett, 1987: 65).

But although this point is well known, it is important to make clear exactly what the parallel involved. One crucial assumption was simply that a language has these basic levels: on the one hand, it has a level of phonology; on the other, a level of grammar. Bloomfield's general model, as we have seen in part in the last section, had been different. In his account, the description of a language had two 'phases' (1935: 138), one concerned with phonetic forms alone, and another which had 'the task of telling what meanings are attached to the several phonetic forms'. The first phase is phonology, which 'defines each phoneme and states what combinations occur'. That his successors could take over unchanged. The second phase is 'semantics', and grammar, as Bloomfield saw it, was only one of two parts into which semantics was 'ordinarily divided'. The other was the lexicon. It was then between grammar and lexicon, as we have seen, that Bloomfield's parallels had been drawn. The morpheme was the basic unit of the lexicon – not, as for Harris and Hockett, of grammar – and to it there corresponded the tagmeme. A morpheme had a lexical meaning, which was a sememe; similarly, a tagmeme had a grammatical meaning, which was an episememe, and so on.

In later years, this model was elaborated by Pike into a theory of three interlocking hierarchies: one phonological, one lexical and one grammatical. The minimal units were again the phoneme, the morpheme and, though now in a different sense, the tagmeme (Pike, 1967 [1954–60]). But Pike was the only scholar in the next generation to develop this aspect of Bloomfield's thought. In his paper in 1942, Harris seems to assume from the beginning that the phoneme and the morpheme are the basic units of language, and in the same year the associated theory of levels was made explicit – without argument – in Hockett's paper on phonology. 'In linguistics', Hockett says, 'there are . . . two basic levels, *phonological* and *grammatical*' (1942: *RiL* 97). This is also implicit in the organisation of Bloch and Trager's *Outline of Linguistic Analysis* (1942), in which the main division is between 'phonetic analysis' (Ch. 3) and 'grammatical analysis' (Chs. 4 and 5). The shift implied is important and seems to have been accepted at once without need of explicit justification.

A second assumption, which is implicit in the opening sentence of Harris's paper, is that the primary need was to develop what Chomsky (1957) later called a 'discovery procedure'. This too did not come from Bloomfield – or, if it did, not from the published work that Harris refers to. Bloomfield's *Language* had defined the morpheme, as it had defined other units. But he did not give a procedural definition, and the criteria by which forms like [naif] and [naiv] are assigned to the same morpheme, while [z] in *knives* is assigned to a different morpheme from the [n] of *oxen*, are not spelled out. His earlier 'Set of postulates' is likewise what its title says it is. In it, Bloomfield made explicit a set of propositions that he took as axiomatic, and interleaved them with a series of definitions that successively underlay or were based on them. He did not specify a series of steps by which linguistic units were to be identified. Indeed it is worth remarking that the order in which topics are introduced – first forms and meanings, then phonemes, then constructions – does not correspond to the successive 'phases' of description as he distinguished them later (1935: as already cited; 1926: *LBA* 130ff.).

But by 1942 priorities had clearly shifted. In his article on phonology, Hockett begins by saying that 'linguistics is a classificatory science' (1942: *RiL* 97). 'The starting-point in such a science', he continues, 'is to define (1) the universe of discourse and (2) the criteria which are used in making the classifications.' In the body of his article, he talks of the 'technique' of analysing utterances in 'biophysical terms' (§3.1), of the 'next step' as the establishment of 'phonological equivalence classes' (§4), of the 'method' of contrastive pairs (§5.21), of the listing of features followed by their classification (§5.31), and in the crucial section on the phoneme he defines it as 'a class of phones' (§6.1) determined by criteria of phonetic similarity, contrastive and complementary distribution, and so on. These last had already been discussed in part in papers such as that of Swadesh on the 'phonemic principle', which, in its section on 'method', had said that phonemes 'can be discovered only by inductive procedure' (1934a: *RiL* 34f.). In Hockett's final section (§10.3), a 'correct statement of the material' is said to emerge finally from a 'trial-and-error process' in which the analyst may 'at certain stages ... work by "feelings", but later he substitutes rigorous criteria' (*RiL* 107).

This kind of theory seems to have been accepted as uncontroversial in phonology, and it is not surprising that Harris should have wanted to propose 'as rigorous [a] method' in morphology. But a third assumption, as important as the others, is that, just as in phonology the phoneme had been treated as a single basic unit, so the morpheme had to be taken as a single basic unit of grammar. We have already seen that it had no such role in Bloomfield's *Language*, and, in abandoning his theory of levels, his successors did not have to base their entire account of morphological and syntactic constructions on any single unit, let alone what had for him been no more than a unit of the lexicon. But once the assumption was made, the morpheme as we find it in his theory could indeed not serve a purpose which it was never meant to serve.

It will be clear now that the changes in morphology which took place in the 1940s were not isolated, and can be understood only as part of the wider process by which Bloomfield's own concept of linguistics was transformed by the next generation. It is therefore worth asking whether the shift away from his account of form and meaning, which was another aspect of that process, also had something to do with it. Briefly, his successors broadly accepted his view of what was required to characterise the meaning of an utterance. As we have seen in §1.1, meaning was for Bloomfield a matter of the 'practical events' (1935: 27) associated with a speech signal. Similarly, in Hockett's later textbook, meanings are 'associative ties between ... morphemes and morpheme-combinations and things or situations, or types of things and situations, in the world around us' (1958: 139). But while broadly accepting Bloomfield's theory of what meanings were, Harris in particular developed the tenets of distributionalism, in which not merely does the study of language start from forms rather than meanings (thus again Bloomfield, 1935: 162), but the entire investigation of meaning is 'put off', in the words of another protagonist, until a formal description has been completed (Hill, 1958: 3). As we have seen in §1.1, this led to a concept of the discipline in which 'microlinguistics' excluded the study of meaning (Trager, 1949), or the 'main research of descriptive linguistics' was into distributions only (Harris, 1951a: 5).

It is not clear from publications how far the argument had got by the early 1940s. But it is easy to see how Bloomfield's own account could have aroused misgivings. As I have suggested earlier, his theory of meaning was essentially a sign theory. Recurring forms are taken to be associated, under the 'fundamental assumption of linguistics', with constant 'features of the practical world'. This is as true of 'grammatical forms', the smallest of which are tagmemes linked with stable 'episememes', as of 'lexical forms', the smallest of which are morphemes which have stable 'sememes'. In this respect, although the notion of what meanings are is different, *Language* is again like the *Introduction*. In the earlier book, the discursive analysis of total experiences similarly leads to the association – I am using this term in a non-technical sense – of recurring elements of experience with recurring formal elements or relations between elements. The main difference, so far as morphology is concerned, is that discursive analysis was seen as 'imperfect' within the word. In Bloomfield's later theory, bound morphemes, which correspond to the earlier formational elements, have meanings as clear cut as morphemes that can form a word on their own.

In this respect, Bloomfield's morpheme was more similar to the 'moneme' as it was explained by Martinet three decades later (Martinet, 1960) than to the morpheme of his immediate successors. In their account there is no 'sememe': even Nida, who is closer to Bloomfield than most, talks more generally of 'semantic domains' and in a chapter that is both separate and late (1946: 166ff.). There seems, in particular, to have been a recognition that the 'fundamental assumption of linguistics', if it were taken to imply that every form did have a constant 'linguistic meaning', was in effect wrong. Take, for example, a morpheme such as plural [-iz, -z -s]. Bloomfield had given a working definition of its meaning ('*more than one* object'). But in a general discussion of the problem of grammatical categories, he himself had pointed to the example of *oats* as compared with *wheat* (Bloomfield, 1935: 271). He does not argue that this is evidence against the sememe. But, if [s] in *oats* is the plural morpheme, what constant feature of meaning does this word have, also found in plurals such as *cats* or *dogs* or *horses*, which *wheat* does not have?

We will return to the problem of meanings in a later section (§3.1), which will deal specifically with the origins of distributionalism. This will consider the meanings of constructions as well as those of morphemes. But the implication for morphology is obvious. In Bloomfield's account, many alternants which (as Harris had put it) 'we wish, because of the grammatical structure, to unite' can in fact be united only by associating them with the same meanings. Thus the [iz] of *horses* and the [(ə)n] of *oxen* were different morphemes united only in that they are related to the same sememe, and, on my reading, the replacement of the vowel in *men* was united with either suffix only in that it was a component of a tagmeme which had the same episememe. But if features of meaning are not stable, uniting elements only at that level is unsafe. Alternants must instead be united by their formal relations: that is, as members of a class of allomorphs.

It is not clear, once again, how far this line of argument may have progressed by 1942. Over the next dozen years, there is no critique of semantic conceptions of the morpheme as able or as complete as that of Bazell (1949) in Europe. But whatever the relative importance of the factors we have discussed, they all lead to an account of grammar which is morpheme-based to a degree that neither Bloomfield's, nor any other in the 1930s, had been. The morpheme is the only basic unit. 'Plural', for example, is the name of a morpheme, and every means by which a plural noun is formed, whether by suffixation or by a change of vowel or with no change at all, must now be reduced to an alternant or allomorph of it. Whatever alternant represents it, its relations to other units must also be the same. So, in words like *men*, the plural morpheme must be said to occupy the same position in the linear structure of the word as it occupies in regular forms like *horses*. As *horses* represents a morpheme 'horse' plus a morpheme 'plural', so 'men' must be the morpheme 'man' plus 'plural'.

The devices by which this reduction was achieved need not concern us: for discussion see, for example, Huddleston (1972). What is more important, for the nature of grammar in general, is that there was now no basis for the traditional division between morphology and syntax. Bloomfield had retained it, as we have seen, on the grounds that morphological and syntactic constructions 'differ radically' (1935: 184). But in the new model they no longer do. The construction of words like *men* and *horses*, once the problem of alternation has been set aside, can be described in precisely the same way as that of the phrases *the men* or *the horses*, in which they are in turn preceded by another morpheme, 'the'. In Harris's *Methods*, which is the most consistent though admittedly the most extreme work of this school, the same term 'morphology' covers the analysis by distributional criteria of both what had formerly been called morphology and what had formerly been called syntax. In the hierarchy of procedures, morphemes are identified first; then they are assigned to distributional classes; then sequences of morphemes, of all sizes, are in turn identified and in turn assigned to classes. Words, with other 'larger sections', are not taken as 'ready-made', but may be arrived at 'in the course of considering sequences of morphemes' (1951a: 281). Alternatively, it might turn out that they are not units at all.

2.4 Morphology in early generative grammar

The Post-Bloomfieldian theory of the morpheme did not end with the Post-Bloomfieldians. Their basic concept is in a certain sense still with us; and although it has from time to time been challenged, even from within the United States, there was no revolutionary at the end of the 1950s who set out to destroy it. The later history is therefore mainly one of continuity, but a continuity which is striking and significant given that so many other things have changed.

The most obvious immediate successor was the account of morphology in Lamb's 'stratificational grammar'. This was first presented in articles that appeared in 1964 (Lamb, 1964a, 1964b), and in its day seemed important. Certainly it was influential enough for foreign commentators at the beginning of the next decade to devote attention to it (e.g. Huddleston, 1972: 360–82; Matthews, 1972a: 199ff. and elsewhere). But despite the initial interest in their ideas, the stratificational school became in the end no more than a coterie. Let us therefore concentrate on the views of Chomsky and his colleague Halle. As we will see in this section, they did not abandon Bloomfieldian ideas in this field, however much they attacked the philosophy of linguistics that had lain behind them. With some qualifications, they retained the morpheme as the basic unit, much as the Post-Bloomfieldians had conceived it. In its treatment of alternations, their work in many ways recalls that of Bloomfield himself.

An early qualification, if indeed it is that, is in Chomsky's unpublished work in the mid-1950s. In this he talks of 'a mapping of words and strings of words into strings of phonemes' (1975a [1955]: 165), which can be simplified and organised 'through the introduction of morphological and morphophonemic levels'. But the organisation is both clearer and more familiar in the first book that he published. In this, he proposed a grammar with three sets of rules: 'rules of phrase structure' (see below §3.3), 'transformational rules' (§3.4) and 'morphophonemic rules' (Chomsky, 1957: 114). Representations of sentences at the level of phrase structure have among their primitives units such as '*past*' (past tense), '*en*' (past participle) and '*S*'' (plural), which form sequences with similar units such as *take* or *be* or *man*. They also include an abstract singular unit 'Ø' (111, rule 4). Sequences in which such units are selected are syntactic phrases, and are characterised by rules like those that characterise any other phrase. When the transformational rules have been applied, the morphophonemic rules will finally 'state the phonemic structure of these morphemes' (32). They are not Chomsky's main concern, and are therefore sketched very briefly. But, for example, *take* + *past* will be rewritten as /tuk/; this rule, he explains later, will 'no doubt' be formulated as 'ey → u in the context t—k + *past*' (58, n. 8). Similarly *hit* + *past* will be rewritten as /hit/, *walk* as /wɔk/, *past* after forms like /wɔk/ as /t/, and so on.

This account of morphemes is essentially Post-Bloomfieldian. As in Harris's treatment, a unit such as '*past*' or '*S*'' is abstracted from its alternant realisations, and neither the rules of syntax nor what remains of the lexicon are concerned with them. Even when a morpheme has just one form, as *walk* has the single form /wɔk/, it is still an abstract unit at a higher level. In syntax, the word is not a central unit. The morpheme '*past*', for instance, is first introduced as one of a potential sequence of 'auxiliary' elements (39, rules (28) (iii), (29) (i)) which are selected in a position before the verb. A sequence such as *past* + *take* is then reordered by a transformation, and it is only at that stage that a 'concatenation operator on the level of words' (symbolised '#') is introduced in place of the 'concatenation operator on the level of phrase structure' (symbolised

'+') (39, n. 5). *Walked*, or '*walk # past*', is thus a word only, as it would be said later, on the surface. The morphophonemic rules are also Post-Bloomfieldian. The term 'morphophonemics' had been used by Hockett, in a passage which Chomsky refers to, of the subsystem of a language which 'ties together the grammatic and phonologic systems'. The morphophonemic system is accordingly a 'code' which, in one direction, can convert 'a flow of morphemes' into 'a flow of phonologic units' (Hockett, 1955: 15–16). That is what Chomsky's rules do, and in ways that Hockett and other Post-Bloomfieldians had already debated. The treatment of /tuk/ as an alternant realising both *take* and the morpheme '*past*' is one that Hockett had mooted in a discussion, 'Morphophonemic troubles with [I[tem and] A[rrangement]' (1954: *RiL* 393f.). Chomsky believed that, by positing a specific rule rewriting /ey/ as /u/, he could save it from the objection that it would obscure a generalisation. The rule rewriting past as /t/ is the second of three which deal separately with each of the regular allomorphs (Chomsky, 1957: 32, rules (19) (iv)-(vi)). There is no basic form, as there was in Bloomfield's treatment, and the default form (/d/) is merely the alternant which appears in contexts that do not require /id/ or /t/.

Finally, the zero morpheme 'Ø' was not so great a step beyond what current Post-Bloomfieldian formulations allowed. At the time, most scholars would have accepted a restriction proposed by Bloch, that 'no morpheme has zero as its only alternant' (Bloch, 1947: *RiL* 245). Although Chomsky gives no rule, the implication is that singular 'Ø', in for instance '*man* + Ø → /man/, was such a morpheme. But every Post-Bloomfieldian accepted that one alternant could be zero: thus, in Bloch's account of *took*, /tuk/ was an allomorph of the verbal morpheme, and was said to be followed by a zero allomorph of the tense. Moreover, there were other morphemes which were associated with no segment in a strict sense. Harris, among others, had proposed that there should be morphemes of intonation (1951a: 52). The morpheme had become in principle the basic unit of syntax, to be justified on syntactic grounds. Its realisation or non-realisation was increasingly subsidiary.

The implications of this became clear in the 1960s. Few generativists discussed intonation; but the Post-Bloomfieldian treatment was translated into Chomsky's format by Stockwell (1960). In the following year, in an article referred to earlier in another context, Hockett floated the suggestion that a passive sentence could be represented as an active plus a morpheme 'passive'. 'Morphemes', he stressed, 'are not composed of, but only (in part) attested by, phonemes'; therefore this would not violate the spirit of the model (Hockett, 1961: 52). In the middle of the decade, such an element is indeed part of the deep structures in Chomsky's *Aspects of the Theory of Syntax* (1965: 103f.), and other wholly abstract units of syntax, such as a morpheme '*I*' distinguishing an imperative sentence and a morpheme '*Q*' distinguishing an interrogative, were proposed by Katz and Postal (1964: 76, 79). These were at once accepted as standard by the generative school.

For morphemes as abstract as these, the realisation had to be given by syntactic transformations. Thus in Katz and Postal's formulation, an underlying structure which included '*Q*' would first be turned, by one transformation, into an interrogative form; then, by another transformation, *Q* would be deleted (1964: 105). Let us, however, return to morphemes such as '*past*' or '*plural*'. In *Syntactic Structures* their realisation belonged, as we have seen, to the 'morphophonemic' level. But the morphophonemic rules were only sketched, and the genius of Chomsky's early work lay, in any case, elsewhere. What is more important is the subsequent marrying of generative syntax, as Chomsky had developed it to this point, with Halle's model of phonology. Neither was concerned directly with morphology, and for nearly a decade and a half the field was a no man's land, attracting little serious attention. But some account of morphology – or what was traditionally called morphology – there had in practice to be; and, since it was not a focus of excitement, it is instructive to see how one was supplied.

Let us remind ourselves of the factors that had influenced the Post-Bloomfieldians. One had been the attempt to develop insights from phonology: just as the phoneme was seen as a class of allophones in complementary distribution, so the morpheme was treated as a class of allomorphs, also in complementary distribution. But for the generativists that particular parallel could have no basis. Linguistics was no longer, in their eyes, a 'classificatory science'. It was a science of rules and levels of representation, and, as Anderson has emphasised in his penetrating study of twentieth-century phonology, of rules especially (Anderson, 1985: 321f.). In phonology, this changed view of the discipline led directly to the rejection not just of the Post-Bloomfieldian criteria for the phoneme, but of any level of representation corresponding to a phonetic transcription. If there were to be parallels between phonology and other components of the grammar they would have to be on a fresh basis.

A more basic aim of the Post-Bloomfieldians had been to reduce each category to a single formal unit: thus again the opening argument of Harris (1942). Here the changes are less clear, since, in the beginning, Chomsky's view of the relation of form to meaning was the same as his predecessors'. A theory of grammar dealt with the formal structure of sentences; a study of how they were used for communication was a separate part of a more general theory (Chomsky, 1957: 102; see below, §3.2). Even when a set of semantic rules was brought within the grammar, they were not merged with the rules of syntax, but formed a separate component which related syntactic descriptions to distinct semantic representations (Chomsky, 1965: 16; 1966a: 13ff.). Within this scheme, a category like plural or past tense had to remain syntactically invariant.

In that sense distributionalism, or the ghost of distributionalism, lived on. But the rules of syntax and semantics presupposed a lexicon, in which features of distribution and of meaning were both entered. According to Chomsky (1965: 84), this was itself part of the 'base component' of a grammar, which was in turn a part of syntax. So, although the main role of the syntactic component was to specify a 'set of abstract formal objects' (16), and for that purpose the Post-Bloomfieldian morpheme would have been a satisfactory minimal unit, it had within it a subcomponent which gave semantic information, to which semantic rules, in their appropriate place, referred. Moreover, they did not refer to the lexicon directly. Instead they operated on syntactic descriptions which, in consequence, had to include, at each stage of their derivation, information about meanings. This plainly opened the possibility that the distinction between distributional and semantic features – between plurality, for example, as a property relevant to agreement in syntax and plurality as an element of meaning – might collapse.

The book I have cited dealt with issues 'at the border of research', and Chomsky warns his reader not to expect definite conclusions (1965: vi). But what we find in the later 1960s, especially in Chomsky and Halle's joint work on phonology, is, not surprisingly, a drift back to the morphology of the 1930s. Certain notions specific to the Post-Bloomfieldians fell away. What took their place was something very like the theory of alternation as Bloomfield himself had conceived it.

One obvious point is that the basic units had a phonological content. As Chomsky described them, these were 'formatives' (1965: 3) and were entered in the lexicon with a specification of all 'aspects of phonetic structure that are not predictable by general rule' (87). This part of their entry took the form of a distinctive feature matrix, which, according to

Halle (1962), was the form all phonological representations should have. With it were entered all other properties that are 'essentially idiosyncratic'. Among these are 'properties of the formative that are relevant for semantic interpretation': 'that is', Chomsky goes on, 'components of a dictionary definition'. For this view of the lexicon as an account of idiosyncratic properties he refers appropriately to Bloomfield (1935 [1933]: 274) and to Sweet (Chomsky, 1965: 214, n. 16). In Bloomfield's terms, the distinctive feature matrix would have been a way of representing the morpheme. Although a dictionary definition had been for him no more than a makeshift device for the description of meaning, the accompanying semantic features correspond to Bloomfield's sememe.

This formulation is clear enough for lexical formatives such as *boy* or *walk*. But how do we deal with a grammatical category such as plural? The regular ending can be represented by a distinctive feature matrix: that of, say, a basic form [z]. So can, for example, the [n] of *oxen*. Both, moreover, are 'aspects of phonetic structure that are not predictable by general rule'. Are they, in that case, different formatives? The problem with this solution is that we want to unite them – I am deliberately echoing Harris's argument from the 1940s – at the level of syntax. But if they are a single formative, what phonological form does it have? Are we to say, for example, that it always has the basic form [z]? Then [z] would have to be replaced by [n] in *oxen*; also by zero in *sheep*, by zero with an accompanying change of [a] to [e] in *men*, and so on. The problem with this solution is that these are once more 'aspects of phonetic structure that are not predictable by general rule'.

Chomsky's book effectively offered two solutions. The first, which is suggested in particular by a discussion of the definite article in German, is that grammatical formatives might be represented by syntactic features alone. Thus, in the phrase *der Bruder*, the initial formative 'might . . . be regarded as consisting of the feature [+ Definite]' (Chomsky, 1965: 233, n. 32). This degenerate complex of features is subsequently expanded by syntactic rules of agreement, and the bundle of features so formed, which implicitly has no inherent phonetic form, would be 'converted to /der/ by rules of phonology' (175). The articles in English were apparently seen as abstract elements of the same kind (108, diagram (59) and 234–5, n. 38), and, on similar lines, a plural formative might be represented in syntax simply by the feature (+ plural]. This minimal bundle of features would then be converted to [z] and so on at the phonological level.

The second solution, which is also suggested by Chomsky's discussion of German, is to say that a category such as plural is not a formative at all. Instead it is a feature assigned by a syntactic rule to lexical formatives. Thus, in *Brüder*, the gender and declensional class are inherent features of a noun whose phonological representation is the distinctive feature matrix underlying *Bruder*. To that initial complex a rule of the base component adds a feature of number and a transformational rule a feature of case, and, on the basis of this enlarged complex, the phonological component will supply the umlaut (Chomsky, 1965: 171–2). Similarly, a rule of the base component might add [+ plural] to the syntactic representations of nouns in English. A form like *men* would then be characterised by the distinctive feature matrix underlying [man], by [+ plural], and by inherent features one of which would determine that, by a rule of the phonological component, [a] would be replaced by [e]. For a regular form like *boys*, the rules of phonology would add [z] to the initial distinctive feature matrix; in *oxen*, a rule referring to another inherent feature would add [n].

This second solution is presented as a restatement of the treatment in a 'traditional grammar', in which 'a particular occurrence of a Noun would be described in terms of its place in a system of paradigms' (170). Each dimension in the paradigm is represented by a syntactic feature that can take a number of values, and the paradigm as a whole by their intersections. Chomsky then argues that this treatment is better than that of an 'Item and Arrangement' grammar, in which plural and the like form sequences of morphemes. One reason is that 'many of these "morphemes" are not phonetically realized' and we must therefore state specific rules which indicate that they are null. 'More generally, the often suppletive character of inflectional systems, as well as the fact that ... the effect of the inflectional categories may be partially or even totally internal, causes cumbersome and inelegant formulation of rules' when they apply to sequences of morphemes in the 'Item and Arrangement' style (173). Furthermore, 'the order of morphemes is often quite arbitrary'. By contrast, his restatement of the traditional approach requires no rule when features are unrealised, 'suppletion and internal modification cause no special difficulty', and the categories are unordered. 'I know', he says, 'of no compensating advantage for the modern descriptivist reanalysis of traditional paradigmatic formulations'. It 'seems', he concludes, '... to be an ill-advised theoretical innovation' (174).

For the first of these defects of morphemic analysis, Chomsky acknowledges a debt to remarks by Halle (232, n. 29). It is therefore a remarkable tribute to the inertia of ideas that, when these scholars together addressed the phonology of English, it was the other, morpheme-based solution that they adopted. In their initial illustration of surface structure, the verb *established* is in the past tense. But tense is not seen as a feature which locates a word in a paradigm. Instead the verb is said to contain a formative '*past*' just like the morpheme '*past*' of *Syntactic Structures* or the Post-Bloomfieldians. This is the terminal element of one branch of a phrase structure tree, just like any other formative (Chomsky & Halle, 1968: 8).

Both lexical and grammatical formatives 'will ... be represented as feature matrices of an abstract sort' (9). But it is clear from what follows that the matrix underlying [t] in *established* will be specified not in the lexicon or by rules of syntax, but by later rules which correspond in part to Chomsky's earlier 'morphophonemic' component. In general, we are told, there are discrepancies between a surface structure which is the optimal output of the syntactic component and one which will serve as an optimal input to the phonological component. We therefore need an intermediate set of rules, called 'readjustment rules', to remove them. For example, readjustment rules 'may somewhat modify the labeled bracketing of surface structure' (10). They may also 'construct new feature matrices for certain strings of lexical and grammatical formatives'. But in the case of '*past*' it seems that it is only here that any phonetic representation will be introduced. 'The readjustment rules would replace *past* by *d*', we are told, except in strong verbs: for '*d*' we are to read 'the distinctive feature matrix representing [d]'. The implication is that '*past*' itself is no more than a complex of syntactic features, perhaps the single feature '[+ past]'.

The formative which is the input to the readjustment rules is therefore, in this instance, essentially the morpheme of the Post-Bloomfieldians. It is a unit of form, located at a specific position in a sequence of forms; but in itself it is without phonetic content. The feature matrix which is their output is essentially the morpheme of Bloomfield's *Language*. It is a basic phonetic form or 'basic alternant' (Bloomfield, 1935: 164), which then undergoes phonetic modification where the rules of phonology require it. The readjustment rules are evidently heterogeneous (see also Chomsky & Halle, 1968: 371f.). But in a case like this they specify what Bloomfield, in the terms of a later article, might have described as 'morpholexical variation' (1939b: §3, *LBA* 352). In Chomsky's words, they deal with 'aspects of phonetic structure that are not predictable by general rule' (see again Chomsky, 1965: 87). Where a formative has a single basic form – or perhaps for every lexical formative – such aspects of phonetic structure will again be detailed in the lexicon. I qualify this last point, since I have found no passage where a case of full suppletion is discussed. Where a formative has two or more basic forms – or conceivably for all grammatical formatives – the phonetic part of the lexical entry will be null, and the so-called 'readjustment rules' will supply them.

In treating this alternation, Bloomfield himself had posited a different basic form. That was because he had decided to relate the alternation in the regular plurals ([iz], [z], [s]) to the reduction of the verb *is* in, for example, *John*[z] *ready* or *Dick*[s] *ready*. The basic alternant there was clearly the unreduced [iz]; therefore that was also the basic form for the plurals, and, in parallel, 'we need not hesitate ... to take [-id] as the basic form' of the past tense suffix (1935: 212). But although his solution was different in this case, the strategy that Bloomfield followed is the same as that of the generativists. Of the alternants in *duke* and *duchess*, [djuwk] was basic because it 'has a much wider range than the other'. It is presumably for that reason in part that Chomsky and Halle took [d] as a basic form for '*past*'. In difficult cases, Bloomfield says that we will 'try, of course, to make the selections of a basic alternant so as to get, in the long run the simplest description of the facts' (164). In Chomsky and Halle's terms, the application of the same rule to both *is* and the suffixes would be a candidate for a 'linguistically significant generalization' (Chomsky, 1965: 42), though apparently one they either did not consider or rejected.

There are further parallels between Chomsky and Halle's 'phonological rules' and Bloomfield's 'phonetic modification'. In his first book, Bloomfield had made clear that variations in form which are associated with a change of meaning, such as the presence or absence of an affix or the variation of vowel in *man* and *men*, are 'to be sharply distinguished from automatic sound-variation' (see again Bloomfield, 1914: 151). But in *Language* the distinction effectively disappeared. The change of vowel in *men* is a feature of phonetic modification. If we interpret Bloomfield's theory strictly, that means that it is a taxeme which forms one component of a tagmeme, which has meaning. The changes by which *duke* become *duch-* are also features of phonetic modification: as such they are taxemes alongside the selection of the *-ess* in *duchess*, its order and so on (1935: 167f.). So too are the changes which describe the automatic alternation of [iz], [z] and [s], or [id], [d] and [t]. So are all forms of sandhi, whether compulsory, like the changes of *a* to *an* before vowels, or optional, like the reduction of *won't you?* to [wowntʃuw], which had been an example of 'automatic sound-variation' in 1914, or the substitution of a 'voiced tongue-flip variant' of the *t* in *at all*. These last examples are cited from the chapter on syntax, where features of sandhi play a part in the syntactic constructions (1935: 186f.).

Chomsky and Halle's general model is different. The 'phonological component' is simply a set of rules which relate a form of representation in which features of selection and order are specified to what they describe as the 'phonetic representation'. But let us look, in particular, at their treatment of strong verbs. In a sequence such as *sing* + *past*, the readjustment rules would not replace the second formative with [d]. Instead they 'would delete the item *past*' and 'would add to the *i* of *sing* a feature specification indicating that it is subject to a later phonological rule which, among other things, happens to convert *i* to æ' (Chomsky & Halle, 1968: 11). In short, they tag [i] – to be more exact, they tag each segment of *sing* (173, convention 2) – with a label saying 'apply to me rule so and so'.

So far this is very like a generative version of a treatment proposed by Bloch some twenty years earlier. In Bloch's terms, the base *sing* has the 'special shape' [saŋ] when it precedes the past tense suffix and, after that base, the suffix itself 'has the phonemic shape zero' (1947: *RiL* 245). A critic might indeed have complained that the solution which Chomsky and Halle propose is just the kind of 'cumbersome and inelegant formulation of rules' that, according to Chomsky himself (1965: 173), the 'Item and Arrangement' account of categories required. But the point which concerns us now is that the rule replacing [i] with [æ] is seen as a phonological rule like any other. To be precise, it is presented as an extension 'to certain lax vowels' (201) of a general 'vowel shift rule' (187ff.) which, for example, converts the 'tense vowel' in [divīyn] to [ǣ]. This rule is also one of four that derives *took* from an underlying [tǣk]. First, 'we . . . apply a rule shifting backness and rounding, which is widely applicable to irregular verbs and other irregular forms' (202f.). The effect of this is to convert [tǣk], to which the readjustment rules have presumably added a feature instructing this rule to operate, to [tɔ̄k]. This form is diphthongised ([tɔ̄wk]), and, by virtue of another special feature which the readjustment rules will have added, undergoes the rule of vowel shift twice. By the first application, [tɔ̄wk] → [tōwk]; compare *verb*[ɔ̄ws] → *verb*[ōws] (187). By the second, [tōwk] in turn is changed to [tūwk]; similarly (186), Chomsky and Halle gratuitously derive [pūwl] (*pool*) from underlying [pōwl]. Finally, [tūwk] → [tuk] 'by a fairly general rule that applies to [ūw] in various contexts' (203, n. 33). All these (to repeat) are 'phonological rules', part of a series which convert surface syntactic structures, or more exactly the output of the readjustment rules, to a speaker's internalised phonetic representation of sentences.

As this last example makes clear, Chomsky and Halle's phonological rules are ordered. But so, in principle, were Bloomfield's 'taxemes'. The 'peculiarity' of a plural like *knives* is described, according to Bloomfield, 'by saying that the final [f] ... of the underlying singular is replaced by [v] before the bound form is added' (1935: 213). This 'descriptive order' is 'a fiction and results simply from our method of describing the forms'. But its effect is to ensure that the alternant of the suffix is [z] and not [s].

'Descriptive order' does not play a wider role in *Language*, and this is the only passage referred to in the index. But Chomsky and Halle's systematic use of ordering develops that of Bloomfield's later treatment of 'Menomini morphophonemics' (1939b). Each morphological element is set up, as in *Language*, 'in a theoretical *basic* form', and the process of description then leads us 'to state the deviations from this basic form which appear when the element is combined with other elements'. If one 'applies [these] statements ... in the order in which we give them, one will arrive finally at the forms of words as they are actually spoken' (§4, *LBA* 352). Bloomfield does not describe these 'deviations from [the] basic forms' as taxemes of 'phonetic modification'. But in the model and terminology of *Language* that is clearly what they would have been. The format in which they are stated is also an equivalent, in ordinary prose, of the generativists' notation for rules. Thus, by the first statement, 'when an element ending in non-syllabic precedes an element beginning with a consonant, a *connective* -e- is inserted' (§10, *LBA* 355). This can be translated directly to the form in which Chomsky and Halle would have written it.

Chomsky and Halle knew Bloomfield's paper and refer to it twice, both for the concept of ordering (1968: 18, n. 4) and for a parallel between basic forms and historical reconstructions (251). Some years earlier, in his first published contribution to generative phonology, Chomsky had described 'Menomini morphophonemics' as 'the first modern example of a segment of a generative grammar with ordered rules' (1964 [1962]: 947). He also refers, in a note, to the discussion of descriptive order in *Language*. But he lays particular stress on Bloomfield's account of order as a 'fiction'. In Chomsky's words, Bloomfield 'regarded ordering of rules as an artifact – an invention of the linguist – as compared with order of constituents, which is "part of language"'. This 'depreciation' of the concept, he goes on, 'is just one aspect of the general antipathy to theory ... that Bloomfield developed and bequeathed to modern linguistics' (n. 35).

But let us look more carefully at what Bloomfield wrote. In talking of order as a fiction, the point that he wanted to make clear is that it does not represent the behaviour of a speaker. 'It goes without saying ... that the speaker who says *knives*, does not "first" replace [f] by [v] and "then" add [-z], but merely utters a form (*knives*) which in certain features resembles and in certain features differs from a certain other form (namely, *knife*)' (1935: 213). That is a point which, at least by the early 1960s, any generativist would have endorsed. In Chomsky's formulation, ordered rules belong to the speaker's competence, and do not represent successive stages in performance. But, in contrast, there is a real sense in which, if one says *these knives*, one is first uttering *these* (a form which bears a partial resemblance to *this*) and then uttering *knives*. There is also arguably a real sense in which, when one utters *knives*, one utters first a form of the root and then a form of the suffix. It is surely in that sense that 'the actual sequence of constituents, and their structural order [for which Bloomfield refers to the sections distinguishing types and parts of word structure] are a part of the language' (note the definite article) and not a fiction.

However we interpret this passage, the parallel between the ordered rules of generative phonology and the ordered 'statements' in Bloomfield's article is clearly acknowledged. But for the remainder Chomsky and Halle scarcely seem to have been conscious that, where morphology was concerned, they were taking over a selection of notions that were largely peculiar to their American predecessors. The notion of a formative as an abstract segment ('*past*' or [+ past]) was plainly Post-Bloomfieldian. It derives directly from the school of 'taxonomic' linguistics, as Chomsky called it, whose general doctrines they most vigorously disparaged. But by the 1960s it was so well established that, despite the tentative critique in Chomsky's work on syntax (1965), a study of phonology, for which the structure of words in syntax was no more than a peripheral concern, could take it for granted. Bloomfield's theory of grammatical forms and lexical forms had by then been dead for many years, and I cannot recall that any generativist discussed it. But the distinction which it imposes on the treatment of morphology lived on. Although they differ in their handling of particular alternations, the feature matrices which represent the underlying shapes of Chomsky and Halle's formatives, whether entered directly in the lexicon or assigned by subsequent 'readjustment rules', correspond to the basic forms of morphemes which were the elementary units of Bloomfield's lexicon. Where they are assigned by readjustment rules, it is because different morphemes which cannot be phonologically related are 'selected', as Bloomfield would have put it, in different words. Where a phonological relation does exist, however irregular, it is represented by a series, if necessary, of what Bloomfield would have described as phonetic modifications.

2.5 Morpheme-based morphology since 1970

How far does Bloomfield's influence extend into the 1970s and 1980s? We are not talking, of course, of direct influence. Where Bloomfieldian ideas survive, they are simply part of what to many scholars is the conventional wisdom of the discipline. To a historian of linguistics, their origin may lie quite clearly in developments in the 1920s and 1930s, when the inherited 'Word and Paradigm' model, as Hockett later called it, was supplanted, in America especially, by models based on the morpheme. To a historian again, it may be clear that the authority of Bloomfield's *Language* was decisive. But three generations later what were at that time innovations are among the elementary things that students of linguistics are first taught. It is the advocate of a word-based model who now has to argue against an inherited tradition.

The most obvious influence is in and through textbooks. Before 1960, genuine textbooks in linguistics scarcely existed, and students were obliged from the beginning, as ideally they should be, to read works of original scholarship. As an undergraduate in my final year in 1956–7, I picked up what I learned of the subject from Saussure's *Cours* (1916), from Bloomfield's *Language*, from the French translation of Trubetzkoy's *Grundzüge* (Troubetzkoy, 1949) and from Martinet's *Economie* (1955), and when I started work as a research student two years later the first books I read were Chomsky's *Syntactic Structures* and Harris's *Methods*. I could have read the first edition of Gleason's *Introduction to Descriptive Linguistics* (1961 [1955]) and perhaps, if I had been at an American university, I would have done so. But I would have been forced very rapidly to go beyond it. From the later 1960s this kind of education has become increasingly rare. Beginners will commonly be directed to derivative treatments, which present the received views of a particular school, or what the writer may conceive to be the views of any scholar who is not a maverick, quite uncritically.

There can be little dispute that, in American textbooks, morphemes are the elementary constituents of grammar. In many, they are also the smallest units of meaning. Take, for example, that of Fromkin and Rodman (1988), which first appeared in 1974. In their chapter on morphology, they point out that 'some words are formed by combining a number of distinct units of meaning' (127). 'The traditional term for the most elemental unit of grammatical form is *morpheme*', and 'may be defined', we are told a couple of paragraphs later, 'as the *minimal linguistic sign*, a grammatical unit that is an arbitrary union of a sound and a meaning and that cannot be further analyzed' (128). The section is indeed headed (127) 'Morphemes: the minimal units of meaning'. They then warn us that, 'as we shall see below, this definition may be too simple', but, they say, 'it will serve our purposes for now'. The problems, as they see them, come in a subsection headed 'Crans and huckles' (129f.). 'To account for bound forms like [the *huckle-* of *huckleberry*], we have to redefine the notion "morpheme"'. To be exact, they do not redefine it, but merely add the qualification that 'some morphemes are not meaningful in isolation but acquire meaning only in combination with other specific morphemes' (129). After giving a few more examples that they see as problematic (the *-ceive* of *receive* or *perceive*, the *-ept* of *inept* and the *-cest* of *incest*, the *straw-* of *strawberry*), they repeat that 'a morpheme, like a word, is a linguistic sign – both its phonemic form and its meaning must be constant' (130).

In a later section, headed 'Inflectional morphology', Fromkin and Rodman deal with a further problem. 'Sentences', they say, 'are combinations of morphemes'; however, 'it is not always possible to assign a meaning to some of these morphemes'. They therefore talk instead of a 'grammatical "meaning"'. The *to* of *He wanted her to go* 'has a grammatical "meaning" as an infinitive marker' (141). Similarly, there are bound morphemes that, 'like *to*, are for the most part purely grammatical markers, representing such concepts as "tense", "number", "gender", "case", and so forth' (142). Finally, in a section on 'The pronunciation of morphemes', they introduce the notions of 'morphophonemic rules' and 'allomorphy'. Their example is the regular plural in English, where the 'pronunciations' [z], [s] and [əz] would be described 'by some linguists' as 'allomorphs of the regular plural morpheme and determined by rule'

(146). Their account of these rules (144–7) follows that of the generative phonologists, which differs from Bloomfield's, as we have seen, largely in that a different form is taken as basic. Exceptions such as plural *men* or past tense *went* 'must be listed separately in our mental dictionaries, as *suppletive forms*' (148). But for a plural like *sheep*, they reject the concept of a 'zero-form'. This is because they 'would like to hold to the definition of a morpheme as a constant sound-meaning form'; they therefore suggest instead that 'the morpheme *sheep* is marked as both singular and plural' in the dictionary (149).

Fromkin and Rodman do not mention Bloomfield's *Language*, in the references for this chapter or for any other. They also differ from him, as can be seen, in details. But their concept of the morpheme is precisely the one that he introduced in his 'Set of postulates' in 1926, and by explicitly placing it within the Saussurean theory of the linguistic sign (122) they make clear that its ultimate inspiration lies in the 'newer trend of linguistic study', as Bloomfield called it in his review of Sapir, for which Saussure had supplied the foundation. Although the first edition of my own introduction to morphology (1974) is flatteringly among the three books recommended in their references (153), their text says nothing about the earlier word-based model, or any notion, such as that of a paradigm or of rules deriving one word from another, which was central to it, or any evidence that critics of morphemic analysis have seen as supporting it. Such ideas get less space than, for instance, religious myths about the origin of language (413ff.).

I have selected this work for illustration because it is a good book of its kind. I have not chosen it as an extreme case, and its authors cannot have intended it to be such. They are simply following a tradition of teaching which was by then unquestioned and had probably been established by the instruction given at Linguistic Institutes before the Second World War. Similarly, in Hockett's *Course* at the end of the 1950s, morphemes are defined more carefully as 'the smallest individually meaningful elements in the utterances of a language' (1958: 123). For Gleason, the morpheme can best be defined as 'the smallest unit which is grammatically pertinent' (1961 [1955]: 52). 'Some morphemes', he adds more cautiously, 'can be usefully described as the smallest meaningful units' (53). Between these books and that of Fromkin and Rodman so much in American linguistics has changed. But the things that students are told when they begin the subject, and that they are perhaps most likely to retain as certainties, have in this respect not changed.

Another factor is the widespread use of what are known as 'morphology problems'. These first appeared in print in Nida's handbook (1946), and since then they too have changed little. They consist of a collection of forms, rarely if ever amounting to a coherent part of any paradigm, and a student has to work out, by inspecting this form of one lexeme and that form of another, and trying to relate recurring bits of words to corresponding features of the English translation, what their grammar is. That is to say, the student is invited, and indeed forced, to look for Bloomfieldian morphemes. The exercises will often include forms that are irregular, and, wherever there is even a hint of a phonetic relation, any student worth their salt will try, by whatever shifts of imagination and ingenuity are needed, to establish a common basic form and a set of phonological modifications. The model is again Bloomfield's, even though, if he had seen some of these problems and the kinds of solution they lead to, he might have felt that it was being abused. It is also, of course, the model of generative phonology, and I have often reflected on a possible connection between the ready acceptance of this theory in the 1960s, and especially the quite extreme applications of it that were fashionable by the end of the decade, and the use of such exercises in teaching. That is perhaps a matter for speculation only. That they reinforce the received view of the morpheme, and in particular the view of the morpheme as a minimal sign or minimal 'same of form and meaning', is certain.

It would be surprising if the way that people are taught did not affect their scholarly thinking later in life. No serious scholar can, of course, imagine that all languages are as the textbooks seem to suggest they are. But it is easy to suppose that that is how ideally they should be, and would be if there were no disturbing factors. Consider, for instance, Chafe's account in *Meaning and the Structure of Language* (1970a). Chafe begins by describing language as 'a system which mediates, in a highly complex way, between the universe of meaning and the universe of sound' (15). But to explain this complexity, and tentatively at least to suggest how language might have evolved, he posits a series of more primitive systems. The first relates just one conceptual unit to one sound (19). The second, which is 'the simplest kind of discrete communication system', relates each of a set of conceptual units to a distinct sound. This is illustrated by what was known of vocal communication in the vervet monkey (22f.). The third system (28f.) differs in that it has the property of duality. But it still establishes a one-to-one relation between semantic primitives and configurations of sounds. The 'semantic structure' of *cats*, which Chafe uses to illustrate it, combines the concepts '*cat*' and '*plural*'; this is converted, by successive processes of 'linearization' and 'symbolization', to a 'phonetic structure' which combines in sequence [kæt] and [s].

'It is possible', Chafe says, 'that language would resemble closely [this third system] were it not for the influence of language change' (30). Change is possible in any system; but 'when it operates on a system with duality . . . it can have an effect which actually modifies the nature of the system itself'. Changes in semantic structure, such as the formation of idioms, are independent of phonetic structure, and phonetic change is similarly independent of meaning. The latter, in particular, 'creates complexities of symbolization with which speakers of a language can cope only if these speakers operate as if they were, in a certain sense, internal reconstruction devices which lead from such forms to an eventual phonetic output' (37). This last statement is subject to 'several reservations'. But the effect of phonetic change is that the process of 'symbolization' no longer leads directly from a linear 'surface structure' to the corresponding 'phonetic structure'. 'Symbolization' as such operates as before, but in the new system it 'is separated from phonetic structure by underlying phonological structures and intervening phonological processes' (39).

Chafe's main aim is to illuminate the nature of language, not to explain its evolution (22f.). But his account rests on the myth of a linguistic Golden Age, in which each utterance is a sequence of perfect signs uniting one form with one meaning. In their evolved or fallen state, languages have lost this simplicity. But the system of signs survives at an underlying level, and the task of the linguist, faced with the kind of data that Chafe cites from an Iroquoian language (31ff.), is to reconstruct, as the generative phonologists were also reconstructing, what an earlier specialist in Iroquoian had called a 'fictitious agglutinating analog' of the actual phonetic forms (Lounsbury, 1953: *RiL* 380). Chafe presents this view with a valuable clarity of insight. But it is also widely reflected – so widely that we may perhaps skip documentation – in a teleological theory of language history in which the main or even the only driving force in morphological change is a striving to restore a simple sign relation that has been lost.

Chafe's education, as he himself describes it, was Bloomfieldian, and the books which he published at this time (see also Chafe, 1970b) are perhaps the last original contribution which is directly and explicitly in that tradition. It is much harder to assess the technical work which has since been done within the generative school. It still continues, and morphology has become the focus of so much excitement, especially in the 1980s, that although one may easily make a subjective judgment of the interest of particular proposals, one cannot tell which scholars will have the greatest influence in the long run, and whose theories will seem, in the perspective of history, to be most important. I am also aware that any assessment I may make will not be wholly dispassionate. In the year in which Chomsky fleetingly described the representation of words by morphemes as an 'ill-advised theoretical innovation', I myself introduced a generative treatment of inflections in which processes of affixation, vowel change and so on were controlled by categories assigned to words (1965; later in Matthews, 1972a). Since most American theories are more morpheme-based than word-based, I find it hard to write as a historian and not as a critic.

It must be said at once that, where the morpheme is basic, it is generally more a distributional unit than a minimal sign. In his work in the 1950s Chomsky had followed Harris in separating the investigation of form from that of meaning, and although the 'formative' of the 1960s was assigned semantic as well as distributional properties, his present views on grammar and meaning do not assume that languages are systems of signs as earlier structuralists had conceived them. Chomsky himself has for many years said little about morphology. But in the article which generative morphologists see as seminal, Halle talks of a list of morphemes which 'must be provided ... with some grammatical information' (1973: 4f.). He does not talk of meanings assigned to them, and although his topic is 'the character of [word formation] rules and their relationship to other parts of the grammar', he is concerned in particular with their relationship to syntax and phonology (3) and not, by implication, to semantics. Where he mentions meanings, they are the idiosyncratic senses of words derived by rules of derivational morphology, and these, as we will see, are supplied separately.

Like Bloomfield's *Language*, Halle's article makes a division between morphology and syntax. It was perhaps the first important American contribution, for some thirty years, to do so. But since, like Bloomfield's *Language*, it proposes an account of morphology based on the morpheme, it raises again the question of which unit categories are basically assigned to. We are told, for example, that *write* must be listed, as a morpheme, with the information that it is a verbal root (4). The rules of morphology then generate a 'dictionary' which will have to contain, among others, the word *write*. But we are later told that it is only in this dictionary that we will find 'such crucial information as', for example, 'that *arrive* is a verb' (10). This is not wholly clear. Does *arrive* not also include a root *arrive*? If so, we can surely say that, since the root is verbal, so too, barring a statement to the contrary, are the words that contain it. Perhaps *arrive* is not a root: on the same page, Halle happily assumes segmentations such as that of *brother* into *bro* + *ther*. But then, if complex words are assigned to categories only in the dictionary, can we not deal similarly with simple words, like *write*?

A similar problem arises for affixes. In Halle's scheme, the dictionary included all morphologically complex words, derived and inflected. For example, the word *writes* will be a dictionary unit, and will be inserted as a whole into appropriate syntactic slots. So too will, for example, *arrival*. But how again are their grammatical properties assigned? According to Halle, words like *arrival* are derived by rules 'in the manner of templates' (10) which will say, for this formation, that a possible form for a derived noun is a sequence 'verb + *al*'. *Arrival* is then by implication a noun, since this rule derives nouns. But we are also told that affixes must be included, with roots, in the initial lists of morphemes (4). One wonders why. Since both the shape of *-al* and its grammatical properties are given by the template, what can a separate listing add? Halle says very little about inflectional affixes except that they too are to be included in the initial list of morphemes (6). Does *writes* then have the properties it has – that it is finite and to be inserted with a singular subject – because they are the properties assigned in that list to *-s*? Or are they, too, assigned by a rule that specifically constructs words of this category?

When I first read this article, I noted on the cover of the journal 'sensible, basically untransformational approach'. Since Halle claimed that he was breaking virtually new ground (3), it would perhaps have been unfair to expect an answer to every question. But given his fundamental decision to derive words from constituent morphemes, there were two ways to proceed. In one possible solution, categories are for the most part given by rules. We would have to assign roots to a part of speech; but, for the rest, a word like *cats* may be derived by a rule which assigns it, as a whole, to the category 'plural'. Similarly, a word like *catty* would be derived by a rule – perhaps like Halle's template – which assigned it as a whole to the category 'adjective'. Since the rule for *cats* adds *-s* to form a plural, it can be interpreted as establishing a secondary relation between the suffix and the category. In my own account of a word-based model, this is called a relation of 'exponence' (Matthews, 1991: Ch. 9). Similarly, the rule for *catty* establishes *-y* as a suffix which can form denominal adjectives. There would be no need for either *-s* or *-y* to be assigned these properties separately.

The other solution would be to ascribe grammatical properties directly to morphemes. The morpheme *cat* would be listed as a noun, *-s* would be listed with the feature 'plural', *-y* would be listed as adjectival. If we wanted to segment forms like *arrive* and *derive*, *-rive* would have to be listed as verbal. Morphemes would then be joined together to form words: noun *cat* + plural *-s*, noun *cat* + adjectival *-y*, and so on. But nothing need be said directly about the properties of the larger units. Since *cats* has a plural morpheme as its inflection, we may deduce that the word is as a whole plural. Since *catty* has an adjectival suffix *-y*, we may deduce that the word as a whole is an adjective.

The 'rule-based' solution (as we may perhaps most usefully call it) was adopted almost immediately in Aronoff's account of derivational morphology (1976). As Aronoff puts it in his summary of Ch. 4, each 'word formation rule' will specify a 'base' and an 'operation'. The bases will be words (Aronoff does not treat *brother* and the like as derived), and for each rule the base must be a member of a specific 'major lexical category'. For example, the base for the derivation of words like *unkind* (63) must be an adjective. The operation is then 'both syntacticosemantic and morphophonological'. It specifies a formal change, such as the addition of a prefix. It also 'specifies the semantics of its output as a compositional function of the meaning of the base, and assigns the output to a specific major lexical category in a specific subcategorization' (85). For example, the operation which derives *unkind* will specify, in particular, that it has a negative meaning and that it is itself an adjective.

In this treatment, an affix like *un-* has a phonetic form and no more. Aronoff argues at the beginning that 'the word is a minimal sign', and 'not merely for the purposes of the syntax' (9). 'What is essential about a morpheme', he says, is 'not that it mean, but rather merely that we be able to recognize it' (15). If such an approach had also been pursued in inflectional morphology, it would have led as nearly as possible – given again the fundamental decision to derive words from their constituents – to the form of word-based treatment that is now advocated by Anderson (1992). But in the work directly inspired by Halle's article, it was in fact the other solution that has tended to prevail. It does not follow again that morphemes must be minimal signs. But a feature like plural, which the Post-Bloomfieldians had converted from a semantic category to the name of an abstract distributional segment, is once more associated with the smallest phonetic form that, in the formula of Gleason (1961), is 'grammatically pertinent'.

For inflections Lieber (1989) gives what is perhaps the clearest account. But the leading proposal was that of Williams (1981). According to Williams, the process of adding an affix to a base 'is "phrase structural"'. For example, *blueishness* will have the constituent structure [[*blue ish*] *ness*] (246). There is accordingly a 'syntax of words' – to borrow the title of a slightly later monograph by Selkirk (1982) – which we must see as parallel to, though separate from, syntax proper. Structures like this will also have 'heads', which Williams sees as similar to the heads of phrases (247f.). In syntax, the head of a construction determines the properties of the whole. For example, *red dust* is a noun phrase because it is headed by *dust*, which is a noun. Similarly, in Williams's reasoning, for words. *Construction*, for example, is a noun because its second constituent is the suffix *-ion*. Therefore *-ion* must be its head, and (he argues) 'we must extend category membership' to it (249). The suffix is accordingly a noun ([*construct* $[ion]_{N}$); given that it is the head, it follows from this that the word too is a noun ([*construct* $[ion]_{N}]_{N}$).

Similarly, as in Lieber's more developed account, for morphosyntactic features. Tense, for example, is a feature said to be borne by various units, 'by words, affixes, and syntactic phrases' (Williams, 1981: 250). On that assumption, Williams expects it to be borne by heads, 'not only in syntax, but also in morphology'. In derived words like *construction*, we have seen that the suffix is the head. Likewise for an inflected word. In a weak past tense, the head is *-ed* and it is by *-ed* that the feature of tense is 'ultimately borne' (251). Similarly, in a comparative like *quicker*, *-er* is the head and it is to *-er* that we assign a feature 'say "[+ comp]"' (252). From the head positions, features 'percolate' or 'float' upwards through the constituency tree until they reach the top node (252f., 264 and elsewhere). *Cited* (250) has as a whole a feature which Williams calls [+ tense], because it has as its head a morpheme which is [+ tense]. *Quicker* is (+ comp] because *-er* is [+ comp].

In these proposals, morphology belongs to a theory of the lexicon, inflectional, as in Halle's 'Prolegomena', as well as derivational. It may indeed seem 'ironic', as Spencer remarks in his acute and lucid survey, that the proponents of what became known as the 'strong lexicalist hypothesis' are committed to 'an essentially Item and Arrangement view of morphology', in which 'discrete morphemes [are] concatenated to form constituents, just as words form phrases in syntax' (1991: 178f.). But a historian will not find it surprising, given the strength of the Bloomfieldian tradition and the reinforcement which Halle's restatement of its basic principles had given to it. Nor it is surprising, if we reflect a little on the history and logic of this model, that both Halle (1973: 6) and, still more decidedly, Williams (1981: 264) should have adopted a 'hypothesis' in which inflectional and derivational morphology are treated identically.

In a treatment like that of Aronoff (1976), the meaning of a derivational formation (for example, that the prefixation of *un-* forms negatives) is given by the rule. The prefix itself is again just a prefix. But let us return once more to Bloomfield's theory. In a word like *unkind*, *un-* is a morpheme and will be associated directly with a sememe ('not X', say). Likewise for inflections: in a word like *cats*, *-s* is a morpheme which is directly associated with the sememe 'more than one'. A derivational affix such as *un-* is thus no different, as a morpheme, from an inflectional affix like *-s*. One immediately asks if there are any grounds on which inflection and derivation can be distinguished.

The answer which Bloomfield had given in his first book rested on his definition of a 'category'. As we saw in §2.1, a 'categoric' distinction is one that has 'become habitual and finally universal in a language' (Bloomfield, 1914: 67). A noun in English must be either plural or singular; therefore number is a category of the language and, since 'it is customary to speak of ... inflection' when the only difference is categoric (140), the difference between *cats* and *cat* is inflectional. But the distinction between *kind* and *unkind* is not categoric: adjectives do not in general have to be marked as positive or negative. Such a relation 'is called derivation' (141).

In Bloomfield's later accounts these notions are far less important. In his 'Set of postulates', the categories of a language are defined as its 'functional meanings and class meanings' (*LBA* 134, §35). But there are no definitions of inflection and derivation, and those of 'functional meaning' and 'class meaning' seem to apply to all constructions. In *Language*, categories are defined in terms that are more like those of the *Introduction*. They are 'large form-classes which completely subdivide either the whole lexicon or some important form-class into form-classes of approximately equal size' (1935: 270). The class of plural substantives is thus a category, while that of *unkind* and the like is not. But Bloomfield does not take this as a basis for distinguishing inflection and derivation. Instead he talks of a distinction between layers of immediate constituents. 'In many languages, ... the structure of a complex word reveals first ... an outer layer of *inflectional* constructions, and then an inner layer of constructions of [as he now calls it] *word-formation*' (222). For example, in *actresses*, 'the outer, inflectional layer is represented by the construction of *actress* with [-iz], and the inner, word-formational layer by the remaining constructions, of *actor* with *-ess* and of *act* with [-ə]'.

This distinction, which 'cannot always be carried out', is 'based on several features' (223). But of the three which Bloomfield goes on to discuss, the first is simply that an inflected form can 'usually' be a constituent, at best, of a larger inflected form. That is, again, inflections are an outer layer. The third feature (§13.13) is the 'derivational unity' of inflectional paradigms. By this Bloomfield means that, in further processes of 'composition or derivation', a 'paradigm as a whole is represented by some one form' (224). For example, in *manslaughter* or *mannish*, both singular *man* and plural *men* are represented by *man*; there are no words *menslaughter* or *mennish*. But that is to say, once more, that inflectional distinctions form the outermost layers. To be precise, they usually do so. At the end of the section, Bloomfield points out, although the formation of diminutives in German is 'a construction of word-formation', there are a 'few instances' in which 'the suffix [-xən] is added to nouns which already have a plural inflection': thus *Kinderchen* as opposed to *Kindchen*. 'If a language', he says, 'contained too many cases of this sort, we should simply say that it did not distinguish such morphologic layers as are denoted by the terms inflection and word-formation' (226).

A reader who was beginning linguistics might indeed be puzzled as to why the construction in [-xən] is assumed to be word-formational. But Bloomfield is in effect employing two criteria. One refers to the distribution of affixes: constructions of word-formation are more central, and inflectional constructions more peripheral. But the second of the 'features' on which the distinction is based is the 'rigid parallelism' (223) of inflectional derivations. 'Nearly all English singular nouns', for example, 'underlie a derived plural noun, and, vice versa, nearly all English plural nouns are derived from a singular noun.' Although Bloomfield does not draw the connection, it is for precisely that reason that these classes are categories. But there is no such 'rigid parallelism' in the case of *kind* and *unkind*, or of German *Kind* and *Kindchen*. In the terms which generativists have used since the end of the 1960s, neither rule is fully productive. It seems that for Bloomfield both criteria were relevant. Where more central constructions are also less productive, the distinction between word-formation and inflection is clear. If there are slight discrepancies, like that of *Kinderchen*, the distinction is there but we must recognise exceptions. If there are serious discrepancies, the distinction cannot, in Bloomfield's words, be 'carried out'.

That, then, is the account that Bloomfield bequeathed to his immediate successors, and through them, since there are few original Post-Bloomfieldian treatments of derivational morphology, to the generativists. Let us therefore return to Halle's 'Prolegomena' (1973). This proposed a morphology with 'three distinct components' (8). The first is again the list of morphemes; this partly corresponds to Bloomfield's lexicon of morphemes. The second is a set of rules of word formation, which we can readily see as corresponding to his statements of constructions. But the third component, to which there is nothing analogous in Bloomfield's theory, is 'a filter containing the idiosyncratic properties of words'. This feature will add the idiosyncratic meanings which we referred to earlier. But it will also exclude many of the words that the other two components will generate. *Arrivation*, for example, will be derived as a 'potential word' (9), as will *derivation*. Both will then pass through the filter. But only the latter will emerge as an 'actual word'. The former will have 'the rule feature [– Lexical Insertion]' (meaning that is is not a word that can appear in a syntactic construction) attached to it.

The effect of this device was to anaesthetise all problems of irregularity in word-formation. In a well-known paper that had been published three years earlier, Chomsky (1970a) had taken note of such irregularities, and had given them as a reason for abandoning his own and others' earlier view, that derived words should be handled by productive rules of syntax. But Halle's filter ensured that they could now be handled by productive rules of morphology. Just as a rule for plurals in *-(e)s* applies to any eligible noun, so a rule which constructs potential nouns in *-ation* will apply, in this model, to any eligible verb. Where it over-generates, the filter makes a correction.

Where did that leave the division between inflection and derivation? In a generative grammar it would have had to be made, if it were made at all, between distinct components or sets of rules. But it is hard to see any real distinction within Halle's rules of 'word formation'. There is no longer a difference in productivity: in Bloomfield's terms, a derivational construction such as that of *observation* or '*arrivation*' will exhibit as rigid a parallelism, between potential rather than actual words, as any inflectional construction. Can one appeal to other differences? Certainly they exist: as Anderson pointed out, inflections, and inflections alone, are directly relevant to syntax (1982: 587). But Anderson's account of inflectional morphology is not morpheme-based (595ff.; Anderson, 1992), so that the logic of his model is different. In Halle's or in Williams's account, the initial assumption is that words of all kinds are constructed from constituent morphemes. If derived words are to be given by a dictionary, they will be first constructed by rules of word formation and then inserted into syntax. But, since inflected words will also be constructed by rules of word formation, there is no reason why they should not be inserted (with, of course, the appropriate inflectional features) similarly. All that remains is a purely formal difference between inner and outer layers. But it was a distinction with no other motive, and Williams easily removed it.

This is perhaps the point at which our story can most safely end. In other contributions there are other echoes: it is hard, for instance, to see in McCarthy's 'noncatenative' morphology much more than an elaboration, in modern dress, of part of Harris's account of discontinuous morphemes (McCarthy, 1982; survey and assessment by Spencer, 1991: 134ff.). But the theory of strict lexicalism is the most important new development in morpheme-based morphology. Of the deeper hypotheses on which it rests, one was an innovation: that derived words must pass through a lexical filter. The other can be traced back to the origins of structuralism, half a century earlier.

This second assumption seems to have been automatic. When I read Lieber's paper on the percolation of morphosyntactic features (1989), I pencilled in my copy of the journal: 'O.K. but why should the features originate in morphemes in the first place?' There might have been substantive reasons, but Lieber does not give them. It was simply taken for granted from the outset. Sixteen years earlier, Halle had begun his 'Prolegomena' by pointing out that speakers know the words of their language. 'They also know' that a word like *trans-form-at-ion-al* 'is composed of the morphemes shown and that these five morphemes cannot be concatenated in most other orders'. Such knowledge must be represented in a grammar: 'hence', he goes on, 'the assumption has been made quite generally that a grammar must include a list of morphemes as well as rules of word formation' (1973: 3). It had been made indeed, first by Bloomfield and then by those who followed him. It is perhaps the clearest tribute to his great work of the 1930s, and the tradition of teaching which developed from it, not that this view should be held, but that it should still appear, to many scholars, to be essentially uncontroversial.

3 *Distributional syntax*

We have seen in chapter 2 how Bloomfield's concept of the morpheme was transformed by his immediate successors (above, §2.3). But we have yet to consider contemporary developments in syntax. Once again a part of Bloomfield's theory was taken from its context and made the foundation of the whole. In morphology it was the morpheme, so that an account of morphology, insofar as it remained distinct from syntax, was reduced to the identification of morphemes and their alternants. In syntax it was, above all, the principle of immediate constituents. From the late 1940s syntax had basically two tasks, one to establish the hierarchical structure of sentences and the other to sort the units of this hierarchy into classes with equivalent distributions. For the same period also saw the firm adoption of distributional criteria. Not merely did the study of language start from form rather than from meaning; but the investigation of form was separated strictly from that of meaning, and necessarily preceded it. It was in syntax that this programme was particularly attractive, and met with the fewest doubts and criticisms.

Of the sections which follow, §3.1 deals with the origins of distributionalism, up to and including the classic Post-Bloomfieldian treatments in the 1950s. In §3.2, we will see how these ideas gave rise, again in the 1950s, to the concept of a generative grammar. This section will concentrate, in particular, on Harris's *Methods* (1951a) and Chomsky's first book (1957). We will then turn to the development of the constituency model, which culminated in the formalisation of phrase structure grammar (§3.3). Finally, in §3.4, we will examine the history of transformational grammar from the 1950s to the early 70s, and try to identify the continuing influence of distributionalism.

3.1 The origins of distributionalism

Until the middle of the twentieth century few scholars, whether in Europe or in America, would have denied that grammar is concerned both with form and with meaning. In Europe, Sweet is perfectly explicit. Language, he says, has two sides – a 'formal side . . . concerned with the outer form of words and sentences', and a 'logical side . . . concerned with their inner meaning'. Grammar deals with neither separately, 'but with the connections between them, these being the real phenomena of language' (1891: 6f.). Likewise Jespersen: of the two branches of grammar, syntax proceeds from the inner aspect to the outer, while morphology proceeds from the outer to the inner (1924: 39–46). Hence syntax is said to take the viewpoint of the speaker, who starts from the meaning that he wants to communicate and must then work out how to express it (46). According to Paul, a sentence is the linguistic expression corresponding to an association of ideas or groups of ideas that has arisen in the speaker's mind; formal devices – such as inflections, intonation, or word order – are the means by which its expression is achieved (1920 [1880]: 121ff.). For Sweet, these are similarly 'ways of indicating the relations between words' (30f.). Such views were not confined to the turn of the century. In the heyday of European structural linguistics, de Groot draws a clear distinction between the order of words, which is a perceptible phenomenon, and the 'syntactic structure' of the word group, which is concerned with meaning and is not perceptible (1949: 54). A later chapter on 'syntactic means' refers specifically to Paul (238ff.). For Tesnière, the whole of structural syntax rests on the relations between the 'linear order' of words and the 'structural order' represented by dependency and other stemmata (1959: 19).

Similar views were normal on the other side of the Atlantic. We have seen how, in his first book, Bloomfield had described a sentence as 'an utterance analyzing an experience into elements' (1914: 60); this analysis establishes relationships among the elements which include the 'primary division of an experience' into subject and predicate, followed by subsidiary divisions into 'subject' (= head) and attribute (61). To these 'logical' or 'discursive' relations Bloomfield added the 'serial' relation (= coordination) and, in particular, 'emotional relations', in which one element, like the pronoun *me* in *It was me they beat* is 'dominant' (113f.). In his chapter on syntax he dealt particularly with the ways in which relations are expressed; these 'formal means' include 'modulation in the sentence' (= stress and intonation), 'cross-referring constructions', 'congruence', 'government' and 'word-order' (176ff.). As for syntactic relations, so too for the elements that ultimately enter into them. The word is a semantic unit (49, 99): 'psychologically a complicative association of those perceptual and emotional elements which we call its meaning or experience content with the auditory and motor elements which constitute the linguistic symbol' (66f.).

The notion that grammar dealt with the expression of meaning was not destroyed by the initial advent of structuralism. In Sapir's treatment (1921), the elements of grammar express 'concrete' and 'relational concepts' (82ff.), and the 'question of form in language' may be addressed from two angles. 'We may either consider the formal methods employed by a language, its "grammatical processes", or we may ascertain the distribution of concepts with reference to formal expression' (57). In Bloomfield's later work, semantics has the task of 'telling what meanings are attached to ... phonetic forms', and has grammar and lexicon as its branches (1935 [1933]: 138). As we have seen in §2.2, the basic lexical unit is the morpheme and its meaning is a 'sememe'; in Bloomfield's terms, this is the smallest 'linguistic form'. The 'smallest meaningful units of grammatical form' are tagmemes, and these in turn have as their meaning an 'episememe'. At each point there is a sign relation, in the sense by then quite usual for a European structuralist, between what Bloomfield called a 'glosseme', which is a 'smallest meaningful unit of linguistic signaling' (264), and a 'noeme', which is the meaning that a glosseme has.

But by the 1950s a different view had arisen. Grammar is seen as separate from semantics, and is concerned with formal patterns only. In Hockett's formulation, which has already been cited more than once, the 'grammatical system' of a language comprises no more than 'a stock of morphemes [morphemes in the new sense of the Post-Bloomfieldians], and the arrangements in which they appear' (1958: 137, and earlier 128f.). For Harris, the study of meaning belonged to another discipline. 'Descriptive linguistics', as (he says) 'the term has come to be used', is 'a particular field of inquiry which deals not with the whole of speech activities', but only with certain regularities. 'These regularities are in the distributional relations' among features of speech, 'i.e. the occurrence of these features relatively to each other within utterances' (1951a: 5). Meaning is thus eliminated, both from the description itself and as a true criterion for analysis (7, esp. n. 4). For Hockett, the 'semantic system' is a peripheral part of the 'design of a language', peripheral because it relates the central subsystem of grammar, which it must therefore take as given, to an aspect of the 'nonspeech world' (1958: 138). Trager and Hill were other important proponents. At the end of a book which deals with the structure of

English in exemplary detail, Hill remarked that 'meaning has been little discussed ... and has never been used as a primary tool of analysis' (1958: 409). This is not to deny its importance, which both he and Hockett make clear. But 'linguists assume' that 'description of meaning must be put off' (3) until an analysis based solely on sounds and their patterning has been completed.

How did this view develop? The impression given at the time, and taken on trust by many scholars since, is that Harris and others were simply following Bloomfield. To the psychologist Carroll, who surveyed the state of American linguistics in the early 1950s, it appeared that 'since the publication of Bloomfield's work in 1933, theoretical discussions among linguists have been largely on matters of refinement ... '. In the next sentence Carroll describes Harris's *Methods* (1951a) as an 'authoritative treatment of the methodology of linguistic analysis, with numerous expansions and modifications of Bloomfield's techniques' (Carroll, 1953: 30). Harris himself says that his work 'owes most ... to the work and friendship of Edward Sapir and of Leonard Bloomfield, and particularly to the latter's book *Language*' (1951a: v). Likewise Hockett and Hill. According to Hockett, 'the influence of American linguistics, and especially that of Leonard Bloomfield, will be apparent on every page' of his book (1958: vii). Hill, like Harris, also mentions Sapir: 'together with all linguists of my generation I owe a pervasive debt to Bloomfield and Sapir, without whose work this book and all of American linguistics would be impossible' (1958: vi). There is in some of this an element of pietas. But in the preface to his last book, Harris refers specifically to 'the distributional (combinatorial) methods of Edward Sapir and of Leonard Bloomfield' as, still, the starting-point for his own work (1991: vi).

We cannot know, from print at least, what Bloomfield would have thought of these acknowledgments. His career ended early and abruptly in 1946, with a stroke which left him unable to work for the remaining years of his life. But in one of his last general papers he continued to make clear that 'in language, forms cannot be separated from meanings' (1943: *LBA* 401). Even in phonology analysis cannot proceed without a knowledge of meanings. An historian therefore has a double problem, whose parts cannot easily be separated. On the one hand, we have to understand why Bloomfield's view was abandoned. How is it that his successors came to believe that forms could and should be described without reference to meanings? On the other hand, we have to try to understand why, in adopting a theory in which the separation of form and meaning was axiomatic, they were so sure they were continuing his work.

The usual answer is that, however central meaning may have been and however important its investigation, Bloomfield's account of how it should be described effectively closed the door to scientific study. 'The statement of meanings', as he had himself said, 'is ... the weak point in language-study, and will remain so until human knowledge advances very far beyond its present state' (1935 [1933]: 140). Elsewhere he lays down the principle that 'linguistic study must always start from the phonetic form and not from the meaning' (162). A further point is that, in order to describe recurrent features in the practical events accompanying a speech signal, which for Bloomfield was the ideal aim of an account of meaning, one apparently had to use terms from outside linguistics. 'In practice', he continues in the first of the passages cited, 'we define the meaning of a linguistic form, wherever we can, in terms of some other science.' Failing that, 'we resort to makeshift devices' (140). Since a scientific account of meaning was for the present unattainable, and would have to depend on advances in human knowledge generally, what was more natural than to start from form alone and make an exhaustive description of it, independently of meaning and before semantic problems are even broached? As Hill saw it (1958: 3), this was 'no more than an application of the principle of working from the more knowable to the less knowable'.

In its final version, Harris's argument is even simpler. 'Language', he says, 'has no external metalanguage in which one could define its elements and their relations.' Therefore they can be established only, as he puts it, 'by their redundancies in the set of utterances, i.e. by the departures from equiprobability in the observable parts of speech and writing' (1991: 3f.). But there is a further element in Harris's thought, whose source perhaps lies in his intellectual formation by Sapir. For one of the major themes of Sapir's treatment of grammar is that the formal processes by which a language expresses concepts do not correspond in any simple fashion to the concepts themselves. There is instead a 'curious lack of accord', as Sapir calls it at one point, 'between function and form' (1921: 89). A word or radical element may express either a concrete idea '(objects, activities, qualities)' or, like an article or preposition, a relational idea. The 'same relational concept may be expressed more than once': for example, in *The farmer kills the duckling*, 'the singularity of *farmer* is both negatively expressed in the noun and positively in the verb'. Equally, 'one element may convey a group of interwoven concepts ... (thus the *-s* of *kills* embodies no less than four logically independent relations)'. In the preceding chapter, he points out that there is no 'logical reason' why the formal structure of a word like *unthinkingly* should be parallel, in terms of the pattern of root and affixes, to that of *reformers*. In another language the concept of manner might be marked by an independent word instead of a suffix, or plurality by a prefix (57f.). Nor, in a given language, are identical functions always expressed in the same way. In one example, plurals are derived in most nouns by reduplication; but in others they are formed with prefixes, in others by internal vowel change, in still others with a suffix (60). From such cases, 'we cannot but conclude that linguistic form may and should be studied as types of patterning, apart from the associated functions'.

This last remark must be read in context. It is not a licence for distributionalism as it was conceived in the 1940s. But a far more serious problem is that constructions do not always bear consistent meanings. Take, for example, that of *I felt cold*. For Bloomfield, this was the 'actor–action' construction, as in sentences like *John ran away*. The meaning of the construction, he explains, is 'roughly this, that whatever is named by the substantive expression [*John*, *I*] *performs* the action named by the finite verb expression' (1935: 185). But 'actor–action' is, as Robins puts it, 'a most imprecise semantic label' (1988: 80). To be exact, a sentence like *John ran away* does describe the performance of an action; *I felt cold* is one of many that do not.

In Bloomfield's first book, it is perfectly clear how such discrepancies were explained. 'Actor' and 'action' are grammatical categories, and it is characteristic of categories that they generalise particular types of experience. 'In the analysis of the total experience into independent elements [see discussion above in §2.1] . . . certain types may become habitual and finally universal in a language'. Thus 'we who speak English always speak of an actor performing an action', even when the total experience is not in fact of that type. The actor–action type 'has been generalised to furnish the mould for all total experiences' (Bloomfield, 1914: 67f.). Sapir talks of categories in much the same way. Language, he says, 'must have its perfectly exclusive pigeon-holes . . . Any concept that asks for expression must submit to the classificatory rules of the game, just as there are statistical surveys in which even the most convinced atheist must perforce be labeled Catholic, Protestant, or Jew or get no hearing' (1921: 99). He does not give syntactic examples. But the state of feeling cold, if it is to be expressed in English, must be classed as an action, even though it is not one.

The answer is less clear in Bloomfield's *Language*. A distinction is again 'categoric' if it is one that is always made (1935: 204). In a formulation which has already been cited in another context, categories are 'large form-classes which completely subdivide either the whole lexicon or some important form-class into form-classes of approximately equal size' (270). In addition, the actor–action construction is said to be that of a 'favorite sentence-form' (172). But although Bloomfield does try, in the passage cited earlier (185), to say 'roughly' what its meaning is, and elsewhere gives a similar working definition of the meaning of a morphological category such as plural, he makes clear that exact accounts will not be easy. 'Having defined [categories] in formal terms, we may have great difficulty in describing their meaning' (271). To illustrate this, he looks briefly at 'some of the more familiar' morphological distinctions. 'The gender-categories of most Indo-European languages ... do not agree with anything in the practical world' (271); 'the categories of *tense* have a surface rationality, ... but even here we soon find that these categories disagree with our non-linguistic analysis' (272), and so on.

The problem is not simply that an exact account of meaning was, for the foreseeable future, unattainable. In the case of the actor–action construction, even makeshift methods lead one to doubt that any unitary account of the constructional meaning, or what Bloomfield called the episememe, can be given. In short, the semantic relations do not reduce to a sign function. Nevertheless, it seems that Bloomfield had no difficulty in defining either this construction or such categories as those of gender in, as he says, 'formal terms'. This formal definition is made independently of meaning; and, since a reference to meaning would at best confuse it, it seems that it must be.

It might be hard to document this argument from Harris's *Methods*. But in his later article on 'Distributional structure', he made clear that, if forms and meanings are considered separately, the structures which result are neither wholly dissimilar nor wholly identical. He does not deny that there is 'a great interconnection between language and meaning, in whatever sense it may be possible to use this word'. But there is no 'one-to-one relation between morphological structure [in *Methods* 'morphology' included what is generally called syntax] and anything else' (1954b: *Papers* 8). The 'correlation between language and meaning is much greater when we consider connected discourse ... However, this is not the same thing as saying that the distributional structure of language (phonology, morphology, and at most a small amount of discourse structure) conforms in some one-to-one way with some independently discoverable structure of meaning' (*Papers* 9). In the preceding section of his paper Harris has argued that a distributional structure does exist (§1, *Papers* 3ff.). It follows that it can be revealed only by a purely distributional analysis. 'Since there is no independently known structure of meanings which exactly parallels linguistic structure, we cannot mix distributional investigations with occasional assists from meaning whenever the going is hard' (*Papers* 9). In a footnote to a later passage, he adds that the distributional analysis must come first. 'It should be clear that only after we discover what kinds of distributional regularities there are among successive elements or sections in discourses can we attempt any organized semantic interpretation of the successions discovered' (n. 19, *Papers* 22).

In summary, an exact account of meaning lay in the future, and, in any case, an analysis which started from form could not rely on meanings as well. But although this may well explain why distributionalism arose as a reaction to Bloomfield's work, it is still not wholly clear why studies such as Harris's *Methods* should have been seen as largely offering no more than what Carroll called 'refinement' or 'expansions and modifications' of it. Surely they were also seeking to correct him, and in a matter that, for Bloomfield, had been central both to his general theory of grammatical and lexical units and to his own conception of his method.

The answer must lie in the way that *Language* was read by his successors. We have seen in the introduction (§1.1) how it was taken as a fresh start in linguistics. It was therefore one thing to have read it as a colleague or reviewer, with a knowledge of the issues that were debated and the conclusions that had been reached before its appearance, and quite another to work through it as a beginning student, coming to it from scratch. As historians, we must try to read it in both modes. For things which in one reading seemed essential to the argument may well have seemed far less important in the other.

If *Language* is read in the first mode it is very hard to interpret Bloomfield's treatment of meaning as inciting his successors to ignore it. In an important endnote, he distinguishes two senses of the term 'semantics', one as the study of 'speech-forms and their meanings' and the other as that of 'meaning or meanings in the abstract' (1935: 513, to §5.1). In the latter sense, 'one is really trying to study the universe in general', a study (we must understand) belonging to other disciplines. In the former sense, which as a linguist he adopts, semantics is 'equivalent to the study of grammar and lexicon'. The distinction is well illustrated in this chapter on substitutes (Ch. 15). These are forms with two elements of meaning; a class meaning and a 'substitution type': for example, the pronoun *I* 'replaces any singular substantive expression' (this gives the class meaning), provided that it 'denotes the speaker ... ' (248). The section which follows takes a look outside linguistics, examining the problems as they 'confront the student of sociology and psychology' (§15.3). Here 'we find at once' that '*I*, *we*, and *you* are based upon the speaker–hearer relation', that '*this*, *here*, *now* and *that*, *there*, *then* represent relations of distance from the speaker or from the speaker and the hearer', and so on. To repeat, these findings lie outside linguistics, being concerned with 'practical circumstances, which the linguist, for his part, cannot accurately define' (end of §15.2). But then, in 'returning to the ground of linguistics' (§15.4), he is able to be 'somewhat bolder' – bolder, that is, than generally in his book – about stating what the meanings are. In fact, he gives a succinct but detailed account (half a page) of the meaning of *he* (251). We may take this as a paradigm of how Bloomfield would have liked the treatment of semantics to be. The reason why other chapters are less bold is that neighbouring sciences had not progressed sufficiently; therefore a linguist has to resort to what are earlier called 'makeshift devices' (140).

Such an approach reflects, in particular, his concern to detach linguistics from psychology. In a passage cited in part at the beginning of this section, Sweet remarks that 'the study of the logical side of language is based on psychology', just as the study of its formal side is based on phonetics. 'But phonetics and psychology do not constitute the science of language, being only preparations for it: language and grammar are concerned not with form and meaning separately, but with the connections between them ... ' (1891: 6f.). For Bloomfield himself, it was essential that linguists should not be embroiled in psychological disputes. We have seen that in his preface he makes clear that we both can and should 'pursue the study of language without reference to any one psychological doctrine' (1935: vii). In his second chapter, he makes clear that the linguist 'is not competent to deal with problems of physiology or psychology'. We must avoid the fault of 'many of the older linguists', who 'vitiated or skimped their reports by trying to state everything in terms of some psychological theory' (32). A linguist has to know something about psychology, and in the paragraphs which follow Bloomfield sketches two alternative theories, the 'mentalistic' and the 'materialistic' or 'mechanistic', a contrast which he returns to in the chapter headed 'meaning' (142ff.). But a linguist's theory must be that of his own science. A striking illustration is the replacement of his earlier Wundtian definition of the sentence (above, §2.1) with one taken from Meillet. Meillet had proposed this from a linguistic viewpoint, in abstraction from both logic and psychology ('au point de vue linguistique, et abstraction faite de toute considération de logique et de psychologie'), a move that Bloomfield had already cited with approval (1931: *LBA* 235). What is defined is a semantic unit – in Bloomfield's terms, the largest 'linguistic form'. But the definition does not depend on a psychological theory, unlike, notably, those of Wundt and of Paul.

Bloomfield's concept of linguistics rested on the 'fundamental assumption' that 'in every speech-community some utterances are alike in form and meaning' (1935: 78, equivalently 144). We thus assume, on the one hand, that there are recurrent or distinctive features of sound. We also assume, on the other hand, that there are recurrent features of meaning; for each form these are 'the *distinctive*, or *linguistic meaning* (the *semantic* features) which are common to all the situations that call forth' its utterance (141). In the state of our knowledge it could strictly be no more than an assumption. But, having made it, linguists could describe linguistic meanings provisionally, and did not have to wait until all other branches of science were 'close to perfection' (78) before they could proceed.

This is not to say that Bloomfield's account was convincing. On this reading, his successors were implicitly subjecting it to one form of critique, and not simply developing it. But what was proposed is an account of meaning within, and central to, linguistics. It was not a theory of linguistic structure in abstraction from meaning, nor an account of meaning in which linguists have to try to 'study the universe in general'. Nor do reviewers of *Language* seem to have found it any way objectionable. Their general assessments have been cited already (§1.1). But it is clear from their silence that, in this respect as in most others, they would have agreed with his own assertion in the preface, that he had 'tried everywhere to present the accepted views . . . ' (1935: viii).

So much if we read Bloomfield in the first mode. Linguistics is presented as an independent, higher-order science, concerned with the conventional linkage between sounds and meanings; but the study of meanings as such has its foundations in other disciplines, of which psychology is the most relevant. That was true however one viewed the nature of meaning, whether mechanistically, as Bloomfield in fact did, or mentalistically, as his readers were free, if they so wished, to prefer. But if we read him in the second mode, the passages which strike us first are those which refer to his general model of the speech-event. This begins with a division between the 'act of speech' and the 'practical events' preceding and following it (23); it is the former with which 'we, as students of language, are chiefly concerned' (25). More precisely, the act of speech is a reaction by the speaker to a stimulus: S → r (small 'r' for linguistic reaction). This is in turn a stimulus that provokes a reaction in the hearer: s → R (small 's' for linguistic stimulus) (25f.). Such a model had been given to him, as he saw it, by psychology (1926: *LBA* 129, with footnote reference to Weiss). We are then told that our concern, 'as students of language', is with 'the speech-event'; 'we distinguish between language, the subject of our study, and real or practical events . . . '. But in the same paragraph the meaning of a speech-utterance (= speech-act, = speech-event) is defined as 'the important things with which [it] is connected, namely the practical events'. This last sentence makes precise reference to the divisions with which the discussion began (27).

Further down the page Bloomfield makes clear that 'to study language' is to study the 'co-ordination of certain sounds with certain meanings'. However, a reader might be forgiven for concluding that, if meaning consists of practical events, and the study of language is distinct from that of practical events, the study of language cannot be concerned with meaning. Nor is this the last remark of that sort. I have cited the passage which leads into a discussion of mentalism and mechanism (32), but without the initial statement that, 'in the division of scientific labor, the linguist deals only with the speech-signal (r . . . s)'. The chapter on phonemes is the next to make use of this model. Bloomfield says there that, 'in principle, the student of language is concerned only with the actual speech'; the preceding sentence makes clear that this means 'the speech-sound'. The study of 'speakers' situations and hearers' responses' – these are explicitly identified with the 'practical events' of the model – 'is equivalent to the sum total of human knowledge' (74). Later in the paragraph he imagines an 'ideal' state of linguistics, which 'would consist of two main investigations: *phonetics*, in which we studied the speech-event without reference to its meaning . . . and *semantics*, in which we studied the relation of [phonetic] features to features of meaning . . . '. But that would be possible only if we had 'an accurate knowledge of every speaker's situation and every hearer's response'. Now it is a note to this section, cited earlier, which makes clear that there is another, non-ideal sense of 'semantics'. It is also this chapter which introduces Bloomfield's 'fundamental assumption of linguistics' (78), precisely so that we can proceed with an imperfect knowledge. But the impression has been left that, for the time being, all the linguist can do is study the speech-signal as such.

It is through this reading that we may perhaps uncover the theoretical authority for distributionalism, if it is to be found at all in Bloomfield's writings. But it is the reading of someone who was young in the 1930s, who did not fully understand the background against which Bloomfield was writing, and who responded instinctively to what was most radical. Nor did distributionalism develop immediately. Even in Harris's first paper on the morpheme, the criterion for morphemic segments is semantic: 'we divide each expression in the given language into the smallest sequences of phonemes which have what we consider the same meaning when they occur in other expressions ... ' (1942: *Papers* 24f.). Likewise, in part, the criterion for grouping alternants into 'morpheme units': 'we take any two or more alternants which have what we consider the same meaning ... and no one of which ever occurs in the same environment as the others' (*Papers* 25). It is not until Harris's *Methods* (written effectively by 1947) that the need to establish morphemes derives simply from the distributional requirement that we should 'stat[e] the limitations of occurrence of [phonemes] over long stretches of speech' (1951a: 156). It is only in a paper published while *Methods* was being written, that Harris proposed a treatment of syntax which relied entirely on the criterion of substitution (1946: esp. *Papers* 45f.).

That such treatments did develop may be due, in part, to practical experience. Bloomfield and Sapir had naturally used distributional criteria, and, without supposing that they could be used exclusively, it would also have been natural, given again that the study of language started from form and not meaning, to see how far they could be pushed. In a moment of reminiscence, Voegelin and his wife imply that Bloomfield himself was willing to push them quite a long way. They recall his advice, 'repeated over and over again' at Linguistic Institutes, 'to postpone consideration of unsolved or unresolved semantic problems until the more formal problems of grammar (in phonology and syntax) were better stated'. 'Most Americanists', they say, 'heeded' it (Voegelin and Voegelin, 1976: 18, 97, n. 7). In particular, they mention work with speakers of Ojibwa 'in which it was found that very explicit formal structure could be obtained with minimum attention to semantics'. We must not fall into the error of associating the exclusion of meaning with the needs of field work. But the further a purely formal analysis is taken, even if it is recognised that in the end it will be insufficient or one-sided, the more its result approaches Harris's concept of distributional structure.

A final factor may have been the technical simplification of Bloomfield's model. As set out in *Language*, it had two levels, those of lexical form and of grammatical form, and two basic units: the morpheme, which was composed of phonemes, and the tagmeme, which was composed of primitive features of grammatical arrangement. Corresponding to each of these there was a unit of meaning, respectively the sememe and the episememe. But in Voegelin and Voegelin's recollection of the 1930s, Bloomfield's units of meaning were 'generally understood at the time (after 1933) to be redundant with formal structure and hence dispensible' (see again their n. 7). The units in question were, I take it, the sememe and the episememe (not, as they say, 'sememe and tagmeme'). The argument then is that, since sememes simply parallel morphemes and episememes likewise parallel tagmemes, they add no information about linguistic structure that is not already there.

It is hard to see why this view should have been general before 1940. Bloomfield's units of form and meaning did not correspond one-to-one: there were alternations, like those of the English plurals, which were precisely among different forms and processes united only in that their meaning was the same. We need not labour this point here, since it has already been discussed in detail in §§2.2 and 2.3. But within ten years of *Language* Harris had proposed a theory of the morpheme in which each set of morphological alternants was brought under a single formal unit. In discussing its development, I raised the possibility that Harris may already have had misgivings about Bloomfield's sememe. But let us now look at the matter the other way round. The meaning of the suffix in, say, *windows* is in this new theory not that of the alternant [z] as such, but that of an abstract morpheme, 'plural', which subsumes all the means by which Bloomfield's sememe, '*more than one* object', was expressed. The sememe is accordingly related to just one formal unit, and, if Bloomfield's sign relation holds, the formal unit is related to just that sememe. This does not mean that an account of semantics will add nothing. But, in morphology at least, it will add no more than an interpretation (to use a term which was to become fashionable much later) to a form of description that is otherwise already complete.

Once this step had been taken, the rest of Bloomfield's model was ripe for reformulation. His account of it had begun, in Ch. 10 of *Language*, with a distinction of four types of 'grammatical arrangement', which together build up 'complex forms' (1935: 162ff.). Of these, 'phonetic modification' included the change of vowel in *geese*; also, for example, that of [-iz] to [-s] in the regular plural suffix of *ducks* (211f.). But in the new theory of the morpheme this is entirely subsumed by the description of allomorphs. 'Modulation' covered features of stress and intonation; for Bloomfield these were 'secondary phonemes ... which do not appear in any morpheme, but only in grammatical arrangements of morphemes' (163). But in the new theory these are said to be morphemes in themselves (thus Harris, 1945: *Papers* 36). 'Selection' referred to the choice of forms: for example, of the substantive in *John!* or the verb in *Run!* or, in *John runs fast*, of *-s* in agreement with *John* (Bloomfield, 1935: 164f.). It is interesting that Harris's next step, though not followed by others, is to reduce all cases of agreement to 'discontinuous morphemes' (again Harris, 1945). The remaining features of grammatical arrangement are those of order. To Hockett, looking back on Bloomfieldian linguistics at the end of the 1960s, that alone is what 'arrangement' ought to have meant (1968: 20f.). But once Harris's theory of the morpheme had been accepted, all that indeed remained were simply the choice of elements (selection) and what Hockett calls the 'geometrical location of elements relative to one another'. That was as true, moreover, of relations within the word, which Bloomfield had still assigned to a separate subfield, as of relations between words.

After distinguishing different kinds of grammatical arrangement, Bloomfield explains that, though the individual features are meaningless, they combine to form tagmemes, or units of grammatical form, which do have meaning (166). But if 'arrangement' is effectively reduced to order, a particularly important notion is that of a 'position' in a tagmeme. Take again his account of the 'actor–action construction' (184f.). For Bloomfield, a construction is a type of grammatical form (169) which characteristically has two positions. In this case, they are the 'actor' position, filled by *John* in the sentence *John ran*, and the 'action' position, filled by *ran*. He then defines 'the positions in which a form can appear' as 'its *functions* or, collectively, its *function*'. Accordingly, the function or functions of *John* would include that of actor in this construction, that of 'goal' in the 'action–goal' construction of *Tell John* (compare 197), and so on. He also uses this framework to make precise the definition of a 'form-class'. When this term first appears, he talks of forms grouped 'by some recognizable phonetic or grammatical feature' (146), and he later gives as one example 'the forms which, when spoken with exclamatory final-pitch, have the meaning of a call' (164). It is now defined as 'all the forms which can fill a given position'. Thus *John, Bill, our horses* ... are members of the form-class defined by the actor position; similarly *ran, fell, ran away* ... of that defined by the action position.

Now in Bloomfield's 'Set of postulates' constructions, like morphemes, had been established by a correspondence between form and meaning. He does not illustrate differences; but, for example, we can say that in *drink milk* and *fresh milk*, whose features of selection are distinguished earlier in *Language* (165), the order of constituents corresponds in one case to an 'action–goal' meaning and in the other to a 'character–substance' meaning. Therefore their constructions are different; therefore *drink* and *fresh* fill different positions and belong to different form-classes. As Bloomfield puts it, the initial assumption is that 'different non-minimum forms may be alike or partly alike as to the order of the constituent forms and as to stimulus–reaction features corresponding to this order' (1926: *LBA* 132). These stimulus–reaction features are defined as the constructional meanings. In *Language* again, the character–substance construction is subdivided into 'quality–substance', as in *fresh milk*, and 'limitation–substance', as in *this milk* (1935: 202). The reason, if we put it in terms of the earlier article, is that in *this fresh milk* a difference in the order of modifiers (*this* before *fresh*, not *fresh* before *this*) corresponds to different 'limiting' and 'descriptive' meanings.

When we return to *Language* it seems clear that Bloomfield's basic theory has not changed. Constructions, to repeat, are tagmemes and tagmemes have meanings, called episememes, just as morphemes have meanings, called sememes. But some of his illustrations might easily suggest that meanings are secondary. In the passage just referred to he does not, in fact, begin by distinguishing the constructions (limitation–substance and quality–substance). Instead he starts from the division between form-classes (limiting adjective and descriptive adjective), which is established 'by the circumstance that when adjectives of both these classes occur in a phrase, the limiting adjective precedes and modifies the group of descriptive adjective plus noun'. This might suggest that the distinction is made simply by the feature of order in phrases such as *this fresh milk*. He then says that the difference between form-classes subdivides the construction. This would suggest that the fundamental distinction is between two sequences of form-classes (member of limiting subclass + substantive expression, member of descriptive subclass + substantive expression), and the difference of meaning between constructions (limitation–substance, quality–substance) is the last thing to be characterised. At the beginning of this section Bloomfield says that 'syntax is obscured ... in most treatises, by the use of philosophical instead of formal definitions of constructions and form-classes' (1935: 201). He means that we cannot establish a grammatical distinction simply by referring to a philosophical distinction; there must also be a formal distinction corresponding to it. But one might plausibly conclude that, starting from the formal features of selection and order, which in themselves are meaningless, one can establish first form-classes and then constructions on the evidence of form alone.

In this light it is tempting to reconsider Bloomfield's sequence of definitions. In theory, positions are elements in a construction; they in turn define form-classes. But if form-classes can in practice distinguish constructions, and classes are in turn still understood to be defined by positions, positions might seem prior to both. Furthermore, there is no term, in the system as it is presented in this chapter, for the meaning of a position. In the 'Set of postulates' this had been called the 'functional meaning': thus 'actor' was the functional meaning of the position in the construction of *John ran* which is occupied by *John*. The functional meanings of a language, with its class-meanings (meanings of form-classes), were said to form its 'categories' (Bloomfield, 1926: *LBA* 133f.). But in *Language* categories are simply 'large form-classes ... '; they are thus composed of forms, not meanings (1935: 270f.). Class-meanings remain, and it is notable that, in the discussion of the character–substance construction and its subtypes, it is the class-meanings (for adjectives in general 'something like "*character* of specimens of a species of objects"', for descriptive adjectives 'roughly "*qualitative* character of specimens"') that correspond to the names given to positions (character, quality). But the term 'functional meaning' disappears. In a later chapter Bloomfield talks of 'positional meanings', such as 'performer of an action' (267). But the term is not put into italics, is not indexed, and is not used when the system is first explained and illustrated.

A more prominent notion is that of function. Functions are defined, in the passage already cited from the syntax chapter, as 'the positions in which a form can appear' (1935: 185; compare 1926: *LBA* 134). Eighty pages later the definition is reformulated, in terms of what are called 'privileges of occurrence'. After talking of lexical forms in isolation, Bloomfield says that a 'lexical form in any actual utterance, as a concrete linguistic form, is always accompanied by some grammatical form: it appears in some function, and these privileges of occurrence make up, collectively, the grammatical *function* of the lexical form' (265). As it is put succinctly in a later monograph, 'a *function* of a form is its privilege of appearing in a certain position of a certain construction' (Bloomfield, 1939a: 26; compare Bloch and Trager 1942: 72, first drafted by Bloomfield (4)). This is a purely formal notion. In his late article on 'Meaning', Bloomfield remarks that to earlier students function was an aspect of language intermediate between form and meaning. 'Thus, a word like *apple* ... functioned as a noun, serving as the subject of verbs ... and so on.' But 'careful study' has shown that these are simply 'formal features which come into being when two or more forms are combined in a larger form'. Thus *apple*, with certain exceptions, always enters into phrases with preceding adjectives (adjective again includes article), and these phrases can 'enter into larger phrases with following finite verb expressions'. 'A form's privilege of occurring in any one position' is once more 'a *function* of that form' (1943: *LBA* 403). A distributionalist need merely add that, by 'position', one means just 'position preceding or following some other class of forms'.

In fact, distributionalism followed, and within a few years of this last paper. In the account developed here, it did not develop solely for theoretical or philosophical reasons. Another important factor is that Bloomfield had himself provided what were effectively models for it. We have seen earlier that, 'having defined' categories 'in formal terms', he then saw 'great difficulty' in some cases 'in defining their meaning' (271). The implication, once more, was that their formal definition could come first, and reference to meaning might confuse it. We have now seen that form-classes could be established, in a way apparently licensed by Bloomfield's own practice, simply by reference to formal features of selection and order. But what more was needed? In the simplified model, a construction is from the formal angle a relation of order among form-classes. So, from that angle their description is complete, without meaning having entered into their analysis.

In developing this argument, I have had to look in detail at the nitty gritty of Bloomfield's exposition, including the forms of words used in discussing specific examples. If we read the book overall, we will still find no sanction for it. But we must try again to put ourselves in the shoes of a young scholar for whom *Language* was a Bible in linguistics. Such scholars were not learning just a general theory, but also how to apply it to specific problems of analysis; and, if one reads the book in that way, it is precisely the nitty gritty that one tends to pore over.

3.2 Generative grammar

Our problem in dealing objectively with the rise of distributionalism is that everyone knows that Harris and his contemporaries were followers of Bloomfield. They themselves said so! We have therefore had to emphasise that there was in fact a discontinuity, before searching for the real continuities that exist. Our problem now is very much the opposite. For everyone knows that Chomsky's theories revolutionised linguistics, and not just in America. Has this not been proclaimed for more than a quarter of a century? We therefore have to begin by reminding ourselves that he did not directly abandon every idea that he had inherited. We will find instead that he often gave them new life.

Let us start with the basic definition of 'a language'. For most European scholars, the language that a linguist sought to describe was an abstraction. It was a system of relations, with at its heart the relation that Hjelmslev called the sign function, seen as underlying the speech of a community. Some Bloomfieldians also described it as a system: 'a system of arbitrary vocal symbols by means of which a social group cooperates' (Bloch & Trager, 1942: 5). For Joos (1948: 99), it was a structure located in a speaker's brain: 'a set of neural patterns in the speech center' (cited, with other definitions, by Hamp, 1957: *s.v.*). Bloomfield's *Language* did not give a definition (nor is there an entry for 'language' in his index). But in his first book he had stressed that 'language' (without the article) is 'merely a set of habits' – 'merely' (we must bear in mind the context in which Bloomfield was writing) in that it is not 'an object or independent organism of some kind' (1914: 259). Forty years later, when Bloomfield's mechanist psychology had come and gone, this notion of a habit was central to Hockett's account. 'A language', as he defined it in his textbook, 'is a complex system of habits' (1958: 137).

But there was another form of definition, whose advantage was perhaps one of method. When we study a language, what we are in practice studying is a certain body of data; and these consist, primarily, of a sample of the linguistic forms, in Bloomfield's sense, that a certain set of speakers might utter. It was therefore practical to define 'a language' as just such a set of utterances. This was Bloomfield's strategy in his 'Set of postulates': having first defined a 'speech-community' (Def. 3), he then says that 'the totality of utterances that can be made in a speech-community is the *language* of that speech-community (1926: Def. 4; *LBA* 130). It was also the line adopted by Harris. In *Methods*, a language or dialect 'comprises the talk which takes place in a language community' (Harris, 1951a: 13), and when, in 'Distributional structure', he says that this structure 'really exist[s] in the language', he means precisely that the relations 'hold in the data investigated' (1954b: *Papers* 6). Finally, in the wake of Harris, a similar line was taken by Chomsky. In the first sentence of *Syntactic Structures*, a language is considered to be 'a set ... of sentences' (Chomsky, 1957: 13). 'All natural languages in their spoken or written form are languages in this sense', and a 'grammar of a language' is a characterisation of such a set of sentences.

In reading these passages we must be careful not to make anachronistic distinctions between a sentence and an utterance. In Bloomfield's 'Set of postulates', an utterance is 'an act of speech' (1926: Def. 1, *LBA* 129); a sentence is in effect a maximal linguistic form 'in any utterance' (Def. 27, *LBA* 132). It follows that an utterance can consist of several sentences: an example, from *Language*, is one which can be divided into three successive sentences *How are you?*, *It's a fine day* and *Are you going to play tennis this afternoon?* (Bloomfield, 1935: 170). In terms of his 'postulates', each of these is a form which, 'in the given utterance, is not part of a larger construction' (*LBA* 133). Moreover, the sentences are literally the parts of the utterance. In the terminology inherited from ancient treatments of language, each is an articulated sound which has a meaning. Similarly, for Bloomfield, each is a 'phonetic form' which has a meaning; that is, a 'linguistic form' (1935: 138). In describing the language of a speech community, we are describing the sounds that can be uttered in that language and their relationship to meanings. That is, once again, we are describing 'the totality of utterances that can be made in a speech-community' (*LBA* 130). But we do so only up to the limits of the sentence.

But for both Harris and Chomsky the terms tended to become synonyms. In Harris's *Methods*, an utterance is defined as 'any stretch of talk, by one person, before and after which there is silence on the part of that person' (Harris, 1951a: 14). But in his review of this book, Householder remarks that, despite that definition, Harris in general 'uses "utterance" to mean what old-fashioned linguists called a "sentence" or "sentence fragment"' (Householder, 1952: 263). This is perhaps even clearer in

'From morpheme to utterance'. The procedure is said to yield 'a compact statement of what sequences of morphemes occur in the language, i.e. a formula for each utterance (sentence) structure in the language' (Harris, 1946: *Papers* 45). Again, 'the final result ... takes the form of one or more sequences of substitution classes ("utterance constructions", "sentence types")' (*Papers* 62).

His pupil went on to use both terms interchangeably, and in all relevant collocations. On the next page of *Syntactic Structures* he talks of grammatical sentences and observed sentences: '... a linguistic theory that attempts to give a general explanation for the notion "grammatical sentence" in terms of "observed sentence"' (Chomsky, 1957: 14). The next paragraph talks of observed utterances and grammatical utterances: 'Any grammar of a language will *project* the finite and somewhat accidental corpus of observed utterances to a set (presumably infinite) of grammatical utterances' (15). This refers to a corpus of utterances; but, on the page before, each grammar is said to be related to a 'corpus of sentences' (see also 49 for both collocations). Chomsky talks at least twice of the speaker's ability 'to produce and understand new utterances' (23); however, speakers are also said to produce sentences. Thus, if a finite state conception of language is adopted, 'we can view the speaker as being essentially a machine' of that type; 'in producing a sentence', he 'begins in the initial state, produces the first word of the sentence' and so on (20). Compare Lees's review of *Syntactic Structures*, where the linguist is seen as modelling the 'kind of device' a speaker uses in his head 'to generate the sentences of his language' (Lees, 1957: 406). At the end of Ch. 4, a grammar is said to associate a sentence with a series of representations at various levels (33); when Chomsky returns to the topic in Ch. 5, it is said to yield representations of utterances (47; see also 59). At the end of this chapter he argues that a grammar is neutral between speaker and hearer; it is 'simply a description of a certain set of utterances, namely, those which it generates'. A few lines later he says that 'a grammar generates all grammatically "possible" utterances', just as a chemical theory 'might be said to generate all physically possible compounds' (48). Naturally, he also says that grammars 'generate sentences'. But in a paper delivered the following year, he again talks of 'a grammar that generates utterances with structural descriptions' (Chomsky, 1962 [1958]: 132; see also 129).

If a language is a set of possible utterances or sentences, a corpus, which is a set of observed utterances or sentences, is a part or subset of it. According to Harris, a descriptive linguist studies distributional regularities in speech (1951a: 5). He must therefore obtain a corpus and adopt research methods which will determine what regularities exist. In his book, such methods are set out 'in the form of successive procedures of analysis imposed by the working linguist upon his data' (1). The procedures are 'ways of arranging the data' (3), which provide a method for identifying all the utterances which occur in a language community as 'relatively few stated arrangements of relatively few stated elements' (1). They lead to a 'compact representation' of utterances (198), or 'a compact statement of what utterances occur in the corpus' (361). 'The over-all purpose of work in descriptive linguistics is to obtain a compact one–one representation of the stock of utterances in the corpus' (366).

At this point, it is important not to read into what Harris is saying the assumptions of what might now be called a 'corpus-based' grammar. For, as he makes clear, a corpus is of interest only as a sample of the language. By 'sample' he means an adequate sample: thus the analysis of one corpus 'becomes of interest only if it is virtually identical with the analysis which would be obtained in like manner from any other sufficiently large corpus of material taken in the same dialect' (13). In that case, the linguist's statements are predictive: 'we can predict the relations among elements in any other corpus of the language on the basis of relations found in our analyzed corpus'. This point was developed still more clearly by Hockett. As he remarks in a paper which will have been written just as Harris's *Methods* was completed, the purpose of classifying data 'is not simply to account for all the utterances' which are in a corpus 'at a given time'. 'Rather, the analysis of the linguistic *scientist*' is to be such 'that the linguist can account also for utterances which are *not* in his corpus at a given time'. That is, 'he must be able to predict what *other* utterances the speaker of a language might produce . . . ' (Hockett, 1948: *RiL* 279). In the paragraphs which follow, Hockett compares 'this analytical process' with 'what goes on in the nervous system of a language learner, particularly, perhaps, that of a child learning his first language'. When the child produces an utterance not already heard, it is, 'of course, a kind of prediction'. Four years later, in one of the few contemporary reactions to the Saussurean concepts of 'langue' and 'parole', Hockett says that an analyst is required to 'produce systematization which *in an operational sense* matches the habits which we ascribe to the speaker'. So, 'just as the speaker can produce any number of new utterances from essentially the same system of underlying habits', our description 'must be capable of producing any number of new utterances, each capable of passing the test of casual acceptance by a native speaker'. Likewise it must match the speaker's ability to understand 'an utterance he has never heard before' (Hockett, 1952b: 98).

A corpus is adequate, then, to the extent that predictions can be made from it. As Hockett put it, 'in theory, at least, with a large enough corpus there would no longer be any discernible discrepancy between utterances the linguist predicted and those sooner or later observed' (1948: *RiL* 280). But this concern for prediction has two important implications, both of which are clear from the discussion by Harris. Firstly, by a corpus one cannot mean an arbitrary or random collection of material. In the first chapter, Harris says that, as far as his procedures are concerned, it does not matter how linguists get their data. We may take down texts, record conversations, or question informants. We may also intervene deliberately: for example, by altering a conversation to obtain repetitions in different environments (1951a: 1). But as he points out in the mid-1950s, we will often 'require for comparison various utterances which occur so infrequently that searching for them in an arbitrary corpus is prohibitively laborious'. 'In particular, investigations of the selections of particular morphemes ... can hardly be carried out without the aid of eliciting' (Harris, 1954b: *Papers* 16). In the last chapter of *Methods*, he talks similarly of the need to bring in 'controlled material'. Thus, given the utterance *What books came?* 'we do not compare it with arbitrary other utterances, but search for utterances which are partly similar, like *What book came? What maps came? What books are you reading?*'. Such comparisons may be elicited 'from an informant, or from oneself, or from some arranged or indexed body of material'; in this way, 'we have an experimental situation in which the linguist tests variations in the utterance stock in respect to a selected utterance'. The reason for these experiments is precisely that 'we are interested in analyzing such a corpus as will serve as a sample of the language' (1951a: 368).

Secondly, we have to adopt what Harris calls techniques of approximation. In his chapter on morpheme classes, he points out that few morphemes will be found in exactly the same environments. 'In a sufficiently large corpus', *Dick*, for example, might have the same distribution as *Tom*; but not *Jack*, which also appears in *Jack of all trades*. A single morpheme will also have different distributions from one corpus to another. For example, *root* might be found in one corpus in *That's the root of the trouble*; in another it might not, but might, however, appear in *The square root of 5929 is 77* (244, nn. 4 and 5). Thus our corpus is not a satisfactory sample for 'the exact environments of morphemes'. Nor will we 'effect a great reduction in the number' of classes by grouping together morphemes with precisely the same distribution. 'We will have to be satisfied with some approximation to such a grouping.' Accordingly, we 'disregard' specific distributional differences. Some will be accidental: for example, if we happen to have recorded *Dick's twelve minutes late*, but not *Tom's twelve minutes late*. Others will not. For example, we would group together *four* and *seven*, even though *He left at two seventy sharp*, on the model of *He left at two forty sharp*, is unlikely to appear in any corpus (245). In an appendix to this chapter, Harris deals particularly with what he calls a 'culturally determined limitation' (253). It 'may "mean nothing" to say *The box will be murdered*'; therefore 'even the largest corpus' will not contain it. The distribution of *box* would thus be partly different from that of *man*. But 'it would be desirable, in grouping the morphemes into classes, to devise such an approximation as would disregard' restrictions of that sort (254).

The reason for making approximations is that, once again, we want our corpus to 'serve as a predictive sample of the language' (244). In his second chapter, Harris remarks that, when we analyse a limited corpus, the features of an element will be defined extensionally, relative to just the 'bits of talking' that have been observed (17). But when a linguist aims to represent 'the language as a whole, he is predicting that the elements set up for his corpus will satisfy all other bits of talking in that language'. The features of an element will then be defined intensionally, in opposition (if I can so render his wording) to those of other elements. This is the only place where Harris uses these terms. But at the syntactic level we could envisage a series of extensional definitions which would simply list all the environments in which, in a particular body of material, such and such a morpheme has been found. If two morphemes appear in exactly the same environments then, and only then, would they be classed together. But what we want are intensional definitions which will tell us how the elements are distributed 'in the language as a whole'. For this the 'usual linguistic corpus' (253) is inadequate; we have to make approximations if our statements are to have any generality. In the section on 'culturally determined limitations', Harris also argues that even if we had an 'exact morpheme classification' its 'predictive usefulness ... need not be greater than that of an approximative one' (254). For cultural factors will change and exact distributions will change with them.

The particular importance of these passages is that, if the methods can succeed, there will be no discrepancy between a predictive account of the language and what Harris calls a compact representation of a corpus. In his final chapter, he points out that, apart from saying that certain sequences of elements do occur in the utterances of a language 'we may also be able to say that certain sequences almost never occur; we may know this from direct testing, or from the fact that the sequence goes counter to the most general regularities of our corpus' (372). The crucial assumption is that we have 'an adequate sample': as Harris puts it in his final chapter on phonology, 'we derive a statement about all the utterances of the language by assuming that our corpus can be taken as a sample of the language' (152). Similarly, for phonology and grammar as a whole, 'the work of analysis leads right up to the statements which enable anyone to synthesize or predict utterances in the language'. 'These statements', he goes on, 'form a deductive system with axiomatically defined initial elements and with theorems concerning the relations among them. The final theorems would indicate the structure of the utterances of the language in terms of the preceding parts of the system.' This constitutes 'the description of the language structure' (372f.).

In the light of this reading of Harris's *Methods*, we can begin to appreciate both the debt that Chomsky owed to older American scholars and his true originality. When Chomsky talks of a grammar it is plainly the same thing as Harris's 'description of the language structure'; indeed he said so (Chomsky, 1961b: 220, n. 5, referring to the passage just cited). In *Methods* Harris had not used the term 'generate'. But in a later article he does: 'a grammer may be viewed as a set of instructions which generates the sentences of the language' (1954a: 260). So does Hockett in an important paper published in the same year. A grammatical description 'must', he says, 'be prescriptive . . . in the sense that by following the statements one must be able to generate any number of utterances in the language'. These will again include not only the utterances of the corpus, but also 'new utterances most, if not all, of which will pass the test of casual acceptance by the native speaker' (Hockett, 1954: *RiL* 398). This too Chomsky cites, adding only that the statements also assign a structure to each sequence (1961b: 221). Earlier in his paper Hockett expounds the form of grammatical description common among Bloomfieldians (the 'Item and Arrangement' model). This is said to set forth 'principles by which one can generate any number of utterances in the language' (*RiL* 390). 'In this sense', Hockett adds, 'it is operationally comparable to the structure of that portion of a human being which enables him to produce utterances in a language; i.e., to speak.' Likewise, in his important review of *Syntactic Structures*, Lees says that, granted the validity of scientific method as he sees it, 'it is not too much to assume that human beings talk in the same way that our grammar "talks"' (1957: 406f.). Hockett's more careful wording seems closer to Chomsky's eventual view of linguistic 'competence' (below, §§4.1–2). Hockett also compares an 'Item and Arrangement' description to a cookbook; similarly, Lees talks in one place of rules which 'provide a recipe for constructing English sentences' (1960a: 2).

By the mid-1950s Harris was beginning to refer to Chomsky in return (1954b: *Papers* 21, n. 3, for the problems of simplicity) and it might perhaps be difficult to decide exactly who was influencing whom. But the essential step had already been taken in Harris's *Methods*. A distributional analysis is meant to determine what combinations of elements occur; hence also, by implication, those that do not occur. This is done, in the first instance, for a corpus. But the corpus is only a sample; for the language as a whole one tries to say, as generally and as succinctly as possible, what combinations 'could occur'. That again implies that other combinations 'could not' occur. Accordingly, the distributional statements separate a set of possible utterances from other arrangements of elements that are not possible; since each utterance will be covered by several successive statements, they also tell us how they are constructed. This is the logical conclusion of Harris's programme, and one which he had himself explicitly formulated.

Chomsky's real contributions lay elsewhere. Firstly, where Harris spoke of 'bits of talking' that occur or do not occur, Chomsky makes clear that the essential property of sentences or utterances is grammaticality. Hockett talks similarly of the grammatical description being 'prescriptive'; it is interesting, in the light of subsequent development of Chomsky's thinking, that he does not require that every utterance so prescribed should meet a test of casual acceptability (Hockett, 1954: passage cited above, *RiL* 398; compare Chomsky, 1965: 11). A language is thus 'the totality of utterances that can be made in a speech-community' (Bloomfield, 1926) in the specific sense that members of the community will recognise them as grammatical. It is not the 'talk' that actually 'takes place', as Harris, at the beginning of *Methods*, had tried to define it. It is an abstract construct, to which quasi-mathematical properties, such as that of being infinite (Chomsky, 1957: 13 *et passim*) can be attributed.

Secondly, he saw clearly what was needed to justify a grammar. The aim of Harris and others had been to develop procedures of analysis which, if rigorously followed, would themselves justify the description resulting from them. 'The work of analysis' thus 'leads right up to the statements which enable anyone to synthesize or predict utterances in the language' (see again Harris, 1951a: 372). Such procedures constitute what Chomsky called a 'discovery procedure' (1957: 50f.). They would provide 'a practical and mechanical method for actually constructing the grammar, given a corpus of utterances'.

Chomsky had in the very beginning shared this aim, which is reflected in his first article (1953). But in syntax it was bound to lead to a procedure for comparing alternative analyses. Take, for example, the phrase *the old man*. Within it there is a sequence *old man*, whose distribution is in this and other contexts similar to that of *man* itself. That might suggest that *old man* is itself a smaller phrase. But to confirm it we have got to show that this division of the unit, into *the* and *old man*, gives a better account of distributions than if, alternatively, we divide it into *the old* and *man*, or directly into *the*, *old* and *man*. As Wells put it in a leading article on 'Immediate constituents', an analysis into constituents 'is never accepted or rejected on its own merits. Our procedure aims only to tell, given two or more mechanically possible dichotomies, . . . how to decide in favor of one of them' (1947b: §8, *RiL* 188). Moreover, we cannot justify the analysis of one phrase, or even of a set of similar phrases, in isolation. 'Ultimately', as Wells puts it later, 'what is accepted or rejected is not the analysis of a single sentence but what we may call the I[mmediate] C[onstituent] *system* of the language, an entire set or system of analyses, complete down to the ultimate constituents, of all the utterances of the language' (§29, *RiL* 193). That is, once more, it is accepted or rejected in comparison with alternatives. In the next paragraph, Wells makes clear that 'we do not propose our account as a mechanical procedure by which the linguist, starting with no other data than the corpus of all the utterances of the language and a knowledge of the morphemes contained in each one, may discover the correct IC-system'.

But what exactly is meant by 'the IC-system' of a language? As Wells describes it, it is 'an entire set or system of analyses . . . of all the utterances of the language' (again §29). So, on the face of it, what is accepted or rejected is a set of representations of utterances, equivalent to what Chomsky later called 'phrase markers'. But how do we 'decide in favor' (§8) of one set rather than another? It would again be pointless to compare each individual 'analysis' with a competing analysis. We have instead to see which set of representations will give us a better overall account of the language. But we can only do that if we compare not the 'analyses' as such, but a set of general statements that can be abstracted from or are implicit in them. In Harris's terms, we have to compare parts of the 'description of the language structure'. In Chomsky's terms, the method that Wells is proposing must be one in which 'ultimately' (§29) we have to evaluate alternative grammars.

But where does that leave the rest of the Bloomfieldian programme? With other scholars of this period, Wells proposes what is in fact a procedure for analysing utterances: in his case, for dividing them into immediate constituents, then these into their immediate constituents, and so on. It is presumably for that reason that Chomsky interprets his article as one of those which have as their 'explicit goal' the development of a discovery procedure (1957: 52, n. 3). The method, then, would seem to be this. First, we take a corpus of utterances and, by following a certain procedure, we arrive at a set of alternative 'IC-systems' for the language of which they are a sample. Our descriptions of these IC-systems are, in effect, grammars. Then we take these systems and, by some criterion of generality or, as Harris would have said, 'compactness' of description, we decide that one is better than the others. But what Chomsky saw clearly, and other Post-Bloomfieldians do not seem to have seen at all, is that, if this second stage is needed, the first is irrelevant. It may be useful for a practising grammarian to have a heuristic procedure. In that way it may be possible, as one works with a language, to propose descriptions which are likely, in the second stage, to come out better. But such procedures are not part of a theory. All a theory must provide is a procedure for assessing alternative grammars.

Chomsky did not engage in direct criticism of Wells's article. But by this kind of reconstructed critique we can see how he had thought his way through to the heart of the problem. To Harris and to several other predecessors, it had seemed essential to prescribe rigorous procedures of analysis. Only thus could a theory of language justify descriptions of particular languages. For Chomsky the basic problem was just the same: how, in his terms, could particular grammars be justified? What he disputed was that a discovery procedure, as he called it, was 'attainable in any interesting way'. He suspects 'that any attempt to meet it will lead into a maze of more and more elaborate and complex analytic procedures that will fail to provide answers for many important questions about the nature of linguistic structure' (1957: 52f.). But rigour might be achieved, as Wells had perhaps seen rather darkly, in another way. First, it was essential that a theory should prescribe the precise form that a grammar should take. The only further requirement was that, 'given a corpus and given two proposed grammars G_1 and G_2', the theory must provide an 'evaluation procedure' which will 'tell us which is the better grammar of the language from which the corpus is drawn' (51).

These were vital contributions, which at once removed the problems that had earlier been thought central, and made central what had earlier been neglected. In particular, the formal nature of a grammar is put centre stage. But in abandoning the particular goals that Harris had set for a distributional theory Chomsky did not abandon distributionalism itself. With Harris's 'Distributional structure', Ch. 9 of *Syntactic Structures* is indeed one of the best apologies for it. For him, as for Harris, 'grammar is best formulated as a self-contained study independent of semantics' (1957: 106). In Ch. 2 he makes clear that 'the notion "grammatical" cannot be identified with "meaningful"' (15). In Ch. 9 he argues at length that differences of meaning are not the basis even for phonemic distinctness (94ff.). Instead he advocates a 'pairs test', which, he says, 'provides us with a clear operational criterion for phonemic distinctness in completely non-semantic terms' (97; see also n. 5). He argues against defining the morpheme as a 'meaning-bearing element' (100), casts doubts on the validity of 'structural meanings' (100, 104f., 108) and stresses that transformations are not characterised by 'synonymity' (101). Not only can a grammar be constructed without appeal to meaning; the suggestion that it can be constructed '*with* appeal to meaning' is 'totally unsupported' (93). 'Investigation of such proposals ... invariably seems to lead to the conclusion that only a purely formal basis can provide a firm and productive foundation for the construction of grammatical theory' (100). 'The motivation for this self-imposed formality requirement for grammars is quite simple – there seems to be no other basis that will yield a rigorous, effective, and "revealing" theory of linguistic structure' (103).

Of the chapters which assess alternative grammars, all but one are, again in Chomsky's words, 'completely formal and non-semantic' (93). Thus the initial argument for the passive transformation (42f.) is that it avoids restating lexical restrictions which hold equally in both the active and the passive constructions. The argument for a transformational treatment of coordination is that it 'simplifies' description; in particular, 'the grammar is enormously simplified' if constituents are so established that the general rule proposed 'holds even approximately' (37). Throughout Ch. 7 ('Some transformations in English'), Chomsky talks of the 'simplest way' to describe constructions (e.g. 61f. on negation), of rules so stated that, when new constructions are brought in, 'almost nothing new is required in the grammar' (66), of the grammar becoming 'much more simple and orderly' (68) if transformations are posited. At the end of this longish chapter he again says that 'our sole concern has been to decrease the complexity of the grammar' (83). In Ch. 9 he acknowledges that the notion of simplicity has been 'left unanalyzed'; but it will not help, with that or any other outstanding problem, to construct the theory 'on a partially semantic basis' (103). Our eventual goal, explained in Ch. 6, is to 'formulate a general theory of linguistic structure in which such notions as "phoneme in L", "phrase in L", "transformation in L" are defined for an arbitrary language L in terms of physical and distributional properties of utterances of L and formal properties of grammars of L' (54). It is in such a theory that simplicity will be defined.

The exception is Ch. 8, in which Chomsky proposes, as a separate criterion, that a grammar should 'provide explanations' (85) for certain semantic facts. But the status of this is again made very clear. On the one hand, we retain a purely formal theory of grammar, and purely formal arguments which, for example, may lead a particular grammar to assign two different representations to the same sequence of phonemes. For instance, /əneym/ will have two analyses at the level of morphology (/ə + neym/ or /ən + eym/); this is not because of their meaning, but is 'an automatic consequence of the attempt to set up the morphology in the simplest possible way' (85). Similarly, *the shooting of the hunters* will have two transformational derivations, from the structure either of *The hunters shoot* or *They shoot the hunters*. Again, 'careful analysis of English shows that we can simplify the grammar' (89) if we so treat them. Such sequences are 'constructional homonyms'. By definition (86), a constructional homonym is simply any form to which a particular grammar has assigned more than one structure.

On the other hand, we can envisage a 'more general theory of language' (102) which will have as subparts both 'a theory of linguistic form' – as, for example, the theory of transformational grammar – and 'a theory of the use of language'. Only there can we address the 'real question' (93) about grammar and meaning, which is: 'How are the syntactic devices available in a given language put to work in the actual use of this language?' Now the examples cited are 'understood ambiguously' by native speakers: /əneym/ as either 'a name' or 'an aim' (85); *the shooting of the hunters* 'analogously to' either *the growling of lions* or *the raising of flowers* (88). These, to repeat, are facts about the 'use' and not the form of such sequences. However, they are explained by a grammar in which, quite independently, the forms are set up as constructional homonyms. They can therefore be seen as independent confirmation that the grammar is right; also that the theory of grammar within which these were the simplest analyses – a theory, therefore, which among other things has levels both of morphology and of transformational derivation – is right.

In this way we test the adequacy of grammars and theories of grammar by 'asking whether or not each case of constructional homonymity is a real case of ambiguity and each case of the proper kind of ambiguity is actually a case of constructional homonymity' (86). More generally, 'we should like the syntactic framework of the language that is isolated and exhibited by the grammar to be able to support semantic description, and we shall naturally rate more highly a theory of formal structure that leads to grammars that meet this requirement more fully' (102). But Chomsky is at pains to stress that, by arguing in this way, 'we have not altered the purely formal character of the theory of grammatical structure itself' (102). On the next page he speaks of language as 'an instrument or tool', whose structure should be described 'with no explicit reference' to its use (103). This formal description 'may be expected to provide insight' into its use – 'i.e., into the process of understanding sentences' (103). But 'systematic semantic considerations are apparently not helpful in determining it in the first place' (108).

There are plainly things here that were new, and were developed further in the next phase. But the approach in general is not so very different from others current in the 1950s. As we have seen earlier, Bloomfield's followers did not think that meaning was unimportant. At worst its description was, again in Hill's words, to be 'put off'. In a section with the title 'Semantics', Hill alludes to the 'familiar ... map of linguistics' drawn by Trager, in which the study of 'microlinguistics', including 'descriptive linguistics', is distinguished from the 'metalinguistic' study of the relations between language and other cultural systems (Trager, 1949; above, §1.1). There was naturally no suggestion there that metalinguistics should not be investigated; merely that it was a separate field, which crossed disciplines and presupposed a description within microlinguistics. Likewise, for Harris, meaning was an object of further study. In his own words, 'when the results of descriptive linguistics are used in other linguistic and social investigations, one of the chief desiderata is the correlation of utterances and their morphemic segments on the one hand with social situations and features of them on the other' (173). Such correlations are equivalent to meanings (187, n. 63). Their study is again 'entirely independent', using 'techniques quite different from those of current descriptive linguistics' (189).

Harris does not suggest that, in the light of such a study, we should look back and assess the adequacy of our 'description of the language structure'. In that respect, Chomsky was taking an important new step. But it is worth comparing his account of constructional homonymy with Harris's explanation of the difference between two predicate constructions. We know that, in the utterance *she made him a good husband because she made him a good wife*, 'there is a difference of meaning between the two occurrences of *made*; and since we know this without any outside information beyond hearing the sentence, it follows that indication of the difference in meaning and in construction can be derived from the structure of the utterance' (Harris, 1951a: 271). The difference cannot be in *made* itself, and must therefore lie in its 'class membership'. Harris then points out that in the second half of the utterance the sequence *him a good wife* can be replaced with *a good wife for him*; this substitution gives us 'an equivalent utterance which we have in our data', and is characteristic of a sequence following a verb of one class. But in the first half we cannot successfully replace *him a good husband* with *a good husband for him*; that would result in 'a meaningless utterance which does not occur in our corpus'. This shows that the verb belongs there to another class. 'We have thus found that the two halves of the original utterance are formally different in the substitutions which can be performed upon them' (273).

Chomsky's treatment is conceptually much clearer. But here as elsewhere he did not abandon the essential goal of distributionalism, or (in any of the work that was published at this stage) the empiricism that pervaded it. His notion of 'grammaticalness' makes clear the true nature of an investigation that talk of utterances which 'appear' or 'do not appear' in a corpus had served, especially in passages like the one just cited, to obscure. But grammaticality was simply the property of being 'acceptable to a native speaker, etc.' (1957: 13). In abandoning the requirement that linguistic theories should provide what he called a 'discovery procedure' he liberated distributionalism from a constraint that was inessential. But what replaced it was the requirement that alternative sets of distributional rules should be evaluated by a measure of simplicity. This was an attempt to rescue the programme, not to destroy it.

3.3 Phrase structure

In a book on Chomsky which was originally published in 1970, Lyons identifies his 'most original, and probably most enduring, contribution to linguistics' as 'the mathematical rigour and precision with which he formalized the properties of alternative systems of grammatical description' (1991 [1970]: 42). A particularly brilliant achievement, and one which has not only endured but has come to dominate the teaching of syntax for the past three decades, was his formalisation of phrase structure grammar. Its influence is especially clear in beginners' textbooks. In Fromkin and Rodman's chapter on syntax, the first twenty-eight pages contain very little that could not have been written on the basis of Chomsky's work in the 1950s (fourth edition, 1988: 162ff.). The main exceptions are an account of lexical subcategorisation dating from 1965 (184), two category labels (N′, S′) which happen to use a bar notation, and half a page on X-bar theory itself (182). Of the remaining seven pages, four deal with transformations, one with the distribution of old and new information, and two with word-order typologies. In their summary, Fromkin and Rodman say that 'linguists often describe sentences in terms of constituent structure trees' (197). To anyone who learns linguistics from their book or others like it, it will seem that only a crank would want to do otherwise.

To have imposed this view of syntax on two generations is a remarkable achievement. It is a tribute, in the first instance, to the ease with which phrase structure grammar can be taught. But that is in turn a tribute to the simplicity and clarity of insight with which Chomsky originally formulated it. Like all ideas it has a history, which we are about to look at. But Chomsky's contribution was so definitive that most of this history, and certainly the part that is most interesting, dates from the 1950s and earlier, and little, and that mostly very straightforward, from afterwards.

For the beginning, we must again go back to Bloomfield's first book. As we have seen in §2.1, the analysis of a 'total experience' proceeded in binary stages (Bloomfield, 1914: 59ff.). Bloomfield describes this as a process of 'division' (61); but, like the similar analysis of Wundt's *Die Sprache*, it is not merely one of division ('Teilung') but of analysis or division into distinct members ('Gliederung'). In *Lean horses run fast*, the sentence does not simply consist of two parts. In addition, the parts stand in a specific relation, in which *lean horses* is subject and *run fast* the predicate. In *lean horses*, there is in turn not just an adjective followed by a noun, but a relation in which *horses* is subject and *lean* its attribute. It is such interrelations, and in particular those of predication and attribution, that syntax studies (167). But in Bloomfield's treatment, as in Wundt's, they hold between units in a hierarchy of what were later to be called 'constituents'.

It is with this concept of the 'Zerlegung einer Gesamtvorstellung', or 'analysis of a total experience', that the history of what we now call phrase structure grammar can conveniently begin. But even in Bloomfield's later book, the hierarchy as such is scarcely the be-all and end-all of syntax. In Bloomfield's account of 'grammatical forms', the central notions are those of grammatical arrangement; of tagmemes as sets of minimal features of arrangement; of episememes as the meanings of tagmemes; of constructions, in particular, as one of three types of grammatical form. Constituents are 'linguistic forms'. Both they and the classes to which they belong ('substantive expression', 'finite verb expression') exist by virtue of the constructions in which words and phrases are arranged.

For a casual reader this may well be partly obscured, both by what came later, in the work of Wells and Harris, and by the order in which these terms were introduced. In his chapter on 'Grammatical forms', Bloomfield begins by pointing out that many linguistic forms can be divided into smaller forms that meet the same criterion (1935: 158ff.). These forms are 'complex', and a linguistic form which recurs as part of two or more such complex forms is a 'constituent' (or 'component') of each of them (160f.). Any linguistic form that is not complex is a 'simple form' or morpheme (161). But Bloomfield then says that it is not enough to reduce each complex form to its 'ultimate constituents': 'we could not understand the forms of a language' on that basis alone. His example is similar to the one used in his *Introduction*. In *Poor John ran away*, 'any English-speaking person who concerns himself with this matter, is sure to tell us' that the sentence has as its 'immediate constituents' *poor John* and *ran away*, that the immediate constituents of *ran away* are *ran* and *away*, and so on. 'Only in this way will a proper analysis (that is, one which takes account of the meanings) lead to the ultimately constituent morphemes' (161).

A reader who pauses at that point might well think that this is the essential first step in a series of definitions. But Bloomfield's general point is simply that the meaning of a complex form depends on something other than the meanings of its component morphemes. 'Every utterance', as he puts it a page later, 'contains some significant features that are not accounted for by the lexicon' (162). He then returns to the example. 'We saw, for instance, that the five morphemes, *John*, *poor*, *ran*, *way*, *a-* which make up the form *Poor John ran away*, do not fully account for the meaning of this utterance.' The 'significant features' which remain are features of arrangement; and these, again, form constructions. A casual reader might also wonder why, in establishing constituents, Bloomfield seems content to rely on nothing firmer than an educated speaker's judgment. But the real argument is that, at each level of this sentence, we find correlations between certain sets of formal features and their recurrent meanings. Thus, once again, the features of selection and so on which relate *poor John* and *ran away* are associated with a meaning which involves the performance of an action.

How then did a model develop in which constituency and the classing or labelling of constituents are the sole primitives? The answer lies first in the development of distributionalism. We have seen in the first section of this chapter how some aspects of Bloomfield's practice might have led his readers to believe that a distributional syntax was desirable (end of §3.1). But let us now look at it the other way round. If, for whatever reason, we do wish to restrict ourselves to a description of distributional structure, our only method is to find which forms can replace each other in a given context. For example, *he* can replace *she* in contexts such as — *came* or *Why did — leave?* Therefore (tentatively) they are members of a class with the same distribution. But it will not be sufficient to restrict the analysis to single words or morphemes. We must also find out which sequences of words or morphemes can replace one another. For example, *he* and *she* can be replaced in the same frames by the longer sequences *your sister* or *that man you detest*. Therefore (tentatively) all are members of a class of sequences with the same distribution. In this way, larger sequences of elements are split into smaller sequences which are classed separately. For example, *Your sister came* can be divided (tentatively) into *your sister*, classed with *she* and so on, and *came*, classed with *arrived yesterday* or *left his hat behind him*.

This was the method followed by Harris (1946, 1951a). Once morphemes have been established and their alternations have been described (1951a: Chs. 12–14), they are assigned to classes, with subclasses where necessary (1951a: 15; 1946: §4.1). We then 'see what sequences of morphemes can be substituted for single morphemes' (1946: *Papers* 53). For example, *good boy* 'can be substituted for *man* anywhere' – within, that is, 'the broad limits of what utterances frequently occur in the culture' (n. 16,

Papers 69). We then write equations showing that a single morpheme class is distributionally equivalent to a sequence of morpheme classes. For example, if *A* is the class of *good* and *N* that of *boy* and *man*, we write *A N* = *N*. In that way, the class *N* is expanded to include not just single morphemes, but also any sequence of morphemes, such as *good boy* or, by other formulae, *your sister* and *that man you detest*, which, within the limits of approximation, have the same distribution.

This procedure 'could be paralleled', as Harris points out, 'by a series of substitutions beginning with the whole utterance and working down, instead of beginning with single morphemes and working up' (*Papers* 62). In that case, we have the 'difficult problem' of finding formal criteria for 'determining the immediate constituents of an utterance'. But in a wider perspective these procedures come to essentially the same thing. Take, for example, a sentence such as *Bill and his brother left*. If we follow Harris's procedure, we might see *Bill and his brother* as a replacement for *she*. Therefore (tentatively) they belong to the same class. As an alternative we could, in principle, see *and his brother left* as a replacement for *came*. Therefore (tentatively) these might go together. But we reject this second analysis because the distributional equations which would result from it are less general. If we follow the opposite procedure, we must begin by asking how the sentence as a whole divides. Are its immediate constituents *Bill and his brother* and *left*, or, among other alternatives, *Bill* and *and his brother left*? But to answer that, we must again ask what can be substituted for what, and which substitutions will lead to the most general classes. For example, *who* can replace *Bill and his brother* in the frame — *left*, but not *Bill* in the frame — *and his brother left*. So, a more general set of classes will result (all else being equal) if *and his brother* is taken with *Bill*.

This complementary treatment was developed by Wells, in the first part of his article on 'Immediate constituents'. In a footnote, Wells acknowledges that 'the central importance of the problem of immediate constituents was driven home to me in many valuable conversations with Zellig S. Harris', who also showed him what were presumably the drafts of *Methods* (Wells, 1947b: n.1, *RiL* 186). This confirms (in passing) that the problem was not seen as centrally important until the 1940s. Harris, in return, acknowledges a debt to Wells for 'several valuable discussions' of his own paper (1946: n. 1, *Papers* 67). We are therefore dealing with closely related work, in which each author knew what the other was doing. But even if it had not been so, the logic of the problem would have dictated similar approaches. The aim was to establish that certain sequences of morphemes were syntactic units, and to do so by the evidence of distribution alone. To be precise, Wells says that 'it is possible in our exposition to leave the factor of meaning out of account until much later' (§8, *RiL* 188). The method, therefore, must be to show that there are sequences about which a distributional generalisation can be made: that is, that they have the same distribution as other sequences. But the only method by which this can be revealed is that of repeated substitution. In Harris's account, as we have seen, the sole operation is 'substitution, repeated time and again' (1946: §1.2, *Papers* 46).

The method, in turn, determines the form of its results. It takes as given the morphemes of a language and a relation of sequence over them. The procedure then divides an utterance into successively smaller subsequences, which, if the method is to work in practice at all, must initially, at least, be continuous. It establishes sets of morphemes and of sequences of morphemes that are distributionally equivalent. It establishes that members of one such set can combine in sequence with members of the same or of another set to form larger sequences which are in turn members either of (one of) the same set(s) or of a third set. In this way, the procedure 'leads up' (Harris, 1951a: 372) to a 'description of the language structure' which will be the equivalent of what Chomsky was to call a phrase structure grammar.

We could easily refer to other Post-Bloomfieldian studies. One is Bloch's on Japanese (1946), which Wells also mentions and which precedes his paper in *RiL*. Another, though it is more than half a decade later, is Hockett's discussion of syntax in 'Two models of grammatical description' (1954). But the continuity with Chomsky's model is already perfectly clear. In a monograph published seven years after *Syntactic Structures*, Postal argued that all 'syntactic conceptions prevalent in the United States', other than those which included transformations, were, 'with certain provisos, versions of the theory of phrase structure grammars in the sense of Chomsky' (1964: 1). But in the case of Harris and others whose work preceded that of Chomsky, it would have made more sense to have put this point the other way round. The model of syntax with which serious study of generative grammars was to begin, and which served as the springboard for the development of the transformational model, was in essence the one implied by the procedures of segmentation, substitution and classification that they had developed.

Why did Chomsky take it over? The answer he gave at the time was that it represented the received method. 'Customarily', he said, 'linguistic description on the syntactic level is formulated in terms of constituent analysis (parsing).' He therefore asked 'what form of grammar is presupposed by description of this sort' (Chomsky, 1957: 26). But among whom was such constituency analysis 'customary'? Among Bloomfieldians certainly; nor was it unnatural that a scholar who was then in his late twenties should see as normal what was actually normal in the particular school in which he had been educated. But Chomsky's reference to 'parsing' shows that he was not thinking of them only. In a paper delivered the following year, he says in passing that 'IC-analysis can be thought of as an attempt to make more rigorous the traditional notion of parsing' (1962 [1958]: 124, n. 2). If that is right, it would be an error to explain phrase structure grammar as a mere continuation of the work of Harris and other contemporaries.

But is it right? The claim was repeated, some years later, in the first textbook introduction to Chomskyan grammar, by Bach. According to Bach, 'phrase-structure rules form a counterpart in the theory of generative grammars to two techniques of linguistic analysis, one old and one rather new'. The old one is 'the schoolroom drill of parsing, that is, of assigning grammatical labels to parts of a sentence'. The new one ' – in reality only a more sophisticated version of parsing – is so-called immediate constituent (IC) analysis'. In illustration, Bach takes the sentence *The man gave me a book*, and gives first an analysis that 'might occur' in a schoolroom drill. In this, the words are assigned to their parts of speech; *the man* is said to be a 'whole subject', and *gave me a book* a 'whole predicate'; within this 'whole predicate', *me* is an indirect object and *a book* a direct object. He then shows how an analysis into constituents might be represented either by a tree or with brackets, each without labels. Finally, he shows how 'we can combine labels such as those used in parsing with nodes in a "tree" or with the brackets for a representation of the "phrase structure" of the sentence'. So, if the analysis is 'continued in more detail', we arrive at a structure in which the sentence is divided into a noun phrase and a verb phrase, the verb phrase into a verb followed by two noun phrases, and so on (Bach, 1964: 33f.).

This is a textbook, and Chomsky himself never wrote anything so naively tendentious. Nevertheless it may help if we look a little further at Bach's illustration. In parsing a sentence, children have always had to identify parts of speech. That is what 'to parse' originally meant – to say of each word what 'part' (in Latin, 'quae pars?') it is. But schoolroom teaching has not generally used terms like 'whole subject' or 'whole predicate'. In the usual practice at least, the subject in Bach's example would have been identified as the noun *man*. One did not talk of a larger subject of which the word was merely one part. The sentence as a whole would have been said to have a subject (*man*), a verb (*gave*), an indirect object (*me*) and a direct object (*book*). Note that there was similarly no concept of a 'whole direct object'. The direct object is the noun *book*.

Were children taught differently in America? In a book published at around the same time, Gleason describes in particular what he calls 'Reed and Kellogg' diagrams (1965: 142ff.). In these, a 'clause base' is represented by a horizontal line, and the main sentence elements are identified along it. For *The ladies own a dog* (to simplify for a moment his initial example), they are a subject *ladies*, a verb *own* and a direct object *dog*; and these are distinguished graphically by writing different kinds of line between them. Words subordinate to these elements are then written underneath the base line. Thus in Gleason's actual example *the*, *three*, *old* and *upstairs* are all written under *ladies* (*the three old ladies upstairs*). Under *dog* three words are written directly: *a*, *boxer* and *with*. But *with* is linked in a different way to *temper*, and under that are written in turn the further subordinates *a* and *mean*. This is the representation of *a boxer dog with a mean temper*. It will be plain that such diagrams show many things that Chomsky's or Bach's phrase structure trees could not show. In another respect they show less: as Gleason points out (143), they were concerned with word relationships, but not directly with word-order.

This system dates from at least the turn of the century, and in the schools was 'generally known simply as "diagramming", there being no other system from which it must be distinguished' (142). At the time when Gleason was writing, it 'continue[d] in use', with abridgement and modification, 'in many school textbooks'. But it is very hard to see how this kind of 'schoolroom drill' could have been thought to have phrase structure grammar as its generative counterpart. A system in which one first identifies the functions of the main words in the sentence and then shows other words as subordinate to them is simply not the same thing as one in which one cuts up sentences into blocks and classifies them.

The origin of phrase structure grammar was, in short, Bloomfieldian constituency analysis, and the origin of that, in turn, was what remained of Bloomfield's model when, first, grammatical arrangement is reduced to selection and order and, secondly, all reference to meaning is taken out. It was, in consequence, a brilliantly simple model. Take, for example,

Bloomfield's 'qualifier-substance' construction. For Bloomfield, this was a semantic unit which existed over and above the sequence of form-classes. But Chomsky does not even use the term. In the phrase marker which will be assigned to *fresh milk*, a member of the class 'adjective' is followed by a member of the class 'noun' and together they form a member of a third class 'noun phrase'. That is all.

The final factor at this stage was the development of transformational grammar. In the next chapter of *Syntactic Structures*, Chomsky discusses the 'Limitations of phrase structure descriptions' (1957: Ch. 5). They do not allow a general account of coordination (35ff.); nor a simple treatment of the auxiliary verbs in English (38ff.); nor a connection between the selectional restrictions found in actives and passives (42f.). In Chomsky's argument, what he called the 'customary' method served in that sense as a straw man. But, unlike the more usual kind of straw man, it was not abandoned when its inadequacies had been demonstrated. Instead it was incorporated in the real man that replaced it. In Chomsky's words, 'we can show quite conclusively that [phrase structure] grammars will be so hopelessly complex that they will be almost uninteresting' (44) unless further rules which relate one phrase marker to another are added to them. In the next paragraph, these rules are said to 'lead to an entirely new conception of linguistic structure'. But, despite the importance of what had been added, it is evident that the conception was not entirely new. The basic relation between units remained that of sequence. The only formal change was that one sequence might now be altered to another sequence. The other syntagmatic relations remained those of constituency. Again, the only change was that one constituency structure might now be altered to another constituency structure. Apart from these relations between phrase markers, the basic paradigmatic relation remained that of membership of the same distributional class. The result, as Haas once put it, was that with the addition of transformations '[phrase structure] is considered to be, on the whole *uncontroversial* as well as *inadequate*' (Haas, 1973: 102).

To understand how this happened, it will be helpful to go back, in particular, to Bloomfieldian treatments of constructional homonymy. For Bloomfield himself it had not been a distinct topic, nor for most earlier scholars. A construction was a meaningful unit from the outset; it was justified by a correlation between recurrent formal features and a meaning; and no special significance attaches to the cases in which different constructions, or complexes of constructions, can be borne by the same sequence of words. But it had become a topic for, in particular, Wells. In a section of his paper headed 'Constructions', he begins by pointing out that, in describing and applying the procedure of analysis in earlier sections, he has sometimes had to add a proviso that the meaning should be held constant. The reason, he explains, is that 'there are many instances of a sequence which in some occurrences has one meaning and in another occurrence has another, and which, moreover, has different analyses into ICs accordingly' (1947b: §30, *RiL* 193). An example, which has since become famous and almost standard in this context, is the sequence *old men and women*. In one meaning, this can be divided into the immediate constituents *old* and *men and women*; in the other, into *old men*, *and* and *women*. 'One of the prime functions of analysis into ICs', as Wells sees it, 'is to reveal a formal difference correlated with the semantic one.'

In Wells's account, a 'construction' is a class of 'occurrences' of sequences which have, among other things, 'a certain meaning in common' (§34, *RiL* 194). So, since the sequence *old men and women* will 'occur' sometimes with one meaning and sometimes with the other, it must belong to two different constructions. However, the definition also allows for a difference in constructions which is not reflected in constituency analyses. *Lady-friend*, for example, is one of a class of compounds of the form 'ÁB' whose occurrences have the meaning 'a B which is identical with or has the property of being (an) A' (§39, *RiL* 196). *Lady-killer*, by contrast, is one of a class with the different meaning 'a B of or connected with (an) A'. Since the meanings are different, occurrences of such compounds must belong to different constructions. Moreover, Wells suggests that *lady-killer* might itself be homonymous. Although the usual meaning is 'killer (in a metaphorical sense) of ladies', there should also be 'a grammatically possible compound *lady-killer* "killer who is a lady"'.

In Wells's terms, both *lady-killer* and *old men and women* exhibit 'homonymous constructions' (§37, *RiL* 195). The difference (§38) is said to be that in the former they are 'wholly homonymous', whereas in the latter they are 'partly homonymous'. But the real difference, as the argument developed over the next decade, is that only the latter can be distinguished naturally within the system that gave birth to phrase structure grammar. As Hockett put it in his later discussion of the 'Item and Arrangement' model, an example like *old men and women* shows that 'hierarchical structure is a "primitive"' (1954: *RiL* 391). That is how it has been used since, and from then on it appears that the result was taken as achieved. But examples such as *lady-friend* and *lady-killer* suggest that something else must also be primitive. On the face of things, it is what Bloomfield called the 'construction'. If such forms are to be distinguished in a grammar, the former must exhibit a construction with one meaning and the latter another construction with another meaning. If *lady-killer* is to be described as homonymous, it must potentially have either.

Hockett's illustration (*RiL* 392f.) is a phrase in Chinese which can mean either 'fried rice' or '(to) fry rice'. But other and better examples were soon available from Chomsky. Take, for instance, the phrase *flying planes* (Chomsky, 1956). This has two meanings, one in which *flying* is traditionally a gerund with an object and one in which it is a modifying participle. In either case it is itself a phrase, and in either case it seems to have the same constituents, *flying* and *planes*. How then was one to describe it?

In the case of *lady-friend* and *lady-killer*, one alternative was to say that there is no syntactic difference. Both forms consist of a noun followed by a noun; in one the second is agentive, and that allows the first to be understood as if it was its object; in the other it is not agentive and a similar meaning is not possible. But in the case of *flying planes* the difference is not just in meaning, but also in distribution. In traditional terms, *planes* as a subject noun takes plural agreement (*Flying planes are dangerous*), but *flying* as a gerund takes the singular. There are also internal differences. In the frame — *is dangerous*, we can substitute *flying fast planes*, but not *fast flying planes*; in the frame — *are dangerous*, the reverse. Even in a syntax that is purely distributional, a distinction has to be made.

The traditional account suggests that we should distinguish the relations between the words. In *Flying planes are dangerous*, the noun is the dominant element of the phrase and *flying* is subordinate to it. Therefore, among other things, it is the noun that determines the agreement. But in *Flying planes is dangerous*, the dominant element is *flying* and it is *planes* that is subordinate. Therefore the agreement is singular, even though *planes* is plural. These relations are, of course, directly representable in other systems of syntax, some of which were being explored in Europe in the same period.

But in accounts of constituency structure the only relation between successive units was that of sequence. A relation between dominant and subordinate constituents could not be shown. The only alternative, therefore, was to make the distinction in terms of the classes to which constituents are assigned. Take, for example, Hockett's illustration from

Chinese. In the meaning 'fried rice', we will classify the whole as a noun phrase. In addition, the constituent meaning 'rice' will be a bare noun. So, using English glosses, the structure can be shown thus: $_{NP}$[$_{V}$[fry] $_{N}$[rice]]. But in the meaning '(to) fry rice', the whole will be a verb phrase; and, in addition, the 'rice' constituent will be a noun phrase. Thus $_{VP}$[$_{V}$[fry] $_{NP}$[rice]].

But the problem posed by *flying planes* is more subtle. In either meaning, we will need to classify it as a noun phrase: $_{NP}$[*flying planes*]. The distinction must therefore be made in terms of the different structures that noun phrases can have. In *Flying planes is dangerous*, we might begin by saying that the whole belongs to a subclass of noun phrases called a 'gerundial phrase': in notation, $_{NP}$[$_{GP}$[*flying planes*]]. We might then say that, within it, *flying* is a 'gerund' (*G*); in addition, *planes* (like 'rice' when Hockett's example means '(to) fry rice') will be a noun phrase. Thus $_{NP}$[$_{GP}$[$_{G}$[*flying*] $_{NP}$[*planes*]]]. In *Flying planes are dangerous*, we might instead class *flying* as a participle (*P*). In addition, *planes* will in this case be a bare noun: $_{NP}$[$_{P}$[*flying*] $_{N}$[*planes*]]. But the distinction between '*G*' and '*P*' effectively adds nothing. They are simply labels: we cannot read into them what is ordinarily implied by the terms 'gerund' and 'participle'. We will find, moreover, that they are labels for the same class. If we call this class '*X*', we will find that 'gerundial phrases' consist of an *X* with or without additional constituents: $_{GP}$[$_{X}$[*flying*] $_{NP}$[*planes*]]; or, for example, $_{GP}$[$_{X}$[*dancing*]]. A noun phrase which is not a 'gerundial phrase' may consist of a noun with or without additional constituents such as an *X*: $_{NP}$[$_{X}$[*flying*] $_{N}$[*planes*]]; or, for example, $_{NP}$[$_{N}$[*planes*]]. In a grammar which deals solely with distributions, there is no need for '*G*' and '*P*' to be distinguished. Nor does the distinction throw light on the meaning. There is no reason why a '*G*' followed by a noun phrase should be understood in the same way as a verb with an object; or why a '*P*' followed by a noun should not.

It took Chomsky's genius to find a way out. Briefly, let us accept that the relations between *flying* and *planes* are different. Let us also accept that the difference cannot be shown by a phrase marker. But it can be shown instead by a succession of phrase markers. If the semantic relation in *Flying planes is dangerous* is like that of a verb and its object, then let us say that it derives, directly or by intermediate stages, from a structure like that of a verb and its object. This initial structure can itself be a phrase marker: it will be like that of the predicate in a sentence such as *They fly planes*. At any intermediate stage the phrase will again be represented by a phrase marker. For example, in the next stage, the structure of the sentence might become that of the noun phrase. At the final stage there will again be a phrase marker. In *Flying planes are dangerous*, the relation may be said to be like that of a verb and its subject. Let us therefore say that its initial structure is like that of a sentence such as *Planes fly*. This again will be a phrase marker; the final structure, and any intermediate structures that are needed, will also be phrase markers.

The consequences will be explored later (§3.4). But the most immediate was that, by adopting this solution, Chomsky effectively protected the constituency model of the Post-Bloomfieldians from any fundamental criticism. There was no objection to it that could not be met by deriving one constituency structure from a series of underlying constituency structures. Therefore its merits were not seriously debated. They were not debated by the Post-Bloomfieldians themselves, since, given their initial objective of developing procedures of analysis, and in particular procedures which, at least as far as possible, did not refer to meanings, there was in reality no other model that they were likely to arrive at. They were not debated by the generativists, since from the very beginning what was in play was not a phrase structure grammar as such, but a transformational grammar founded on phrase structure grammar.

As I remarked towards the beginning of this section, the history of phrase structure theories is straightforward after the 1950s. Nor does it belong entirely to the United States, since Chomsky's influence has been world-wide and the response to it, both collaborative and critical, has also been world-wide. But, within the United States, two later episodes can be singled out. In both, limitations which had in effect been introduced by Chomsky himself were eliminated.

The first kind of limitation was inherent in his initial formalisation. Briefly, a phrase structure grammar was interpreted as a rewrite system (Chomsky, 1957: 26f.); and, for reasons which at this distance of time it is scarcely worth going into, it was necessary to exclude any rule of the form $X \rightarrow Y\ X$, or $X \rightarrow X\ Y$, or $X \rightarrow X\ Y\ X$, in which the rightmost or the leftmost constituent was assigned to the same class as the whole. In addition, Chomsky excluded any rule which did not rewrite an element as a finite sequence of other elements. There could therefore be no rule of the form, for example, $X \rightarrow Y_n$, meaning that an X could consist of a sequence of any number of Ys.

The first restriction is in Bach's textbook (1964: 35), and seemed to Postal to be 'very natural' (1964: 16); the second was thought to follow from the requirement that a grammar itself should be finite. But, as Postal pointed out, they excluded any satisfactory account of coordination. In a phrase like *Bill and his brother*, the structure is apparently: $_{NP}$[$_{NP}$[*Bill*] *and* $_{NP}$[*his brother*]]. But we cannot write a rule *NP* → *NP and NP*, since it would violate the first restriction. In addition, any number of noun phrases can be coordinated in this way: *Bill and his brother and me*, *Bill and his brother and my aunt and me*, and so on. But we cannot write a rule, say, $NP \rightarrow and\ NP_n$, since it would have to be understood as the equivalent of an infinite set of rules, one coordinating two noun phrases, one three, one four ... (Postal, 1964: 16; 23f., against Wells; 110, against Halliday). The conclusion, for Postal and others, was that coordination had to be handled by a transformation which would derive a phrase marker such as that of *Bill and his brother came* from those of *Bill came* and *His brother came*.

In fact both hang-ups could be, and were, rapidly removed. By 1965, Chomsky had himself proposed that coordination should be handled by 'rule schemata': these were precisely in the form $X \rightarrow and\ X_n$ (Chomsky, 1965: 99; 224, n. 7 to 134; 225, n. 11 to 137). A few years later, McCawley pointed out that the other restriction 'could be obviated if [phrase structure rules] operated directly in terms of IC-trees rather than through the intermediate stage of a rewriting rule derivation' (1976 [1968a]: 39). In retrospect, it may seem odd that Postal should have founded an argument for transformations on mere details of formalisation. But in the early 1960s the word 'mere' could not be used in that context. I remember vividly, from a year spent in America in 1963–4, how Chomsky's admirers and followers (of whom I was one) took seriously the need for formalisation, and were mesmerised by the account that he had originally given.

The second episode is the development of the 'X-bar' system, sketched in part by Chomsky (1970a: 210f.) and elaborated by Jackendoff (1977). The essential feature of this system is that the categories to which phrases are assigned are no longer simple. In the earlier account, a phrase like *my brother* was a noun phrase and, within it, *brother* was a noun. But 'noun phrase', like 'noun', is a primitive category, and there is therefore no more connection between it and 'noun' than between it and the category of *my*. In the new account a category such as 'noun phrase' was analysed into components. Firstly, *my brother* was itself a noun (*N*); in that sense, it belonged to the same class as *brother*. But, secondly, it was a noun at a higher level ($\bar{N}$, say, as opposed to unbarred *N*). The relation between *my* and *brother* was then asymmetrical. The noun is the head of the phrase: in

Jackendoff's definition (1977: 30), a 'head' of a phrase belonging to a category '*X*' is a lower level '*X*' within it. *My* is a constituent accompanying the head, and thus definable as subsidiary to it.

In this way, Chomsky and Jackendoff successfully reduced to an analysis of categories a relation which Chomsky's original account of phrase structure grammar had ignored. But it was a solution to a problem that had been created by Bloomfield's work in the 1930s, and that Harris, in particular, had in part addressed. Moreover, it was a solution basically in Bloomfield's or in Harris's terms. That is to say, it did not treat the category of a head as primitive. Instead it and the relations which it implies were defined on the basis of a configuration of categories.

Let us go back again to Bloomfield. In his first book, he distinguished two main kinds of 'logical relation': predication, which was the relation established by the primary division of a total experience, and attribution, which was that established by every subsequent division (Bloomfield, 1914: 61). In both, one term (the 'predicate', the 'attribute') stands in an asymmetrical relation to the other, called in either case 'the subject'. But in *Language* these matters are treated differently. 'Predication' is merely the 'common name' for 'favorite sentence-forms' (equivalently, full sentences) that have two parts (Bloomfield, 1935: 173). A subject is defined, in terms that cannot have seemed satisfactory even then, as 'the more object-like component' of a predication. The predicate is 'the other part'. Attribution is defined in another chapter, as part of a general typology of constructions. Moreover, it is defined in a more limited sense than in the *Introduction*. As Bloomfield puts it, a construction is 'exocentric' if the phrase as a whole 'belong[s] to a form-class other than that of any constituent' (194). If it 'belong[s] to the same form-class as one (or more) of the constituents', the construction is 'endocentric', and if it belongs to the same form-class as just one, it is 'subordinative' or 'attributive'. For instance, the construction of *poor John* is attributive, since both *poor John* and *John* are 'proper noun expression[s]', but the form-class of *poor* is different. By a further definition, *John* is the 'head' (195).

But in this account the 'exocentric' constructions include relations that had also been seen as asymmetrical. Take, for instance, the construction of *beside John* or *with me* (194). In such phrases, 'the constituents are a prepositional expression and an accusative expression', but the whole 'has a function different from either of these, appearing in entirely different syntactic positions'. Therefore the 'relation-axis' construction, as Bloomfield calls it, is exocentric. But he then says that these and other phrases are 'characterized' by one of their constituents. Although a phrase with an exocentric construction 'has a function different from the function of any constituent, yet one of these constituents is usually peculiar to the construction and serves to characterize the resultant phrase'. For example, 'finite verbs, prepositions, and subordinating conjunctions regularly appear' in constructions of this kind, 'and suffice to characterize them'. But although this passage would have made perfect sense to anyone familiar with the work of earlier grammarians, it is not in fact clear how such constituents have a characterising role. Neither the formal relation of sequence nor the semantic relation between the 'relation' and 'axis' positions has been described any differently from that of any other construction. Why then is *beside John* characterised by *beside* and not *John*?

Such was the treatment that Bloomfield bequeathed to his successors. His account of predication was not taken further – not surprisingly, since the term was merely the common name for a kind of sentence structure, and was moreover 'superfluous' for any language which 'has only one type of bipartite sentence' (again 173). But the strategy in general finds an echo, years later, in Chomsky's conception of subjects and objects. The problem by then was to identify the roles that a noun phrase can play in the semantics of a sentence. For example, in the structure underlying *I persuaded John to be examined by a specialist*, it must be shown that *John* is both 'the logical Direct-Object of the embedded sentence' and 'the Direct-Object of the [main] Verb Phrase' (Chomsky, 1965: 23). As Chomsky pointed out, these are terms that refer to functions or relations, not to categories. But his solution was still to take categories alone as primitive, and to try to define a set of 'grammatical functions' and 'grammatical relations' over them. For example, a direct object is a noun phrase that is an immediate constituent of a verb phrase. It is defined as the direct object 'of' that verb phrase; that is its 'function'. It is also defined as the direct object of the main verb of the verb phrase; that is a 'grammatical relation' (Chomsky, 1965: 70ff.).

The topic of heads was touched on very little in the earlier years of generative grammar. But Bloomfield's concept of endocentricity had meanwhile been developed in an interesting way by Harris. As we have seen already, Harris's basic procedure in the 1940s had been to take single morphemes and see what sequences of morphemes could be substituted for them. For example, *good boy* could, in a wide range of contexts, replace *man*. This and other substitutions lead us to the general statement that a single noun is distributionally equivalent to an adjective followed by a noun: in Harris's notation, $A\ N = N$ (1946: *Papers* 53; 1951a: 265). Similarly, sequences which consist of an adjective followed by the suffix *-ly* (*A ly*) can in general be substituted for a simple adverb (*D*): thus $A\ ly = D$ (1951a: 263). Harris is not directly concerned with the typology of constructions, and his own use of the term 'construction' (at least in *Methods*) is different (1951a: Ch. 18). But in a footnote he remarks that 'sequences of the type $XY = Y$ are called endocentric constructions, and the *X* in *XY* is then called the head of the construction' (276, n. 33). In the earlier article, this is said to be a result 'implicit' in the formulae (*Papers* 64). So, in phrases like *good boy* the noun is the head; but in a word like *largely* there is no head.

As Harris makes clear, the equations hold for classes. The second formula 'does not state that', for example, '*large* + *ly* has the same distribution as *quite*', but that, in general, '$A + ly$ has the same distribution as *D*' (1951a: 263, n. 1). In Bloomfield's terms, we are again talking of the form-class of the whole being, or not being, the same as that of a constituent. But Harris then addresses a problem that Bloomfield possibly could not have seen. Take, for example, a word like *boyhood* (1951a: 265f.). It consists of a noun (*N*) plus a noun-forming suffix (in Harris's notation, *Nn*). In addition, sequences like *boy* + *hood* can be substituted in many contexts for a single noun, like *life*. That gives us the formula: $N + Nn = N$. But one context in which *boyhood* cannot replace a simple noun is, of course, before *-hood*: there are no forms such as *boyhoodhood.* In Harris's terms, the substitution is 'non-repeatable'. He therefore distinguishes the two '*N*'s in the formula by raised numbers. 'We can write $N^1\ Nn = N^2$ to indicate [that] *N Nn* (which equals N^2 not N^1) cannot be substituted for the *N* of *N Nn* itself.' Similarly, a plural such as *boys* or *boyhoods* can in many contexts replace a singular. But there are no words *boys-es* or *boyhoods-es*: therefore Harris writes N^2 *-s* = N^3. At a higher level, a determiner (*T*) plus a noun can also replace a single noun. But not only is this non-repeatable (*the some cheeses*); it is also impossible in our original sequence *A N* (*Swiss some cheeses*). Harris deals with this by writing the new formula as $T\ N^3 = N^4$. The original formula, where the substitution is repeatable, is now $A\ N^3 = N^3$. In this way, all the sequences are, in Bloomfield's terms, assigned to the same form-class. But they are assigned to it at different levels, and thus the differences in their distribution can also be registered.

Chomsky says at one point that in formulating phrase structure rules he had 'done nothing more than modify Harris' "Morpheme to Utterance" procedures ... showing how these ideas can provide us with a grammar' which is generative (1962 [1958]: 129). But the system of raised numerals is one idea that got left by the wayside, and was not picked up again until the 'X-bar' system was developed in the 1970s. Why it was neglected, no one seems to have said: a possible reason is that this was another cramping effect of Chomsky's initial conception of a grammar as a restricted form of rewrite system. What is, however, more interesting is that, when Chomsky did pick it up, the system of barring was used to solve not only the problem of representing heads in endocentric phrases, which his own initial account had not addressed, but also the question that Bloomfield had left unanswered in the 1930s, of how an exocentric phrase might also be said to be 'characterised' by one constituent. For verb phrases this is already clear in Chomsky's own sketch: just as the configuration of constituents and categories defines the *N* as the head of the '$\bar{\bar{N}}$' *several of John's proofs of that theorem*, so it also defines the *V* as the head of the '$\bar{\bar{V}}$' *proved the theorem* (Chomsky, 1970a: 211). Jackendoff extended this to prepositional phrases. Thus, in *beside John*, the preposition characterises the whole precisely in that it is a *P* which is the head of a larger *P* with two or three bars.

Chomsky remarks that the system is 'reminiscent' of that of Harris. If we were to consider the matter in detail, that is perhaps the most that could be concluded. But like Harris's treatment of the more limited topic of endocentricity, or Bloomfield's treatment of the same topic, and like Chomsky's own attempt to define 'functions' such as subject and direct object, it again adopts the general strategy of taking constituency relations as the only primitive, and trying to define other relations over them. For anyone who approaches syntax from a different angle, it is a very Bloomfieldian solution to a Bloomfieldian problem.

3.4 The heyday of transformations

Around 1970 David Crystal, who was then editing a series of readers for Penguin Books, received a proposal for a volume on transformational syntax which did not include a single paper by Chomsky. At the time this seemed strange, and indeed unacceptable. A few years later and it would again have been unthinkable. But it is a reminder of how far the theory of transformational grammar, though Chomsky's invention and developed largely by him or under his supervision until the mid-1960s, had at the end of the decade acquired a momentum which was effectively independent of him. Its culmination was the attempt by many scholars to develop what they called a 'generative semantics'. They failed, and with their failure, which was apparent to most observers before the mid-1970s, the flowering of transformations ended. From then onwards, their role has progressively contracted and withered.

It may seem strange at first sight that I should include the history of transformational grammar in the 1960s in a chapter on distributionalism. For two of the main changes that were made in the middle of the decade were, firstly, the incorporation into a generative grammar of rules that assigned meanings to sentences; and, secondly, the distinction between deep structure, as a representation of syntactic structure angled towards meaning, and surface structure. But the distributionalist view was not, once more, that meanings should not be studied. What was essential was that formal relations should be described first, without reference to meaning, and that meanings should be tackled later. That view was reflected both in Chomsky's revision of his model (1965) and in many of his followers' reactions to it.

Let us begin with the original arguments for transformations. They were technically arguments against phrase structure grammar; and not surprisingly, in view of the limited aims of Post-Bloomfieldian theories of constituency structure and the tightly restricted formalisation that Chomsky had derived from them, they were of more than one kind.

One kind rested entirely on the formalisation. A striking example, referred to already in the last section, was the demonstration that phrase structure grammars, conceived as Chomsky had originally conceived them, could not give a straightforward description of any structure in which phrases were coordinated. Other kinds of argument were also partly technical. In particular, Chomsky's formulation of phrase structure grammar did not allow discontinuous constituents. Hence, in forms like *has been singing*, there could not be a phrase whose constituents were the morphemes '*have*' and '*-en*', or another whose constituents were '*be*' and '*-ing*'. Chomsky's implicit remedy for this (1957: 39) became known as the 'affix-hopping' transformation. Again, though *take* and *up* could form a phrase in *I will take up his offer*, they could not when they were separated in *I will take his offer up*. This too led to an early application of transformations (Chomsky, 1957: 75f.; 1961a: 23).

As arguments against Chomsky's model of phrase structure, these were impeccable. The only question, which was seen at the time as being open at least in principle, was whether adding transformations to it was the right remedy. But let us look more closely at the case of phrasal verbs. In the examples I have given, there were two reasons for saying that the syntactic relations were the same. One was distributional. In either sentence, *take* (. . .) *up* can be replaced by other forms like *set* (. . .) *up*, *set* (. . .) *out* or *turn* (. . .) *down*. But in neither can we substitute, for instance, *leave* (. . .) *up*, or *leave* (. . .) *down*, or *wash* (. . .) *in*. The 'selectional restrictions', as Chomsky called them, are parallel. The other reason was semantic. In whichever order, *take* (. . .) *up* means the same. Likewise, in *I will turn his offer down*, the phrasal *turn* (. . .) *down* has the same figurative or idiomatic meaning that it bears in *I will turn down his offer*. Both the meanings and the distributional restrictions are parallel.

Now consider *the shooting of the hunters*. Again there might be two reasons for saying that this had two different constructions. The first was that it had two different meanings. In one meaning, it was understood 'with "hunters" as the subject, analogously to' *the growling of lions*; in the other, with the same word 'as the object, analogously to' *the raising of flowers* (Chomsky, 1957: 88). The distributional reason was that the 'selection' of *shoot* and *hunter* could be paralleled elsewhere in two different structures. In one, the noun preceded a finite form of the verb: for example, *The hunters were shooting*. In that structure, we can substitute *growl* and *lion*, *roar* and *tiger*, and so on, but not, for example, *raise* and *flower*. In the other, the noun followed a finite form of the verb: for example, *They were shooting the hunters*. In that structure, we can substitute *raise* and *flower*, or *pick* and *tomato*; but not *growl* and *lion*, or *roar* and *tiger*. Again the evidence of meaning and the patterns of distribution ran parallel.

The history of transformational grammar from the beginning until the early 1970s in large part reflects the ways in which these kinds of arguments were exploited. It is sometimes difficult to trace, since the criteria for analysis were not always acknowledged to be such, and crucial changes in practice, though evident from the ways in which particular cases were dealt with, were not always stated or justified explicitly. But, in outline, there was a gradual progression from a theory which accounted for distributional regularities to one in which any similarity or difference, whether distributional or semantic, was explained in transformational terms.

For the very beginning, we must again go back to Harris. In a paper published shortly after *Methods*, Harris suggested a technique for the analysis of connected texts which, among other things, assumed that a grammar of the language would establish distributional regularities across contrasting sentences. 'For example, given any English sentence of the form N_1 V N_2 (e.g. *The boss fired Jim*), we can get a sentence with the noun phrases in the reverse order N_2 V N_1 ... by changing the suffixes around the verb: *Jim was fired by the boss*' (Harris, 1952: *Papers* 110). The advantage of using such 'grammatical information' was that one could establish equivalences between parts of a text which could not be established directly from the text itself. For example, Harris's specimen text (*Papers* 118) has one sentence which begins *Millions of consumer bottles of X- have been sold*... and another beginning *Every year we sell more bottles of X-* ... 'Grammatically, *have been sold* is *sell* + past + passive ... Grammatically also, V + passive + *by* N is equivalent to V + passive alone.' That is, for any sentence of the form *X is sold by us*, there is another of the form *X is sold.* We can therefore 'match' the fragment *we sell bottles* in the second sentence with *bottles are sold* in the first (*Papers* 137).

Where equivalences are given by a grammar they are called 'grammatical transformations' (*Papers* 127ff.). But it was only five years later, in what must in origin have been one of the denser presidential addresses given to the Linguistic Society of America, that Harris made clear the nature of the grammar that he had presupposed. A 'transformation', as Harris defined it, is basically the difference between 'two or more constructions (or sequences of constructions)' which 'contain the same classes' and which 'occur with the same n-tuples of members of these classes in the same sentence environment' (1957: *Papers* 147). Take, for example, the phrase *the distant storm.* A statement of its construction will refer to, among other things, the classes A (adjective) and N (noun), and these are represented, in this instance, by the pair of members *distant* (A) and *storm* (N). Now take the sentence *The storm is distant.* Its construction is different; but not only does it involve the same classes A and N, but the same pairs of individual adjectives and nouns are found in this construction as in the other. *Recent* and *events* co-occur naturally (*the recent events*, *The events are recent*), as do *green* and *table* (*the green table*, *The table is green*), and so on; other pairs, like *green* and *events* or *wooden* and *storm*, do not. Harris does not discuss this example in detail. But, on such evidence, we 'say that the constructions are transforms of each other, and that each may be derived from [the other] by a particular transformation'. Thus, in a later and shorter definition, 'the difference between any two constructions which are satisfied by the same n-tuples of their word classes comprises a transformation' (*Papers* 194).

In the course of a long article, Harris identifies many different transformations in English, among them those involving pronouns or more generally 'pro-morphemes'; those which relate one single sentence to another (such as an active to a passive); those combining two or more sentences into one (for instance, by coordination); many others, like the one just illustrated, which relate sentences to noun phrases. But the basic criterion is throughout the same, and is throughout distributional. Constructions are related transformationally if, for two or more classes that are part of each, the observed limitations on the co-occurrence of words in one construction are the same as in the other. To be precise, they are related if 'the n-tuples ... which satisfy one construction' (*Papers* 147) are at least a proper subset of those satisfying the other. In his final section, Harris shows how, of the multitude of constructions that can be related by this criterion, the majority can be derived, by a series of irreducible operations that he describes as 'elementary transformations', from a set of minimal sentence constructions that define the 'kernel' of the language (*Papers* 194ff.). From the criterion by which transformations in general have been established, it follows that, 'in addition to exhibiting the minimal sentence constructions, the kernel sentences are ... also the domain of the major restrictions of co-occurrence in the language' (*Papers* 199).

As Chomsky remarked, his own approach to syntax had 'developed directly out of' Harris's work on discourse analysis (1962 [1958]: 124). It was to be expected, therefore, that although the approach in Harris's article was 'somewhat different' (Chomsky, 1957: 44, n. 8), and was, in particular, within a 'different general framework' (1962 [1958]: 136, n. 21), arguments from lexical co-occurrence should again play an important role. Let us look then at his treatment of what he calls, from the outset, 'the active–passive relation'. Chomsky begins by pointing out that the complex of morphemes *be* + *en*, which for him (as for Harris) distinguishes the passive, is subject to 'heavy restrictions'. It can be selected only if the verb is transitive, cannot be selected if the verb is followed by a noun phrase, and must be selected if the verb 'is transitive and is followed by the prepositional phrase *by* + *NP*' (1957: 42). 'Finally', Chomsky adds, a 'full-fledged grammar' will have to include 'many restrictions on the choice of [verbs] in terms of subject and object'. For example, the grammar will have to 'permit' such sentences as *John admires sincerity* and *Sincerity frightens John*, while 'excluding the "inverse" non-sentences' *Sincerity admires John* or *John frightens sincerity*. But 'this whole network of restrictions fails completely' if the verb is passive. Instead 'the "selectional dependencies" are in the opposite order' (43). In a phrase structure grammar, we would therefore have to state the same restrictions twice, once in one order, when *be* + *en* is not selected, and again, in the reverse order, when it is. 'This inelegant duplication, as well as the special restrictions involving the element *be* + *en*, can be avoided only' if we derive passives from actives by a transformation.

Syntactic Structures is a short book and this is the only point in it at which an argument of that kind is spelt out. But the importance of selectional restrictions will emerge more clearly if we look at the then unpublished work which underlies it. In a long chapter on the 'Transformational analysis of English', Chomsky refers to selectional restrictions not only in the active and passive, but in many other cases where a transformation is proposed. In sentences like *I saw the play and so did he*, 'no noun can appear as the final element ... unless it can appear before "saw"'. Thus 'there is a selectional relation between the main verb of the first conjunct and the noun phrase of the second' (Chomsky, 1975a [1955]: 423). The 'simplest way to provide for this selectional relation' is by the transformation which is called, there and in *Syntactic Structures*, 'T_{so}' (Chomsky, 1957: 65, 113). In phrases like *John's flying*, the 'selectional relation ... is just that between subject and verb' (1975a [1955]: 464); in *growling of lions* and *reading of good literature* we again 'find' in one 'the selectional relation verb–subject' and, in the other, 'the selectional relation verb–object' (467). If the construction of *The detective brought the suspect in* were to be added to a phrase structure grammar, 'the whole set of restrictions that must be stated for constructions' of the type *The detective brought in the suspect* 'would have to be repeated' (475). That again 'suggests that we relate these constructions transformationally'. In sentences like *I consider John incompetent*, 'the complement and the object ... have heavy selectional restrictions which suggest transformational analysis' (505); by means of it, we can make 'an important saving' (507). In other sentences with a complement, like *I found the boy studying in the library*, 'the motive for [a] transformational analysis lies in the heavy selectional restrictions ... that hold between the object and the complement, duplicating the selection of subject and predicate' in simple sentences (516). Between nouns and modifying adjectives 'there are ... a variety of selectional restrictions' (539); but these do not have to be restated if such phrases are derived from sentences with a predicative adjective. With a possessive modifier, 'we have' *John's toothache* and *John has toothache*, 'but not' *victory's toothache* or *victory has toothache*. This shows the 'essential simplification' achieved by relating such forms transformationally (536f.).

Why should a grammar deal with selectional restrictions? The short answer is that a generative grammar was a set of rules which described the distribution of elements; and, just as major classes such as noun and verb have different distributions, so do smaller classes such as those of *victory* and *sincerity*, or *John* and *Mary*. If, therefore, we can distinguish sentences from non-sentences by rules that refer to parts of speech, 'we can just as well distinguish "John plays golf" from "golf plays John" by rules involving such syntactic subcategories as Animate Noun, etc.'. Chomsky saw no 'fundamental difference'. 'No general procedure has ever been offered for isolating such categories as Noun, Adjective, etc., that would not equally well apply to such subcategories as are necessary to make finer distinctions' (1961b: 235, n. 29). In later work, he pointed out that categories like 'Human', which were involved in 'selectional rules', might also be involved in rules of other kinds: for example, those excluding *the book who you read* or *Who you met is John* (1965: 150).

Given that the grammar was an account of distributions, and that Chomsky's general object was to make it as simple as possible, it is not surprising that transformations should so often have been justified by evidence of selectional restrictions. But, in retrospect, this raised two questions that did not find satisfactory answers. Firstly, how important was it that the restrictions which apply to one construction should derive exactly from the other? Would there still be a transformation if there was no more than a larger or smaller overlap? Secondly, how far should the description of selectional restrictions be taken? *Sincere*, for example, has a distribution resembling that of *honest*. But they are not identical: compare *He made an honest woman of her* with *He made a sincere woman of her*. Was there to be a rule for this, and would it again affect the argument for deriving an attributive adjective from a predicative?

Let us take the second question first. In earlier work, Harris had made clear that any account of distributions would be an approximation (above, §3.2). Nor did his test for transformations require that selectional restrictions should be absolute. Take, for example, the construction of *He met us*. The triple ⟨*he*, *meet*, *we*⟩ 'certainly' satisfies it, and as certainly satisfies the transformed construction of *his meeting us*. Other triples might be said to satisfy both 'doubtfully': for example, ⟨*moon*, *eat*, *cheese*⟩. We might say of others that they satisfy them 'hardly at all': for example, ⟨*soup*, *drink*, *abstraction*⟩. But what matters is merely that the same triples should have a similar standing in both transforms. We do not require 'a yes-or-no decision on whether any given n-tuple is in the set' that satisfies the constructions. 'We can accept graded decisions' (Harris, 1957: *Papers* 148).

In Chomsky's terms, that means that we can accept what were called 'degrees of grammaticalness'. As Chomsky put it, a form such as *Sincerity admires John* was 'certainly more grammatical' than, for instance, *Of admires John*. But at the same time it was 'clearly less grammatical' than *John admires sincerity* (1957: 43f., n. 7). Likewise for his example *Golf plays John*. On the one hand, he acknowledges that it 'can be a perfectly perspicuous utterance'. In that way, it would again be different from *Of plays John*. On the other hand, such a form can only bear an 'analogic or imposed interpretation'. It is perspicuous 'precisely because of the series of steps that we must take in interpreting it – a series of steps that is initiated by the recognition that this phrase deviates from a . . . grammatical rule'. 'No such steps are necessary in the case of the nondeviant' *John plays golf* (Chomsky, 1961b: 234f.).

Both in this paper and in his unpublished work, Chomsky tried to represent this gradation formally by means of a hierarchy of classes. Both *Of plays John* and *Golf plays John* break rules; but the first breaks a rule for the distribution of a major category, while the one that is broken by the second involves no more than a subsidiary division among nouns. Therefore both are ungrammatical, but on this basis the second is assigned a lesser degree of ungrammaticalness (1961b: 237; 1975a: Ch. 5). In later work, he sought to refine this by invoking a specific distinction between 'selectional rules', like that excluding *Sincerity admires John*, and others which were described as 'strict' subcategorisation rules (1965: 148ff.). But where, as Chomsky put it, should 'continued refinement of the category hierarchy . . . come to an end'? This was not, he said, 'obvious' (1961b: 237, n. 32). But wasn't it? Take again *He made a sincere woman of her*. This too will receive what Chomsky called an 'analogic or imposed interpretation', 'by virtue of [its] relation' (again 1961b: 234) to *He made an honest woman of her*. On that evidence, it is marginally 'deviant'; and, on the face of it, a grammar has in principle to deal with that and any similar difference in the distribution of individual words. Moreover, Chomsky himself raised a more interesting possibility.

'As the grammatical rules become more detailed, we may find that grammar is converging with what has been called logical grammar.' By this he meant that we will 'seem to be studying small overlapping categories of formatives, where each category can be characterized by what we can now (given the grammar) recognize as a semantic feature of some sort'. If so, he said, 'so much the better' (again 1961b: 237, n. 32).

Our other question was, in effect, how far a transformation could have exceptions. For Harris, the answer had been clear. There is a transformation only if, in his terms, 'all the n-tuples ... which satisfy one construction ... also satisfy the other' (1957: *Papers* 147). But alongside transformations proper, Harris also talked of 'quasi-transformations'. These are of various kinds (§4.5, *Papers* 192–4), but among them there are many where 'the set of n-tuples that satisfies one construction is only partly similar to the set that satisfies the other construction'. For example, 'there are some subclasses for which' we find a relation like that of *people in groups* to *groups of people*. Other cases involve derived words. For example, there are quasi-transformations between the constructions of *walk slowly* and *slow walker*, or *He pushed with energy* and *He pushed energetically*.

In Harris's account, a quasi-transformation was still not a transformation. But he also pointed out that many such relations were productive: 'that is, co-occurrences which are present in one of the two constructions but lacking in the other frequently appear in the second as new formations' (*Papers* 193). He gives no illustration; but, for instance, by analogy with *He wakes early* → *He is an early waker*, we might find *He breakfasts early* → *He is an early breakfaster*. Moreover, it became clear by the early 1960s that many relations that both Harris and Chomsky had described as transformations were, strictly speaking, quasi-transformations. There are verbs that take what is apparently a transitive construction, but have no corresponding passive: Chomsky had already striven with some of these in his unpublished work (1975a: 565ff.). He also noted that there were apparent passives without corresponding actives. Similarly, there were predicative adjectives (like *awake*) that were not used in the attributive construction, and attributives (like *main*) that were not used predicatively. The difference between what Harris had called transformations and quasi-transformations seemed more and more one of degree.

Why then should they be handled differently? Suppose that two constructions share a set of collocations: of *slow* with *walk*, of *run* with *quick*, of *wake* with *early*, and so on. Others will be restricted to one construction or the other, and in some way that must be shown. But, for the shared set, which will be simpler – to set out selectional rules twice, once for each construction, or to posit a transformational rule and give them only once? There is no straightforward answer. But, in many cases at least, the generalisation that would be achieved by a transformation would outweigh whatever generalisations might be impaired by having to distinguish exceptions to it.

This argument was not spelled out, at least (so far as I can discover) in print. But, among Chomsky's followers, Lees in particular seems in practice to have had no hesitancy in rejecting Harris's test. In a footnote to his review of *Syntactic Structures*, he assumes that *He is an early riser* is a transform of *He rises early* (1957: 387f., n. 19); and in his later monograph on nominalisation he includes other lexical relations that were obvious quasi-transformations. Some of the most striking discrepancies are in his lists of compounds (1960a: Ch. 4). *Doorway*, for instance, is seen as a transform of *The way is a door*; compare *girlfriend* from *The friend is a girl* (126–7). In the same list, *snap course* is apparently from *The course is a snap*. In other lists, *small talk* is implicitly a transform of *The talk is small* (130), *jitterbug* and *peptalk* of *The bug jitters* and *The talk peps* (137); *masterstroke* of *The master strokes* (139); *dewlap* of [*John*] *lapped the dew* (154). Lees was not worried when his rules derived a compound that does not 'happen commonly to be used'. In his view, it was nevertheless grammatical (121). Nor did he seem to be worried if his proposed source had a strikingly lower degree of grammaticalness.

But by this stage the semantic argument had also moved on. In the beginning, Harris and Chomsky had implied that distributional arguments were sufficient: for the general similarities and the differences between their views see above, §3.2. But Harris remarked that 'some major element of meaning seems to be held constant under transformation'. There might be 'differences in emphasis or style, as between the active and the passive'; also 'specific meaning differences . . . as between assertion and question'. But leaving these aside, 'transforms seem to hold invariant what might be interpreted as the information content' (1957: *Papers* 149f.). At the end of his paper, Harris reports the 'immediate impression' that 'many sentences which are transforms of each other have more or less the same meaning, except for different external grammatical status'. Therefore they had a special role, outside 'structural linguistics' and 'transformation theory', when semantics is considered (*Papers* 202).

Harris also mentioned cases of constructional homonymy (*Papers* 190, 199), acknowledging the contribution of Chomsky (210, n. 65). But the argument changes as soon as judgments of ambiguity are used to test the adequacy of a grammar. Take, for example, *It roasted well.* This can have two meanings: either something (e.g. a new oven) performed the process of roasting well, or something (e.g. a joint of beef) underwent the process well. As Lees presented the argument that Chomsky had given in *Syntactic Structures*, it was one of the 'external, empirical requirements' for a grammar 'that it explicate our intuitive understanding of ambiguous sentences by providing two or more different automatic derivations for them' (Lees, 1957: 382–3). How then is it to explicate our understanding of this sentence? The grammar itself was simply a set of rules for the distribution of morphemes: it could not itself say anything about meanings. Therefore there were two alternatives. Either the morphemes must be different – that is, *roast* must be a lexical homonym – or the homonymy must be syntactic. The solution is easy. In one case, we can derive the sentence by a transformation which deletes a direct object: *It roasted* [e.g. *the joint*] *well.* That explains why, in one meaning, the verb is understood as transitive. In the other case, we can relate it to a form in which the subject, *it*, is itself a direct object: [e.g. *the oven*] *roasted it well.* That explains why the verb can also be understood as if its sense were passive. This may or may not make the grammar simpler. But if it is 'an external condition ... on a useful grammar' that it should explicate our understanding of ambiguities (again Lees, 1957: 383), then, as an argument for transformations, it can stand on its own.

This is another implication that was not precisely spelled out. But it is instructive to look, in particular, at what was said about constructions with an adjective and an infinitive. In an article on this topic, Lees remarks at the outset that sentences like *It's too hot to eat* 'exhibit ... [a] grammatical ambiguit[y]'. They 'are judged ... to differ in grammatical structure' in the same way as, for instance, *It's too humid to play* and *He's too old to send* (1960b: 213). But by whom are they so 'judged'? In the light of earlier discussion, we might expect to be told, first, that they are judged by speakers to be ambiguous: that is, to have two different meanings. We might then be told that, in Lees's view, this can be explained by constructional homonymy – as, in the sections that follow, he argues is the case. But what Lees actually wrote could easily be taken to imply that the 'grammatical ambiguity' is itself a datum. In a later and briefer discussion, Chomsky says that, 'to achieve ... descriptive adequacy', a grammar 'would have to assign structural descriptions indicating that', in *John is easy to please*, '*John* ... is the direct object of *please*', while, in *John is eager to please*, 'it is the logical subject of *please*' (1964 [1962]: 928). To say that a grammar will not achieve descriptive adequacy is to say that it will not 'give a correct account of the linguistic intuition of the native speaker' (924). Thus grammars might be justified directly by appeal to, among other things, a speaker's knowledge of differences in meaning.

By the time this last contribution was published, a correct account of meaning was no longer seen as 'external' to a grammar. In the beginning Chomsky had followed Harris, as we have seen, in excluding semantics from a 'linguistic theory'. Questions of meaning should then 'be studied in some more general theory of language' (Chomsky, 1957: 102). In the early 1960s, a grammar therefore consisted simply of a 'syntactic component' and a 'phonological component' (Chomsky, 1964 [1962]: 915). But in the middle of the decade, he adopted a position which is much more similar to that which had been taken, at the end of the 1950s, by Hockett. The syntactic component remained central; and, as earlier, it comprised a set of rules that 'specify the well-formed strings of minimal syntactically functioning units ... and assign structural information of various kinds' (Chomsky, 1965: 3). The phonological component continued to relate 'a structure generated by the syntactic component to a phonetically represented signal' (16). The latter had already been called the 'phonetic representation' of a sentence. But, just as Hockett had envisaged a 'peripheral' semantic component (1958: 137f.), so Chomsky now included in the grammar a component which 'relates a structure generated by the syntactic component to a certain semantic representation'. The grammar itself was therefore no longer simply an account of distributional structure, and would be wrong if judgments of meaning were not explicated.

The changes that generative grammar underwent at this time have been described by able commentators, Lyons (1991 [1970]: 78ff.) among them. But, in essence, what Chomsky and those associated with him did was to tie together the proposal that a grammar should have a semantic component with his earlier, distributional theory of levels of syntax. These notions were logically independent, and were to be separated again, in Chomsky's own thought, almost immediately. But they were tied together very cleverly, and in a way that fitted beautifully with the ways in which the arguments for transformations had developed.

In Chomsky's earlier theory of levels, the crucial notions had been those of a 'phrase marker' (or 'P-marker') and a 'transformation marker' (or 'T-marker'). The former was simply a phrase structure tree: a phrase structure grammar, as opposed to a transformational grammar, was accordingly one which represented a sentence on that level only. A T-marker was a set of relations established, by transformational rules, over a set of P-markers. As Chomsky himself explained it in the 1970s, 'the T-marker of a sentence *S* provides a record of the P-markers of the elementary strings from which *S* is derived ... and also a record of the "history of derivation" of *S*' (1975a: 15f.). For example, the T-marker of *The old man was taken* might record that it is derived from two 'elementary strings', *someone* + *past* + *take* + *the* + *man* and *the* + *man* + *past* + *be* + *old*. Each of these has its own P-marker, and the sentence then has a 'history of derivation' in which, first, the two P-markers are conflated into one; the adjective *old* is moved, in one or more stages, to before *man*; then the whole structure is turned into the passive; then the agent, *by someone*, is deleted; then, finally, the morphemes *past* and *be* and *en* and *take* are rearranged. The result of each rule is itself a P-marker, to be defined by the transformation itself.

In Chomsky's published writings, this was generally not explained (thus, for example, Chomsky, 1961a: 17, n. 22). But how would such a T-marker have related to the new level of 'semantic representation'? Of the transformations that he had originally posited, most, like the passive, or the rule for coordination, or the one that derived attributive adjectives, could still be seen as establishing relations, in Harris's sense, between different constructions. Since different constructions were potentially associated with different meanings, any of these might enter into a semantic rule. But there were other transformations that simply derived one representation of a construction from another. In our example, the passive verb *was taken* will be represented, at one stage in its derivational history, by a partial P-marker in which *be* and *en* form a constituent: [[*past* [*be en*]] *take*]. But in the final stage, by Chomsky's 'auxiliary' or 'affix-hopping' transformation, it has another representation in which the elements are rearranged: [[*be past*] [*take en*]]. In Chomsky's model, transformations like this were distinguished as 'obligatory' (1957: 45), and, when rules for meanings were added, plainly would not enter into them.

It is hardly surprising that a form of representation that had been justified by formal arguments should turn out to be semantically heterogeneous. But, even in Chomsky's original view of the relation between grammar and meaning, it would be nice if aspects of syntactic structure that were relevant to understanding a sentence were distinguished systematically from those that were not. Moreover, there were transformations whose formal status might be said to vary. In *Syntactic Structures*, Chomsky had established two transformational rules, 'T_{seb}^{ob}' and 'T_{sep}^{op}', both moving the 'particle' of a phrasal verb after its object. The only difference was that the first applied when the object was a pronoun, and was obligatory, while the second applied to any other object, and was not (Chomsky, 1957: 75f., 112). But, that difference apart, were they not in reality the same transformation?

One way to sharpen the question was to ask whether a sentence derived by 'T_{sep}^{op}' was in any sense less basic than one to which it did not apply. With Harris, Chomsky had sought to distinguish a kernel within a language: for example, a sentence such as *Someone took the man* was a 'kernel sentence', while *The man was taken*, which was derived by an optional passive and an optional agent-deleting transformation, was for that reason not a kernel sentence. In such a case, the order of words in one construction could be said to underlie that of the other. But just as an active structure would in this way be represented as more basic than a passive, so, for other reasons, the initial representation of auxiliary elements, in which affixes were ordered before the roots to which they belonged, was thereby seen as underlying the final representation in which they were rearranged. It was therefore appropriate to make an exception for obligatory transformations. In Chomsky's definition, a kernel sentence was one that is 'produced when we apply obligatory transformations to the terminal strings of the [phrase structure] grammar' (1957: 45). *Someone took the man* accordingly remains part of the kernel, since the only transformation that applies is the obligatory rule for auxiliaries. *The man was taken* is not a kernel sentence, since other transformations apply that are not obligatory.

In which sense does a structure in which the members of a phrasal verb are adjacent underlie one in which they have been separated? By Chomsky's definition, *I took it up* must be a kernel sentence, since the only transformations that apply are again the rule for verbal affixes and the equally obligatory 'T_{seb}^{ob}'. In either case, the transformation can be said to specify how a single construction must be realised. But *I took his offer up* is not part of the kernel: it is derived by 'T_{sep}^{op}', and, since there is also a sentence *I took up his offer*, 'T_{sep}^{op}' is not obligatory. In Harris's terms, the transformation is another that establishes a relation between different constructions. But is it? An alternative view is that there is throughout a single construction; but, when the object is a pronoun, it can be realised by only one arrangement of the verb and particle, whereas, if the object is not a pronoun, it can in principle be realised by either.

For contemporary arguments see, in particular, Katz & Postal, 1964: Ch. 3; Chomsky, 1966a: 59ff. I should perhaps stress that in the last few paragraphs I have tried to pick out and interpret what I believe to be historically important, and not to give a blow-by-blow summary. But the nature of the problem was in fact explained only as a prelude to the proposed solution. Briefly, the 'syntactic description' of a sentence – what replaced, that is, the original T-marker – was reduced to a pair of phrase markers. One was assigned by what is called the 'base component' of a grammar, which included, among other things, a set of phrase structure rules. For a sentence like *The old man was taken*, this will indicate already that the construction has to be passive; that *old*, or a structure which includes it, is subordinate to *man*; that what will be the agent of the passive is null. In general, it supplies the basis for the rules of the semantic component; and, in that sense, was what Chomsky called for the first time a 'deep structure'. The other was a 'surface structure'. This was derived by transformations, which accordingly supplied a realisation at another level – unique if all the rules were obligatory, or one of a set if some were optional – for the deep structure of either kernel or non-kernel sentences.

In later work, Chomsky was apt to say that, at this time, 'it was postulated that deep structures give all the information required for determining the meaning of sentences' (1976: 81). He has also tended to stress that the term 'deep', as used to refer to an initial phrase marker, had a purely 'technical' status (Chomsky & Lasnik, 1977: 428, n. 6) within a given theory. But although this may quite possibly describe his real intentions in the middle 1960s, especially as recollected ten years later after his theory had changed, it is not in fact how he put it. What was 'postulated' was that an initial phrase marker would correctly represent the 'deep structure', and, if we leave aside gross misunderstandings, as for example by literary semioticians such as Kristeva (1969), 'deep' had just the implications that readers thought it had.

Let us look, in particular, at the lectures which Chomsky gave to the Linguistic Institute in 1964. In an introductory discussion of 'Assumptions and goals', he defines or redefines a generative grammar as 'a system of rules that relate signals to semantic interpretations of these signals' (1966a: 12). The term 'signal' is thus used interchangeably with 'phonetic representation of a sentence', and 'semantic interpretation' interchangeably with 'semantic representation'. Chomsky then says that, if this is what a grammar has to do, 'the theory of generative grammar must provide a general, language-independent means for representing ... signals and semantic interpretations'. There must, in short, be both a 'universal phonetics' and a 'universal semantics'. But, despite what he believes to be some 'interesting' suggestions by colleagues of his, he recognises that 'the problems of universal semantics still remain veiled in their traditional obscurity' (13). He therefore introduces instead the 'neutral technical notion of "syntactic description"'. This is a construct intermediate between meanings and phonetic representations. It will therefore be a basis for talking about meanings insofar as that is possible. For, 'although there is little one can say about the language-independent system of semantic representation, a great deal is known about conditions that semantic representations must meet, in particular cases'.

It is clear some pages later that at this point Chomsky did not believe that he had said anything 'in any way controversial' (17). Nor did he see very much that was controversial in what follows. A 'syntactic description', as he defines it, is 'an (abstract) object of some sort, associated with [a] sentence, that uniquely determines its semantic interpretation ... as well as its phonetic form' (13). There must therefore be some 'aspect' of a syntactic description that 'determines [the] phonetic form' of a sentence; this 'aspect', by definition, is its surface structure (16). Correspondingly, there must be an aspect of a syntactic description that 'determines [the] semantic interpretation'; and this 'aspect' is, again by definition, the 'deep structure'. The only substantive assumption that Chomsky admits to making is that 'deep structures must in general be distinct from surface structures' (18). That, he says, 'is surely much too obvious to require elaborate defense'.

We must again remind ourselves that this is from a chapter on 'Goals and assumptions'. Similarly, in *Aspects of the Theory of Syntax*, deep and surface structure are in a chapter headed 'Methodological preliminaries' (Chomsky, 1965: Ch. 1). But let us now return, in this light, to the topic of constructional homonymy. According to Chomsky, a deep structure must, by definition, 'uniquely determine' a semantic representation of a sentence. In alternative terms, it will be part of an 'abstract formal object[ ] ... which incorporates all information relevant to a single interpretation of a particular sentence' (Chomsky, 1965: 16). By hypothesis, 'the deep structures that determine semantic interpretation are ... phrase markers generated by the base component' (1966a: 70). So, if a sentence can be shown to have two or more different 'semantic interpretations', the rules of the base component must assign to it two or more different initial phrase markers. Not only does the grammar have to distinguish the kinds of sentence that Lees had earlier called 'grammatically ambiguous'; but, if Chomsky's postulate is to hold, they have to be distinguished at that level.

This fitted very neatly with the way the argument had been going earlier. But it was also bound to bring to a head the problem of what constitutes a grammatical ambiguity. In terms of Chomsky's new conception of a grammar, sentences would be represented as ambiguous if they had more than one semantic 'representation' or semantic 'interpretation'. But by what criteria was it to be decided that they had?

One answer that might conceivably have been given was that semantic representations were simply projections of deep structures. As in the 1950s, we establish rules of syntax by which we describe the distributional structure of the language as simply as we can. These will now assign to each sentence one or more initial phrase markers. For each such marker, we then ask what aspects of the meaning of the sentence, or of its meaning when it is understood in a certain way, are 'determined' by it. These define its semantic representation; and, as in the 1950s, we can argue that the more real ambiguities are explicated by the rules that are proposed, the better the individual grammar, and the better our account of what it means for a grammar to be simpler, will be. But a more exciting view was that semantic representations could be established independently of syntax. In an article which dealt principally with lexical meaning, Katz and Fodor had already argued that 'empirical data for the construction of a semantic theory' are provided by a speaker's 'ability to interpret sentences' (1963: 176). So, among other things, the '[semantic interpretations] must mark each semantic ambiguity that a speaker can detect' (183). Let us return then to examples like *It is too hot to eat*. If we can show that speakers see this as 'semantically ambiguous', an adequate grammar must assign to it two different 'semantic interpretations'. Therefore, independently of any other argument, it must assign two different deep structures.

But what exactly is the evidence for 'semantic ambiguity'? According to Katz and Fodor, a particular 'facet of the speaker's semantic ability' is that of 'disambiguat[ing] parts of a sentence in terms of other parts'. For example, if *The bill is large* is placed in the context — *but need not be paid*, it will be understood that *the bill* refers to an order to pay a debt and not, for example, to the beak of a bird (175). Similarly, if *It is too hot to eat* is placed in the context — *and too windy*, it will be understood as being about the weather and not the food; if it is placed in the context — *and has too much garlic*, the opposite. But Bolinger showed very quickly (1965) that this test would distinguish lexical ambiguities indefinitely; and, although it was remarked less at the time, there was again no obvious limit when it was applied to ambiguities in relationships. Take, for example, *It roasted well.* A speaker can 'disambiguate' this easily: *It roasted well and tasted delicious*, *It roasted well until it broke down.* Now take *It slid out*. This could mean that it happened under external pressure: that is how a speaker will understand it in a context such as — *easily when I pushed it*. Or it could mean that it was done deliberately: thus in the context — *and crawled away*. But that is not all. On another 'reading' there was neither deliberate action nor external pressure: *It slid out gradually over fifty years*. In this way we can find evidence for ever finer shades of 'semantic ambiguity'.

The particular interest of ambiguities is that, since deep structures were said to 'uniquely determine' semantic interpretations, any 'semantic ambiguity' must be reflected in some difference, either lexical or syntactic, at that level. But another facet of the speaker's 'semantic ability', according to Katz and Fodor, is a skill in 'paraphrasing'. For example, speakers can answer questions like 'How can what [is said] be rephrased?' (1963: 175). So, to account for this ability, 'semantic interpretations' must also 'suitably relate sentences that speakers know to be paraphrases of each other' (183). Let us therefore consider, for example, an active and passive. *Everyone read the book* can be 'rephrased' as *The book was read by everyone*. So, their 'semantic interpretations' must be 'related'; and that must mean that they are either the same or in large part similar. Is it not then tempting to propose, independently again of any consideration of the simplicity of rules of syntax, that their deep structures are also related?

As matters stood, this was no more than a temptation. By definition, each deep structure 'determined' a semantic representation; but there was no requirement that a single semantic representation should be determined by a single deep structure, or even by a set of deep structures that were syntactically similar. But in the year after Katz and Fodor's article, Katz and Postal had proposed a 'heuristic principle' which, they said, was 'based on the general character of linguistic descriptions'. To discover the syntactic derivation of a sentence, 'look', they suggested, 'for simple paraphrases ... which are not paraphrases by virtue of synonymous expressions'. To judge from Katz and Fodor's notion of a 'paraphrase', on which Katz and Postal offer no advance, most actives are in that sense paraphrases of the corresponding passives. Then, 'on finding [such paraphrases], construct grammatical rules that relate the original sentence and its paraphrases in such a way that each of these sentences has [in terms of the model they were assuming at that time] the same sequence of underlying P-markers' (Katz & Postal, 1964: 157). In terms of the new model, look for any sentences that a speaker will recognise as saying the same thing (compare again Katz & Fodor, 1963: 175), and try to justify rules that will assign a common initial phrase marker to them.

Katz and Postal stress that this is no more than a heuristic principle. 'Of course', they say, ' ... it is still necessary to find *independent syntactic justification*' for whatever rules are proposed. But what exactly did that mean? The obvious answer is that the rules must at least distinguish what is grammatical from what is ungrammatical. But as we have seen earlier in this section, these were not perceived as absolute properties. There were 'degrees of grammaticalness' and they too should be explicated by syntactic rules, to a level of detail that remained open. Moreover, Chomsky had already suggested that, the more the rules dealt with fine details of distribution, the more they might converge with 'what has been called logical grammar' (again Chomsky, 1961b: 237, n. 32). Suppose then that we have two different accounts of syntax, formally explaining the same distributional facts. Suppose, in addition, that one converges more closely with an independent account of semantics. Which is the better?

In Chomsky's earlier account, a grammar dealt with distributions only. Therefore we might have preferred whichever was the simpler. But if a grammar also has a semantic component, we can no longer consider syntax in isolation. As Katz and Postal themselves point out, we must in principle 'assess the adequacy of a full linguistic description in terms of its over-all simplicity and explanatory power' (1964: 3). It follows that syntactic rules can have no 'independent ... justification' apart from the bare requirement that, at some level of detail, they should distinguish strings of words that constitute grammatical sentences from those that do not. Given that the 'heuristic principle' was concerned with what were now deep structures as opposed to surface structures, and that it was now a requirement, and not just a heuristic principle, that deep structures should distinguish sentences that were ambiguous, that was no check at all.

The floodgates were now open, and in the next few years the water joyously burst through. In an important paper, Lakoff argued that sentences with an instrumental, like *He sliced the salami with a knife*, had the same deep structures as 'synonymous' sentences like *He used a knife to slice the salami* (Lakoff, 1968). In keeping with earlier principles, he insisted that their 'synonymy' was not a sufficient argument; there had, in addition, to be 'empirical syntactic evidence' (7). But the evidence consisted simply of the demonstration that, where sentences have this sense in common, they both share certain properties that reflect their meaning and are distinguished by similar properties from other sentences whose sense is different. For example, the verb that describes what is done with the instrument must have the feature '+ ACTIVITY' (13f.); the noun phrase which refers to the instrument cannot be a reflexive with the agent noun phrase as its antecedent (16); a sentence describing the deliberate use of an instrument is distinguished from one that describes an accident in that the latter cannot include adverbs such as *carefully* (9). Moreover, Lakoff does not say what the deep structure should be. He simply argues that if such structures have a set of properties that he sees as 'emerg[ing]' from the work of Katz and Postal and from Chomsky's *Aspects of the Theory of Syntax* (4), they have to be the same. Otherwise such 'generalizations about selectional restrictions and co-occurrence' (23) will be missed.

The properties of deep structure, as Lakoff saw them, were that 'basic grammatical relations (e.g. subject-of, object-of)' should be defined over them; that generalisations of the kind he uses in evidence must be stateable; that 'lexical items are assigned to their appropriate categories'; and, finally, that they are the 'input to the transformational rules' (again 1968: 4). It will be noted that these do not include the property of uniquely determining semantic representations, by which Chomsky had actually defined them. Nor does Lakoff refer to that later. But even with this omission, they are sufficient in his eyes to justify a form of argument in which the identity of sentences at an underlying level is established without consideration not just of the simplicity, but even of the nature of the rules that would be required to generate them. The generalisations have to be stated; according to current concepts of deep structure they had to be stated at that level; and that could not be done unless, at that level, the sentences had the same syntax. As Lakoff saw it, this was a type of argument that 'differ[ed] considerably' (24) from those that 'ha[d] been used in transformational research so far'.

This still falls short of saying that sentences have the same deep structure if they are 'synonymous'. We must also show that, at some level of detail, there is some distributional peculiarity that they share. But what if these features of distribution are themselves seen as, in Lakoff's words, a 'semantic phenomenon'? In that case, he presents us in effect with two alternatives (26f.). Firstly, they might be described by rules that are among those which derive 'semantic readings' from deep structures; in the technical work of Katz and his associates, these were known as 'projection rules'. But then (Lakoff argued) they would have to operate on structures that were syntactically alike; otherwise the generalisations would again be missed. We therefore arrive at the same conclusion, that, for these sentences with this sense in common, the deep structures must be identical. The second alternative was that they might be stated 'not in terms of projection rules, but in terms of well-formedness conditions on semantic readings' themselves. For example, a sentence like *I knew the answer with a slide rule*, where the verb does not have the feature '+ ACTIVITY', might still have a deep structure different from that of *I used a slide rule to know the answer*. The 'projection rules' would then derive the same 'reading' for both; but, finally, an 'appropriate well-formedness constraint' would indicate that both sentences were 'semantically ill-formed' (27).

I have chosen this article for discussion partly because generative semantics was Lakoff's invention more perhaps than anyone else's, and partly because, in this last argument, although he says that he was raising no more than a possibility (28f.), he was plainly only an inch away from advocating it. All that was required was, firstly, that we should agree that the restrictions which he invokes – on instrumentals occurring with verbs that are not '+ ACTIVITY', and so on – have to do with meaning. This Lakoff did in fact believe (26). Secondly and crucially, we have to reconsider the directional relationship between semantic representations and deep structures. As we have seen from the lectures that Chomsky published in 1966, and that (it is worth remarking) had been heard by Lakoff and most other participants in this debate, the basic task of a generative grammar was to relate 'phonetic signals' to their meanings. 'Syntactic descriptions', of which deep structures were part, were then presented as intermediate constructs which would enable us to talk about structures that determined meanings, even though we lacked, as yet, a theory of universal semantics that would allow us to represent them directly (thus again Chomsky, 1966a: 13). Given such constructs, a representation of the meaning of a sentence could be derived, in principle, from that part of its syntactic description that would, by that token, be its deep structure.

But although the nature of universal semantics was indeed obscure, Katz and Fodor had at least shown, to the satisfaction of most generativists, what kinds of fact were vital to the semantic description of a particular language. If a sentence was judged to be 'semantically ambiguous', it had to have two or more distinct 'semantic interpretations'; if two or more sentences were judged to be 'paraphrases', they had to have the same 'semantic interpretation', and so on. But if we know so much about the conditions that particular 'semantic interpretations' must meet, why do we need to start from Chomsky's intermediate structure? We find, for example, that a sentence like *I knew the answer with a slide rule* is judged to be 'semantically anomalous' (compare again Katz & Fodor, 1963: 175); a sentence like *I found the answer with a slide rule* is not. Therefore the latter must have a 'semantic interpretation', while the former must either be assigned no interpretation or assigned one which is deviant. Can we not write rules which do this directly – not rules which 'interpret' an intermediate deep structure, but rules which generate, or impose 'well-formedness conditions' on, the representations of meanings themselves?

Many other studies were already tending to this conclusion. Let us take first the requirement in Lakoff's list (1968: 4) that 'basic grammatical relations' should be defined over deep structures. For Chomsky, these had involved in particular the functions of 'logical subject' and 'logical object' (1965; above §3.3). But in a paper in the following year, Fillmore had argued that subject and object were not 'among the syntactic functions to which semantic rules [rules, that is, deriving semantic representations from deep structures] were sensitive' (1966: 21), and in a major contribution to a theory of universal grammar he now developed in detail a proposal in which the rules of what Chomsky had called the base component specified a series of abstract 'syntactic-semantic' functions by which noun phrases were related to verbs as agentives, instrumentals, datives, and so on (1968: §3). For example, *the key* is an instrumental in both *John opened the door with the key* and *John used a key to open the door* (25). It is again an instrumental in *The key opened the door*, while in the other two *John*, though having the same 'surface' role as subject, is an agentive. Agentive and the like are 'concepts' which directly 'identify certain types of judgments human beings are capable of making' about events (24).

At the very end of his paper, Fillmore considers the objection that his account is 'too strongly motivated by semantic considerations' (88). But is there, he asks, 'a "level" of syntactic description that is discoverable one language at a time on the basis of purely syntactic criteria'? If we can 'discover a semantically justified universal syntactic theory' such as he is proposing, and convert 'these "semantic deep structures" into the surface forms of sentences', Chomsky's 'syntactic deep structure' may well be an 'artificial intermediate level' that we can dispense with.

Another property of Chomsky's base component was that it included a lexicon assigning dictionary words to categories. But in discussing sundry 'residual problems', Chomsky himself had spoken of the 'meaning relation, approaching a variety of paraphrase', between pairs of sentences like *John strikes me as pompous* and *I regard John as pompous*, or *John bought the book from Bill* and *Bill sold the book to John*. In the beginning, Harris had suggested that for this second pair it might be possible to talk at least of a 'quasi-transformation' (1957: *Papers* 189; also 1952; *Papers* 134). But in Chomsky's model, such relations were not 'expressible in transformational terms', and accordingly suggested 'the need for an even more abstract notion of grammatical function and grammatical relation' than any he had proposed (Chomsky, 1965: 162). He did not explore a solution to this problem; but the obvious implication was that, just as he had defined such functions as 'logical subject' or 'logical direct object' over the deep structures of sentences, so there had to be a still more abstract form of representation over which these still more abstract functions could in turn be defined. At this level, phrases such as *John*, *the book* and *Bill* must bear the same relation to some element, or complex of elements, which must underlie both *sell* and *buy*.

In a minor paper published two years later, Gruber proposed, for different reasons, that certain configurations of features that represent verbs should be 'generated in the base component independently of particular words' (1967: 947). We have also seen how Lakoff had argued that a sentence in which an instrument is marked by *with* should have the same underlying structure as one with the verb *use*. But such straws in the wind were immediately overtaken by a flood of papers from McCawley. In two of them, he argued briefly (1968a) and at length (1968b) that Chomsky's selectional restrictions (by which, for example, *Sincerity admires John* was excluded as ungrammatical) had nothing to do with syntax. From that it follows that there was no need, at least, to assign words to the categories involved in such restrictions by lexical entries which were part of his base component. In another paper, which by chance was published first, he argued, with Fillmore but more forcefully, that deep structures were an artefact. 'One could propose' instead that 'there is simply a single system of processes which convert [semantic representations into surface structures] and that none of the intermediate stages in the conversion ... is entitled to any special status such as that which Chomsky ascribes to "deep structure"' (McCawley, 1976 [1967]: 105). Finally, in the last of the series to be written (see 1976: v, on the order in which they are reprinted), McCawley virtually assumes not just that Gruber's concept of a structure underlying lexical items was correct, but that, in the kind of grammar now proposed, such structures should themselves be derived by transformations from underlying structures resembling those of syntax. Thus, in a classic illustration, the configuration which is associated in the lexicon with *kill* is derived from a semantic representation with four nested 'semantic predicates' (CAUSE, BECOME, NOT, ALIVE), by successive operations which in effect reduce them to one (McCawley, 1976 [1968c]: 157f.). In this way all the properties of Chomskyan deep structures, as seen by Lakoff (1968: 4) or as presented by Chomsky himself, were now thrown over.

By the end of the decade the bandwaggon was rolling at full speed, and all that remained was for it to fall over the precipice. But if we ask how it had got going, or why, in general, transformational grammar was by then so seriously out of hand, it seems possible, in the light of this survey, to offer both a short-term and a long-term answer.

The short-term explanation is the one that the proponents of generative semantics might themselves have given, that they were simply carrying to their logical conclusion ideas that were implicit in Chomsky's *Aspects of the Theory of Syntax*. This was a rich and in places contradictory book, full of tentative suggestions and throw-off passages – like the one on *buy* and *sell* or *strike ... as* and *regard ... as* – that he himself would sometimes take further and sometimes not. As we will see at the beginning of the next chapter, the notion that deep structures uniquely determine semantic representations, which was first presented as true by definition, was already being reprocessed into a factual hypothesis, which Chomsky was soon to reject. But such things were there for any reader to see, and it was to be expected that many would choose to develop them. The unsurprising result was that investigations of deep structure were to probe ever deeper. As McCawley reported within two years, 'virtually every advance achieved within this framework has required the setting up of deep structures which are further removed from the superficial form of sentences than had previously been thought to be necessary' (1976 [1967]: 103).

The long-term explanation is more contentious; but, as I at least have tried to interpret this story, the rationale for much that was argued in the 1960s lies in the decision by an earlier generation of American scholars to divorce the study of form from that of meaning. In general, this led to a view of language in which an account of syntax could be justified on purely distributional grounds; and, when meaning was eventually tackled, to a concept of levels in which a 'semantic representation' of a sentence, and with it of the construction of a sentence, was a formal object to be characterised by a grammar alongside, but separately from, a representation of its syntax. This was assumed by the 'generative semanticists', who proposed precisely that a grammar should generate such objects and derive syntactic descriptions from them, as by those who opposed them.

It also led to the notion that, in justifying grammars, distributional and semantic arguments were independent. On the one hand, a grammar had to generate 'all and only the grammatical sentences of a language', to a degree of grammaticalness that was left open. Consequently, any difference in the distribution of words was potentially evidence for, or constituted 'independent syntactic justification' of, grammatical rules. On the other hand, a grammar might be expected to explain some aspects of the meanings of sentences; and, once a 'semantic component' had been incorporated in it, one could argue, quite apart from any 'syntactic' evidence, that a sentence was 'semantically ambiguous', that two sentences were 'paraphrases' or 'synonymous', that a sequence of words was 'semantically anomalous', and so on. A grammar then gave an integrated account of findings of both kinds.

But just as, in the distributional method, the analysis of form proceeded without appeal to meanings, so, conversely, the analysis of meanings was unconstrained by reference to form. Therefore any 'ambiguity' and so on was potentially relevant. Take, for example, the treatment of compounds. We saw earlier in this chapter (§3.3) how Wells (1947b) had distinguished the 'constructions' of *lady-friend* and *lady-killer*. This was based on a semantic difference, which Wells's formal criteria did not explicate. In the early days of generative grammar, differences like this were picked up with a vengeance by Lees (1960a). *Flour mill*, for example, was 'ambiguous' (117) because it could potentially mean either 'a mill which produces flour' or 'a mill powered by flour'. According to the programme of *Syntactic Structures*, this would be explained by formal rules that took account of 'selectional restrictions'. Ten years later, Lees carried the analysis yet further. For example, in *briefcase* and *coffee cream* 'we understand the spatial relations oppositely: the briefs go into the case, but the cream into the coffee'. In *car thief*, the second noun 'represents someone who actually does something to or with what is represented by' the first; in compounds like *water pistol* the head nouns are 'inanimates representing objects which do nothing but instead can be *used* by someone to do something', and so on (Lees, 1970: 140). Where then should one stop? A water pistol does, when it is fired, emit water; in *hour glass*, which Lees lists with it, *glass* does not 'represent' something that emits hours. Is that not also a distinction that the grammar must draw?

Finally, the belief that 'syntactic' and semantic criteria were independent made it seem marvellous when they coincided. In a paper on the 'surface verb' *remind*, published when the excitement over generative semantics was at its height, Postal sets out very clearly a programme of research in which syntactic descriptions that are ever more remote from surface structures will eventually converge with semantic representations (1970a: 101ff.). The former are established by arguments for transformations, which 'have usually been wholly or largely justified on assumptions independent of hypotheses about the Semantic Representations of sentences' (102). If then, deeper and deeper representations 'do come, in a clear sense, closer and closer to Semantic Representation, this is a fundamental empirical fact about human language'. A quarter of a century after the separation of form and meaning was proposed, that was still the spirit and essence of distributionalism.

4 *Chomsky's philosophy of grammar*

Chomsky's first article appeared in 1953; forty years later, when this book is published, he will barely have reached a normal age of retirement. It would be astonishing if, over these four decades, his views had not changed, even on general topics and even touching matters central to his thought. In the beginning, for example, he believed that the study of meaning was separate from that of grammar, and concerned with the 'use' of sentences. Some years later, he thought it obvious that sentences had 'intrinsic meanings' that were determined by grammatical rules. At still later stages, that belief was gradually reversed. At no moment, however, have his views changed comprehensively and suddenly. They have changed as the clouds change in the sky, or as the key changes in a classical sonata movement. Nor, in some ways, have they changed entirely. As in a sonata movement, new ideas have often been at once new and a development of perhaps a fragment of what has preceded.

The aim of this chapter is to try and trace the evolution of Chomsky's general ideas. It will be well to acknowledge at the outset that this is not easy, and that any account that might be given, barring the most slavish and unpenetrating chronicle, is liable to seem in part misleading to others who have read his works differently. One reason is that Chomsky's career is not over: his ideas are still developing, and, even if scholars are less eager than before to publish their reactions, anyone with a serious interest in the nature of language must still try to decide for or against them. It is therefore much harder than in earlier chapters to separate an account of history from either an encomium or celebration of what has been achieved or a form of polemic. Another reason is that the changes in Chomsky's thought have rarely been linear. In following his work, one has often had the impression that, at a certain time or in a certain book, he has plainly said so and so. Then, at a later time or in a later book, he is evidently saying something different. But when, in the light of this, one looks again at what had been written earlier, one finds that it was not as unambiguous as one had supposed. Sometimes there is an inconsistency or marginal expression of doubt; and this, one can now see, was the seed from which a new conception has come. Sometimes there is a pregnant vagueness, which has later given birth to a new clarification. It is therefore rarely that old theory is explicitly abandoned. Instead it is often reworked or reshaped into new theory, or may fade, perhaps for a period only, into the background.

Take, for example, the concept of deep structure. It was introduced, as we have seen, in the mid-1960s, as part of the reworking of an earlier theory, in which the notion of a kernel sentence had figured prominently. That notion was never explicitly abandoned; on the contrary, Chomsky thought that it had 'an important intuitive significance' (1965: 18). But it had no natural place in the revised theory, and thereafter, until now at least, one has heard no more of it. A new concept was then based on the relation of syntax to semantics. The passages in question have been cited in the last chapter (§3.4), and make clear that deep structure was, by definition, the aspect of a syntactic description of a sentence that determines its semantic interpretation; that it was one of a set of notions that were not 'in any way controversial'; and that the task of a substantive theory was to say, among other things, what properties the structures that will meet this definition have.

Five years later, both the model and the presentation of the problem had changed. Firstly, the previous account was no longer uncontroversial. On the contrary, 'it goes without saying that none of the assumptions' embodied in it 'is self-evident, and that all are open to empirical challenge' (Chomsky, 1970b [1972a: 66]). This even includes, for example, the notions of a 'semantic' and a 'phonetic interpretation'. Chomsky then proceeds to challenge the specific assumption that deep structures do determine the meanings of sentences. Formerly, to repeat, they did so by definition; Chomsky had then made the substantive assertion that they 'must in general be distinct from surface structures', and must therefore form a distinct level of representation. But now it is assumed that there is a distinct level of representation which has, in other respects, the same properties that Chomsky's substantive theory had attributed to the level of deep structure under the old definition. That is simply a hypothesis. He then considers the further proposition that the representation of sentences at that level determines their meanings. That is now another hypothesis, and Chomsky adduces a series of examples (1972a: 88ff.) which suggest that they are, in fact, determined partly by their surface structures.

This was in appearance a rather important shift. But when one searches in the notes to what had been written in the 1960s, one finds that Chomsky had never entirely believed what he had said. There is no qualification in the lectures at the 1964 Linguistic Institute (Chomsky, 1966a), which is the main source I have cited; nor in the chapter on 'Methodological preliminaries' in *Aspects of the Theory of Syntax*, where again the notion of deep structure is defined (Chomsky, 1965: 16). But in a note to a later chapter, the 'assumption' that semantic interpretation depends only on the underlying structure (136) is said to be a 'claim' that 'seems ... somewhat too strong'. 'For example, it seems clear that the order of "quantifiers" in surface structures sometimes plays a role in the semantic interpretation' (224, n. 9). Problems with quantifiers are among those discussed in 1970 (Chomsky, 1972a: 103ff.), and we are told, in general, that the material for that discussion is 'drawn in large part' from lectures given in and before the summer of 1966 (88, n. 20). One might indeed add that the example Chomsky gave in 1965 was already familiar from the chapter on semantics in *Syntactic Structures* (1957: 100f.). It would appear, therefore, that he did not see this as an 'assumption' that was true by definition, but was already treating it as part of a theory that could be challenged.

How are we to interpret all this? In a way, the story is simple if we just ignore the passages that were cited in the last chapter. What is constant from the 1950s is that there are transformations; and, in the middle 1960s, it is suggested that the structures on which they operate have the formal properties that Chomsky describes. At the same time semantic representations are incorporated in the grammar, and it is further suggested, as a hypothesis, that they are determined by the same structures. Then this hypothesis is tested; it is found to be inadequate; therefore, in 1970, a new one is proposed. This story is not only simple, it is also the one that in later discussion Chomsky himself invites us to believe. But if it is true, why did he define 'deep structure' in the way he plainly did define it? It seems that, for a moment at least, he was hoping to reconcile two different senses of the term 'deep'. In one sense ('deep_a'), it means 'having to do with meaning rather than form'. Thus, in particular, a representation of the syntax of a sentence is 'deep_a' if it determines its semantic representation. In the other sense ('deep_b') it meant 'syntactically underlying'. Thus, in particular, a syntactic representation of a sentence is 'deep_b' if it is the source from which, by transformations, its surface constituency structure is derived. How wonderful it would then be if the same representations were 'deep' in both senses! If that is so, we can define 'deep' as '$deep_a$': that is the intuitively exciting sense of 'deep', as opposed to the merely technical. But structures which are '$deep_a$' are also '$deep_b$'. Therefore the whole theory of transformational syntax, which had originally been developed as part of a grammar without a semantic component, slots in beautifully with the new proposal to add one.

Hence the definitions which we have cited, which were presumably formulated in 1964 or earlier. Briefly, a grammar with both a semantic and a syntactic component must have a level of syntactic representation that is '$deep_a$'. That is to say, there must be syntactic representations of sentences to which their semantic representations are related by semantic rules. Therefore the existence of '$deep_a$' structures is uncontroversial; and, by hypothesis, they are also '$deep_b$'. But no sooner is this in the press than Chomsky is forced to acknowledge that the hypothesis is wrong. For example, there are problems with quantifiers, with the location of the main stress in the sentence (Chomsky, 1972a: 89ff.), and so on. He could, at that point, have continued to define 'deep' as '$deep_a$'. He could then have argued that, in a transformational account of syntax, the structures that were '$deep_a$' were not just the underlying representations of sentences, but their syntactic descriptions as wholes. '$Deep_a$' therefore simply does not equal '$deep_b$'. One could even have seen it as an objection to transformational syntax that it failed to identify naturally the structures that were '$deep_a$'. But instead Chomsky chose to proceed as if he had never in fact defined 'deep' as he had. 'Deep' from then on simply means '$deep_b$'. As he explains in the mid 1970s, with all the patience of a man who is so woefully misunderstood, it is merely a technical notion in a specific theory of syntax. The hypothesis is therefore turned on its head. Instead of asking whether structures which are '$deep_a$' are also, in fact, '$deep_b$', we have to ask whether, on the assumption that a transformational syntax is correct, the structures which are '$deep_b$' are also, in fact, '$deep_a$'.

Many of Chomsky's critics have found this kind of thing quite maddening, since they do not know, even at times within the same book, what view or formulation they are supposed to be addressing. For myself, I confess I find it fascinating. It is the testimony of a mind that is always fruitful and always on the move, and that often moves too fast for considered and orderly publication. It is also one of the things that makes this chapter worth writing. But at the same time it is very hard to demonstrate that my understanding of the history is right. By a judicious choice of quotations, Chomsky's intellectual development can be presented as no more than an elaboration or unfolding of ideas that were already there, in embryo, in the 1950s. At worst, it will be acknowledged that there have been false starts and some wayward insights on the way. By taking another selection of quotations, one can argue that on the contrary he has changed his mind repeatedly, and has sought to conceal it by what amounts at best to rhetorical opportunism. The interpretation which I will give does not agree with either of these. But like them it is based on judgment.

4.1 The early Chomsky

Chomsky's early concept of grammar has been explored in some detail in earlier chapters. Briefly, a grammar is a formal device that generates the sentences of a language. For example, a grammar of English must generate the sentences of English. A 'language' in turn is simply a set, finite or infinite, of sentences. For example, the language we call 'English' is a set of sentences of which *I came home, Bill left* or *The girl from next door left her ring on the sideboard* are all members. Each sentence is represented as a finite sequence of elements, and the 'fundamental aim in the linguistic analysis of a language' (Chomsky, 1957: 13) is thus to separate 'grammatical sequences' from 'ungrammatical sequences'. For example, a grammar of English will distinguish sequences which are grammatical in English, such as *I came home*, from those that are not grammatical in English, such as *I home came* or *I cape hope*.

We have seen in §3.2 how this account in part derives from and in part differs from those that had been current in the Bloomfieldian school. But one important innovation is that 'languages' do not only include what Chomsky called 'natural languages'. English is a 'language', since, even 'in [its] spoken ... form', each sentence is 'representable as a finite sequence' of elementary units, which at first were phonemes (again Chomsky, 1957: 13). But so too was any other set of sequences or 'strings' of elements. For example, 'the set of "sentences" of some formalized system of mathematics can be considered a language'. So too, by implication, could the 'languages', as they were already called in technical usage, in which computers are programmed. In general, there is an infinite set of 'languages' that need not in any other way resemble 'natural languages', as well as an infinite set that do. In this light it is possible, firstly, to compare classes of 'languages' in the abstract. For example,

Chomsky gives a formal definition of a 'terminal language', which is one of a class that can be generated by a specific form of phrase structure grammar. He also gives a formal definition of a 'finite state language', which can be generated by what is called a 'finite state Markov process'. It can then be proved that whereas 'every finite state language is a terminal language' (that is, every set of strings that can be generated by a finite state Markov process can also be generated by this form of phrase structure grammar), the reverse is not true: 'there are terminal languages which are not finite state languages'. This means that 'description in terms of phrase structure is essentially more powerful than description in terms of [finite state processes]' (Chomsky, 1957: 30).

Secondly, it is possible to compare 'natural languages' with formal 'languages' of this kind. For example, Chomsky shows that, under certain assumptions about what is and is not a grammatical sentence in English, the 'natural language' called 'English' can be represented as a set of strings which is not a member of the class of 'finite state languages' (Chomsky, 1957: 21ff.). I have put this rather carefully: in Chomsky's own words, the 'remark' that 'English is not a finite state language' can, 'under any reasonable delimitation of the set of sentences of the language, ... be regarded as a theorem concerning English' (21). We might then ask whether, in the same terms, English is a 'terminal language'. Chomsky offered no demonstration that it was not. 'Of course', he says, 'there are languages (in our general sense) that cannot be described in terms of phrase structure ..., but I do not know whether or not English is itself literally outside the range of such analysis' (34).

Finally, in this and other discussion of linguistic structure, 'our fundamental concern ... is the problem of justification of grammars' (Chomsky, 1957: 49). The weakest requirement that is considered is that a linguistic theory should provide a practical 'evaluation procedure', which, given two grammars based on the same corpus of utterances, will 'tell us which is the better' account of the 'language from which the corpus is drawn' (51). To that end, we must complete 'three main tasks' (53f.). The first is to 'state precisely (if possible, with operational, behavioral tests) the external criteria of adequacy for grammars'. For example, we must be able to test how far a proposed grammar of English gives a correct account of what is and is not, or what is more and what is less, 'grammatical in English'. The second task is to 'characterize the form of grammars in a general and explicit way'. For example, we must give an account of a transformational grammar as complete and explicit as those of a finite state Markov process or a phrase structure grammar. Thirdly, 'we must analyze and define the notion of simplicity that we intend to use in choosing among grammars'. As Chomsky explained more fully in work that was then unpublished, the strategy was to establish notational conventions for grammars in such a way that a reduction in their length will reflect what he calls 'real simplicity' (1975a [1955]: 118). For all these tasks considerations of meaning are irrelevant. Grammaticalness 'cannot be identified' with being '"meaningful" or "significant" in any semantic sense' (Chomsky, 1957: 15); grammars themselves say nothing about meanings; and the 'correspondences between formal and semantic features' belong to a 'more general theory of language' (102) of which a theory of grammar is no more than a part.

This account of Chomsky's early ideas is based on contributions written in the mid-1950s. I have set aside his first article (1953), which he himself lists among those that sought to develop a 'discovery procedure' (Chomsky, 1957: 52, n. 3). But the views in *Syntactic Structures* are also those of his underlying work, *The Logical Structure of Linguistic Theory*, whose published recension is said to date from 1955–6 (Chomsky, 1975a: 4). In a preface, which must presumably have been written somewhat later, readers are told that they 'may find *Syntactic Structures* a helpful introduction' to it (59). Similar views appear in part in two further articles published before *Syntactic Structures*. One is a strong attack on the notion that semantic criteria are relevant to, in particular, phonology (Chomsky, 1955a). Compare Chomsky, 1957: 94f.; 1975a: 88ff.; but this is the best discussion and was delivered at a conference whose published proceedings include the discussion that followed. The other (1956) deals in greater technical detail with the comparison of finite state Markov processes, phrase structure grammars, and transformational grammars. One cannot help remarking again that, for a scholar who was twenty-seven in 1955, this is an outstanding body of work. The part that was published is also very lucid, and it is unlikely that anyone who has read it would disagree with what I have said so far.

But to someone who is not familiar with it, or has looked at it only through the medium of later exegesis or hagiography, it may seem that, in the final paragraph, I have laid too much stress on ideas that connect the early Chomsky with Harris and other Post-Bloomfieldians, and have omitted things that, in the context of the 1950s, were more revolutionary. In particular, I have said nothing about the psychological reality of grammars, or the nature of what was later called a 'faculty of language'. I have accordingly given the impression that the justification of grammars was a purely methodological problem. But in many accounts of the 'Chomskyan revolution' what is said is precisely this: that the Post-Bloomfieldians were indeed interested only in the development of methods and procedures for arriving at a description, whereas Chomsky's interest, from the very beginning, was in describing the grammar that had been internalised (to use a term that dates from the end of the 1950s) by a speaker.

The truth is more complicated, and can be recovered only with some care. But, on the one hand, Chomsky's connection with Harris is undeniable. He had been his pupil when *Methods in Structural Linguistics* was prepared for the press, and is first known to scholarship for having helped with the typescript (Harris, 1951a: v). Years later he was to say that he learned linguistics from it (for the source see Newmeyer, 1980: 33). The driving aim of this work, with that of other leading American linguists since the war years, had been the rigorous validation of descriptions of languages, and Chomsky's earliest work was naturally in the same vein. On the other hand, he laid far more stress than Harris or anyone else in the mid-1950s on the linguistic abilities of the speaker. The references for this will be examined in a moment. It is also true that, by at least the end of the decade, he had begun to conceive of the status of linguistic descriptions in a new way.

The question for a historian is how and why he came to do so. It is difficult to answer for two reasons. One is that there is no single issue: we are dealing with a spectrum of ideas, some of which appear in Chomsky's early writings, while others are developed in print five or even ten years later. Another problem is the discrepancy between what he actually wrote in the middle 1950s, both in *Syntactic Structures* and in his long unpublished book, and what he later says he was thinking at the time. The main source for the latter is the introduction added in 1975 to the published version of *The Logical Structure of Linguistic Theory* (Chomsky, 1975a: 1–53). In this he sought to weave together an outline of the 'central concepts of the manuscript' with a brief account of 'some of the theoretical modifications introduced in work' of the intervening twenty years. He also sought to 'reconstruct what [he] had in mind while writing [it]' (1–2). These are ostensibly the topics of two different sections (§§II–III), between which, as he remarks, there is 'a certain amount of redundancy'. But the effect of his exposition is to suggest that what was said later in the course of 'theoretical modifications' was in fact exactly what he had always 'had in mind', but simply did not write. For example, there is nothing in the work itself about the acquisition of language. Unlike many of Chomsky's publications, it is well indexed and all nine references (*s.v.* 'language') are to the later introduction. Nevertheless Chomsky says that 'the "realist interpretation" of linguistic theory is assumed throughout'. In this interpretation, 'the principles of [a] theory specify the schematism brought to bear by the child in language acquisition' (45).

This is the kind of autobiographical recollection that, on principle, one can neither wholly trust nor wholly mistrust. On the one hand it is easy for any scholar, even one whose mind is far less full of ideas than Chomsky's, to become convinced that their mature beliefs were clear and fully worked out at a stage when in fact they were still being formed. I have found this in my own experience, when I could have sworn that I said things in early publications that are not in fact there. In this respect Chomsky too is only human – as may have been sensed already in the account he gave at the same time in the 1970s (see also Chomsky, 1975a: 16f.) of what he had originally said about deep structure. On the other hand, it may be thought improbable that such a recollection is without foundation. Even if Chomsky's later ideas had not been born, they may have been in gestation.

In his own account, the reason why he did not at first express them was that 'to raise this issue seemed to me, at the time, too audacious' (Chomsky 1975a: 35). I will therefore try to give an account that may be read in either of two ways. Briefly, as we look at Chomsky's writings from the mid to the late 1950s, we can see a gradual and explicable progression of ideas. That is simply to say that what he argues at one stage goes beyond what he has argued earlier, and in a way that seems sometimes to clarify and sometimes to amend it. This is what I will be mainly concerned to bring out. One may then interpret this progression in one of two senses. In one interpretation it reflects the real development of his thinking: allowing, that is, for normal gaps between conception and publication, it shows the steps by which what was originally obscure or subsidiary was followed through and made central. That is undoubtedly the interpretation that most commentators would have accepted before Chomsky himself set out, some twenty years later, to 'overcome' what he claimed to be 'misunderstandings' (1975a: 45f.). On the other reading, it shows how Chomsky progressively introduced a complex of ideas that he had formed at the beginning, when he was in his mid-twenties, and had sagely decided he would not immediately be able to publish. Instead he chose to reveal them bit by bit, first the less audacious bits and then the more so, until, after some years and with a twitch of the last veil, his philosophy stood naked before us. I think I have to make clear that I am myself inclined to prefer the first interpretation. A sufficient reason is that it seems to me to show his genius in a far more favourable light. But others can, if they wish, maintain the second.

Let us begin with what little was said by Post-Bloomfieldian scholars. In reviewing Harris's *Methods*, Householder drew a distinction that was cited for years afterwards, between two views of the status of linguistic descriptions. In what he called the 'hocus pocus' view, they were a product of a linguist's method and, if the method changed, they would change also. In the other or 'God's Truth' view, a linguist was seeking to describe what was in some sense the real structure of the language (Householder, 1952: 260f.). If one takes this second view, the choice of method clearly cannot be arbitrary. One must be able to make a reasoned choice between methods or criteria that lead towards a true description of the language and others that do not.

On Householder's reading, 'many, many parts' of Harris's book seemed 'pure hocus-pocus' (261). That is the usual interpretation of his work, and there is in general no call to dispute it. But in his paper on 'Distributional structure', which was published two years after Householder's review, he devotes one section to a discussion of the 'Reality of the structure' (1954b: §1.2, *Papers* 6–8). He asks first whether the structure really exists 'in the language'. By a 'language' he means, as we have seen in §3.2, a set of utterances, and his answer is that it does exist, 'as much as any scientific structure really obtains in the data which it describes'. But he then asks whether it really exists 'in the speakers'. 'Clearly', he says, 'certain behaviors of the speakers indicate perception along the lines of the distributional structure.' He cites, for example, the way people imitate sounds in a foreign language; also 'evidences of perception of sounds in terms of their morphophonemic memberships'. For the last point he refers to Sapir's well-known paper on the psychological reality of phonemes (1933). 'A reasonable expectation', he goes on, 'is that the distributional structure should exist in the speakers in the sense of reflecting their speaking habits.' Evidence for this can 'be found in experimental psychology work', with the qualification, however, that 'different speakers differ in the details of distributional perception'. For example, some may 'associate the stem of *nation* with that of *native*' while others do not.

Harris then discusses the specific proposal that, as he puts it, we should 'measure the [speakers'] habits by the new utterances which had not been used in the structural description'. As he remarks in the next paragraph, 'the position of the speakers is . . . similar to that of the linguist'. They too have 'heard (and used) a great many utterances' which, they perceive, have 'parts which occur in various combinations'. They then 'produce new combinations': 'the formation of new utterances in the language is therefore based on the distributional relations – as changeably perceived by the speakers – among the parts of the previously heard utterances'. By a 'habit' Harris means a 'predisposition to form new combinations along particular distributional lines rather than others'; accordingly, 'we know about its existence in the speakers' if 'new formations of the type in question have been formed' by them. For example, the formation of *analyticity* as a term of philosophy confirmed the existence, at that moment, of a habit – that is, a 'readiness to combine [the elements *-ic* and *-ity*] productively' – which also corresponds to part of the linguist's description of distributions.

For this proposal Harris refers to a review by Hockett (1952b), which has already been cited in §3.2. In this, Hockett had talked of the requirement that, in analysing a language, we should 'produce systematization which *in an operational sense* matches the habits which we ascribe to the speaker'. So, in particular, our system must match the ability of speakers to produce and understand new utterances that they have not heard previously (Hockett, 1952b). Such discussion was rare, and Harris's in particular makes contact with the philosophy of the period in the way that Householder's, for example, does not. But they do show that the issue of reality was in the air – and in the mind particularly of Chomsky's teacher – at a time when his own thoughts, which from the beginning are historically more important, were being formed.

What then did he say? One thing that is obvious is that at an early stage he too drew a parallel between a grammar and the ability of a speaker to produce new utterances. The grammar, in his words, 'will *project* the finite and somewhat accidental corpus of utterances to a set (presumably infinite) of grammatical utterances' (Chomsky, 1957: 15). As we have seen in §3.2, where such passages were also cited, this is an extension and a clarification of what Harris and Hockett had been saying. 'In this respect', he goes on, 'a grammar mirrors the behavior of the speaker who, on the basis of a finite and accidental experience with language, can produce or understand an indefinite number of new sentences.' In the published recension of *The Logical Structure of Linguistic Theory*, a similar point is placed right at the beginning. 'We are antecedently interested', he says, 'in developing a theory that will shed some light' on certain facts. The first fact or series of facts concerns this ability. A speaker can produce new utterances on the basis of a limited experience of the language, and can also, Chomsky adds, 'distinguish a certain set of "grammatical" utterances, among utterances that he has never heard and might never produce' (1975a [1955]: 61).

Another fact, as Chomsky puts it, is that 'the speaker has developed a large store of knowledge about his language and a mass of feelings and understandings that we might call 'intuitions about linguistic form"' (62). Thus 'any speaker of English knows', for example, that *keep* and *coop* 'begin with the same "sound"', that *Are they coming* 'is the question corresponding to' *They are coming*, and that *They are flying planes* can be understood in different ways. In the index to the published version (which was not prepared by Chomsky himself), this passage is entered under 'language, knowledge of', along with passages in the introduction which reflect the concept of a speaker's 'tacit knowledge' which Chomsky introduced in the 1960s. But that is surely misleading. For what he is talking about here is precisely 'knowledge about' the language, and the 'intuitions' that are referred to are the subjects of explicit judgments that speakers may volunteer or that may be elicited from them as informants. Nor does he say anything else that looks forward clearly to what he was to say in the future. The problem for a linguistic theory, as he explains it, is to give a general account of 'projection, ambiguity, sentence type, etc., that will provide automatically' for such intuitions (62). But by 'the grammar of a language *L*' we simply mean 'that theory of *L* that attempts to deal with such problems wholly in terms of the formal properties of utterances' (63). The term 'language' is not defined at this point. But the entity about which the speaker has a 'store of knowledge and a mass of feelings and understandings' is again represented later as 'a set ... of strings in a finite alphabet' (71).

In saying that our central problem is to 'shed some light' on these matters, Chomsky says more than any Post-Bloomfieldian had said. But how do we assess how far we have succeeded in doing so? Suppose, for example, that speakers tell us that *the shooting of the hunters* is ambiguous; this fact is accordingly one thing on which we would like to 'shed light'. But it is not enough to write a grammar in which, in whatever way, two different structures are assigned to it. That may shed no light at all, but make a distinction which, in a phrase which soon became part of the everyday vocabulary of linguistics, is merely 'ad hoc'. Instead we have to show that the distinction has a systematic basis. Then, in a view which was current at the time, we can claim to have explained it.

In Chomsky's account, the minimal requirement is that the form of grammar should be able to generate the sentences that we believe to be grammatical. Thus, if we accept the 'theorem' that 'English is not a finite state language', we must accept that 'no theory of linguistic structure based exclusively on Markov process models and the like, will be able to explain or account for the ability of a speaker to produce and understand new utterances, while he rejects other sequences as not belonging to the language' (Chomsky, 1957: 23). Beyond that, however, his essential requirement was that a grammar should be simple. In the case of *the shooting of the hunters*, we try to state rules which will give as simple an account as possible of the distribution of verbs like *shoot*, of nouns like *hunter*, and so on. As we saw in §3.4, that requires us, in particular, to give rules for 'selectional restrictions'. This we do quite independently of any evidence of what a speaker knows about its structure, or about its meaning. We do it, as Harris too had said it should be done, on distributional evidence only. But we then find that the simplest grammar will assign two different structures to *the shooting of the hunters*, in one of which it is related to *the hunters are shooting*, in the other to *were shooting the hunters*. Since this finding rests on arguments independent of the speaker's statement that it is ambiguous, we claim that the grammar explains the ambiguity.

The references for Chomsky's notion of simplicity have been given already. In particular, I have referred in §3.2 to the many passages in *Syntactic Structures* in which, on the basis of a notion of simplicity which he acknowledges to have been 'left unanalyzed' (103), he argues that the rules will be simpler if a transformation is posited. I have also referred in another context (§3.4) to places in *The Logical Structure of Linguistic Theory* where a transformation is explicitly said to simplify the rules for 'selectional restrictions'. The main differences in this respect between the two books are, firstly, that one treatment is enormously longer and fuller; and, secondly, that where in *Syntactic Structures* the case for transformations is at first based on this kind of argument only, in the unpublished work, the first draft of which must date from a year or so earlier, arguments from ambiguities and so on appear from the outset (Chomsky, 1975a: 294ff.). I have also referred, earlier in this section, to a passage in which Chomsky talked of the notion of 'real simplicity' that underlay an evaluation measure. If we ask how we assess two different grammars of the same kind, the immediate answer, in part, is that our theory includes a measure of certain formal properties. In Chomsky's published account these were referred to by 'the word "simplicity"' (1957: 53). But if we then ask how we assess two alternative measures, the answer implied is that we prefer the one that reflects 'real simplicity'. That is, a theory of the kind that Chomsky was exploring is better the more it 'will turn simpler grammars (in some partially understood, presystematic sense of this notion) into shorter grammars' (again 1975a: 118).

In a footnote to his book in the 'Modern Masters' series, Lyons refers to a comment by Chomsky in which he said (this is Lyons's wording) that he was 'not himself aware of any change over the years with respect to the role of simplicity measures and intuition'. In the text, Lyons had remarked that 'in *Syntactic Structures* Chomsky claims that one of the main reasons for preferring a transformational grammar to a phrase structure grammar is that the former is, in a certain sense, simpler than the latter'. This can hardly be disputed by anyone who has read it with an open mind; nor will it be disputed that 'in his later publications' (we are talking now of the period up to the late 1960s) 'Chomsky attaches far less importance to the notion of "simplicity"' (Lyons, 1991 [1970]: 62). But according to Chomsky's comment (63, n. 1), confusion may have been caused by the fact that *Syntactic Structures* was (in Chomsky's words) 'a rather watered-down version of earlier work (at that time unpublishable)'. For that reason, he says, it 'emphasized weak rather than strong generative capacity'.

But this remark of Chomsky's is surely not quite to the point. The 'weak generative capacity' of a theory is defined in the 1960s as the class of languages – that is, sets of sentences – that grammars of the form proposed can generate (Chomsky, 1965: 60). The term was not used in the 1950s; but, for example, the weak generative capacity of finite state Markov processes is such that, if Chomsky's argument held, they were inadequate for English. This particular argument is not, as it happens, in his then 'unpublishable' work (1975a); but it has nothing whatever to do with the case for transformations. To rephrase what is said in *Syntactic Structures*, Chomsky '[did] not know' (34) whether English was within the weak generative capacity of phrase structure grammars. Instead he argued, in the first instance, that a grammar which included transformations would be simpler.

By the 'strong generative capacity' of a theory, Chomsky refers to the class of 'system[s] of structural descriptions' that grammars of the form proposed can assign to the sets of sentences they can generate (again 1965: 60). Although this too was not a term used in the 1950s, we can again see how what was said at the time might be rephrased. For example, it is within the strong generative capacity of a transformational grammar to assign two different structural descriptions to phrases like *the shooting of the hunters*, while 'there is no good way' (Chomsky, 1957: 88) for phrase structure grammars to do so. This was the only kind of argument about the generative capacity of phrase structure and transformational grammars, and it is precisely about 'strong generative capacity'. Other arguments are indeed 'emphasised' more; but they are not about weak generative capacity. As we have seen, they are about simplicity.

Let us now return to the topic of intuition. The word appears rarely in *Syntactic Structures*: in particular, Chomsky does not say at the outset, as he does in the published recension of his longer work, that a major object is to 'shed light' on a speaker's 'intuitions about linguistic form'. It is in that respect, if any, that the thesis is 'watered down'. But let us look back to the account he had given of phonological analysis. According to many scholars, this involved an appeal to meaning. For example, we want to know if *pit* and *bit* begin with the same phoneme; therefore we ask if they mean the same. But Chomsky argues that, since there are phonemically distinct forms with the same meaning (such as /ekənamiks/ and /iykənamiks/) and phonemically identical forms with different meanings (like the two meanings of *bank*), this cannot be right (1955a: 143f.; 1957: 95). Instead, with Harris and others, he advocates what was called a 'pair test'. For example, we want to 'discover whether there is a phonemic difference', in certain dialects of English, between forms like *latter* and *ladder*. We therefore take two utterances, one containing one form and the other the other; we perhaps record them on tape; and we 'play them repeatedly in random order to an informant, and see whether he can consistently and correctly identify them' (1955a: 144; compare 1957: 96). 'The pair test', Chomsky says, 'is one of the operational cornerstones for linguistic theory' (1955a: 145).

How does this relate to intuition? 'The major goal of methodological work in linguistics', as Chomsky puts it in this article, 'is to avoid intuition about linguistic form, replacing it by some explicit and systematic account' (1955a: 149). In the words of *Syntactic Structures* (94), 'the major goal of grammatical theory is to replace [an] obscure reliance on intuition by some rigorous and objective approach'. This is what the pair test offered. Until it is developed, 'we have only our intuition that *pit* and *pull* begin with the same phoneme, while *pit* and *bit* do not' (1955a: 148). Chomsky stresses once more that there is 'nothing semantic about' this. The pair test thus 'enables us to avoid this reliance on intuition' (149). It 'provides us with a clear operational criterion for phonemic distinctness' (1957: 97), again 'in completely non-semantic terms'.

The problem was to develop a similarly 'rigorous and objective approach' in syntax. Take first the question of grammaticalness. Before we develop an account of this notion 'as a part of linguistic theory', we again 'have only our intuition about form to tell us that *this is a round square* is a grammatical (though nonsensical) sentence, whereas *this are a round square* is not' (1955a: 148f.). Again Chomsky stresses that 'there is nothing semantic about this intuition'. But in the case of this and 'many other linguistic notions', 'an effective way to replace intuition about form has yet to be demonstrated'. All that Chomsky says, in this article, is that 'there is no reason to introduce "meaning" into such a conception of linguistic theory'. If the appeal to it is 'irrelevant at other points in the theory' (as he has argued in the case of phonemic distinctness), 'we are entitled to say that [it] functions as a dangerous bypass . . .'. It is dangerous because 'it gives the illusion of being a real explanation', when in fact it is 'merely avoidance of the problem'.

It would be unsafe to attempt too close an analysis of *The Logical Structure of Linguistic Theory*. The version in print was not revised for publication until the 1970s, and, even in those circulating in the 1950s, it was a series of time-exposed snapshots of thoughts developing. But it is not difficult to see where the heart of the problem lay. On the one hand, Chomsky wanted to argue that a grammar should assign appropriate structural descriptions to, for example, *the shooting of the hunters*. In the terms in which the example is discussed in this work, there is an 'intuitively felt difference in structure that is not properly accounted for' (1975a: 296) in a phrase structure grammar. That is because 'the relevant distinction . . . is . . . in the relation between the verb and the noun of the following prepositional phrase'; and all a phrase structure grammar can do is distinguish the verb as either transitive or intransitive (297). As most scholars would have seen it, intuitions like this involve judgments of meaning. The speaker knows, in Chomsky's own words, that 'many sentences can be understood in several ways', that they 'are ambiguous' (62). Similarly – or similarly to all appearances – Wells had argued eight years earlier that phrases like *old men and women* had two different meanings, and that the semantic difference correlated with a formal distinction revealed by immediate constituent analysis (1947b: *RiL* 193).

On the other hand, Chomsky had argued that to appeal to meaning was to avoid the problem. We could not simply say that we need a transformational grammar because phrases like this differ in meaning in this kind of way. Nor could we appeal directly to 'intuitions about linguistic form'. Therefore we could not simply say that we need a transformational grammar because a speaker knows intuitively that the phrase has these different structures. If arguments that might be taken in either of these ways seem to be offered at the beginning of his chapter on transformations, they must, if Chomsky is to be true to his principles, be no more than a *captatio benevolentiae*. We have to find some 'rigorous and objective approach' by which an 'obscure reliance on intuition' can be avoided.

This is in effect the dilemma that the programme of *Syntactic Structures* tried so brilliantly to resolve. As Chomsky explains earlier in a more general context, we first assign descriptions to sentences at the transformational and other levels 'so as to lead to the simplest grammar'. For example, we simplify the rules for *the shooting of the hunters* by allowing alternative descriptions of its syntax. We then find that 'there are, in specific instances, correspondences with strong intuition about language structure'. For example, speakers have strong intuitions about the ambiguity of *the shooting of the hunters*. 'This result' may then 'be interpreted as giving an explanation, in terms of a theory of linguistic structure, for these intuitions of the native speaker' (Chomsky, 1975a: 294). But although this solution was a beautiful extension of the distributional method, and for that reason (if we accept Chomsky's later assurance that he was concealing his true beliefs) would have been well calculated rhetorically to put his programme over, it is hard to see how an ultimate reliance on intuition could have been said to be avoided. In his article in 1955, Chomsky had stressed that such avoidance was essential; moreover, he referred to intuitions not just about matters such as ambiguity, but even about grammaticality. We had, as he had said, to replace reliance on intuition with some 'explicit and systematic' account. But it now seems that we are treating judgments of all kinds as part of our data. As Lees said in this review of *Syntactic Structures*, 'the empirical data which a linguistic theory must explain consists not only of the noises which talking people produce, but also of various kinds of judgments they can make and feelings they may have about linguistic data'. These judgments, 'sometimes referred to as linguistic intuitions', are, he repeats, 'part of the linguistic data to be accounted for' (Lees, 1957: 376).

Early readers of *Syntactic Structures* searched in vain for a clear statement that this was so. But the issue came up several times in the discussion at the Third Texas Conference in 1958. Towards the end, Chomsky says that he 'dislike[s] reliance on intuition as much as anyone, but if we are in such a bad state that it is only intuition that we are using, then', he feels, 'we should admit it'. We must, however, 'try to refine it by testing'. If we can then 'get to a point where we have refined our basis by theoretical investigations and operational tests', he will be 'very happy to stop saying that we start with the intuition of the native speaker' (Hill, ed. 1962: [1958]: 177f.). An example of such refinement would perhaps be the procedures which are envisaged a little later to 'elicit differential responses' bearing on grammaticalness (181). But for the moment reliance on the speakers' intuitions cannot be avoided. 'Intuition', Chomsky said, 'is just what I think I am describing.' 'The empirical data that I want to explain', he goes on, 'are the native speaker's intuitions' (158). If that is not accepted as 'the purpose of linguistic study', he is 'lost' (168). These remarks are almost all from interchanges with Hill, who drew him out repeatedly on this point. In another passage, Hill remarks that 'if I took some of your statements literally, I would say that you are not studying language at all, but some form of psychology, the intuitions of native speakers'. 'That', Chomsky replied, 'is studying language' (167).

Moreover, it seems hard to deny that some of these intuitions are about meaning. In *The Logical Structure of Linguistic Theory*, Chomsky had talked, as we have seen, of 'intuitions about linguistic form'. Since these were distinguished at this time from intuitions about meaning, the implication seems to have been that, if speakers say that phrases like *the shooting of the hunters* are ambiguous, they are simply telling us that they have two different formal constructions. In *Syntactic Structures* he does not generally talk of intuitions. But 'what we are suggesting', in the chapter on the explanatory power of theories, 'is that the notion of "understanding a sentence" be explained in part' in terms of its representation on successive linguistic levels (87). This is made clearer in the following chapter, on 'Syntax and semantics'. What he was saying, Chomsky remarks, is that both grammars and theories of grammar can be judged 'in terms of their ability to explain a variety of facts about the way in which sentences are used and understood'. 'In other words', he goes on, 'we would like the syntactic framework of the language that is isolated and exhibited by the grammar to be able to support semantic description, and we shall naturally rate more highly a theory of formal structure that leads to grammars that meet this requirement more fully' (102).

In short, it was clear to Chomsky at least by the Third Texas Conference that our object in studying language was to account for intuitions. It was also clear at least when *Syntactic Structures* went to the press that a theory of grammar might be assessed directly by semantic criteria. But what in that case is the status of the grammar itself? In the view that Chomsky had inherited from Harris, it was again a formal characterisation of the distributional structure of a certain set of sentences. It said nothing itself about meaning, or about the psychological basis for the intuitive judgments that speakers make. That is as true of the grammar of *Syntactic Structures* as of Harris's 'description of the language structure'. But Harris himself had also asked how far this structure existed 'in the speakers' (see again Harris, 1954b). In retrospect at least, it seems surprising that Chomsky did not immediately follow him.

In his own account, the issue of 'the "psychological analogue" to the methodological problem of constructing linguistic theory' did lie 'in the immediate background' of his thinking (see again 1975a: 35). The implication is that it would once more have been 'too audacious' to say even as much as Harris had said on the subject. He also points out that the issue was 'raised explicitly' in Lees's review (1957) of his book. But if Lees's remarks are any reflection of what Chomsky himself was thinking, they confirm that he had not yet clearly formulated his mature view. In a section on the implications for learning theory, Lees talks of 'the speaker's generation of the grammatical sentences of his language'. 'We cannot look', he says, 'into a human speaker's head to see just what kind of device he uses there with which to generate' them; however, we can 'construct a model which . . . generates those sentences in the same way as the human speaker'. This model is by implication the grammar. Granted the method as Lees goes on to describe it, 'it is not too much to assume that human beings talk in the same way that our grammar "talks"' (Lees, 1957: 406f.). In later years, Chomsky was to complain that he had been misunderstood in just this sense. In speaking of a device that generated sentences, he stressed that he was saying nothing about their actual production by a speaker. But if he was indeed misunderstood, it was because most scholars had read Lees's review before they read his own book, and had pardonably assumed that what Lees said was the gospel he too was preaching.

In the development of his own thinking – or, if we prefer, in the progressive unveiling of the 'background' to it – the crucial stage is marked by his review in 1959 of Skinner's *Verbal Behavior*. Before this he had said at one point that grammars were concerned with neither 'the process of producing utterances' nor 'the "inverse" process of analyzing and reconstructing the structure of given utterances'. 'In fact, these two tasks which the speaker and hearer must perform are essentially the same, and are both outside the scope' of the form of grammar he proposes (1957: 48). This does not say quite what he says later: in particular, a grammar is still 'simply a description of a certain set of utterances'. But it is at least not incompatible with it. At another point, however, he says that 'if we can adopt' a finite state conception of language, 'we can view the speaker as being essentially a machine of the type considered'. 'In producing a sentence', a speaker would then 'begin[ ] in the initial state, produce[ ] the first word of the sentence, thereby switching into a second state' and so on (1957: 20). This seems to be entirely compatible with what Lees says in his review. In short, one has the impression that, very understandably, he was still sorting out his ideas.

But in reviewing Skinner Chomsky had to consider seriously both what enables speakers to do what they can do and how they acquire this ability. After describing a grammar in the terms by now familiar, he points out that 'the construction of a grammar ... does not in itself provide an account of ... actual behavior'. Instead it – that is, 'the construction of a grammar' – merely characterises abstractly the ability of one who has mastered the language to distinguish sentences from nonsentences, to understand new sentences (in part), to note certain ambiguities, etc.' (Chomsky, 1959: 56). But the word 'merely' conceals the beginning of an argument that was in fact new. For in the paragraph that follows Chomsky takes it as an assumption that a speaker or listener has 'acquired the capacity characterised abstractly by the grammar' (56f.). The task of someone who is speaking is then to 'select a particular compatible set of optional rules': so, by implication, what the grammar characterises is itself a series of rules. 'A child who learns a language' has thus 'in some sense constructed a grammar for himself'. It is a 'fact' (next paragraph) that 'all normal children acquire essentially comparable grammars of great complexity'. That is, what the grammar characterises is itself a grammar.

This argument did not become central – alternatively, Chomsky prudently refrained from presenting it as central – until six years later, in the first chapter of *Aspects of the Theory of Syntax*. But once he started to think in this way, it must have become clear that both grammars and theories of grammar had to be justified in a new way. Suppose once more that we are considering whether English is better described by a phrase structure or a transformational grammar. The initial question can no longer be: which form of grammar is simpler? Instead we have to ask directly which is right – which, that is, correctly represents the rules that speakers themselves have 'in some sense constructed'. Suppose that we are trying to develop an evaluation measure that will choose between alternative transformational grammars. The initial criterion cannot be that grammars which are shorter must in some 'real' sense be simpler. Instead it must be that they give a truer account of the speakers' own 'grammars'. In this framework, there is no place for an independent appeal to simplicity, not even to the 'explanatory power' of grammars that are simpler.

Instead there are two ways in which an individual grammar may be justified. Firstly, it may be confirmed directly by our data. That is, we will know, from spontaneous evidence of speakers' intuitions or by quizzing them and forcing them to introspect, that it is, so far as we can tell, empirically correct. In the terms which Chomsky was to introduce in *Aspects of the Theory of Syntax*, this establishes that it is 'descriptively adequate' (Chomsky, 1965: 24). Secondly, it may be justified indirectly, by a theory of grammar. Such a theory specifies a certain form of grammar and an evaluation measure, and we can then show that, for a given language, our particular grammar is, so far as we can tell, the best that it makes available. But the theory must itself be justified empirically. That is, we must show that other theories do not lead to grammars which are truer accounts of speakers' 'grammars'. In the terms of *Aspects of the Theory of Syntax*, this would establish that the theory is 'explanatorily adequate' (Chomsky, 1965: 25).

In the mid-1960s Chomsky was to complain that his notion of simplicity had been 'grossly misunderstood' (1965: 38). All he was talking about was a 'simplicity measure' internal to a linguistic theory, which, being internal to it, was part of an empirical hypothesis. That was indeed one sense, as we have seen, in which the term had been used in *Syntactic Structures* (again Chomsky, 1957: 53). But it had also been used, time and time again, in arguing, ahead of any formulation of an evaluation measure, that, in particular, a transformational grammar would be simpler than a phrase structure grammar. On both points he had surely been understood perfectly. But, as his concept of the psychological reality of grammars had developed, the latter form of argument, however vital it had seemed in establishing his theory of syntax in the first place, had to be abandoned.

4.2 Chomsky's classic period

In his account of the battle of El Alamein, Liddell Hart (1970: 315) comments on Montgomery's 'adaptability and versatility' in devising a fresh plan when his initial thrust had failed. It was 'a better tribute to his generalship' than his own habit of talking as if everything had gone as he intended. One might say much the same of Chomsky, both in the period from the mid-1950s to the early 1960s and, as we will see, in a later period that extends roughly over the 1970s. Between these, however, lies what we may call his classic phase. It is classic for various reasons. Firstly, although it was very brief, it was immensely productive. A space of four years saw the publication first of *Aspects of the Theory of Syntax* (1965); then of his lectures to the 1964 Linguistic Institute (Chomsky, 1966a) and, in the same year, an excursion into the history of linguistics (Chomsky, 1966b); finally, of an important set of lectures given to a general audience (Chomsky, 1972b [1968]) and the culmination of his joint work with Halle on phonology (Chomsky & Halle, 1968). Few scholars can have published so much, of such value and on such varied topics, in such a short time.

Secondly, it is this work that won Chomsky his academic reputation outside linguistics. His following within the discipline, if we leave aside Lees, Halle and a handful of others, dates from around 1960; from a time, that is, when his general ideas (or his public exposition of them) had almost reached their mature state. But when these ideas were finally unveiled, they attracted attention far beyond, in philosophy and psychology especially but even, by the 1970s, in disciplines not apparently concerned with language at all. A quarter of a century later, the view that many people have of Chomskyan linguistics is still rooted in what he said in the 1960s and in the huge amount of secondary discussion devoted to it. This includes many linguists, especially when their own interests are different and they have learned these ideas through textbooks.

Finally, the ideas themselves have a classic elegance and neatness. In later years it became clear that they were too neat by half, and few of them, and those only the most general, were to survive unmodified for more than a decade. But at the time they were remarkably easy to teach, even to students who found Chomsky's own exposition, especially in *Aspects of the Theory of Syntax*, very difficult. As ideas changed, it was therefore natural both for commentators and for Chomsky himself to take this period as the starting-point and then show how or why this aspect or that aspect of the original theory had been, or would have to be, modified. By the 1980s it was time for a new synthesis. But the earlier one had been so beautiful that many who had originally been attracted by it seemed reluctant to let it slip into history.

Of the ideas in question, some were already adumbrated in Chomsky's review of Skinner (see §4.1). But for the rest the most important change was the addition to a generative grammar of rules relating syntactic structures to meanings. There had been no such rules in *Syntactic Structures*, whose programme had originated, as we have seen, in an attempt to develop a grammar of explanatory power which would be based on distributional facts only. But in the wake, it seems, of his review of Skinner, Chomsky had begun to talk of a grammar as representing part of what he called a speaker's 'competence' in a language. 'Each normal human', as he remarked to the Ninth International Congress of Linguists, 'has developed for himself a thorough competence in his native language.' 'This competence', he says, 'can be represented, to an as yet undetermined extent, as a system of rules that we can call the *grammar* of his language' (1964 [1962]: 915). The grammar proposed at that stage still contained no more than 'a *syntactic component* and a *phonological component*'. But since anyone who is competent in a language evidently knows what words and utterances mean, a grammar will be much more nearly a complete account of their competence if it deals with meanings also. Chomsky did not say that this was his reasoning. But in the year in which this lecture was published, Katz and Postal argued that 'a linguistic description must reconstruct the principles underlying the ability of speakers to communicate with one another'. Accordingly, they set out to develop an 'integrated conception of the nature' of such descriptions, in which they sought to extend work on generative grammar 'by bringing it in line with recent developments in semantics' (1964: 1). In his lectures to the Linguistic Institute that summer, Chomsky (1966a [1964]) immediately followed them.

In commenting later on this and related developments, Chomsky remarks that the 'approach' in *Syntactic Structures* and *The Logical Structure of Linguistic Theory* 'was vague about the notion "semantic representation"' (1975a: 22). Indeed neither the term nor the concept appears in them. What is more interesting, however, is the reply he had made a little earlier to a paper by Bar-Hillel (1954) on logical syntax and semantics. The gist of Bar-Hillel's proposal was that, in descriptions of ordinary languages, '*logical analysis*, based upon the relation of *direct consequence*, will have to be given equal rights with *distributional analysis*' (232). Take, for example, the synonymy (as it was assumed) of *oculist* and *eye doctor*. A distributional analysis will show that each can be substituted for the other in certain contexts. The same is true, for example, of *oculist* and *dentist*. But a logical analysis will add that *oculist* and *eye doctor* stand in a relationship of formal consequence. They are '*logically*' substitutable (or substitutable '*salva veritate*'), whereas *oculist* and *dentist* are only '*distributionally* substitutable' (or substitutable '*salva significatione*') (233f.). Through the work of logicians, semantics had now 'become a well-defined, rigorous field'; and just as this had 'caused Carnap to reintroduce it into logic', so it should 'cause descriptive linguists to follow [his] lead' (237).

Chomsky's reply (1955b) is of a piece with his article on 'Semantic considerations in grammar' (1955a), cited in the last section. In Bar-Hillel's argument as he saw it, 'there are certain "rigorous, structural procedures", over and above distributional procedures', that linguists ought to import from logic (38). We also need 'a new approach ... that will yield reliable techniques of elicitation for the establishment of synonymy and the like' (37; Bar-Hillel, 1954: 237). But in the absence of what Chomsky calls 'an adequate operational, behavioral account of synonymy' (37), the procedure Bar-Hillel is recommending is simply to list, for example, such meaning postulates as *An oculist is an eye doctor*. 'If a linguist has qualms about establishing or using somehow the fact that *oculist* and *eye-doctor* are synonyms, he can avoid all fear of mentalism by the formal procedure of setting down this fact as a meaning postulate' (38). If he is 'concerned about the question why [this] is a meaning postulate, while *Washington is the capital of the United States* is not, he can be assured that there is a rigorous procedure for making this distinction, namely, to list the former sentence under the heading "meaning postulates" and not to list the latter'. But 'such an ad-hoc approach to the problem ... will be of no help to linguists, who are interested in the *general grounds*' on which relations are established. If we have 'an operational account', this procedure of 'arbitrary listing' will not be needed (39). But if we do not have such an account, it is 'obviously useless'.

This article is not mentioned in *Syntactic Structures*; nor, so far as I can discover, in any of Chomsky's later publications. It is also neglected in the official history of transformational-generative grammar by Newmeyer (1980). But if we compare these views with those that Chomsky appeared to hold with equal conviction ten years later, it is hard not to conclude that, for the moment at least, he had pretty well completely changed his mind. For the proposal of Katz and his collaborators was precisely to enlarge a generative grammar by what Bar-Hillel had called a 'logical analysis'. *Oculist* and *eye doctor*, let us say, are synonymous. For example, *Smith is an eye doctor* is a 'direct consequence' of *Smith is an oculist*, and vice versa. We therefore assign the same semantic features to them. To be precise, we add to the grammar a dictionary in which *oculist* is assigned a set of features identical to those resulting from the amalgamation, by what was called a 'projection rule', of the features of *eye* and *doctor*. By further applications of that rule, *Smith is an oculist* and *Smith is an eye doctor* will then have identical 'readings' or semantic representations. No 'operational, behavioral account' lies behind this. Speakers are simply said to know that such sentences are synonymous, or are 'paraphrases' of each other, and the grammar must represent that knowledge.

At the same time, Chomsky cut loose from his earlier notion that an account of meaning is concerned with the use of sentences. In *Syntactic Structures*, he had compared language to an 'instrument or tool', whose structure could initially be described 'with no explicit reference to the way in which this instrument is put to use' (1957: 103). Thus, to develop the analogy, one might in principle describe the structure of a knife – handle, blade and so on – without reference to the fact that it is used for cutting. For language, this was the field of grammar, and of syntax especially, as Chomsky conceived it at that time. To study meaning was then to study what the speakers of a language did with this instrument. 'How', as Chomsky put it, 'are the syntactic devices available in a given language put to work in the actual use of this language?' (93). It is hardly surprising that he said nothing, even vaguely, about 'semantic representations'. For the notion does not belong in that kind of theory.

But by the mid 1960s the distinction between language and the use of language had been redrawn. We have seen already how a grammar could be said to represent, 'to an as yet undetermined extent', a speaker's 'competence in his native language' (see again Chomsky, 1964 [1962]: 915). But in the work that followed the qualification was implicitly removed. By 'competence' we mean 'the speaker-hearer's knowledge of his language' (Chomsky, 1965: 4), and this must naturally include a knowledge of the meanings of its words and sentences, as well as of their form. There is therefore a potential discrepancy between this aspect of a speaker's 'knowledge' and 'the actual use of language in concrete situations'. Suppose, for instance, that I utter the sentence *It is very warm in here*, meaning in the 'concrete situation' that I am feeling too hot and would like the heating turned down. Then suppose that in another 'concrete situation' I utter the same sentence, meaning this time that I feel snug and comfortable. It is tempting to argue that this has nothing to do with my underlying knowledge of its meaning. I 'know', as a native speaker-hearer, how the meaning of this sentence differs, in isolation, from those of other sentences such as *It is very cold in here* or *It is very warm outside*. This is what Chomsky was later to call, in *Language and Mind* and elsewhere, its 'intrinsic meaning', and a description of that meaning, which is by definition an abstraction from any specific situation in which the sentence might be uttered, can with perfect propriety be called its 'semantic representation' or, with further implications, its 'semantic interpretation'. The rest is then precisely a matter of 'actual use ... in concrete situations'. In Chomsky's terms (again 1965: 4), it is a matter not of 'competence', but of 'performance'.

I have said that it is 'tempting to argue' in this way. Certainly many did so, and although Chomsky's own remarks on the nature of semantic representations were at best programmatic, it does not seem unlikely that for a brief period in the mid-1960s, before he began to reflect more seriously on the problem, he too would have argued in the same way. There is therefore a distinction, within the treatment of meaning, between what belongs to the characterisation of the 'instrument' (the speaker's 'competence') and what belongs again to the use the speaker makes of it. The knife, if we may resume the analogy, is used for cutting. I might on one occasion use it for one job, say to cut string; on another occasion in another way, say to slice onions. That is still contingent, or, in Chomsky's terms, a matter of 'performance'. But I 'know', in general, that a knife is used for cutting. Therefore an account of the instrument must be more than a description of its physical components – handle, metal projection with a point and a sharp edge, and so on. It must also say what, in abstraction, it is for. When applied to language, this leads to a distinction very similar to that which Bloomfield tried to draw in the 1930s between the total meaning of an utterance and the specifically '*distinctive*, or *linguistic* meaning' (Bloomfield, 1935: 141) of forms. The latter was supposed to be common to all the situations in which a form was uttered. For example, in describing the linguistic meaning of *It is very warm in here* we would identify it as a statement about the temperature in some enclosed space, in abstraction from whether, on specific occasions, it is intended as a compliment to a host, a hint to open the window, or whatever. The linguistic meaning of a complex form can then be derived from simpler components. In Bloomfield's terminology, morphemes are associated in the lexicon with sememes, and contructions are associated in the grammar with further meanings, called episememes. As Chomsky put it, a lexical entry must specify the 'properties of the formative that are relevant for semantic interpretation' (1965: 88). These are the 'components of the dictionary definition'. From these properties and an account of syntactic structures the semantic interpretation of any larger form, up to and including the 'intrinsic meaning' of a sentence, may be derived.

The remaining ideas of Chomsky's classic period were more explicitly developed, and involve, in particular, the reinterpretation of linguistic theory as a theory of the acquisition of language. We have already seen how Hockett and Harris had compared the task of a linguist seeking to analyse a language to that of a child who has to learn it (Hockett, 1948: *RiL* 279; Harris, 1954b: *Papers* 7). We have also seen how Chomsky had talked, in his review of Skinner, of a speaker having 'in some sense constructed' a grammar (1959: 57). In the case of Hockett and Harris, these remarks make no more than a comparison: it would be wrong to pretend, as Chomsky was to do for his own ends in a passage we will come back to later in this section, that the 'taxonomic, data-processing approach of modern linguistics' represented an 'empiricist view' of learning (Chomsky, 1965: 52). But his review of Skinner was the first straw in a new wind. In the work that followed not only was a grammar reified as a set of rules constructed in a child's mind. A theory of grammar was in turn reified, as an innate structure that partly determines how this will be done.

The reification is made clear in *Aspects of the Theory of Syntax*. In a passage which is arguably one of the most important that he has ever written, Chomsky begins by assuming that children learning a language construct systems of rules. 'Clearly', in his own words, 'a child who has learned a language has developed an internal representation of a system of rules that determine how sentences are to be formed, used, and understood' (Chomsky, 1965: 25). He therefore uses 'the term "grammar" with a systematic ambiguity'. 'First', he says, it refers to 'the native speaker's internally represented "theory of his language"'; then 'second, to the linguist's account of this'. Using the term in this way, 'we can say that the child has developed and internally represented a generative grammar'. Again, 'the child constructs a grammar' (there is now no qualifying 'in some sense'): 'that is, a theory of the language ...'. Chomsky then uses the term 'linguistic theory' with a similar 'systematic ambiguity'. From what has been said, it follows that 'the child must have a method for devising an appropriate grammar'. That is (by implication, since this is the sentence that immediately follows), 'he must possess, first, a linguistic theory that specifies the form of a grammar of a possible human language, and, second, a strategy for selecting a grammar of the appropriate form that is compatible with the primary linguistic data'. So, 'as a long-range task for general linguistics, we might set the problem of developing an account of this innate linguistic theory that provides the basis for language learning'.

My immediate reaction to this passage is on record, in one of the few serious reviews that Chomsky's book received (Matthews, 1967: 121f.). As a historian, over a quarter of a century later, I find it even more remarkable. In the first place, it effectively changed the real, and still more the ostensible, direction of linguistic theory. For the majority of scholars, and increasingly not just in the United States, the goal has since become essentially what Chomsky said it should be at this time, and for every one who has taken the trouble to think the idea through, there are doubtless a dozen, especially in Chomsky's own to an outsider overwhelmingly conformist country, who recite and teach it. For many linguists, to be committed to theory can only mean to be committed to this.

Secondly, Chomsky achieved this major change of direction without apparently having to change anything else. A 'grammar' was now, in one sense, something internal to a speaker. Let us call this a grammar in sense 1, or 'grammar$_1$'. In another sense, a 'grammar' was, as it had previously been, a series of statements constructed by a linguist. Let us call that a grammar in sense 2, or 'grammar$_2$'. The main point, therefore, was that a grammar$_2$ was now to be interpreted not just as a characterisation of a language – that is, of a set of potential utterances in the sense of Bloomfield, Harris or *Syntactic Structures* – but as an account of what enables a speaker to speak and understand it. A grammar$_2$ is thus an account of, or description of, or theory about, a grammar$_1$. But at the same time it was assumed that grammars$_1$ had essentially the properties that grammars$_2$

already had. They too were 'system[s] of rules'. They too had levels or components, such as a phonological component or a level of surface structure. They too, by implication, were internally consistent and free of redundancy. They too were constructed by the speaker in a maximally simple form, given some definition of simplicity. Under such assumptions, the practice of writing $grammars_2$ could continue unchanged. All that had happened was that our object in writing them had been redefined.

As for grammars, so for theories of grammar. A theory in one sense ('$theory_1$') is now seen as internal to a child. This is the 'innate linguistic theory that provides the basis for language learning'. In another sense ('$theory_2$') it is a hypothesis put forward by a linguist; and, in Chomsky's 'long-range' programme, such a $theory_2$ is now an account of, or hypothesis about, a $theory_1$ that (we assume) all normal children share. But it is further assumed that this 'innate linguistic theory' has essentially the character that $theories_2$ had had in the 1950s. It specifies 'the form of the grammar of a possible human language': correspondingly, as Chomsky puts it later, $theories_2$ which aim to give an adequate account of it must 'provide for ... an enumeration of the class G_1, G_2 ... of generative grammars' (1965: 31). It also specifies 'a strategy for selecting a grammar of the appropriate form' (25). So, a $theory_2$ that aims to give an adequate account of it must provide an evaluation measure: 'a specification', as Chomsky puts it, 'of a function m such that $m(i)$ is an integer associated with the grammar G_i as its value' (31). The later passage lists three other things that 'a child who is capable of language learning must have'. For example, children must have 'some initial delimitation of a class of possible hypotheses about language structure' (30). So, a $theory_2$ which aims to represent this $theory_1$ must provide for ... an enumeration of the class SD_1, SD_2, ... of possible structural descriptions'.

The reification is thus complete on both levels. A $theory_2$ is now interpreted as a linguist's account of the child's $theory_1$, a $grammar_2$ as an account of a resulting $grammar_1$. But both the $theory_1$ and the resulting $grammars_1$ are assumed to have the properties that $theories_2$ and $grammars_2$ had had in Chomsky's earlier work, before he resolved to interpret them in this way or (if one accepts his own assurances about his real beliefs in the 1950s) before he finally dared to reveal to the world that that was how he was interpreting them. Therefore the ways in practice in which $theories_2$ and $grammars_2$ were developed did not change in the slightest. In the three remaining chapters of Chomsky's own book no evidence is used or argument adduced that would not be acceptable in principle to someone who still thought that the aims of generative grammar should be, in these respects, as they had been (or had been presented as being) in *Syntactic Structures*. Although the whole object is ostensibly to propose a theory of the acquisition of language, the index (*s.v.* 'language learning') records just one passing reference in these chapters (171f.) to it.

Finally, it is remarkable that Chomsky offered so little justification for what he said. Take first the proposition that, to be an adequate account of the child's theory$_1$, a theory$_2$ had to provide for an evaluation measure. This was scarcely, in the event, uncontroversial. A few years later, one of Chomsky's followers pointed out that 'it is not evident that any notion of "evaluation measure" is needed to explicate learning'. It might be that 'each time the child revises his grammar he simply selects at random one of a set of possible modifications'; accordingly, the 'explication of language learning' would require instead 'a characterization of the possible revisions which a learner may make in his grammars' (McCawley, 1968d: [1976: 172]). Yet it seems that Chomsky thought this aspect of the reification quite straightforward. A child had to have a method for arriving at a grammar. In the account he had given in the 1950s, linguists' grammars (grammars$_2$) were justified by an evaluation procedure. So, he seems to have assumed that the child's 'strategy for selecting a grammar' should be characterised in the same way.

Let us now turn to the most basic proposition, that a child internalises a system of rules. The notion of a rule is introduced quite casually in Chomsky's early work. In *Syntactic Structures*, it first appears in the chapter on 'Phrase structure': each 'rule $X \rightarrow Y$', as Chomsky calls it, is interpreted as 'the instruction "rewrite X as Y"' (1957: 26). In the published version of *The Logical Structure of Linguistic Theory* these are at first called 'statements' (1975a [1955]: 67). But 'rule' appears at the beginning of the second chapter. A grammar, he says, can be considered a theory; a theory proposes general laws; and an utterance is a consequence of a grammar if its structure 'conforms to the grammatical rules, or the laws, of the theory' (77). The notion that a grammar included rules would have been familiar to anyone, and the conception of it as in its entirety a set or system of rules seems to have been introduced without comment. It is worth remarking that when the longer work was finally published, the indexer seems to have decided that a general entry for the term was not needed.

Whether or not this had been controversial, it rapidly became clear that the notion of internalised rules was. The knowledge that they were said to constitute was unconscious, and although subjects might again have intuitions about the grammar of particular sentences – even 'tacit knowledge' that, as Chomsky argued, might be brought to a level of consciousness – it was neither argued nor suggested that by similar methods (see 1965: 21ff.) a linguist might elicit an awareness of the rules themselves. Nor was it a notion that had been justified in another discipline. As Milner reminds us in his recent treatise on linguistic theory, 'la notion de "règle inconnue"', though since adopted by so-called 'cognitive scientists' especially, 'n'a qu'un seul appui dans les sciences, c'est la linguistique de [MIT]' (1989: 252). The term 'internalise' is also used in what seems virtually to have been a new sense. Of the citations in the Supplement to the *OED*, those earlier than 1959, when it starts to appear in Chomsky's writings, are in or derive from psychoanalysis. The sense as defined is 'to transfer to a subjectively formed image (the emotions connected with some object)' (Burchfield, 1976: *s.v.*; see also citations *s.vv.* 'internalisation', 'internalised'). But a grammar is an external object only in the sense of what I have called a $grammar_2$, and there is no suggestion that a learner 'internalises' (feelings about) that. The Supplement rightly distinguishes Chomsky's usage as a new sense, specific to linguistics (*s.v.* 'internalise', §b).

A historian is not, of course, concerned with whether this idea was good or bad. But, in retrospect, it seems surprising that Chomsky should have presented it as uncontroversial. In the passage on 'systematic ambiguities' (1965: 25), he begins with the adverb 'clearly'. 'Clearly' (to repeat), 'a child who has learned a language has developed an internal representation of a system of rules . . . '. In an earlier passage, 'obviously' is used instead: 'Obviously', Chomsky says, 'every speaker of a language has mastered and internalized a generative grammar that expresses his knowledge of his language' (8). It is worth reminding ourselves again that this central idea is among those introduced in a chapter with the disarming title 'Methodological preliminaries'. Was this simply a delightful disingenuousness? Or had Chomsky lived with this conception so long (at least, on the evidence of published writings, since his review of Skinner) that, when he came to develop it systematically, he believed that anyone of sense and good will would accept it?

Of the ideas associated with it, the most important was that a linguistic theory should not only investigate linguistic universals, but should 'attribute[ ] tacit knowledge of these universals to the child'. That linguists were concerned with the general properties of languages was not, of course, new. Nor was it, by the middle 1960s, a concern that was merely implicit. This is a point that has been covered earlier, at the relevant stage in §1.1. But two things were new, and have come to dominate Chomsky's thought. The first is that a 'tacit knowledge' of universals was part of an 'innate schema' that children bring to learning their native language. The second was that this schema had to be detailed and specific. 'For the present', Chomsky said, 'we cannot come at all close to making a hypothesis . . . that is rich, detailed, and specific enough to account for the fact of language acquisition' (1965: 27). Therefore our main task must be to develop one.

These passages are cited from the beginning of a section on 'Formal and substantive universals', in which Chomsky argues that what I have called a theory$_2$, if it is to give an account of the 'innate schema', should concern itself with universals of all kinds. There is 'no doubt', he says, that that is so (30). By implication, the innate schema might include 'tacit knowledge' of distinctive features in phonology, or, following 'traditional universal grammar', of an 'underlying syntactic structure of each language' (28). A child might also tacitly know various 'abstract conditions' that a grammar$_1$ must meet. For example, it might include a requirement that there should be transformations relating deep and surface structures, or that rules in phonology should apply cyclically (29). Another possibility is that it might include conditions on the semantic level: for example, that 'artifacts are defined in terms of certain human goals, needs and functions instead of solely in terms of physical properties'. 'Formal constraints of this sort', he goes on, ' . . . may severely limit the choice (by the child, or the linguist) of a descriptive grammar' (29f.).

When we compare this tentative list with the proposals that Chomsky was to make in the 1970s and 1980s, it seems clear that, however exciting his idea may have been, he was still essentially groping for some substance to attach to it. What then, on the published evidence, were the arguments that had led him to it?

In the passages already cited he assumes that there must be an 'innate linguistic theory' (25) and asks how 'detailed and specific' it is (27). But he answers this question immediately with the assertion that the 'facts of language acquisition' can only be accounted for by a hypothesis so 'rich, detailed, and specific' that 'for the present we cannot come at all close' to it. The implication, once more, is that Chomsky thought that this was obvious. Certainly there is nothing earlier in the chapter to support it. Apart from the fact that children do learn languages, which has been rendered in the preceding section by the proposition that they construct generative grammars, the 'facts of language acquisition' have not been discussed.

Chomsky's later arguments are well known, and it is very difficult, in seeking to make sense of this chapter, not to read them into it. But as historians we must make the effort; and, if we do, we find very little that does not rest simply on the problems of linguistics in developing what I have distinguished as grammars$_2$ and theories$_2$, and the reification of these as grammars$_1$ and children's theories$_1$. Let us look, in particular, at an argument in the following section about what is needed for a theory$_2$ to explain the acquisition of language. A theory is said to achieve what Chomsky calls 'descriptive adequacy' (34) if, in effect, it specifies the form and interpretation of generative grammars. As Chomsky puts it, in a passage already referred to, it must provide for an enumeration of a class of possible grammars, a class of possible structural descriptions, and so on (30). It is said to achieve 'explanatory adequacy' (34) if it also specifies an evaluation measure. But this, we are at once told, is 'misleading in one important respect'. For a theory might be descriptively adequate, but yet so unspecific that the mere addition of an evaluation measure would not suffice to make it explanatorily adequate. In Chomsky's words, it might 'provide such a wide range of potential grammars that there is no possibility of discovering a formal property distinguishing [correct] grammars, in general, from among the mass of grammars compatible with whatever data are available'. Before a grammar can be selected by an evaluation measure, we require 'a precise and narrow delimitation' of the class of possible grammars: that is, 'a restrictive and rich hypothesis concerning the universal properties that determine the form of language' (35).

The implication is that an evaluation measure will not work unless the rest of the theory specifies the kinds of universals – underlying syntactic structure, cyclical application of rules in phonology, and so on – that Chomsky has been talking about in the preceding section. But for this to have any bearing on a theory of the acquisition of language, we have to assume not only that children construct grammars, but that, in doing so, they too unconsciously employ an evaluation measure to select an optimal grammar. That is, we have to assume the reification of linguistic theory as it had been conceived in *Syntactic Structures*. Later in the chapter, in a section with the title 'Linguistic theory and language learning', Chomsky draws a distinction between two views of learning in general, one 'rationalist' and the other 'empiricist'. His own discussion of language learning is 'rationalistic', he says, in its 'assumption that various formal and substantive universals are intrinsic properties of the language-acquisition system' (53). But in seeking to justify this 'assumption' he begins by asking whether an 'empiricist' proposal can 'succeed in producing grammars within the given constraints of time and access' (54). That is, he assumes that children have a 'language acquisition device', as he has called it earlier, that 'produc[es] grammars'. An 'empiricist' proposal specifies 'inductive procedures'; so the procedures developed 'within taxonomic linguistics' (that is, by Harris and others) are reified as proposals of that kind. But, he says, 'it seems to have been demonstrated beyond any reasonable doubt' that such methods are 'intrinsically incapable of yielding the systems of grammatical knowledge that must be attributed to the speaker of a language'. In support of this he cites a series of references, from his own 'Three models' paper (1956) onwards, whose common feature seems to be that they argue for a transformational syntax. The apparent assumption is that the grammar to be 'attributed to' speakers 'must be' a reification of a transformational grammar.

In the next paragraph he raises the possibility that a 'rationalist' hypothesis might be tested. A theory of the kind he is proposing will 'attribute[ ] possession of certain linguistic universals to a language-acquisition system' (55). We can therefore conceive of 'symbolic systems' that would fall outside the range of languages so defined; these should be hard to learn, and, 'in principle, one might try to determine whether [such systems] do pose inordinately difficult problems for language learning'. But as the argument continues it becomes clear that we must again assume that a theory$_2$ can be reified as a theory$_1$. For illustration, Chomsky takes the proposal that 'grammatical transformations are necessarily "structure-dependent"'. In advancing it, we would 'predict that although a language might form interrogatives, for example, by interchanging the order of certain categories', it could not do so by a mechanical reversal of the order of words, 'or interchange of odd and even words, or insertion of a marker in the middle of a sentence' (56). Let us assume then that there are, in fact, no languages that falsify this prediction. If a theory$_2$ is to characterise the range of languages actually spoken, this restriction on transformations is then part of it. But that tells us nothing about a 'language acquisition device' unless we assume precisely what Chomsky was proposing to test: that there is such a device and that it incorporates a theory$_1$ with whatever properties linguists will agree are appropriate to what is now a theory$_2$.

The point that is of greatest interest to a historian is not that these arguments were tendentious, but that they confirm that Chomsky's view of the development of language in the child was, at this early stage, no more than an inspired leap in the dark. 'It may well be', as he remarks at the end of this section, 'that the general features of language structure reflect ... the general character of [our] capacity to acquire knowledge' (59). It may well be right, accordingly, to attribute linguistic universals to an innate theory$_1$. It 'seem[ed] to' Chomsky 'that the problem of clarifying this issue and of sharpening our understanding of its many facets provides the most interesting and important reason' for the study of grammar. But the wording of this passage acknowledges that the clarification and sharpening had yet to come.

The line the argument was to take is clearer in the second chapter of *Language and Mind* (1972b [1968]). In the first place, Chomsky is no longer appealing to any universals whatever. In 1965 he had talked of a wide range, from the structure-dependence of transformations and the cyclical principle in phonology to the way in which artefacts are defined and the hypothesis that there is a 'general underlying syntactic structure'. The implication that most readers read into this last suggestion was that a set of rules beginning 'S $\rightarrow$ NP + Predicate-Phrase' (Chomsky, 1965: 106) were to be seen as part of the child's 'innate schema'. Whatever exactly he intended, by 1968 the hunt for a universal base component was in full cry. But the argument in *Language and Mind* is based entirely on hypotheses about what Chomsky had called 'formal universals'. These include the cyclical principle (1972b: 43ff.), now tentatively extended to syntax (45ff.); structure-dependence (62ff.); also a more specific condition called the 'A-over-A principle' (51ff.). This was a precursor of what later became the principle of 'subjacency'; and with its appearance it was evident that Chomsky now knew what kinds of evidence might be found to support what he had said.

Secondly, it became clear that the argument was basically an appeal to incredulity. Take, for example, Chomsky's discussion of the cyclical principle in syntax. His pupil Ross, whose thesis on 'Constraints on variables in syntax' must have been conceived when *Aspects of the Theory of Syntax* was being written, had suggested that the results for pronouns in English might make sense in terms of such a principle (Ross, 1969). As Chomsky saw it, it was 'quite impossible' to explain the facts 'in terms of "habits" and "dispositions" and "analogy"' (48). 'Rather', he says, 'it seems that certain abstract and in part universal principles governing human mental faculties must be postulated to explain the phenomena in question'. The chain of reasoning is perhaps not fully spelled out. But what is implied is that it is 'impossible' to explain the facts of English without postulating that a speaker has an internal 'grammar' which incorporates 'certain abstract ... principles'. It is equally 'impossible' to explain how that could be so unless we postulate that these abstract principles are in part innate: that is, 'in part universal'. The argument is similar in the case of structure-dependence. It is a 'simple fact that grammatical transformations are invariably' so dependent (61); there is 'no a priori reason' why that should be so (62); and, if we seek to explain it, 'it is difficult to avoid the conclusion that ... the reliance on structure-dependent operations must be determined ... by a restrictive initial schematism of some sort that directs [a language-learner's] attempts to acquire linguistic competence' (63). Any other conclusion is, in short, seen as at best implausible.

Finally, in looking for the kinds of 'abstract principle' that were needed, Chomsky had by then identified the fields of grammar from which, as the argument developed, almost all his basic evidence was to come. The interpretation of pronouns is one (44ff.); others are the 'movement' of *wh*-words (49ff.), followed by noun phrases with a prepositional complement (55), followed by the interpretation of infinitives with a 'deleted' subject (57f.). He had spoken at the outset of the need for concentrated 'small-scale studies' (1965: 26), and from the early 1970s onwards he was to concentrate on these constructions almost exclusively.

4.3 The period of transition

In the early 1980s Chomsky remarked of the methodological chapter of *Aspects of the Theory of Syntax* that, if he 'ever rewrote' the book, he '[did] not think [he] would rewrite that discussion in almost any respect' (Chomsky, Huybregts & van Riemsdijk, 1982: 62). It is easy to see why he should have said this. The passages which we have just discussed, in which he argues or conjectures that a knowledge of linguistic universals is innate, are the heart of his life's work. He will be remembered for this in a hundred or perhaps five hundred years' time, as Schleicher is now remembered for conceiving of a language as an organism, or William of Occam for his razor. But they are not the whole of the chapter. It also includes, for example, a theory of levels in which, just as surface structures determine a phonetic interpretation for each sentence, so deep structures determine a semantic interpretation (see again Chomsky, 1965: 16). As we have seen already, that view of deep structure was soon abandoned. In the same passage he makes clear that the semantic component of a grammar is 'purely interpretive'. By the mid-1970s, at the latest, that was no longer true. By 1980 the very notion of an 'integrated theory of linguistic descriptions', as Katz and Postal had conceived it in the 1960s, was effectively ditched.

To an observer in the early 1970s, it would have seemed unlikely that any fundamental change was under way. For most generativists, the main issue was whether the semantic component of a grammar was 'interpretive', as Chomsky had said, or 'generative'. The case for generative semantics had been variously made by Lakoff, McCawley and others; and one important element in it, as we have seen in §3.4, was that there was no level of deep structure. Against this Chomsky himself had argued not so much that generative semantics was wrong, but that many of the proposals that had been made amounted to no more than 'notational variants' (Chomsky, 1972a [1970b]: 69ff.) of the theory he had set out in 1965. This he now began to refer to, 'merely for convenience of discussion' (1972a: 66), as the 'Standard Theory'. At the same time he began to argue that this 'Standard Theory' had, in one respect, to be amended. We have already seen how, at the time, he had doubted whether deep structures did entirely determine semantic interpretations (again Chomsky, 1965: 224, n. 9). He now argued that semantic interpretation involved properties of both deep and surface structures; this was supported by his pupil Jackendoff (1972), and characterises the first version of what Chomsky called an 'Extended Standard Theory' (Chomsky, 1972a: 136).

This was tied in with a further argument, about the scope of transformations. For the generative semanticists, the role of what had been the transformational component of a grammar was enormously extended. For example, most of the lexicon was now derived syntactically from more abstract elements. It also seemed that new forms of rule were needed. By the end of the 1960s, Lakoff in particular was arguing the case for 'global rules' referring not just to the structure on which they operate, but potentially to the entire derivation of which it is part (Lakoff, 1970). Transformational rules as earlier conceived were just the simplest or a degenerate instance. But in the same years Chomsky's work was taking quite the opposite direction. In 'Remarks on nominalization' (Chomsky, 1970a), he argued specifically that derived nouns should be removed from the scope of transformational syntax. As we have seen in our introductory survey (§1.1), this was to lead not just to the development of 'lexical morphology' but, by the 1980s, to an extension of the lexicon at the expense of other kinds of transformation. In the preamble to this paper, Chomsky addressed more generally the balance, or what he called the 'trading relation' (185), among the various components of a grammar. For illustration, he discusses a specific construction (that of *John felt angry*), which, he argues, would be better described directly by the base component of a grammar (that is, as a copular or 'prepredicative' verb with an adjective following) than by transformational reduction of a structure like *John felt* [*John was angry*] (186f.). In contrast, generative semanticists were beginning to multiply levels of embedding with what soon seemed reckless abandon.

By the middle of the decade generative semantics was played out, and although the sound of battle had not quite died down, a dispassionate reader of Chomsky's *Reflections on Language* (1976 [1975]), would probably have judged that those who had campaigned beneath the banner of 'interpretive semantics' had won. In his own publications, Chomsky himself had by then returned in particular to the search for specific principles of 'universal grammar'. This had begun, as we have seen, in *Language and Mind* and in Ross's thesis, with the postulation of the 'A-over-A principle'. But in a long and important paper on 'Conditions on transformations' (Chomsky, 1973), he proposed a more far-reaching proposal, in which the application of rules was constrained by a pair of interacting principles, called the 'subjacency' and (as it was formulated at that time) the 'specified subject' conditions. Successive versions of these principles were to be the main theme of his technical research for the rest of the decade, and were associated soon afterwards with an ingenious device by which, in any structure that had been derived by a transformation, 'traces' were left, in the form of a phrase with no phonetic content, of any element that had been moved. This led directly to a further dismantling of the 'Standard Theory'. It was tentative at first; but plainly, in the interpretation of (let us say) a passive sentence, a semantic rule might as easily identify an agent and patient by locating their 'traces' in a surface structure as it might by referring to their original positions in deep structure. Therefore the rules for semantic interpretation might, in the end, not need to refer at all to the level of structure that, ten years before, had been defined as determining it. As Chomsky put it in 1975, he was already 'tend[ing] to believe' that 'a suitably enriched notion of surface structure suffices to determine the meanings of sentences under interpretive rules' (1976 [1975: 83).

Finally, at the philosophical level, it was at last clear what the argument for an 'innate' knowledge of grammar was. In the beginning Chomsky had boldly reified linguistic theory as he knew it, and with it (as we have seen in the last section) any feature that might be supposed to be universal. In searching for evidence to support this, he had also referred in passing to the practical problems facing a learner, to the 'constraints of time and access' (1965: 54) and the 'degenerate' character, as he described it in *Language and Mind*, of the 'evidence' that children had to work with (1972b [1968]: 27). But by the mid-1970s the argument was simply that a learner seemed to know things that could not be explained by any other plausible hypothesis. In forming questions, for example, a child 'unerringly makes use of [a] structure-dependent rule' (1976 [1975]: 32). Why so? The 'hypothesis' that rules are structure-dependent is 'far more complex' (31) than its opposite. There 'seems to be no explanation in terms of "communicative efficiency" or similar considerations' (32), and it is 'certainly absurd to argue that children are trained' to conform to this principle. The 'only reasonable conclusion', Chomsky argued, is that it must be part of the innate 'U[niversal] G[rammar]'. It is not in effect claimed that the 'evidence' is degenerate, but simply that, on this point, none exists. Nor does it matter how long the development of a speaker's 'grammar' takes. To 'facilitate the discussion', we can adopt the 'simplifying assumption' that it is instantaneous (14f.).

In summary, a great deal had been done in the first half of the 1970s both to clarify and support the philosophical argument of *Aspects of the Theory of Syntax* and to elaborate and correct in detail the original model for the relation of syntax and semantics. By 1977 our observer would also have noted that the need for most of the transformations that had been posited in the 1950s and 1960s, and with them anything like the accepted discrepancies between deep and surface structures, had been eliminated. This related beautifully to a feeling that had been growing since 1970 that what Chomsky had called the 'weak generative capacity' of grammars (1965: 60) had to be cut back. At the end of the 1960s Peters and Ritchie had announced a theorem (1969; proof in Peters & Ritchie, 1973) which confirmed in effect that transformational grammars imposed no restriction on the class of formal languages that could be generated. It therefore seemed important to many that the 'power' of rules of syntax should be reduced, and by 1977, with the limitation implied by the subjacency and other principles and the establishment of surface structures as the sole input to semantic interpretation, it seemed that the aim might be achieved. Nevertheless, to most observers, the new theory was yet another in the line initiated twelve years earlier in *Aspects of the Theory of Syntax*. Chomsky himself still referred to it as the 'so-called "extended standard theory"', or 'EST' (1977a: 1; compare 1977b: 71). I recall that some onlookers with a knowledge of Latin remarked that the 'EST' was by then an 'ERAT'. But its replacement was often referred to (for example, by Bach, 1977: 135 in commenting on Chomsky, 1977b) as the 'Revised Extended Standard Theory' or 'REST', and discussion tended still to link it with the issues at the beginning of the decade.

So much for the apparent history of this period. It would be easy to expand and elaborate such a sketch, and as a straightforward account of what people saw as happening it would not be untrue. But it does little to explain the upheaval that was to hit Chomsky's followers by the early 1980s. The roots of this lie deep, and I must confess at once that, like others, I did not appreciate till the end of the decade how far the foundations of so much that had been taken for granted had been crumbling. But, with hindsight, we can perhaps attempt to lay them bare.

Let us begin with the notion of 'semantic representations'. We have seen in §1.1 how the attempt to develop a generative semantics had effectively destroyed the very idea with which it had started. As McCawley remarked in 1975, 'strictly speaking, generative semanticists are not engaged in "generative grammar"' (McCawley, 1982: 11). The main reason was that, if one tried to apply the tests for semantic representations that had been proposed in the 1960s, the results inexorably depended on the beliefs of individual speakers and other matters that a grammar excluded. Chomsky himself argued against the generative semanticists in general and, it might have been thought, was against them in this matter too. But the theory they were undermining had not, in origin, been his. It was that of Katz and Fodor; its assumptions had been basically those of earlier structuralist accounts of meaning; and, like other long established assumptions, especially in fields which have ceased for several years to be a major focus of research, they seemed at the time to be uncontroversial. But it seems that as soon as Chomsky began to think about them he too realised that they would not hold.

In *Language and Mind*, the most important assumption was still 'obvious'. 'It is quite obvious', Chomsky said, 'that sentences have an intrinsic meaning determined by linguistic rule.' The system of rules was internalised by a speaker and determined 'both the phonetic shape of the sentence and its intrinsic semantic content' (1972b [1968]: 115). The meanings assigned to individual 'formatives' contributed to this semantic representation, just as the phonological forms assigned to them contributed to its phonetic representation. So, for example, did the 'grammatical functions', such as 'Subject-of' or 'Object-of', that were defined over phrase structure trees. The implication was, once more, that linguists could and should distinguish what Bloomfield had called 'linguistic meanings' from the endless meanings or nuances that sentences might take on in specific circumstances.

Bloomfield had seen this as part of a 'fundamental assumption'. But its empirical basis was by no means 'obvious' and by the end of the 1960s Chomsky was already questioning it. In a lecture delivered in 1969, he remarked that 'the notion "representation of meaning" or "semantic representation" is . . . highly controversial'. 'It is not at all clear', he goes on, 'that it is possible to distinguish sharply between the contribution of grammar to the determination of meaning, and the contribution of so-called "pragmatic considerations", questions of fact and belief and context of utterance' (1972b: 111; for date of lecture, vii). In one of his papers in 1970, he begins by assuming that a sentence has an 'inherent meaning' (1970b [1972a: 63]). But with other assumptions this is no longer thought to be self-evident. 'One might argue that nonlinguistic beliefs, intentions of the speaker, and other factors enter into the interpretation of utterances in so intimate – and perhaps so fluctuating and indefinite – a fashion that it is hopeless and misguided to attempt to represent independently the "purely grammatical" component of meaning, the various "readings" of expressions' as Katz and his collaborators had conceived them, and so on (67; see also n. 4).

These are presented as doubts, and, strictly speaking, were still doubts seven years later. But by then they were much sharper. In the course of a conversation recorded in 1976, Chomsky begins by ascribing this aspect of the 'Standard Theory' to Fodor and Katz. 'They', he says, 'developed an analogy between phonetics and semantics' (Chomsky, 1979 [1977]: 141). It was by implication their idea that 'semantic representation would be based on a universal system of semantic categories'. It is Katz who 'takes the view' that such a system should aim to characterise 'the semantic properties of all utterances of all languages, independent of all extralinguistic considerations'.

But to the Chomsky of the 1970s it was 'not at all clear that there exists such a universal system'. Some individual features might be universal (141f.). 'If so, then these aspects of the theory of meaning can be taken to fall within the "generative grammar"'. But, beyond these, there were 'good reasons for being skeptical about such a program'. Again, it 'seems that other cognitive systems – in particular, our system of beliefs concerning things in the world and their behavior – play an essential part in our judgments of meaning and reference'. It is 'not at all clear that much will remain' if we try to isolate 'the purely linguistic components' of meaning (142).

What then was the right view? One alternative might have been to return to the theory of the 1950s. A generative grammar would be restricted again to syntax and phonology, and the primary aim of syntax would be to account for distributions. As in the 1950s, we would prefer a grammar which described sentences in a way that would facilitate a subsequent account of their meanings. But semantic interpretation would lie entirely outside it. In investigating the meaning of sentences, Chomsky, like McCawley and the other generative semanticists, would not be 'engaged in "generative grammar"'. Instead one would be looking at the ways in which the sentences of a language are used, and that is inextricably bound up with the circumstances in which they are uttered on concrete occasions, with the beliefs of speakers and the 'extralinguistic knowledge' that they share with others, and with specific communicative 'intentions'.

This alternative was not considered at the time and it is easy to see why Chomsky himself would not have been attracted to it. For in the conversation I have cited, he accepts that some semantic features may be universal and ascribable to grammar. They include 'traditional notions like "agent of action", "instrument"', and so on, the subject of what were to become, in the opaque terminology of the 1980s, 'θ-roles'. It also seemed 'reasonable to suppose that semantic relations between words like *persuade*, *intend*, *believe*, can be expressed in purely linguistic terms'. For example, 'if I persuade you to go, then you intend to go'. It also seemed likely that 'the fundamental properties of quantifiers ... and anaphora' could be 'expressed in part on the level of semantic representation, separate from extralinguistic considerations' (again Chomsky, 1979: 141–2). He was therefore driven to a theory intermediate between the one he had inherited from Harris and the one that Katz had apparently sold to him in the 1960s. A language, in the sense of what was characterised by a grammar, did have some specific semantic features. But his 'own speculation' was that they amounted to 'a bare framework ... altogether insufficient for characterizing what is ordinarily called "the meaning of a linguistic expression"' (1979: 143).

In practice, it was already limited to what Chomsky called 'logical form'. The term had been introduced in *Reflections on Language*, and was associated with a restriction of grammar, as conceived in the 1960s, to what Chomsky now called 'sentence grammar'. Logical form or 'LF' was a level of sentence grammar, and was derived from surface structures by 'certain rules of semantic interpretation' labelled (1976: 105) as rules 'SR–1'. These rules 'assign the scope of logical operators ("not", "each", "who", etc.) and fix their meaning, assign antecedents to such anaphoric expressions as reciprocals . . . and necessarily bound anaphors', and so on (104). That is, they dealt with aspects of grammatical meaning that, as we have seen, were still thought to be candidates for linguistic universals. Beyond these, there were other semantic rules, labelled 'SR–2'. They in turn interpreted logical forms, 'interacting with other cognitive structures', to derive 'fuller representations of meaning' (105). But they did not belong to sentence grammar. 'The theory of grammar – or more precisely "sentence grammar" – ends', Chomsky said, with logical form.

The subsequent fate of 'logical form' belongs to our final period (§4.4). But for the moment it was evident that, if 'sentence grammar' dealt with no more than some aspects of grammatical meaning, much of what had originally been called the speaker's 'competence' now lay outside it. 'Competence' was, by definition, 'the speaker-hearer's knowledge of his language' (1965: 4), and that would surely have to include the semantic rules which were not part of sentence grammar (SR–2) as well as those that were. In 1977, when Chomsky talks of a 'grammatical competence', it seems that he still intended these rules to be included. But, in addition, a speaker 'attains a system of "pragmatic competence" interacting with his grammatical competence' (1977a: 3). This interaction evidently involved the 'SR–2' component especially; and in that sense pragmatic competence was separate, as Chomsky had made clear in *Reflections on Language*, from the autonomous system that he had called 'sentence grammar'. Moreover, there was a further possibility that it too might differ from language to language. This point was, according to Chomsky, 'far from clear'. But if it was true, the original notion of 'competence' – that is, of the speaker's knowledge of a particular language – seemed to split up into three parts. One was characterised by the so-called 'sentence grammar'. Another was characterised by the 'SR–2' component, operating at a level at which, as Chomsky had repeated in conversation in 1976, other 'cognitive systems' were 'inextricably involve[d]' (1979: 145). Another would be characterised by one of these other 'cognitive systems'.

These developments were rather hard to interpret, especially for readers educated in the methodological certainties of the 1960s. In Chomsky's own work, they were covered with qualifications ('my own, quite tentative, belief', 'my own speculation', 'it would be reasonable to say that'), very different from the 'clearly's and 'obviously's of his classic phase. But, in retrospect, it seems clear that behind the superficial history of these years – the replacement of the 'Standard Theory' by the '(R)EST', the refinement of universal grammar, even the emergence of 'logical form' – we were witnessing the dissolution of ideas that went back to the 1940s and that in 1965 Chomsky still at bottom accepted. The central Post-Bloomfieldian idea was, once more, that forms could be described separately from meanings. This had been the foundation for generative grammar in the 1950s, as we have seen in §3.2 especially. But it was also implicit in the generative grammar of the 1960s. The syntactic component again assigned a structural description to any string of formatives that formed a sentence. The other components were 'purely interpretive'. Accordingly, it fell to the syntactic component to distinguish all and only the strings of formatives that were grammatical.

But by 1965 there were two qualifications. The first was that, within the syntactic component, the transformational rules could act as a filter on the output of the base rules. This seemed at the time to be a purely technical matter. But, briefly, transformations would in general derive surface structures from underlying structures. So, among other things, they derive clauses and phrases from embedded structures like those of sentences. Let us suppose that, in so doing, they delete a 'boundary symbol' which marks off such structures. We can then say that if, at the end of the transformations, such a boundary symbol has not been deleted, the resulting string of formatives is ungrammatical. As Chomsky put it, the resulting surface structure was not well formed. Therefore, he said, the underlying structure from which it was derived, though generated by the base component, was not in fact a deep structure (1965: 138f.).

It is perhaps worth noting that at this stage Chomsky still assumed that grammars had to give a unified account of grammaticality. A grammatical sentence was a sequence of formatives to which the rules of syntax assigned at least one deep structure. In principle, deep structures were assigned by the base rules; so, if a structure assigned by such rules failed to pass the 'filter', it was apparently necessary to say, as in the passage referred to, that it was not after all a deep structure. But in reality a sentence was grammatical if it had a 'well-formed' representation on both levels, both underlying and surface. Moreover, it was not immediately evident at which level specific cases should be dealt with. Take, for example, the construction of a verb with a *that*-clause. At one point, Chomsky assigns to *believe* a feature that allows it to appear, in underlying structures, before *that* plus an embedded sentence (1965: 94). But *elapse*, for instance, does not have this feature; therefore a sequence like *I elapse that it is true* would have no underlying structure and would be ungrammatical for that reason. But there was plainly an alternative. Let both *believe* and *elapse* appear quite freely at the underlying level. But *believe* allows a transformation which, if it does nothing else, deletes the 'boundary symbols' in a sentence such as *I believe that it is true*. *Elapse* does not allow this transformation; therefore, though the base rules will have assigned an underlying structure to *I elapse that it is true*, the corresponding boundary symbols will not be deleted, and the surface structure will be 'ill-formed'. In a real sense the solutions are equivalent. But in technical terms, what was well-formed and what was ill-formed could be distinguished at either level.

The second qualification had to do with 'competence' and 'performance'. In the beginning, in the 1950s, a grammar was said to generate the sentences of a language. Sentences were forms that were 'grammatical', and to be grammatical was once more to be 'acceptable to a native speaker, etc.' (Chomsky, 1957: 13). But in the 1960s Chomsky made a distinction between grammaticality and acceptability. A sentence, he argued, might be perfectly grammatical. That is, no rule of the speaker's competence would exclude it. But it might nevertheless be unacceptable. That is, it might not be 'perfectly natural or immediately comprehensible', or might seem 'bizarre or outlandish' (1965: 10). This could be due to other factors bearing on 'performance'. These involved not grammar, but rather 'memory limitations, intonational and stylistic factors, "iconic" elements of discourse . . . and so on' (11).

What was acceptable was therefore determined jointly by the grammar and these other factors that were external to it. Moreover, there was again the possibility that the same facts might be explicable at either level. Take, for example, the case of what were known as 'heavy noun phrases'. A sentence like *The detective brought the man in* is acceptable, and by implication grammatical. But one would not normally say *The detective brought the man who was accused of having stolen the automobile in*. Why not? The example was one that had flummoxed Chomsky in the 1950s (1975a [1955]: 477f.). Since the phenomenon was systematic, 'we might expect that a grammar should be able to state it'. 'But', he went on, 'it may turn out to involve probabilistic considerations for which our system has no place as it now stands.' By 1965 he had decided that the explanation lay outside the grammar. 'It would be quite impossible', in this and other cases that he discusses, 'to characterize the unacceptable sentences [that is, to characterize them as unacceptable] in grammatical terms' (again 1965: 11). But was it strictly impossible? The most one could perhaps have said was that there was no solution in Chomsky's theory of grammar as it then stood. But the facts themselves were not self-evidently facts about competence or facts about performance. So, if the theory of grammar were to change, their explanation might, in principle, change with it.

These qualifications were separate and unconnected, and by referring to them in the context of the 1970s I run the risk of reading into them far more than was intended at the time. But, as we look back, they were the first signs that the unified concept of a grammar might begin to fall apart.

The next step was to see the semantic component as another 'filter'. It assigned interpretations to the structures assigned by rules of syntax, and it had always been understood that such interpretations might be 'anomalous'. That is to say, a sentence might be 'well-formed' in syntax, but 'deviant' (to use a term which is deliberately all-embracing) in meaning. But what exactly was the scope of semantic deviance? In the beginning, it had been assumed that being grammatical and being meaningful were different things: see again *Syntactic Structures* (1957: 15). Therefore each set of rules dealt initially with what were seen as separate phenomena. Technically, however, it was possible for a sequence of formatives to be 'ill-formed' by virtue of semantic rules alone. It might be assigned a potential deep structure; from this a well-formed surface structure might be derived; but, finally, no semantic interpretation would be assigned to it.

The possibility was first exploited in the early days of generative semantics (§3.4). But in 1970 Chomsky too invited us to 'notice that in general rules of semantic interpretation have a "filtering function" analogous to that of rules of transformation in the standard theory' (1970b [1972a: 109]). The example that gave rise to this remark can be passed over. But let us take, for instance, the treatment of reciprocals. At the beginning of the decade, a sentence like *They knew each other* was seen as derived, by transformation, from a structure like that of *They each knew the other*. If one could not, for example, say *They said that John knew each other*, it was because the transformation was constrained by a general principle, hypothetically 'innate'. But there was an alternative. Suppose that both these sentences are syntactically 'well-formed'. But let us then say that an equivalent principle constrains the rules of semantic interpretation. In *They knew each other*, the reciprocal *each other* can be interpreted by reference to *they* as its antecedent. But in *They said that John knew each other* it cannot; and, since the singular *John* cannot be taken as an antecedent either, it has no interpretation. Therefore it is 'filtered out'.

This change was in fact made without comment. In 'Conditions on transformations' it was still a transformation that was constrained (1973 [1977a: 89ff.]). But two years later it was a rule of 'reciprocal interpretation' (1975b [1977a: 178]). In either case, the forms that are excluded are 'ungrammatical'. That is, at some level a rule of grammar would fail to cover them. But it did not seem to matter, in principle, what kind of rule it was. In terms that Chomsky uses in inverted commas in the second article, something might be ungrammatical because it was 'unsemantic', not because it was 'unsyntactic' (discussion of example (13), 1977a: 177f.).

It is hardly surprising that by this stage Chomsky was beginning to deny that the distinction between syntax and semantics was self-evident. In *Reflections on Language*, he remarks that a form like *The police think who the FBI discovered that Bill shot* is ungrammatical. Is this distinction syntactic or semantic? Chomsky was 'not persuaded that the question makes very much sense, or that any reasonably clear criteria exist to settle it' (1976 [1975]: 95). 'Personally', he says, 'I have no intuitions' that will supply an answer. 'I can make the judgment that certain sentences are fine and others deviant ... but have no further intuitions that provide me, in such cases as these, with the basis for these judgments.' It was an 'open and perhaps interesting question', as he saw it, 'to establish sharper criteria that will help to make the questions "syntactic or semantic?" more precise' in such cases.

Where did that leave the earlier concept of levels? It is obvious, firstly, that the semantic component of the 'sentence grammar' was no longer purely interpretive. Thus, by the time the famous controversy between interpretive and generative semantics had reached a stalemate, the former was in practice no more 'interpretive' than the latter was 'generative'. In *Reflections on Language* and other contributions in the same year, Chomsky still talked of 'rules of semantic interpretation' (1976: 104). But he soon acknowledged that this was 'in fact misleading'. 'They are more properly described as rules concerned with the syntax of L[ogical] F[orm]' (1977b: 72).

Secondly, there was no longer a single account of how the elements of a language were formally related. A form that would originally have been seen as ungrammatical could now be treated in at least four ways. It might be said to be grammatical – that is, in accordance with the rules of sentence grammar – but excluded as 'unnatural' or 'bizarre' by other factors. Alternatively, it might be ungrammatical on any of three levels. It might be contrary to one of the old rules of syntax, either one concerned (we might say) with the syntax of deep structures or one concerned with the syntax of surface structures. Alternatively, it might be contrary to one of the new rules concerned with the syntax of logical forms. A rule like that which linked *each other* to an antecedent was soon described by Chomsky as a 'rule of construal' (1977a: 6; 1977b: 72). It was a rule concerned with meaning. But, like a rule of syntax, it too indicated when *x* could and could not stand in a construction with *y*. The original objective of a generative grammar had thus been dispersed across a spectrum of levels.

Finally, what was the rationale behind these various sets of rules? In the middle of the decade, Chomsky represented the structure of the whole in terms of a flow-chart (1976: 105; compare 1975b: 195). First the base rules specified a set of 'initial phrase markers'; then transformational rules converted these to surface structures (filtering out some); then the 'SR–1' component converted these to logical forms (filtering out more); then, he said, the 'SR–2' component, in consort with 'other cognitive structures', derived 'fuller representations of meaning'. But it was hard to see a natural division at any point. Historically, the object of the whole had been to relate phonetic forms to intrinsic meanings. But the operation of the 'SR–2' component was now bound up with other non-linguistic systems, and it was 'not clear at all' exactly what grammatical competence contributed. The 'SR–1' rules dealt with logical forms. But what exactly were they? When first defined, they were said to 'incorporate whatever features of sentence structure (1) enter directly into semantic interpretation and (2) are strictly determined by properties of (sentence-) grammar' (Chomsky, 1975b [1977a: 166f.]). But what was '(sentence-) grammar'? The answer (1976: 104) was that it was the part of grammar in the original sense that stopped at logical forms. And surely 'features of sentence structure' were also the province of syntax. Within syntax, the 'initial phrase markers' had once been deep structures that determined semantic interpretations. But what now belonged to them and what to surface structure? At all points in this scheme, the divisions seemed to be not substantive but entirely technical.

At the same time, Chomsky drew a separate distinction between 'core grammar', as he called it, and (by implication) other parts of grammar that were not 'core'. Core grammar was defined at the time by reference simply to a set of rules (1977a: 6; 1977b: 72). It included two transformations, one moving noun phrases and the other *wh*-phrases; also three 'rules of construal', dealing with the interpretation of *each other* and of pronouns (1977b). It therefore cut across the division, within sentence grammar, between syntactic rules and rules assigning logical forms. Moreover, there seemed no reason why these rules should be separate from others. They were simply the ones which dealt, as it happened, with the phenomenon in which Chomsky was, at the time, mainly interested. On the face of it, that was the only distinguishing feature that they had.

How worrying was all this? In the years of which I am talking, textbooks were appearing that still looked back to the concept of levels in the 1960s. It is hard to see how any student reading them and turning unaided to Chomsky's current articles could have made real sense of what was going on. But it seems that in his own mind the preoccupations that had inspired his earlier work had by then ceased to be relevant. The primary aim of linguistic theory had ceased to be the justification of a linguist's description. The first test was no longer whether a grammar generated all and only the potential utterances of a language. It was no longer important to separate the study of distributions from that of meanings. Within the sentence grammar it was an open question whether something was 'syntactic' (that is, to be handled technically by base rules and transformations) or 'semantic' (that is, to be handled technically by rules assigning logical forms).

Most important, one no longer needed to look at grammars as wholes. At the beginning of the 1970s, Chomsky had still talked of a grammar as 'a tightly organised system'. 'A modification of one part generally involves widespread modifications of other facets' (1970a [1972a: 13]). But since then all his detailed work had been directed to establishing the validity of the subjacency and other principles. Let us therefore reflect again on the logic of such arguments. Speakers were found to know, for example, that they could not say things like *They said that John knew each other* or *Who did he like John's pictures of?* The patterns are systematic; so, failing other explanations, Chomsky said that we must posit principles of universal grammar that account for them. The task then is to discover exactly what these are. To do this, we must certainly look at other relevant data. Throughout the decade, rules and principles were reformulated in more abstract terms, to cover a widening range of cases. But data that they could not account for were not relevant. That universal principles existed was taken to be true from the outset. One would not deny that by citing data that did not fit. The problem, again, was purely to discover their nature and their scope. That is, all that mattered was 'core grammar', defined precisely as the part of grammar that could be shown to fall under these rules and principles.

Little of this was wholly clear at the time. The butterfly of the 1980s had yet to emerge from the chrysalis of the 1970s. But behind the relatively superficial changes that had led from the 'Standard Theory' to the '(R)EST', the aims of grammar were in fact being radically transformed.

4.4 The new programme

The 1980s were marked externally by the emergence of a new Chomskyan school, largely different in both personnel and character from the old school that had disintegrated in the 1970s. One major difference, as we remarked in §1.1, is that it is not so dominantly American. It includes a number of established scholars from Europe and elsewhere, who have made influential studies of their own languages. Even Chomsky himself, in whose writings on syntax virtually all examples are from English up to the early 1980s, has made crucial use of their findings.

The new Chomskyan school is also addressing a different problem. For a generative grammarian in the 1960s, the goal was to develop an all-embracing theory of linguistic rules and levels of representation, and within this framework to write generative grammars of particular languages. Naturally, one could not work on a whole language at once. One had to choose a particular problem, like coordination or the rules for what was called 'pronominalisation', and try to find a solution which would fit with what was known of the rest. But the unquestioned assumption was that it should fit; that the rules proposed should eventually form part of an integrated grammar, by which every sentence is assigned an analysis and every string that is not a sentence is excluded. In the light of what has been posited for a particular language, one can confirm or falsify a theory of rules in general. The unquestioned assumption was that it should impose restrictions either on the class of languages that could be generated or at least on the class of derivations that were possible. Hence a theory, like a grammar, had to be tested as a whole.

To judge from textbooks, this is the way transformational syntax was still taught throughout the 1970s. In studying a language, an investigator must begin with a set of data bearing on a particular point: this will include both sentences and other forms that are known to be non-sentences. The problem, therefore, is to devise a rule which will distinguish one from the other. When such a rule has been proposed, we have a duty to look for counter examples. If they are found it must, as it stands, be invalid; therefore we must amend it or go back to the drawing board. When we have devised a fragment of a grammar that accounts for this body of data, we will try to extend it by bringing in others. Again they will consist of sentences and non-sentences; and although we are well aware that, at a later stage in our attempt to develop a total grammar, we may have to change any of the rules that have been posited earlier, the crucial test is once more that, for the data we have before us, what is grammatical should be precisely distinguished from what is ungrammatical. Research proceeds in the manner of an army systematically reducing a territory. Each successive topic is a new stronghold, that we must storm or lay siege to.

The method is well illustrated in a textbook at the end of the 1970s, by Perlmutter and Soames (1979). But it is scarcely how the new Chomskyan school works. The primary or immediate aim is not, in reality, to write a generative grammar. It is to explore directly the principles of 'universal grammar', like subjacency or what was known at the beginning of the 1980s as 'opacity'. We therefore begin by looking for facts that hypotheses about such principles might explain. For example, speakers of English know that such and such a form is unconstruable; they cannot have been taught this nor, it seems, have induced it from speech that they have heard; so, it may be genetically determined. Therefore we try to formulate a principle that will cover it. We then look for other things that are known to speakers of English and that might be tied in with it. We also look at similar things that are known to speakers of other languages. But we will not need to write an exhaustive grammar for any of them. Nor will we need to deal immediately with every fact that, in the old view, might have been thought to invalidate our hypothesis. Some may simply be idiosyncrasies, which speakers have learned as such. Research will therefore proceed in the manner of the German army advancing across France in 1940. We throw our whole weight at a particular range of problems. So long as progress continues and is spectacular, the rest can be set aside.

Of the developments that inaugurated this *Blitzforschung*, the most important was the proposal that universal grammar should include 'parameters'. Let us begin, for example, with Chomsky's notion of an 'anaphor'. The term was introduced at the end of the 1980s, and refers to pronominal expressions which must have an antecedent (Chomsky, 1980: 174). For example, *each other* is an anaphor; and, as we have seen already, a series of studies stretching back into the 1970s had sought to show how the identification of its antecedent was genetically constrained. But over languages in general the term 'anaphor' was clearly a variable. In English its extension includes *each other* and the reflexives in *-self*; in Latin, for example, *se*, and so on. Children acquiring English will hypothetically know that the interpretation of anaphors is constrained in such and such a way. But they will have to work out from the speech they are exposed to what the anaphors of English are.

This point is obvious, and it is only perhaps the limited scope of Chomsky's studies in the 1970s that had stopped it being exploited further. But let us turn next to the notion of subjacency. This had been defined from the outset by reference to what was called a 'cyclic node': briefly, one position was 'subjacent' to another only if such a 'node' dominated it (Chomsky, 1973 [1977a: 102]). But what counted as a 'cyclic node'? Chomsky assumed at first that it was one which was labelled 'S[entence]' or N[oun] P[hrase]' (1973 [1977a: 85, n. 8]). But this left open the possibility that there might be others: four years later, he explored a suggestion that both '$\bar{S}$' (a clause with a complementiser) and '$\bar{\bar{S}}$' (a 'topicalised' phrase plus, on the analysis he adopted, an '$\bar{S}$') might be cyclic (1977b: 73, 91ff.). In addition, it left open the possibility that the extension of the term might vary across languages. This point is less obvious, and at the time there are few signs that it was appreciated. But, again, a child acquiring a language might 'know' that there are universal principles whose operation depends on how this term is defined. But children would then have to establish which of 'S' or '$\bar{S}$' or '$\bar{\bar{S}}$' and so on were cyclic categories in the particular language they were hearing.

Such ideas were not developed until the very end of the decade, and we must therefore be careful not to underestimate the depth of insight that may have been involved. But once the step was taken it finally got the investigation of 'universal grammar' off the hook. Take, for example, reflexives. Rules had been proposed quite early for English, and in a paper on 'The method of universal grammar' Postal, for example, had sought to generalise the principle that seemed to operate (1970b: 116ff.). But for anyone who knew a language as familiar as Latin there were obvious counter examples. Although it too is clearly a reflexive in meaning, Latin *se* did not entirely obey the constraints that had been proposed for English *-self*. How then could universality be claimed for them?

Ten years later the answer was precisely that universal grammar incorporates alternatives. As Chomsky presents the argument in *Rules and Representations*, we have 'no reasonable alternative', on the one hand, 'but to suppose' that some properties of languages are 'part of the genotype'. On the other hand, people do learn different languages and, 'as translators are well aware, there need be no point-by-point comparison' between them. 'What we should expect to discover', accordingly, 'is a system of universal grammar with highly restrictive principles that narrowly constrain the class of attainable grammars, but with parameters that remain open to be fixed by experience' (Chomsky, 1980: 66). These parameters, he tells us later, involve 'options for base ordering, for the scope and conditions of application of [a rule that moves an element], for what counts as an "anaphor", and much else' (179). So, to return to our example, the principles that govern Latin *se* and English *-self* might be the same at a very abstract level. But children acquiring such languages will 'fix' certain 'parameters' quite differently.

Rules and Representations is based on lectures aimed at a general academic audience, and Chomsky did not explore this idea in detail. But his next book, which is based on technical lectures first given a few months later, made clear just how rapidly his thought had moved. A parameter might, for example, concern a single term in universal grammar. In certain kinds of construction, Chomsky had posited a zero pronoun 'PRO'; this is an element that may or may not have an antecedent. It would appear without an antecedent in, for instance, *It is unclear how* [PRO] *to be happy*. Similarly, it is posited in the corresponding Italian sentence *Non è chiaro come* [PRO] *essere allegri*. But in Italian the adjective (*allegri*) is plural. So, when it has no antecedent the features of 'PRO' are subject to 'parametric variation'. In Italian it has the feature 'plural': that is, Italian children will have to fix the parameter to this value. But in English, he says, the value is 'singular' (Chomsky, 1981: 61).

At the other extreme, the 'order of major constituents' is a parameter (34). So is a general distinction between 'configurational' languages, in which there are fixed orders and a surface hierarchy of constituents, and a contrasting type that is 'non-configurational' (128ff.). This is said to reduce to 'the parameter [± configurational]' (135). Another parameter has, as one of its consequences, the distinction between languages in which a subject is or is not obligatory (27). This is one of a 'clustering of properties' related to what Chomsky calls 'the pro-drop parameter' (240). For example, the subject may be 'missing' in Italian (*l'ha mangiato* '[ ] has eaten it'); there may be 'inversion' of the verb and subject in simple sentences (*l'ha mangiato Giovanni* 'John has eaten it'); there are also differences in, for example, the syntax of Italian *chi* and English *who*. In Chomsky's analysis, these are all connected, directly or indirectly, to a basic parameter that involves the relation to subjects of richly versus poorly inflected verbs (241ff., 253ff.). In such ways, it is possible for 'a change in a single parameter' to have 'proliferating effects' (344) throughout the language.

It was clear at this point that a theory of universal grammar was no longer directly vulnerable to conflicting evidence. Suppose that, in a particular language, we discover facts that seem to run contrary to it. It might indeed be that the theory is wrong. But it might be that we have simply discovered a new parameter. Therefore our best strategy is not to scrap the principle that has been proposed. Instead we take the variation on board, and look for other things that may be connected with it. In this light, it is not surprising that the methods of the new Chomskyan school depart so radically from those of the old. In former times the focus was on writing rules; and though inductive methods as such had been abandoned, it still seems to have been assumed, even in Chomsky's own writings, that the route to linguistic universals lay through individual grammars. In writing such grammars, counter examples matter. But the new school is concerned directly with universal grammar; and, if we accept its premiss, we do not have to be perturbed by them.

For the rest of Chomsky's ideas in the 1980s, it will often be simpler to turn to the more general and more organised account in *Knowledge of Language* (Chomsky, 1986) This has a lucidity that 'the Pisa lectures', as they are subtitled everywhere except on the cover and title page, lack. It also introduced a central change of terminology, and we have reached a point at which we too should make it. Finally, it incorporates another of Chomsky's own accounts of his earlier thinking. But in other respects it stands to the 'Pisa lectures' somewhat as, in the 1960s, *Language and Mind* stood to *Aspects of the Theory of Syntax*. There are new things in it, but the earlier work was the breakthrough.

Let us start with the change of terminology. In the 1950s, Chomsky had taken over what was essentially Bloomfield's definition of a language: it was a set of sentences or utterances (see above, §3.2). A 'grammar' was then a characterisation of such a language, and was 'generative' in the sense that it was a formal system that, among other things, defined its membership. As Chomsky observes, 'the study of generative grammar' originally 'developed from the confluence of . . . structuralist grammar [to be precise, he says 'traditional and structuralist grammar'], and the study of formal systems' (1986: 29). It was therefore 'easy to see how one might take over from the study of formal languages the idea that the "language" is somehow given as a set of sentences or sentence-meaning pairs, while the grammar is some characterization of this infinite set of objects' (30).

By the use of the impersonal 'one', Chomsky may be trying to insinuate that he himself had never really quite said such things. Earlier in the same section, he again seeks to argue that the history of this period is 'in part obscured by accidents of publishing history' and that 'specifically linguistic work . . . not publishable at the time' would have revealed the truth (28; 48f., n. 17). *Syntactic Structures*, he now tells us, was 'actually course notes for an undergraduate course at MIT and hence presented from a point of view related to interests of these students'. But we have seen how, by the middle of the 1960s, the theory of grammar had been reified as a theory about 'grammars' said to be 'internalised' by speakers. If that view is adopted, to study 'a language' is essentially to study the properties of an internalised 'grammar'. To study the properties of 'language' in general is likewise to study the properties of such 'grammars': that is, with the further assumption that Chomsky made in *Aspects of the Theory of Syntax*, to study an innate 'theory of grammar'.

Chomsky had clearly been content with this terminology throughout the 1970s. But it had two disadvantages. On the one hand, the term 'grammar' had to be used with what he had called a 'systematic ambiguity'. That is, it referred both to a 'grammar' in the earlier sense and to the object that it was now supposed to describe. On the other hand, a 'language' was now peripheral to the investigation: as Chomsky had come to see it by the end of the decade, it was 'a derivative and perhaps not very interesting concept' (1980: 90), something 'epiphenomenal' (1980: 83, 122f.). But this conflicts with ordinary usage, in which 'language' is precisely what a linguist is studying. Nor had Chomsky himself avoided that usage. 'Knowing a grammar' may indeed have been 'the fundamental cognitive relation' (1980: 70); but in *Reflections on Language*, for example, he refers directly to 'the acquisition of a cognitive system such as language' (1976: 10), to 'knowing a language L' or 'cognizing L' (164), and so on.

As soon as Chomsky felt that it was necessary to be strict about this, it must have been obvious that something closer to ordinary usage would be better. A speaker knows a language: so, 'an element of [his or her] mind' is an 'internalized language' or 'I-language' (1986: 22). This 'state of mind', equivalent to what I distinguished in §4.2 as a 'grammar$_1$', is now what the linguist's generative grammar [that is, what I distinguished as a 'grammar$_2$'] attempts to characterise (40). So, in that sense of 'language', language is indeed the object of inquiry, speakers can be said to know or 'cognize' I-languages, and so forth. What then of the 'epiphenomenon' that had earlier been called a 'language'? In the new terminology, this is an 'externalized language' or 'E-language' (20), and is 'now regarded [that is, by students of I-language] as an epiphenomenon at best' (25).

In the version of history that Chomsky wishes to bequeath to posterity, E-language was 'the object of study in most of traditional or structuralist grammar or behavioral psychology' (25). In this story, even Saussure is included (19). The development of generative grammar then saw a 'conceptual shift' from E-language to I-language (24; compare 3). By implication it is dated to the mid-1950s, though by what was, 'in part, a historical accident' (29), the original choice of terms had been 'misleading'. Why then was it only after more than twenty years – or at least fifteen on an alternative view of the history – that he finally decided he had to change them?

A possible answer is that the original notion of a child 'constructing a grammar' had come to seem meaningless. In the mid-1970s, Chomsky had already begun to talk of a parallel between the acquisition of language and the growth of physical organs. 'Human cognitive systems', such as language, 'prove to be no less marvelous and intricate than the physical structures that develop in the life of the organism' (Chomsky, 1976: 10). 'Why', he goes on, 'should we not study the acquisition of a cognitive structure ... more or less as we study some complex bodily organ?' We can then talk analogously of 'the growth of language' (11), rather than the learning of language; and what is grown is then a 'mental organ'. 'The theory of language', as the matter is summarised later, 'is simply that part of human psychology that is concerned with one particular "mental organ", human language' (36). In keeping with this, Chomsky began to cast doubt on the notion of 'learning' a language. As he puts the argument in *Rules and Representations*, we do not talk of learning in the case of physical organs. Is there a reason why we should talk differently in the case of language? 'Perhaps', he answers, 'but it is not obvious.' In this case too, it seems that 'the final structure attained and its integration into a complex system of organs is largely determined by our genetic program'. 'It is entirely possible that significant components of such cognitive states [as language] are "wired in" . . . ' (Chomsky, 1980: 134f).

When it was first put forward, this idea seemed like another leap in the dark. But by the early 1980s, Chomsky had developed a framework which could be said to support it. What was 'wired in' was universal grammar: that is, a specific set of universal principles. But these principles include parameters. As the image is developed in *Knowledge of Language*, the wiring incorporates 'a finite set of switches, each of which has a finite number of positions' (Chomsky, 1986: 146). The switches can be set only in the light of experience; but when this is done, a major part of what had earlier been called a grammar ('grammar_1') is automatically determined. It has not been 'constructed'. The alternative 'grammars' were there already, and, by setting the switches, the 'learner', as the child had formerly been conceived, has simply reduced them to one. In particular, there is no sense in which children have to construct rules. The analogy between the 'learner' and the linguist constructing or devising a grammar of a language, which had originally tempted Chomsky into using the term with 'systematic ambiguity', no longer holds.

In Chomsky's account of the history, the 'principles-and-parameters model' represents a 'second conceptual shift' (1986: 6, 145). It is 'more theory-internal' than the first (6); but 'during the past [five to six] years', in which it had emerged, it had led to 'an unmistakable sense of energy and anticipation' like that which he had felt in the 1950s (5). To an observer who has followed the progress of his thought from outside, it certainly makes sense of things that in the 1970s had seemed obscure and puzzling. But in the same passage, Chomsky also remarks that it had led to a sense of 'uncertainty'. He does not immediately say where this lies. To judge from his book as a whole, he was thinking of the choice between specific theories of universal grammar, not the general topics with which this history deals. But to an outsider at least, there are uncertainties at that level too. Although it is unlikely that after only six years I have arrived at a mature historical understanding, it may be helpful if, in the remainder of this section, I move gradually from what now seems clear to what, to me again, seems less worked out.

Of the notions not already discussed, the clearest is that of 'core language'. This is another that had been introduced, as we have seen, in the mid-1970s; but 'core grammar', as it was called at that stage, had at first been given what appeared to be an ad hoc definition. It merely referred to a certain set of rules of movement and of 'construal', with the general principles thought to constrain them (again Chomsky, 1977a: 6; 1977b: 72). But by 1981 a systematic definition had been attached to it. It was simply the projection, in any individual grammar, of universal grammar. In Chomsky's 'highly idealized picture' (1981: 7), universal grammar is 'taken to be a characterization of the child's pre-linguistic state'. Alternatively, since here the 'systematic ambiguity' has not been removed, it is that state. Each parameter of universal grammar is then 'fixed in one of the permitted ways', and a 'core grammar', or (we must now say) a 'core language', is the part of an internalised language that is thus determined (Chomsky, 1981: 7, 137; 1986: 147).

As a further fall-out from the same 'conceptual shift', Chomsky found a new rationale for theories of levels. In his classic model of the 1960s, levels of representation had had a priori definitions: 'semantic interpretations' represented the meanings of sentences; 'deep structures' were defined as determining semantic interpretations, and so on. By the mid-1970s, as we have seen in §4.3, this scheme had broken down. Levels of representation were simply defined by different components of a grammar, and Chomsky himself was seeking to deny that a priori definitions had ever been given.

But there was, of course, another view of levels. In Harris's *Methods*, they had in effect been defined by successive procedures. For example, there was no a priori definition of the morpheme (say, as the smallest unit that would enter into relations between form and meaning); nor could there have been. Instead there were procedures from which morphemes resulted – that is, which would lead to a representation of a sentence as composed of morpheme *a* plus morpheme *b* and so on. In Chomsky's early theory, levels are correspondingly defined by sets of rules relating one representation to another. For example, there is a 'mapping ... that carries strings of phonemes into strings of phones' (Chomsky, 1975a [1955]: 159), and the crucial question for a theory of phonemes was the nature of that mapping. Similarly for levels of syntax. Transformations established a mapping from a set of phrase structure trees or 'P-markers' to a set of what Chomsky called 'transformation markers' or 'T-markers' (see above, §3.4). The reason why both levels of representation were established was that both phrase structure rules and transformational rules were needed, they were separate, and they were formally different.

The new theory of the 1980s was again a theory of interrelated components, or, as they were now called, 'modules'. The term 'modularity' was first used of the mind in general: to say that 'the mind is modular in character' is to say that it is 'a system of distinct thought interacting systems' (Chomsky, 1980: 28). The 'language faculty', as Chomsky had conceived it since the mid-1960s, is one of these systems within a larger system. But Chomsky's 'guess' (59) was that this faculty is itself modular. That is, 'what we normally think of as knowledge of language might consist of quite disparate cognitive systems that interweave in normal cognitive development' (58). Thus he thinks it 'makes sense, in particular, 'to distinguish what is sometimes called "grammatical competence" from "pragmatic competence"' (59). As we have seen, these terms had in fact been distinguished by Chomsky himself some five years earlier.

What of the divisions within what he had earlier called a 'sentence grammar'? In his next book, he remarks that grammar has in turn a 'modular character' (Chomsky, 1981: 7). The modules are, of course, genetically determined. That is, they are the modules of universal grammar. But universal grammar is more precisely a system of 'interacting systems' (5), which, we are told, 'can be considered from various points of view'. From one point of view, we can distinguish 'the various subcomponents of the rule system of grammar'. These are superficially the old levels: 'syntax', divided into a 'categorial component' and a 'transformational component', and so on. The most obvious change from the 1970s is that the lexicon is a separate component alongside the others. But 'from another point of view, which has become increasingly important in recent years, we can isolate subsystems of principles'. These are 'bounding theory', which includes the principles of subjacency; 'θ-theory', which deals with the assignment to noun phrases of roles such as agent, and so on. The whole system, Chomsky says, is 'highly modular', in that 'the complexity of observed phonemena is traced to the interaction of partly independent subtheories, each with its own abstract structure' (1981: 135).

It is clear both from this last remark, and from the organisation of the whole book, that the subsystems of principles are the vital part of this structure. They are the modules that constitute universal grammar, and are distinguished from each other in supposedly the way that larger modules are distinguished in the mind in general, by the different principles that operate. But what of the levels that Chomsky had carried over from his earlier work? Their status does not seem to have been spelled out at this stage. All we are explicitly told is that they are the parts of universal grammar when it is considered 'from another point of view'. But the implication, which emerges more clearly five years later, is that they are simply derivative.

Let us take for illustration a discussion of differences between English and Chinese, in respect of '*wh*-movement' (Chomsky, 1986: 75f., 152ff.). In English, this is said to take place in the assignment to sentences of S-structures: these were the nearest equivalent, since the late 1970s, of the old 'surface structures'. In Chinese, there seems at first to be no movement; but, following a native scholar, Chomsky says that the same operation takes place 'not overtly ... but rather in the mapping of S-structure to the level of L[ogical] F[orm]' (75). So, if this is right, there is at least one point in universal grammar at which a parameter will define a difference between 'S-structure' and 'LF'. That is, it will allow the possibility that a certain operation, which is known to be constrained by universal principles, is restricted in different languages to either one or the other. But then what other kind of justification do such levels need? Levels of representation are 'determined', as Chomsky puts it at one point, 'by the interaction of [the] principles' that makes up 'bounding theory', 'θ-theory', and so on (1986: 155).

The specific levels that Chomsky assumed throughout the 1980s still recall those of the 'EST' of the mid-1970s, which in turn derived from the 'Standard Theory' of the 1960s. 'S-structures' are merely less superficial than the old surface structures. 'D-structures' have the same place in the scheme as the old deep structures, though in practice they are less 'deep' than even Chomsky's underlying structures had ever been. Finally 'LF' was in origin an abbreviation for the old 'logical form'. But since the basis for the model has changed, there has been little in it that can be taken as given. Principles and parameters that had at first been thought to establish different levels may in the end prove not to. Hence there might no longer be a need for certain components to be separated. Equally, a new account of some 'subtheory' might suggest a new component.

That much is straightforward, even though, by the end of the decade, neither possibility had been realised. But if there was no a priori scheme of levels, there was also no clear sense in which the categorial and transformational components are 'syntactic', while the 'LF-component', as it is called at the same stage in the early 1980s (Chomsky, 1981: 5, 135), was by implication not 'syntactic'.

Let us look in that light at what happened to the notion of 'logical form'. It was introduced, as we have seen, as a form of semantic interpretation. 'I use the ... term', as Chomsky puts it in the introduction to his *Essays on Form and Interpretation*, 'to refer to those aspects of semantic representation that are strictly determined by grammar, abstracted from other cognitive systems' (1977a: 5). Although there is no citable definition in *Reflections on Language*, that is also plainly what had been meant there (Chomsky, 1976 [1975]: 104f.). But we have also seen how, by 1977, Chomsky was beginning to talk of rules for 'the syntax of logical forms'. As he remarks four pages later in the same introduction, 'strictly speaking, we might say that the rules mapping [what is now S-structure] to LF are not "semantic rules" but rather rules concerned with the syntax of LF'. That is, he goes on, they are 'rules that give the representations that are directly interpreted through the theories of meaning, reference, and language use, in interaction with other cognitive structures beyond the grammar' (1977a: 9f.).

Three years later, 'LF' (as the level is now called) is still a 'mental representation[ ] of ... meaning', parallel to 'phonetic form' (subsequently 'PF') as a representation of the form of sentences (Chomsky, 1980: 143). But in later work Chomsky begins to talk instead of an 'interface'. If we 'assume' that universal grammar has 'three fundamental components', two of which are PF and LF, 'it is reasonable to suppose' that these 'stand at the interface of grammatical competence, one mentally represented system, and other systems' (1981: 17f.). This is how both levels are again described in *Knowledge of Language*. 'PF and LF constitute the "interface" between language and other cognitive systems, yielding direct representations of sound ... and meaning ... as language and other systems interact' (Chomsky, 1986: 68). The 'LF representation' is the 'interface between syntax (in the broad sense) and the systems of language use' (76, identically 98). Is it then itself a level of syntax? Sometimes Chomsky implied that it is not. In his account of the 'subcomponents of the rule system', syntax is the categorial component plus the transformational component (again 1981: 5, 135). So, for example, one can contrast 'syntactic movement' with 'movement in the LF-component' (1981: 66, 197), or talk of the 'syntactic and LF components of the language' (1986: 162). But in other places LF was included in syntax. In the earlier book Chomsky talks at one point of 'each syntactic level (LF, D-structure, S-structure)' (1981: 335); similarly in the later (1986: 84). It is perhaps worth a note in passing that in this second passage and elsewhere (1986: 155) PF is also called 'surface structure'. As D-structures and S-structures were always potentially identical, so are S-structures and 'LF-representations'. There are examples in both books (1981: 19, 21, 35; 1986: 75f. especially).

In citing these passages I am not trying to suggest that Chomsky was confused or inconsistent, but rather to illustrate what now seemed to be true, that in the 'principles-and-parameters model' to call one level 'syntactic' and another 'semantic' no longer made any real sense. In the logic of the model as it emerges in these books, there can be levels of representation within core language to the extent that different complexes of principles or different values of parameters distinguish them. Insofar as they were like those envisaged before what Chomsky calls his second 'conceptual shift', we could perhaps continue to use the old names. But if I have understood the logic correctly, they were mere names.

Where did that leave the account of meaning? Chomsky as always is primarily a student of syntax, or of 'grammar' in a traditional sense. Therefore we can expect, as always, little more than programmatic statements and passing remarks. Nor is there any strict need for a grammarian to go beyond that. The theory of meaning is another topic; and although, as Chomsky stresses in a popular work, he does not 'make a sharp distinction between philosophy and science' (1988: 2), it does seem to involve arguments that cannot be resolved empirically, and are in the domain of philosophy as it is now conceived. For students of grammar the basic problem is simply to decide what aspects of meaning are relevant to their own work.

In the tradition which we have been examining in this book, the earliest answer is that of Bloomfield's *Language*. Briefly, we must assume that there are recurrent forms with recurrent meanings. These linguistic meanings can be analysed into lexical meanings ('sememes' in his terminology) and grammatical meanings ('episememes'). In that sense, linguistic meanings were (as it was later said) 'compositional'. It is unfortunate that commentators have tended to focus on Bloomfield's reductionist account of meaning in the wider sense, to the exclusion of his 'fundamental assumption' and its consequences. These remained in the tradition, waiting to resurface.

The next answer was that of the Post-Bloomfieldians, which Chomsky followed in the 1950s. In *Knowledge of Language*, he stresses that at this time he was 'primarily concerned with the problem of designing the theory of linguistic structure ... so that the rule systems selected will be adequate to explain semantic properties of expressions' (Chomsky, 1986: 205, n. 10). That is true, in the sense that, as he put it in *The Logical Structure of Linguistic Theory*, he was concerned to 'shed light' on 'intuitions about linguistic form', such as that *They are flying planes* is ambiguous (see above, §4.1). But a crucial feature of the explanation was that the rule systems must be justified without reference to meaning. That is what Harris and others also advocated, and in discussing examples like *old men and women* they were addressing the problem of meaning in the same way. Chomsky simply did more than anyone else to deliver on the promise.

The next answer was that of Katz, Fodor and Postal. As I have interpreted it, this was in essence a structuralist answer, like that of Bloomfield. More obviously, however, it was an attempt to integrate into a generative grammar an account of the meanings of sentences in which, as Harris had put it at one point in *Methods in Structural Linguistics*, 'the meaning of each morpheme in the utterance will be defined in such a way that the sum of the meanings of the constituent morphemes is the meaning of the utterance' (Harris, 1951a: 190). Chomsky endorsed their view in the 1960s, but had abandoned it, along with most of the so-called 'Standard Theory' that went with it, by the early to mid-1970s.

The answer that emerged in the early 1980s is perhaps more reminiscent of one which might have been articulated before the advent of structuralism. 'Meaning' in one sense is what lies beyond the 'interface' called 'LF'. Towards the end of the 'Pisa lectures', Chomsky talks of 'the interpretation' of 'LF' (1981: 324; compare 1986: 76 especially). But even the 'step in the process of interpretation' that he describes there 'is not to be confused with what might be called "real semantics"'. Instead it is 'in effect an extension of syntax, the construction of another level of mental representation beyond LF, ... this further level then entering into "real semantic interpretation"'. By 'real semantics', Chomsky means 'the study of the relation between language or language use and the world'. Similarly, in *Knowledge of Language*, he talks, as we have seen, of LF as an 'interface between syntax ... and the systems of language use' (again Chomsky, 1986: 76, 98). Elsewhere in the same book, it is described as an interface between language and other cognitive systems, including 'conceptual systems and pragmatic systems' (68); between 'formal structure' and 'other components of the mind/brain which interact with the language faculty ... in the use of language in thought, interpretation, and expression' (157).

There are hints in these wordings of many different semantic theories – quite properly, since 'real semantics' is not Chomsky's concern. In the verbal discussion printed with the 'Managua lectures', he says that there are 'no very good theories of meaning' anyway (1988: 191). But he goes on to stress that his own work is, of course, concerned with meaning. In particular, he says a great deal in these lectures about lexical meaning. At a distance of four years from this last book, and eleven from the publication of the 'Pisa lectures', there are perhaps few commentators who will still seek to understand the 'principles-and-parameters' model in the light of what he said in 1965. But the distinction between real semantics and this new conception of linguistic meaning would surely perplex them.

The earlier model was in part undermined in what I have called the period of 'transition' (§4.3). But of the developments that belong to the 1980s, the one that is potentially the most important concerns the interaction of the levels of syntax, in the 'broad' sense of *Knowledge of Language*, with the lexicon. In 1965 (let us remind ourselves) a lexicon was part of the 'base component' that generated deep structures. That was still true in *Reflections on Language* (see again Chomsky, 1976: 105). But when the 'principles-and-parameters' model was introduced, it became a component on a par with 'syntax', the LF-component and the PF-component (Chomsky, 1981: 5). Furthermore, these other levels are normally considered in abstraction from it. They are said to be the 'three fundamental components' of universal grammar, and their relations are shown together in a flow chart (1981: 17; compare 1986: 67f.). Chomsky also makes clear that universal grammar allows a finite set of possible core languages. That is, 'there are finitely many parameters and each has a finite number of values' (1986: 149; compare 1981: 11). But this is specifically 'apart from the lexicon'. The lexicon too is subject to universal principles; but there is no closed set of possible lexical components.

One rather obvious interpretation was that the 'fundamental components' form one module, and the lexicon another. What matters more, however, is the role played by the lexicon in determining how syntax will develop. To borrow terms from another tradition, each lexeme has a valency. For example, a verb like *give* 'takes' (to use a term that goes back to the beginnings of Western linguistics) a direct object and an indirect object. For Apollonius Dyscolus, whose work on syntax is the first we have, that meant that its construction derived from its meaning. A sentence would not be complete and congruent if such a verb were not construed with one noun in one case and another in another case (trans. Householder, 1981: book 3; exposition Matthews, 1990b: 285ff., 296ff.).

In the 1980s Chomsky moved towards this. In his earlier work, the rules of the 'categorial component' had specified a set of structures whose elements were the parts of speech N[oun], V[erb] and so on. There was then a 'lexical rule' (Chomsky, 1965: 84) which 'inserted' specific lexical elements at the places in these structures where they were permitted. But he now introduced a 'guiding principle' by which 'representations at each syntactic level ... are projected from the lexicon, in that they observe the subcategorization properties of lexical items' (Chomsky, 1981: 29). If it holds, 'the role of the categorial component of the base is reduced', he says, 'to a minimum'. 'It will simply express language-particular idiosyncra[s]ies that are not determined by the lexicon' (31).

I have to confess that when I reviewed Hudson's more radical proposals in *Word Grammar*, I still believed that Chomsky's view was as it had been before (Hudson, 1984; Matthews, 1985). For one reader, therefore, the significance of this principle had evidently not sunk in. But the argument is spelled out more clearly in his next book, and the nature of the lexicon itself is explored further.

The general aim is again to develop a theory of universal grammar (perhaps more strictly of universal 'syntax'?) such that core languages derive, on the analogy of setting switches, by no more than the fixing of parameters. Thus a child will no longer have to 'construct' specific rules. Chomsky points to two ways to achieve this. Firstly, we may say of certain kinds of element that, as a class, they require other elements. In the ancient view, for instance, an adverb in general requires or 'seeks' (ζητεῖ) a verb; conversely a verb can take an adverb. In the same way – though he naturally does not draw the parallel – Chomsky says that $\bar{N}$s 'take[ ] a determiner'. This is 'a general property of language': to be precise, it is one of many such relations that in effect make up his 1980s formulation of 'X-bar theory' (Chomsky, 1986: 82; compare especially Chomsky, 1988: 68ff.). Therefore children do not have to work it out.

Secondly, if there are differences among members of a word class, they are determined by the lexicon. For example, *see* is 'lexically characterised as a transitive verb'; hence 'it must have an object, syntactically represented as a complement in a Verb Phrase', at each of the levels of D-structure, S-structure and LF. Lexical properties are thus projected onto 'every syntactic level' (Chomsky, 1986: 84). What then is the status of these properties? A grammarian in the ancient tradition would say that they are properties of meaning – 'meaning' in a sense, of course, in which semantics is not opposed to syntax. For good measure, the property of belonging to a specific part of speech would also be one of meaning.

For specific lexical properties, it is clear that Chomsky is essentially saying the same. In a section on the lexicon, he begins by distinguishing two kinds of 'selectional' features. One he calls 'semantic selection' (or 's-selection'). For example, the entry in the lexicon for *hit* 'will specify that it takes a complement with the semantic role of recipient of action (patient), and that its subject has the semantic role of agent' (1986: 86). The other he calls 'categorial selection' (or 'c-selection'). For example, '*hit* takes an NP complement'. But does this too need to be specified? As Chomsky remarks, its 'specification seems redundant; if *hit* s-selects a patient, then this element will be an NP'. To the extent that c-selection follows from it, 'the lexicon can be restricted to s-selection'.

In the pages that follow (86–92), Chomsky tries to show how the 'syntactic' valency (as another tradition would describe it) may in general be reduced to 'semantic' valency. The details need not concern us. But if this is successful, the old Bloomfieldian distinction of form and meaning may finally be near to collapse.

I remarked in §4.2 that Chomsky's concept of universal grammar seems to have been at first a leap in the dark. It would perhaps be unreasonable to suggest that it is still that. But how far is a commitment to his programme still essentially a matter of faith?

We seem at present to be in an age of live and let live, in which each school gets on with its own thing. But if Chomsky and his followers are right, the detailed theory that has emerged since 1980 must for any linguist be by far the most exciting thing there is. As he puts it in his purplest vein, 'we are beginning to see into the hidden nature of the mind ... really for the first time in history'. 'It is possible that ... we are approaching a situation that is comparable with the physical sciences in the seventeenth century, when the great scientific revolution took place......' (Chomsky, 1988: 91f.). Faced with such rhetoric, any linguist who did not agree might be expected, for their own satisfaction at least, to say why. But in practice there has been little published debate. On the one hand, there are born-again scholars whose academic life is driven by his ideas. On the other hand, there are those who, through what might in another theology be called invincible ignorance, seem content to have nothing to do with them.

It is hard to comment as a historian without lapsing into a style that is more like that of a critical review. For that reason I have inserted a line space before these final paragraphs. But if we look back over Chomsky's career, it does seem that he is a scholar whose assumptions and goals have never in fact been open to direct argument.

It is possible that this ultimately comes from Harris. Take, for example, the attempt by Harris and his contemporaries in the 1940s to reduce intonation to the model of phonemes and morphemes. As he remarks at one point, only some intonations may be reducible: for example, the 'assertion or command intonations' may be, but not 'the ones for excitement or for irony' (1951b: 303). But could that be evidence that the attempt is mistaken? By implication, it would appear not. Some intonations are seen as 'part of language', while others are what Harris calls 'gestural sounds'. Which are which is 'simply the question of which of them can be described like the other elements of language – as combinations and sequences of phonemic elements'. That is, 'at least some of the distinction' is precisely 'a matter of the linguist's methods of analysis'. By implication, the method itself cannot be attacked by any direct appeal to facts.

This appeal to the method finds an echo in a passage in *Syntactic Structures*, according to which we 'let the grammar itself decide', in doubtful cases, whether sequences are grammatical (Chomsky, 1957: 14). Some sequences are 'definitely sentences' and others 'definitely non-sentences'. A grammar is therefore 'set up in the simplest way' to account for these, and in the intermediate cases, where our evidence is not definite, sequences will be either generated or not generated. As Chomsky puts it, 'this is a familiar feature of explication'. But consider the plight of someone who wants to argue that grammars should not be – or, if we are talking of internalised 'grammars$_1$', are not – determinate. They cannot simply point to cases, though there are many, where the judgments of speakers are doubtful. That would be water off Chomsky's back.

In later work, he began to develop a doctrine that, in many applications, may have seemed innocuous. Take, for example, a rule that deals with an inflection or a vowel alternation. It may have exceptions, in the sense in which grammarians have always used this term. But these need not invalidate the generalisation. As he and Halle put it in the preface to their joint work on phonology, 'counterexamples to a grammatical rule are of interest only if they lead to the construction of a new grammar of even greater generality or if they show some underlying principle is fallacious or misformulated' (Chomsky & Halle, 1968: ix). Otherwise citation of them is 'beside the point'.

In the context of their book, that meant in particular that it was no use citing exceptions to their rules for English stress. Counter examples would again be interesting only if they led to more general stress rules. But now suppose that some poor souls had wanted to argue that stress in English was for the most part free. Chomsky and Halle had them disqualified from the start. Either one played the game by their rules, in which case one could only join in the hunt for deeper generalisations; or, in the light of their conception of the goals of linguistic research, one could not be taken seriously.

The problem for the would-be critic of universal grammar is that it has come to be defended in the same way. Suppose that in some language one discovers counter examples to Chomsky's principles. For example, the hypothesis appears to predict that speakers will not say and accept things like *They knew that each other had seen it*; but, from our evidence, it seems that they do. How then can one argue?

One can clearly play the game as Chomsky has prescribed it. So, if the language is one not previously studied in this context, one might hope to work in some set of parameters that will cover the new facts. Perhaps it may be better to propose a different set of principles altogether. That too is legitimate: it is like proposing a more general set of stress rules. But the reason for postulating a universal grammar is that in particular languages there are things that speakers cannot know from experience. To be precise, this is said to be a 'near certainty' (Chomsky, 1981: 3). Suppose then that one is minded to cast doubt on that argument. At first sight, one course might be to argue that the knowledge of particular speakers is not, in fact, correctly characterised. For example, it is claimed that there are principles which explain, among other things, why speakers of English reject 'anaphors' as the subject of a finite clause. So, one looks for counter examples. One might remark, as has indeed been remarked, that if occasion warrants people will quite happily say things like *They knew that each other had seen it*. Therefore it might be suggested that the matter is more indeterminate, and that the true explanation may be of another kind. Alternatively, one might show that the principles make wider predictions about what is grammatical in English or about how forms must be construed, and that some of these are wrong.

But all this would again be water off Chomsky's back. Once more, speakers know that certain forms are wrong. For example, they just cannot accept a reflexive as the subject of a finite clause (*They knew that themselves had seen it*). In such a case, their knowledge of the language is 'radically underdetermined by evidence available to [a] language learner' and it is a near certainty that it 'must ... be attributed' to universal grammar (Chomsky, 1981: 3).

Accept that, and counter examples are again irrelevant unless they lead to a better theory of the same kind. In the case we have envisaged, the principles will account for a certain range of facts. Therefore, for Chomsky, they will explain them, in the same sense that, in generative phonology, the stress rules would have been said to explain the stress on all the words for which they got it right. Naturally there may be other facts that the principles do not account for. But these are simply things that, as yet, we have not explained. Anyone who tries to argue beyond that is again in the position of someone who wanted to argue that the stress in English is free. If we think we can do it, it is because we are assuming that, 'if something is unexplained, then nothing is explained' (Chomsky, 1981: 149). Such arguments are 'unfortunately all too common in the linguistic literature' (that is, as it was then), but the assumption 'can only be regarded as pathological'.

These remarks are cited from a note excoriating a brief review of mine (Matthews, 1980). I am therefore anxious to make clear that my aim as a historian is not polemic but simply that of elucidating what I take to be Chomsky's view. Nor do I wish to suggest that, in principle, the hypothesis that there is a genetically determined universal grammar could not, in the end, be acknowledged to have been wrong. It might be, for example, that as more and more languages are studied, and either more and more parameters are admitted, or more and more rules have to be seen as lying outside core language, the problems facing a child who must choose among all possible syntaxes and knows the structure of every possible lexicon will turn out to be as daunting as the problems that appeared to justify the hypothesis in the first place. Nor, finally, is any historian of ideas likely to disparage acts of faith. That is so often the way in which progress in science has been made.

Faith is a beautiful thing, which a non-believer can only regard with awe. At the time of writing, that seems to be how matters stand. There are many who share Chomsky's faith, and for them 'The research program of modern linguistics' (Chomsky, 1988: Ch. 2) must without arrogance be his programme. Others cannot bring themselves to accept that it has empirical content. 'C'est magnifique, mais peut-être ce n'est pas la linguistique.' But all they can do is watch and wait.

References

Akmajian, A. & Heny, F. (1975). *An Introduction to the Principles of Transformational Syntax* (Cambridge, Mass.: MIT Press).

Anderson, S. R. (1982). Where's morphology? *LIn* 13: 571–612.

(1985). *Phonology in the Twentieth Century: Theories of Rules and Theories of Representations* (University of Chicago Press).

(1992). *A-Morphous Morphology* (Cambridge University Press).

Andresen, J. T. (1990). *Linguistics in America 1769–1924: a Critical History* (London: Routledge).

Aronoff, M. (1976). *Word Formation in Generative Grammar* (Cambridge, Mass.: MIT Press).

Bach. E. (1964). *An Introduction to Transformational Grammars* (New York: Holt, Rinehart & Winston).

(1974). *Syntactic Theory* (New York: Holt, Rinehart & Winston).

(1977). Comments on the paper by Chomsky. In Culicover *et al.* (eds.), 1977: 133–55.

Bach, E. & Harms, R. T. (eds.) (1968). *Universals in Linguistic Theory* (New York: Holt, Rinehart & Winston).

Bar-Hillel, Y. (1954). Logical syntax and semantics. *Lg* 30: 230–7.

Bazell, C. E. (1949). On the problem of the morpheme. *Archivum Linguisticum* 1: 1–15. Reprinted in Hamp *et al.* (eds.), 1966: 216–26.

(1953). *Linguistic Form* (Istanbul: Istanbul Press).

Bloch, B. (1946). Studies in colloquial Japanese II: syntax. *Lg* 22: 20–48. Reprinted in *RiL* 154–84.

(1947). English verb inflection. *Lg* 23: 399–418. Reprinted in *RiL* 243–54.

(1948). A set of postulates for phonemic analysis. *Lg* 24: 3–46.

(1949). Leonard Bloomfield. *Lg* 25: 87–94. Reprinted *LBA* 524–32.

Bloch, B. & Trager, G. L. (1942). *Outline of Linguistic Analysis* (Baltimore: Linguistic Society of America).

Bloomfield, L. (1914). *An Introduction to the Study of Language* (London: Bell), [US edn New York: Holt].

(1915). Sentence and word. *Transactions of the American Philological Association* 45: 65–75. Reprinted in *LBA* 60–9.

(1917). Subject and predicate. *Transactions of the American Philological Association* 47: 13–22. Reprinted in *LBA* 70–7.

(1922). Review of Sapir, 1921. *The Classical Weekly* 15: 142–3. Reprinted in *LBA* 91–4.
Review of Saussure, 1922 [1916] *Modern Language Journal* 8: 317–19. Reprinted in *LBA* 106–8.
(1925). Why a linguistic society? *Lg* 1: 1–5. Reprinted in *LBA* 109–12.
(1926). A set of postulates for the science of language. *Lg* 2: 153–64. Reprinted in *LBA* 128–38, *RiL* 26–31.
(1927). On recent work on general linguistics. *Modern Philology* 25: 211–30. Reprinted in *LBA* 173–90.
(1930). Linguistics as a science. *Studies in Philology* 27: 553–7. Reprinted in *LBA* 227–30.
(1931). Review of Ries, *Was ist ein Satz? Lg* 7: 204–9. Reprinted in *LBA* 231–6.
(1934). Review of Havers, *Handbuch der erklärenden Syntax*. *Lg* 10: 32–9. Reprinted in *LBA* 281–8.
(1935). *Language* (London: Allen & Unwin), [US edn New York: Holt, 1933].
(1936). Language or ideas? *Lg* 12: 89–95. Reprinted in *LBA* 322–8.
(1939a). *Linguistic Aspects of Science* (International Encyclopaedia of Unified Science, Vol. 1.4) (University of Chicago Press).
(1939b). Menomini morphophonemics. In *Etudes phonologiques dédiées à la mémoire de M. le Prince N. S. Trubetzkoy, Travaux du Cercle Linguistique de Prague* 8: 105–15. Reprinted in *LBA* 351–62.
(1942). Philosophical aspects of language. In *Studies in the History of Culture* (Menasha, Wis.: George Banta Publishing Co.), 173–7. Reprinted in *LBA* 396–9.
(1943). Meaning. *Monatshefte für deutschen Unterricht* 35: 101–6. Reprinted in *LBA* 400–5.
(1944). Review of Bodmer, *The Loom of Language*. *American Speech* 19: 211–13. Reprinted in *LBA* 410–12.
(1946). Twenty-one years of the Linguistic Society. *Lg* 22: 1–3. Reprinted in *LBA* 491–4.
Boas, F. (1911). Introduction. In *Handbook of American Indian Languages*, Part 1 (Washington: Government Printing Office). Reprinted, with introduction by Stuart, C. I. J. M. (Washington: Georgetown University Press, n. d.).
Bolinger, D. L. (1961). Syntactic blends and other matters. *Lg* 37: 366–81.
(1965). The atomization of meaning. *Lg* 41: 555–73.
(1975). *Aspects of Language*, second edn (New York: Harcourt Brace Jovanovich), [first edn 1968].
Bolling, G. M. (1929). Linguistics and philology. *Lg* 5: 27–32..
(1935). Review of Bloomfield, 1935. *Lg* 11: 251–2. Reprinted in *LBA* 277–8.
Bresnan, J. (1978). A realistic transformational grammar. In Halle, M., Bresnan, J. & Miller, G. A. (eds.), *Linguistic Theory and Psychological Reality* (Cambridge, Mass.: MIT Press), 1–59.
Brown, R. (1970). *Psycholinguistics: Selected Papers*, with Gilman, A. *et al.* (New York: Macmillan).
(1973). *A First Language: the Early Stages* (Cambridge, Mass.: Harvard University Press).

Burchfield, R. W. (ed.) (1976). *A Supplement to the Oxford English Dictionary*, Vol. 2 (Oxford: Clarendon Press).

Carroll, J. B. (1953). *The Study of Language: a Survey of Linguistics and Related Disciplines in America* (Cambridge, Mass.: Harvard University Press).

(ed.) (1956). *Language, Thought and Reality: Selected Writings of Benjamin Lee Whorf* (Cambridge, Mass.: MIT Press).

Chafe, W. L. (1970a). *Meaning and the Structure of Language* (University of Chicago Press).

(1970b). *A Semantically Based Sketch of Onondaga* (Baltimore, Supplement to *IJAL* 36, 2).

Chomsky, N. (1953). Systems of syntactic analysis. *Journal of Symbolic Logic* 18: 242–56.

(1955a). Semantic considerations in grammar. In Weinstein, R. M. (ed.), *Report of the Sixth Annual Round Table Meeting on Linguistics and Language Teaching* (*MSLL*) (Washington: Georgetown University Press), 141–50.

(1955b). Logical syntax and semantics: their linguistic relevance. *Lg* 31: 36–45.

(1956). Three models for the description of language. *I.R.E. Transactions on Information Theory* IT–2: 113–24.

(1957). *Syntactic Structures* (The Hague: Mouton).

(1959). Review of Skinner, *Verbal Behavior Lg* 35: 26–58. Reprinted in Fodor & Katz (eds.), 1964: 547–78.

(1961a). On the notion 'rule of grammar'. In Jakobson, R. (ed.), *Structure of Language and its Mathematical Aspects* (Providence: American Mathematical Society), 6–24. Reprinted in Fodor & Katz (eds.), 1964: 119–36.

(1961b). Some methodological remarks on generative grammar. *Word* 17: 219–39.

(1962). A transformational approach to syntax. In Hill (ed.), 1962 [1958]: 124–58. Reprinted in Fodor & Katz (eds.), 1964: 211–45.

(1964). The logical basis of linguistic theory. In Lunt, H. G. (ed.), *Proceedings of the Ninth International Congress of Linguists, Cambridge, Mass., August 27–31, 1962* (The Hague: Mouton), 914–78.

(1965). *Aspects of the Theory of Syntax* (Cambridge, Mass.: MIT Press).

(1966a). *Topics in the Theory of Generative Grammar* (The Hague: Mouton). [Also in Sebeok, T. A. (ed.), *Current Trends in Linguistics*, Vol. 3: *Theoretical Foundations* (The Hague: Mouton, 1966), 1–60.]

(1966b). *Cartesian Linguistics* (New York: Harper & Row).

(1970a). Remarks on nominalization. In Jacobs & Rosenbaum (eds.), 1970: 184–221. Reprinted in Chomsky, 1972a: 11–61.

(1970b). Deep structure, surface structure, and semantic interpretation. In Jakobson, R. & Kawamoto, S. (eds.), *Studies in General and Oriental Linguistics Presented to Shiro Hattori on the Occasion of his Sixtieth Birthday* (Tokyo: TEC Co.), 52–91. Reprinted in Chomsky, 1972a: 62–119.

(1972a). *Studies on Semantics in Generative Grammar* (The Hague: Mouton).

(1972b). *Language and Mind*, enlarged edn (New York: Harcourt Brace Jovanovich), [first edn of Chs. 1–3, 1968].

(1973). Conditions on transformations. In Anderson, S. R. & Kiparsky, P.

(eds.), *A Festschrift for Morris Halle* (New York: Holt, Rinehart & Winston), 232–86. Reprinted in Chomsky, 1977a: 81–160.
(1975a). *The Logical Structure of Linguistic Theory* (University of Chicago Press). [Typescript described as dating from 1955–6.]
(1975b). Conditions on rules of grammar. In Cole, R. (ed.), *Current Issues in Linguistic Theory* (Bloomington: Indiana University Press, 1977 [1975]), 3–50. Reprinted in Chomsky, 1977a: 163–210.
(1976). *Reflections on Language* (London: Fontana/Maurice Temple Smith) [US edn 1975].
(1977a). *Essays on Form and Interpretation* (New York: North-Holland).
(1977b). On wh-movement. In Culicover *et al.* (eds.), 1977: 71–132.
(1979). *Language and Responsibility*, based on conversations with Mitsou Ronat, trans. Viertel, J. (Hassocks: Harvester Press) [French edn, *Dialogues avec Mitsou Ronat* (Paris: Flammarion, 1977)].
(1980). *Rules and Representations* (Oxford: Blackwell).
(1981). *Lectures on Government and Binding* (Dordrecht: Foris).
(1986). *Knowledge of Language: its Nature, Origin, and Use* (New York: Praeger).
(1988). *Language and Problems of Knowledge: the Managua Lectures* (Cambridge, Mass.: MIT Press).
Chomsky, N. & Halle, M. (1968). *The Sound Pattern of English* (New York: Harper & Row).
Chomsky, N., Huybregts, R. & van Riemsdijk, H. (1982). *The Generative Enterprise* (Dordrecht: Foris).
Chomsky, N. & Lasnik, H. (1977). Filters and control. *LIn* 8: 425–504.
Coleman, L. & Kay, P. (1981). Prototype semantics. *Lg* 57: 26–44.
Collitz, H. (1925). The scope and aims of linguistic science. Summary in *Lg* 1: 14–16.
Comrie, B. (1981). *Language Universals and Linguistic Typology: Syntax and Morphology* (Oxford: Blackwell).
Croft, W. (1990). *Typology and Universals* (Cambridge University Press).
Culicover, P. W. (1976). *Syntax* (New York: Academic Press).
Culicover, P. W., Wasow, T. & Akmajian, A. (eds.), (1977). *Formal Syntax* (New York: Academic Press).
Darnell, R. (1990). *Edward Sapir: Linguist, Anthropologist, Humanist* (Berkeley: University of California Press).
De Groot, A. W. (1949). *Structurele Syntaxis* (The Hague: Servire).
Debrunner, A. (1936). Review of Bloomfield, 1933 (1935). *Indogermanische Forschungen* 54: 148–9. Reprinted in *LBA* 278–80.
Edgerton, F. (1933). Review of Bloomfield, 1933 (1935). *JAOS* 53: 295–7. Reprinted in *LBA* 258–60.
Fillmore, C. J. (1966). A proposal concerning English prepositions. In Dinneen, F. P. (ed.), *Report of the Seventh Annual Round Table Meeting on Linguistics and Language Studies* (*MSLL*) (Washington: Georgetown University Press), 19–33.
(1968). The case for case. In Bach & Harms (eds.), 1968: 1–88.

Firth, J. R. (1951). General linguistics and descriptive grammar. *TPhS* 69–87. Reprinted in Firth, *Papers in Linguistics 1934–51* (London: Oxford University Press, 1957), 216–28.

Fodor, J. A. & Katz, J. J. (eds.), (1964). *The Structure of Language: Readings in the Philosophy of Language* (Englewood Cliffs: Prentice-Hall).

Fodor, J. D. (1977). *Semantics: Theories of Meaning in Generative Grammar* (New York: Crowell).

Fries, C. C. (1954). Meaning and linguistic analysis. *Lg* 30: 57–68.

Fromkin, V. & Rodman, R. (1988). *An Introduction to Language*, fourth edn (New York: Holt, Rinehart & Winston), [first edn. 1974].

Gabelentz, G. von der (1981). *Die Sprachwissenschaft, ihre Aufgaben, Methoden und bisherige Ergebnisse* (Leipzig: Tauchnitz).

Gleason, H. A. (1961). *An Introduction to Descriptive Linguistics*, second edn (New York: Holt, Rinehart & Winston), [first edn 1955].

(1965). *Linguistics and English Grammar* (New York: Holt, Rinehart & Winston).

Gleitman, L. R. (1965). Coordinating conjunctions in English. *Lg* 41: 260–93. Reprinted in Reibel & Schane (eds.), 1969: 80–112.

Greenberg, J. H. (ed.), (1963). *Universals of Language: Report of a Conference held at Dobbs Ferry, New York April 13–15, 1961* (Cambridge, Mass.: MIT Press).

(ed.) (1978). *Universals of Human Language*, Vol. 1: *Method and Theory* (Stanford University Press).

Gruber, J. S. (1967). Look and see. *Lg* 43: 937–47.

Haas, W. (1954). On defining linguistic units. *TPhS* 54–84.

(1973). Review article on Lyons, 1968. *JL* 9: 71–113.

Hall, R. A. (1990). *A Life for Language: a Biographical Memoir of Leonard Bloomfield* (Amsterdam: Benjamins).

Halle, M. (1959). *The Sound Pattern of Russian* (The Hague: Mouton).

(1961). On the role of simplicity in linguistic descriptions. In Jakobson (ed.), 1961: 89–94.

(1962). Phonology in generative grammar. *Word* 18: 54–72.

(1973). Prolegomena to a theory of word formation. *LIn* 4: 3–16.

Hamp, E. P. (1957). *A Glossary of American Technical Linguistic Usage 1925–1950* (Utrecht/Antwerp: Spectrum).

Hamp, E. P., Householder, F. W. & Austerlitz, R. (eds.), (1966). *Readings in Linguistics II* (University of Chicago Press).

Harms, R. T. (1968). *Introduction to Phonological Theory* (Englewood Cliffs: Prentice-Hall).

Harris, Z. S. (1942). Morpheme alternants in linguistic analysis. *Lg* 18: 169–80. Reprinted in Harris, *Papers* 23–35; *RiL* 109–15.

(1945). Discontinuous morphemes. *Lg* 21: 121–7. Reprinted in Harris, *Papers* 36–44.

(1946). From morpheme to utterance. *Lg* 22: 161–83. Reprinted in Harris, *Papers* 45–70; *RiL* 142–53.

(1951a). *Methods in Structural Linguistics* (University of Chicago Press). Reissued as *Structural Linguistics* (1960).

(1951b). Review of Mandelbaum (ed.), 1949. *Lg* 27: 288–333.
(1952). Discourse analysis. *Lg* 28: 1–30. Reprinted in Harris, *Papers* 107–42; Fodor & Katz (eds.), 1964: 355–83.
(1954a). Transfer grammar. *IJAL* 20: 259–70.
(1954b). Distributional structure. *Word* 10: 146–62. Reprinted in Harris, *Papers* 3–22; Fodor & Katz (eds.), 1964: 33–49.
(1955). From phoneme to morpheme. *Lg* 31: 190–222.
(1957). Co-occurrence and transformation in linguistic structure. *Lg* 33: 283–340. Reprinted in Harris, *Papers* 143–210; Fodor & Katz (eds.), 1964: 155–210.
(1981). *Papers on Syntax*, ed. Hiż, H. (Dordrecht: Reidel).
(1991). *A Theory of Language and Information* (Oxford: Clarendon Press).
Haugen, E. (1950). The analysis of linguistic borrowing. *Lg* 26: 210–31.
(1951). Directions in modern linguistics. *Lg* 27: 211–22. Reprinted in *RiL* 357–63.
Hawkins, J. A. (1990). A parsing theory of word order universals. *LIn* 21: 223–61.
Hill, A. A. (1936). Phonetic and phonemic change. *Lg* 12: 15–22. Reprinted in *RiL* 81–4.
(1958). *Introduction to Linguistic Structures: from Sound to Sentence in English* (New York: Harcourt Brace).
(1961). Grammaticality. *Word* 17: 1–10.
(ed.) (1962). *Third Texas Conference on Problems of Linguistic Analysis in English, May 9–12, 1958* (Austin: University of Texas).
Hjelmslev, L. (1928). *Principes de grammaire générale* (Copenhagen: Høst).
Hockett, C. F. (1942). A system of descriptive phonology. *Lg* 18: 3–21. Reprinted in *RiL* 97–107.
(1947). Problems of morphemic analysis. *Lg* 23: 321–43. Reprinted in *RiL* 229–42.
(1948). A note on 'structure'. *IJAL* 14: 269–71. Reprinted in *RiL* 279–80.
(1949). Two fundamental problems in phonemics. *SIL* 7: 29–51.
(1950a). Which approach in linguistics is 'scientific'? *SIL* 8: 53–7.
(1950b). Age-grading and linguistic continuity. *Lg* 26: 449–57.
(1952a). A formal statement of morphemic analysis. *SIL* 10: 27–39.
(1952b). Review of *Recherches structurales 1949*. *IJAL* 18: 86–99.
(1954). Two models of grammatical description. *Word* 10: 210–31. Reprinted in *RiL* 386–99.
(1955). *A Manual of Phonology* (Baltimore, Supplement to *IJAL* 21, 4).
(1958). *A Course in Modern Linguistics* (New York: Macmillan).
(1961). Linguistic elements and their relations. *Lg* 37: 29–53.
(1968). *The State of the Art* (The Hague: Mouton).
(ed.) (1970). *A Leonard Bloomfield Anthology* (Bloomington: Indiana University Press).
(1980). Preserving the heritage. In Davis, B. H. & O'Cain, R. K. (eds.), *First Person Singular: Papers from the Conference on an Oral Archive for the History of American Linguistics* (Amsterdam: Benjamins), 99–107.

(1987). *Refurbishing our Foundations* (Amsterdam: Benjamins).
Hoenigswald, H. M. (1944). Internal reconstruction. *SIL* 2: 78–87.
(1946). Sound change and linguistic structure. *Lg* 22: 138–43. Reprinted in *RiL* 139–41.
(1950). The principal step in historical grammar. *Lg* 26: 357–64. Reprinted in *RiL* 298–302.
(1960). *Language Change and Linguistic Reconstruction* (University of Chicago Press).
Horrocks, G. C. (1987). *Generative Grammar* (London: Longman).
Householder, F. W. (1952). Review of Harris, 1951a. *IJAL* 18: 260–8.
(1965). On some recent claims in phonological theory. *JL* 1: 13–34.
(1981). *The Syntax of Apollonius Dyscolus*, translated, and with commentary (Amsterdam: Benjamins).
Huddleston, R. D. (1972). The development of a non-process model in American structural linguistics. *Lingua* 30: 333–84.
(1976). *An Introduction to English Transformational Syntax* (London: Longman).
Hudson, R. A. (1984). *Word Grammar* (Oxford: Blackwell).
Hymes, D. (1961). Alfred Louis Kroeber. *Lg* 37: 1–28.
Hymes, D. & Fought, J. (1981). *American Structuralism* (The Hague: Mouton), [first published in Sebeok, T. A. (ed.), *Current Trends in Linguistics*, Vol. 13: *Historiography of Linguistics* (The Hague: Mouton, 1975), 903–1176].
Jackendoff, R. S. (1972). *Semantic Interpretation in Generative Grammar* (Cambridge, Mass.: MIT Press).
(1977). *$\bar{X}$ Syntax: a Study of Phrase Structure* (Cambridge, Mass.: MIT Press).
Jacobs, R. A. & Rosenbaum, P. S. (eds.) (1970). *Readings in English Transformational Grammar* (Waltham, Mass.: Ginn).
Jakobson, R. (1948). Russian conjugation. *Word* 4: 155–67. Reprinted in Jakobson, *Selected Papers*, Vol. 2: *Word and Language* (The Hague: Mouton, 1971), 119–29.
(ed.) (1961). *Structure of Language and its Mathematical Aspects* (Providence: American Mathematical Society).
Jakobson, R., Fant, C. G. M. & Halle, M. (1952). *Preliminaries to Speech Analysis: the Distinctive Features and their Correlates* (Cambridge, Mass.: MIT Press).
Jakobson, R. & Halle, M. (1956). *Fundamentals of Language* (The Hague: Mouton).
Jespersen, O. (1922). *Language: its Nature Development and Origin* (London: Allen & Unwin).
(1924). *The Philosophy of Grammar* (London: Allen & Unwin).
(1942). *A Modern English Grammar on Historical Principles*, Vol. 6 (Copenhagen: Munksgaard).
Joos, M. (1948). *Acoustic Phonetics* (Baltimore: Supplement to *Lg* 24, 2).
(1950). Description of language design. *Journal of the Acoustical Society of America* 22: 701–8. Reprinted in *RiL* 349–56.
(ed.) (1958). *Readings in Linguistics: the Development of Linguistics in America since 1925*, second edn (New York: American Council of Learned Societies).

Katz, J. J. & Fodor, J. A. (1963). The structure of a semantic theory. *Lg* 39: 170–210. Reprinted in Fodor & Katz (eds.), 1964: 479–518.

Katz, J. J. & Postal, P. M. (1964). *An Integrated Theory of Linguistic Descriptions* (Cambridge, Mass.: MIT Press).

Kent, R. G. (1934). Review of Bloomfield, 1933 (1935). *Lg* 10: 40–8. Reprinted in *LBA* 266–74.

King, R. D. (1969). *Historical Linguistics and Generative Grammar* (Englewood Cliffs: Prentice-Hall).

Koerner, K. (1989). *Practicing Linguistic Historiography* (Amsterdam: Benjamins).

Kristeva, J. (1969). Σημειωτική: *recherches pour une sémanalyse* (Paris: Seuil).

Kroesch, S. (1933). Review of Bloomfield, 1933 (1935). *Journal of English and Germanic Philology* 32: 594–7. Reprinted in *LBA* 260–4.

Kuhn, T. S. (1962). *The Structure of Scientific Revolutions* (University of Chicago Press).

Labov, W. (1963). The social motivation of a sound change. *Word* 19: 273–309. Reprinted in Labov, 1972: Ch. 1.

(1965). On the mechanism of linguistic change. In Kreidler, C. W. (ed.), *Report of the Sixteenth Annual Round Table Meeting on Linguistics and Language Studies* (*MSLL*) (Washington: Georgetown University Press), 91–114. Reprinted in Labov, 1972: Ch. 7.

(1966). *The Social Stratification of English in New York City* (Washington, D.C.: Center for Applied Linguistics).

(1972). *Sociolinguistic Patterns* (Philadelphia: University of Pennsylvania Press).

Lakoff, G. P. (1968). Instrumental adverbs and the concept of deep structure. *FL* 4: 4–29.

(1970). Global rules. *Lg* 46: 627–39.

(1971a). Presupposition and relative well-formedness. In Steinberg & Jakobovits (eds.), 1971: 329–40.

(1971b). On generative semantics. In Steinberg & Jakobovits (eds.), 1971: 232–96.

(1987). *Women, Fire, and Dangerous Things: What Categories Reveal about the Mind* (University of Chicago Press).

Lakoff, G. P. & Peters, P. S. (1969). Phrasal conjunction and symmetric predicates. In Reibel & Schane (eds.), 1969: 113–42, [originally in Harvard Computation Laboratory, Report NSF–17 (1966)].

Lamb, S. M. (1964a). On alternation, transformation, realization, and stratification. In Stuart, C. I. J. M. (ed.), *Report of the Fifteenth Annual (First International) Round Table Meeting on Linguistics and Language Studies* (*MSLL*) (Washington: Georgetown University Press), 105–22.

(1964b). The sememic approach to structural semantics. In Romney, A. K. & D'Andrade, R. G. (eds.), *Transcultural Studies in Cognition* (*American Anthropologist* 66, Part 2), 57–78.

(1966). *Outline of Stratificational Grammar* (Washington: Georgetown University Press).

Langacker, R. W. (1967). *Language and its Structure: some Fundamental Linguistic Concepts* (New York: Harcourt Brace Jovanovich).
(1969). On pronominalization and the chain of command. In Reibel & Schane (eds.), 1969: 160–86.
(1991). *Concept, Image, and Symbol: the Cognitive Basis of Grammar* (Berlin: Mouton de Gruyter).
Lees, R. B. (1957). Review of Chomsky, 1957. *Lg* 33: 375–408.
(1960a). *The Grammar of English Nominalizations* (Bloomington: Supplement to *IJAL* 26, 3).
(1960b). A multiply ambiguous adjectival construction in English. *Lg* 36: 207–21.
(1961). Grammatical analysis of the English comparative construction. *Word* 17: 171–85. Reprinted in Reibel & Schane (eds.), 1969: 303–15.
(1970). On very deep grammatical structure. In Jacobs & Rosenbaum (eds.), 1970: 134–42.
Lees, R. B. & Klima, E. S. (1963). Rules for English pronominalization. *Lg* 39: 17–28. Reprinted in Reibel & Schane (eds.), 1969: 145–59.
Lehmann, W. P. (ed.) (1978). *Syntactic Typology: Studies in the Phenomenology of Language* (Hassocks: Harvester Press).
Lepschy, G. C. (1982). *A Survey of Structural Linguistics* (London: André Deutsch), [first published Faber & Faber, 1970].
Liddell Hart, B. H. (1970). *History of the Second World War* (London: Cassell).
Lieber, R. (1989). On percolation. *Yearbook of Morphology* 2: 95–138.
Longacre, R. E. (1964). *Grammar Discovery Procedures* (The Hague: Mouton).
Lounsbury, F. G. (1953). *Oneida Verb Morphology* (New Haven: Yale University Press). Introduction, 'The method of descriptive morphology', reprinted in *RiL* 379–85.
Lyons, J. (1968). *Introduction to Theoretical Linguistics* (Cambridge University Press).
(1991). *Chomsky*, third edn (London: Fontana), [first edn 1970].
McCarthy, J. J. (1982). Prosodic templates, morphemic templates, and morphemic tiers. In van der Hulst, H. & Smith, N. (eds.), *The Structure of Phonological Representations*, Part 1 (Dordrecht: Foris), 191–223.
McCawley, J. D. (1967). Meaning and the description of languages. *Kotoba na Uchū* 2: 10–18, 38–48, 51–7. Reprinted in McCawley, 1976: 99–120.
(1968a). Concerning the base component of a transformational grammar. *FL* 4: 243–69. Reprinted in McCawley, 1976: 35–58.
(1968b). The role of semantics in a grammar. In Bach & Harms (eds.), 1968: 124–69. Reprinted in McCawley, 1976: 59–98.
(1968c). Lexical insertion in a transformational grammar without deep structure. *Papers from the Fourth Regional Meeting of the Chicago Linguistic Society* 71–80. Reprinted in McCawley, 1976: 155–66.
(1968d). Review of Sebeok (ed.), *Current Trends in Linguistics*, Vol. 3. *Lg* 44: 556–93. Reprinted in McCawley, 1976: 167–205.
(1975). Review article on Chomsky, 1972a. *Studies in English Linguistics* 3: 209–311. Reprinted in McCawley, 1982: 10–127.

(1976). *Grammar and Meaning: Papers on Syntactic and Semantic Topics* (New York: Academic Press).
(1982). *Thirty Million Theories of Grammar* (London: Croom Helm).
Mandelbaum, D. G. (ed.) (1949). *Selected Writings of Edward Sapir in Language, Culture, and Personality* (Berkeley: University of California Press).
Martinet, A. (1955). *Economie des changements phonétiques* (Berne: Francke).
(1960). *Eléments de linguistique générale* (Paris: Colin).
Matthews, P. H. (1965). The inflectional component of a word-and-paradigm grammar. *JL* 1: 139–71.
(1967). Review of Chomsky, 1965. *JL* 3: 119–52.
(1972a). *Inflectional Morphology: a Theoretical Study Based on Aspects of Latin Verb Conjugation* (Cambridge University Press).
(1972b). Review of Jacobs & Rosenbaum (eds.), 1970. *JL* 8: 125–36.
(1980). Review of Chomsky, 1980. *Times Literary Supplement*, 21 November.
(1985). Review of Hudson, 1984. *Times Literary Supplement*, 4 January.
(1986). Distributional syntax. In Bynon, T. & Palmer, F. R. (eds.), *Studies in the History of Western Linguistics in Honour of R. H. Robins* (Cambridge University Press), 245–77.
(1990a). Language as a mental faculty: Chomsky's progress. In Collinge, N. E. (ed.), *An Encyclopaedia of Language* (London: Routledge), 112–38.
(1990b). La linguistica greco-latina. In Lepschy, G. C. (ed.), *Storia della linguistica*, Vol. 1 (Bologna: Il Mulino), 187–310.
(1991). *Morphology*, second edn (Cambridge University Press), [first edn 1974].
(1992). Bloomfield's morphology and its successors. *TPhS* 90: 121–86.
Meillet, A. (1933). Review of Bloomfield, 1933 (1935). *Bulletin de la Société de Linguistique* 34, 3: 1–2. Reprinted in *LBA* 264–5.
(1937). *Introduction à l'étude comparative des langues indo-européennes*, eighth edn (Paris: Hachette), [first edn 1912].
Miller, G. A. (1951). *Language and Communication* (New York: McGraw-Hill).
Milner, J.-C. (1989). *Introduction à une science du langage* (Paris: Seuil).
Mounin, G. (1972). *La Linguistique du XXe siècle* (Paris: Presses Universitaires de France).
Newmeyer, F. J. (1980). *Linguistic Theory in America: the First Quarter-Century of Transformational Generative Grammar* (New York: Academic Press).
(1983). *Grammatical Theory: its Limits and Possibilities* (University of Chicago Press).
Nida, E. A. (1946). *Morphology* (Ann Arbor: University of Michigan Press).
Partee, B. (1975). Montague grammar and transformational grammar. *LIn* 6: 203–300.
Paul, H. (1920). *Prinzipien der Sprachgeschichte*, fifth edn (Halle: Niemeyer), [first edn 1880].
Percival, W. K. (1976). On the historical source of immediate constituent analysis. In McCawley, J. D. (ed.), *Notes from the Linguistic Underground* (New York: Academic Press), 229–42.

Perlmutter, D. M. & Soames, S. (1979). *Syntactic Argumentation and the Structure of English* (Berkeley: University of California Press).

Peters, P. S. & Ritchie, R. W. (1969). A note on the universal base hypothesis. *JL* 5: 150–2.

(1973). On the generative power of transformational grammars. *Information Sciences* 6: 49–83.

Pike, K. L. (1938). Taxemes and immediate constituents. *Lg* 14: 65–82.

(1947). Grammatical prerequisites to phonemic analysis. *Word* 3: 155–72.

(1952). More on grammatical prerequisites. *Word* 8: 106–21.

(1967). *Language in Relation to a Unified Theory of the Structure of Human Behavior*, second edn (The Hague: Mouton), [first edn, 3 vols., 1954–60].

Popper, K. (1959). *The Logic of Scientific Discovery* (London: Hutchinson).

Postal, P. M. (1964). *Constituent Structure: a Study of Contemporary Models of Syntactic Description* (Bloomington: Supplement to *IJAL* 30, 1).

(1970a). On the surface verb 'remind'. *LIn* 1: 37–120.

(1970b). The method of universal grammar. In Garvin, P. L. (ed.), *Method and Theory in Linguistics* (The Hague: Mouton), 113–31.

Reibel, D. A. & Schane, S. A. (eds.) (1969). *Modern Studies in English: Readings in Transformational Grammar* (Englewood Cliffs: Prentice-Hall).

Ries, J. (1927). *Was ist Syntax?* Second edn (Prague: Taussig & Taussig) [first edn 1894].

(1931). *Was ist ein Satz?* (Prague: Taussig & Taussig).

Robins, R. H. (1988). Leonard Bloomfield: the man and the man of science. *TPhS* 86: 63–87.

(1990). *A Short History of Linguistics*, third edn (London: Longman), [first edn 1967].

Ross, J. R. (1969). On the cyclic nature of English pronominalization. In Reibel & Schane (eds.), 1969: 187–200.

(1970). Gapping and the order of constituents. In Bierwisch, M. & Heidolph, K. E. (eds.), *Progress in Linguistics: a Collection of Papers* (The Hague: Mouton), 249–59.

Sampson, G. (1980). *Schools of Linguistics: Competition and Evolution* (London: Hutchinson).

Sapir, E. (1921). *Language: an Introduction to the Study of Speech* (New York: Harcourt Brace), paperback edn London: Rupert Hart-Davis, n.d.

(1924). The grammarian and his language. *American Mercury* 1: 149–55. Reprinted in Mandelbaum (ed.), 1949: 150–9.

(1925). Sound patterns in language. *Lg* 1: 37–51. Reprinted in Mandelbaum (ed.), 1949: 33–45; *RiL* 19–25.

(1929). The status of linguistics as a science. *Lg* 5: 207–14. Reprinted in Mandelbaum (ed.), 1949: 160–6.

(1930). *Totality* (Baltimore: Supplement to *Lg*).

(1933). La Réalité psychologique des phonèmes. In Delacroix, H. *et al.*, *Psychologie du langage* (Paris: Félix Alcan). Reprinted in English, 'The psychological reality of phonemes', Mandelbaum (ed.), 1949: 46–60.

(1944). Grading. *Philosophy of Science* 11: 93–116. Reprinted in Mandelbaum (ed.), 1949: 122–49.
Sapir, E. & Swadesh, M. (1932). *The Expression of the Ending-point Relation in English, French and German*, ed. Morris, A. V. (Baltimore: Supplement to *Lg*).
Saussure, F. de (1916). *Cours de linguistique générale* (Paris: Payot).
Selkirk, E. O. (1982). *The Syntax of Words* (Cambridge, Mass.: MIT Press).
Sellar, W. C. & Yeatman, R. J. (1930). *1066 and All That* (London: Methuen).
Sells, P. (1985). *Lectures on Contemporary Syntactic Theories: an Introduction to Government-Binding Theory, Generalized Phrase Structure Grammar, and Lexical-Functional Grammar* (Stanford: Center for the Study of Language and Information, Stanford University).
Smith, C. S. (1964). Determiners and relative clauses in a generative grammar of English. *Lg* 40: 37–52. Reprinted in Reibel & Schane (eds.), 1969: 247–63.
Spencer, A. (1991). *Morphological Theory: an Introduction to Word Structure in Generative Grammar* (Oxford: Blackwell).
Steinberg, D. D. & Jakobovits, L. A. (1971). *Semantics: an Interdisciplinary Reader in Philosophy, Linguistics and Psychology* (Cambridge University Press).
Stockwell, R. P. (1960). The place of intonation in a generative grammar of English. *Lg* 36: 360–7.
Sturtevant, E. H. (1934). Review of Bloomfield, 1933 (1935). *The Classical Weekly* 27: 159–60. Reprinted in *LBA* 265–6.
Swadesh, M. (1934a). The phonemic principle. *Lg* 10: 117–29. Reprinted in *RiL* 32–7.
(1934b). The phonetics of Chitimacha. *Lg* 10: 345–62.
Swadesh, M. & Voegelin, C. F. (1939). A problem in phonological alternation. *Lg* 15: 1–10. Reprinted in *RiL* 88–92.
Sweet, H. (1891). *A New English Grammar, Logical and Historical*, Part 1 (Oxford: Clarendon Press).
Tesnière, L. (1959). *Eléments de syntaxe structurale* (Paris: Klincksieck).
Trager, G. L. (1934). The phonemes of Russian. *Lg* 10: 334–44.
(1949). *The Field of Linguistics* (Norman, Okla.: *SIL*, Occasional Papers 1).
(1963). *Linguistics is Linguistics* (Buffalo: *SIL*, Occasional Papers 10).
Trager, G. L. & Smith, H. L. (1951). *An Outline of English Structure* (Norman, Okla.: *SIL*, Occasional Papers 3).
Troubetzkoy, N. S. (1949). *Principes de phonologie*, trans. Cantineau, J. (Paris: Klincksieck).
Voegelin, C. F. & Voegelin, F. M. (1976). Some recent (and not so recent) attempts to interpret semantics of native languages in North America. In Chafe, W. L. (ed.), *American Indian Languages and American Linguistics* (Lisse: Peter de Ridder Press), 75–98.
Wackernagel, J. (1926). *Vorlesungen über Syntax*, 2 vols. (Basle: Birkhäuser).
Weinreich, U. (1953). *Languages in Contact* (New York: Linguistic Circle of New York). Reissued The Hague: Mouton, 1963.
Weinreich, U., Labov, W. & Herzog, M. I. (1968). Empirical foundations for a

theory of language change. In Lehmann, W. P. & Malkiel, Y. (eds.), *Directions for Historical Linguistics* (Austin: University of Texas Press), 95–188.
Weiss, A. P. (1925). Linguistics and psychology. *Lg* 1: 52–7.
Wells, R. S. (1947a). De Saussure's system of linguistics. *Word* 3: 1–31. Reprinted in *RiL* 1–18.
(1947b). Immediate constituents. *Lg* 23: 81–117. Reprinted in *RiL* 186–207.
Williams, E. (1981). On the notions 'lexically related' and 'head of a word'. *LIn* 12: 245–74.
Wundt, W. (1911–12). *Völkerpsychologie: eine Untersuchung der Entwicklungsgesetze von Sprache, Mythus und Sitte*, Vol. 1: *Die Sprache*, third edn. (Leipzig: Engelmann), [first edn 1900].

Index